Corpus

of the

Mosaics of Turkey

Uludağ University Press

Uludağ University Mosaic Research Center Series – 2

CORPUS of the MOSAICS of TURKEY

Volume I

Edited by

Mustafa Şahin, David Parrish, Werner Jobst

Republic of Turkey
Ministry of Culture and Tourism

Uludağ University

AIEMA Türkiye

Centre national de la recherche scientifique

Institut Francais
d'Etudes Anatoliennes

COLLÈGE DE FRANCE
—1530—

The Getty

CORPUS of the MOSAICS of TURKEY

Volume I

LYCIA

XANTHOS, Part 1
The East Basilica

Marie-Patricia RAYNAUD

with the assistance of the
Getty Foundation
desteğiyle basılmıştır

CORPUS OF THE MOSAICS OF TURKEY
Volume I

LYCIA

XANTHOS, Part 1
The East Basilica

Marie-Patricia RAYNAUD

Set: ISBN 978-975-6149-49-2
Volume I: ISBN 978-975-6149-50-8

Editorial Committee: Mustafa Şahin, David Parrish, Werner Jobst
Hélène Morlier (publication consultant and layout)
David Parrish (translation into English)
Derya Şahin (translation into Turkish)

Cover: photo and drawing M.-P. Raynaud - layout Christophe Bailly

Published with the assistance of the Getty Foundation

AIEMA-Türkiye @ Mosaic Research Center, Uludağ Üniversitesi, Bursa
CNRS (Centre national de la recherche scientifique), Paris
COLLÈGE DE FRANCE, Orient et Méditerranée, Centre d'histoire et de civilisation de Byzance, UMR 8167, Paris
IFEA (Institut français d'études anatoliennes), Istanbul
INVISU, l'information visuelle et textuelle en histoire de l'art, USR 3103 du CNRS, INHA, Paris

Printed by
Graphis Matbaa

Production and Distribution
Zero Prod. Ltd.
Abdullah Sokak 17, Taksim 34433 Istanbul-Turkey
Tel: +90 (212) 244 75 21   Fax: +90 (212) 244 32 09
info@zerobooksonline.com   www.zerobooksonline.com

TABLE OF CONTENTS

Acknowledgments		9
Foreword		
AIEMA-Turkiye, the Corpus of the Mosaics of Turkey	M. Şahin, D. Parrish	11
I. Introduction		
History of the site: "la Lycie byzantine"	J.-P. Sodini	17
Excavations in Xanthos: "redécouvrir Xanthos"	J. des Courtils	23
II. Catalogue	M.-P. Raynaud	29
Roman period		32
Early Byzantine period (phases 1 and 2)		35
Middle Byzantine period		120
III. A Synthesis of the pavements	M.-P. Raynaud	129
IV. Turkish abstract of the Synthesis		147
V. Addenda	M.-P. Raynaud	167
Abbreviations		168
Bibliography and abbreviations		168
Table of cube densities		176
Individual Mosaic Entry or Fiche		177
Table of sites		178
Photographic Credits		182
List of illustration		182
About the author		185

Fold-out plan A: Early Byzantine East Basilica, Phase 1
Fold-out plan B: Early Byzantine East Basilica, Phase 2
Fold-out plan C: Medieval building

La publication des pavements (*opera sectilia* et mosaïques) de la basilique Est de Xanthos, que nous pouvons raisonnablement considérer comme la cathédrale de Xanthos, même si la résidence épiscopale n'a pas été fouillée, constitue le premier volume de la publication de cet édifice dont j'ai dirigé la fouille et guidé la publication. Le second volume qui comportera la publication de la fouille proprement dite traitera des phases de l'édifice, de l'époque paléochrétienne jusqu'à l'époque ottomane, donnant pour chacune les éléments en notre possession (restes architecturaux, matériel dateur) et leur reconstitution. Il intégrera également les mosaïques en insistant moins sur leur description mais davantage sur les données de fouille qu'elles livrent et leur liaison avec le contexte architectural.

Je suis très reconnaissant à la section turque de l'AIEMA et à son président, notre collègue Mustafa Şahin, directeur du Département archéologique de l'université Uludağ à Bursa ainsi qu'à notre collègue David Parrish, professeur à la Purdue University de West Lafayette (Indiana), qui ont été les co-fondateurs du *Corpus des mosaïques de Turquie*, d'avoir accepté d'accueillir dans le premier volume de ce corpus la publication des mosaïques de la cathédrale de Xanthos.

Je remercie enfin Madame Marie-Patricia Raynaud, ingénieure d'études au CNRS, qui a mené cette publication (dessins et textes) avec sa rigueur coutumière et sa large connaissance des mosaïques et des *opera sectilia* du monde antique.

Jean-Pierre Sodini,
Professeur émérite de l'université de Paris I (Panthéon-Sorbonne), Paris
Membre de l'Académie des inscriptions et belles-lettres

Aknowledgements - Remerciements

J'ai entrepris l'étude des mosaïques de la basilique Est de Xanthos (considérée comme la cathédrale) en 1986 à la demande de Jean-Pierre Sodini, alors que j'appartenais au Centre Henri Stern (AOROC UMR 8546, CNRS-ENS, Paris). Jean-Pierre Darmon, alors responsable de ce centre, a bien voulu soutenir ce programme. Il a aussi participé avec Christian Le Roy au jury du DEA que j'ai présenté en 1992 sous la direction de Jean-Pierre Sodini, à l'Université Paris I-Sorbonne («Les mosaïques de la Basilique épiscopale de Xanthos [Turquie]»). Je remercie Jean-Pierre Sodini de m'avoir aidé dans mon enquête bibliographique et de m'avoir invité à faire connaître mes premiers resultats dans des articles et au cours de séminaires. Je lui sais gré également d'avoir rédigé l'introduction historique de ce volume et d'avoir suivi de près sa préparation.

Mes séjours à Xanthos ont toujours été rendus agréables par les équipes de la mission française, sous la direction de Christian Le Roy d'abord, de Jacques des Courtils ensuite, a qui je suis reconnaissante d'avoir accepté de rédiger pour ce volume un historique des fouilles.

La présente publication a été réalisée dans le cadre du Centre d'histoire et civilisation de Byzance (UMR 8167, CNRS-Collège de France, Paris) auquel j'appartiens depuis 2006. Je tiens à remercier Jean-Claude Cheynet ainsi que les membres du conseil scientifique pour leur soutien généreux en moyens financiers et missions, ainsi que Lydie Simon. Ma gratitude va aussi aux membres de ce labo dont les conseils m'ont été précieux.

Ce volume peut voir le jour dans le cadre du Corpus des mosaïques de Turquie lancé par la branche turque de l'AIEMA créée en 2005 à l'instigation de Mustafa Şahin, David Parrish et Werner Jobst ; leur enthousiasme et leur énergie ont stimulé grandement la publication de ce volume.

Je suis très reconnaissante à David Parrish d'avoir beaucoup amélioré mon texte en anglais et de l'avoir rendu clair et précis. Grâces lui soient également rendues pour avoir obtenu auprès de la Getty Foundation l'aide financière nécessaire à l'impression de ce volume. Que cette institution soit remerciée pour l'intérêt qu'elle porte à la toute nouvelle entreprise du Corpus des mosaïques de Turquie.

Ma reconnaissance va aussi à Aksel Tibet qui a relu mon texte et à Madame Nora Şeni, directrice de L'IFEA d'Istanbul, qui a accepté d'apporter le soutien de cette institution à la publication ce livre.

Beaucoup d'amis m'ont soutenu dans la préparation de ce volume. En premier lieu Hélène Morlier, toujours prête à m'encourager, m'aider dans les recherches bibliographiques, relire les textes, et qui a de plus réalisé la maquette de l'ouvrage. Tous les détails de fond et de forme ont été discutés ensemble, et outre son amitié et son humour, sa longue expérience dans l'édition du *Recueil de mosaïques de la Gaule* et l'élaboration du *Bulletin de l'AIEMA* a été essentielle. Christophe Bailly a une nouvelle fois fait la preuve de son talent en réalisant la couverture.

Marie-Geneviève Froidevaux, qui réalise les plans de la basilique Est depuis 1994, a été une interlocutrice avisée pour toute la documentation graphique. Un travail en commun a permis de présenter les dessins des mosaïques dans leur contexte architectural, et rendre ainsi lisible le décor dans son cadre. Qu'elle soit remerciée pour son aide, et pour m'avoir permis d'utiliser son travail ici, avant la prochaine publication archéologique du monument. Merci à ceux qui avaient travaillé sur les pavements de l'église avant mon arrivée, en particulier Jean-Luc Biscop, Annie Toto et Gérard Bernard. Merci aussi à Bernard Noël Chagny pour m'avoir gracieusement permis d'utiliser une de ses excellentes vues prises par cerf-volant.

Les restaurateurs de mosaïques m'ont beaucoup appris sur le terrain, surtout Patrick Blanc, Laurence Krougly et Şehrigül Yesil Erdek, tandis que les spécialistes de la bibliographie m'ont donné leurs « clefs », tout particulièrement Anne Cavé (bibliothèque d'archéologie, ENS Paris), Michèle Tahri (mise en ligne bénévole et efficace du *Bulletin de l'AIEMA*, en cours), et Anne-Marie Manière-Levêque (archéologue à Xanthos).

Ma gratitude s'adresse aussi à Pat Witts pour les multiples discussions sur des questions de fond *via* courrier électronique, à Christian Saunier pour les relectures du français, à Derya Şahin pour les traductions en turc, ainsi qu'à Brigitte Pittarakis et Abdelatif Arcalıoğlu pour leurs relectures, Iki Çay, Belkis et Simit pour leurs conseils en informatique, sans oublier Louis et Jacqueline Dubois pour leur réconfort et soutien.

Pour conclure merci à Didier Dubois, à son humour, sa patience, son esprit critique, son indéfectible soutien – et à sa perche photographique –, sans lequel tout cela serait encore « dans les cartons ».

Enfin, une pensée émue à mes parents qui m'ont fait découvrir et aimer la Turquie, et à qui je dédie ce livre.

Marie-Pat. RAYNAUD

1. Map of Turkey.

Foreword

With the publication of this volume, Turkey officially joins several other countries in the Mediterranean world and in Western Europe that have launched a systematic inventory of mosaics found on their soil. The present project is an ambitious one, taking as its model well established series of this type, such as the *Recueil général des mosaïques de la Gaule* (with some 20 volumes covering mosaics of ancient and medieval France) or the *Mosaici antichi in Italia* (also with numerous fascicles). Organization of the *Corpus of the Mosaics of Turkey* began in 2004, when mosaic scholars from six different nations met at the Istanbul headquarters of the American Research Institute in Turkey (ARIT) and started planning the forthcoming corpus. Over thirty years ago, Elisabeth Alföldi-Rosenbaum and Volker Michael Strocka had conceived the idea of forming a Turkish corpus, aided at a later date by Werner Jobst and Sheila Campbell. However, that initiative did not continue subsequently.

More recently, the time has seemed ripe to relaunch the notion of a systematic inventory, as the mosaics of Anatolia have become better known to the scholarly world, in part because of the spectacular new discoveries in this medium at the site of Zeugma on the Euphrates River, and because the 70th anniversary of the important mosaic excavations at Antioch-on-the-Orontes was near. In addition, the outstanding mosaics from the Palace of the Byzantine Emperors in Constantinople-Istanbul had been restored a decade before and reset in their original location, with new archaeological soundings to confirm their date in the first half of the 6th century CE. At the first and second organizational meetings of the Turkish Corpus, it was decided to divide that country into 18 historical regions where individual research teams would focus their efforts, and to establish a national Mosaic Research Center at Uludağ University in Bursa – all under the guidance of a small group of co-directors of the project. It was further agreed that the Corpus volumes not only would employ a standardized format for documenting pavements, but also that these publications would be in multiple languages, with the texts appearing in English, French or German and with a substantial summary or synthesis translated into Turkish, thereby making them more accessible to young local scholars. In other cases, the main text would be Turkish, with a synthesis written in English. This research program was strongly endorsed by AIEMA, the International Association for the Study of Ancient Mosaics, based in Paris.

Among the Turkish archaeological sites with mosaics thoroughly studied and ready for publication is Xanthos (located in the region of Lycia in southwestern Turkey), where several monuments have yielded excellent pavements of the Late Antique to Early Byzantine periods and later. The current volume, written by Marie-Pat Raynaud and dealing with mosaics in the East Basilica at Xanthos, offers the opportunity to examine the mosaic program of an entire church and its adjacent baptistery, from its beginnings in Early Byzantine times and during its subsequent evolution over five centuries into the medieval era. Both the technique of *tessellatum* (pavements made of small, regularly cut cubes or tesserae of stone or other materials, set in mortar) and that of *sectile* (variously shaped marble pieces or plaques forming a geometric pattern in a floor) are present in this building. The author studied these works of art meticulously, marshaling all available archaeological evidence to reconstruct fragmentary designs, and demonstrating the pavements' chronological sequence. Ms. Raynaud was able to distinguish the characteristics of several individual workshops decorating the East Basilica and its annex, and she also showed how the mosaics are related to their architectural setting. They reflect liturgical and other religious functions and give visual emphasis to paths of circulation by the occupants. The few pictorial and figural pavements also have symbolic associations.

We cite two other significant features of the present volume, one being its superb illustration. Numerous color photographs, reconstruction drawings of mosaics, and precise, elegant ground plans accompany the text, bringing these works of art to life and giving visual pleasure to the reader. Ms. Raynaud also views the mosaics and *sectile* pavements within a larger art-historical context: she makes extensive comparisons with contemporary developments in other parts of the eastern Mediterranean and shows how the mosaics of Xanthos reflect broader currents in this artistic medium. In all of its qualities, this volume very ably initiates the present *Corpus of the Mosaics of Turkey* and sets a high standard for the monographs to follow.

Finally, we note that the publication of this book coincides with preparations for the next international colloquium of AIEMA, to be held at Bursa, Turkey, in October, 2009. In several respects, Turkey is coming of age in the modern history of mosaic studies.

Dr. Mustafa ŞAHİN
Director of AIEMA Turkiye, Director of the Archaeology Department, Uludağ Universitesi, Bursa, Turkey

Dr. David PARRISH
Co-Director of AIEMA Turkiye,
Professor of Art History, Department of Visual and Performing Arts, Purdue University, West Lafayette, Indiana, USA

2. Plan of Xanthos by G. Scharf, 1843-44.

Önsöz

Türkiye, bu cildin basımıyla resmi olarak kendi topraklarında bulunan mozaiklerin sistematik envanterini tutan Akdeniz Dünyası ve Batı Avrupa ülkelerine katılmış olmaktadır. Sunulan bu proje modeli de *"Recueil général des mosaïques de la Gaule"* (Antik ve Ortaçağ Fransa'sının mozaiklerini kapsayan 20 cilt ile) veya *Mosaici antichi in Italia (yine birden fazla fasikül ile)* bu türde daha önce kendini kanıtlamış seriler gibi oldukça ciddi projelerden birisidir. 2004 yılında Türkiye Mozaik Corpus organizasyonu, 6 değişik ülkeden mozaik uzmanlarının Türkiye'deki American Reasearch Institute'un merkezinde corpus'u planlamalarıyla başladı. Otuz yıldan fazla bir zaman önce, Elisabeth Alföldi-Rosenbaum ve Volker Michael Strocka "Türkiye Korpusu"nu yapmayı tasarlamışlardı, onlardan daha sonra ise Werner Jobst ve Sheila Campbell aynı fikir üzerinde durdu. Ancak bu kişisel girişimler süreklilik gösteremedi..

Bu proje için uygun bir zamandı, zira Zeugma am Euphrate çevresindeki yeni keşifler ve Antiocheia a.O'deki önemli mozaik kazılarının 70. yıldönümü sebebiyle Anadolu mozaikleri bilim dünyası tarafından daha iyi tanınmaya başlanmıştı. Ayrıca yeni arkeolojik çalışmalarla 6. yüzyıla tarihlenen İstanbul'daki Bizans İmparatorlarının Sarayında bulunan göz alıcı mozaikler on yıl önce restore edilmiş ve orijinal yerlerine yerleştirilmiştir. Birinci ve ikinci Türkiye Corpusu toplantısında, yönetici yardımcılarından oluşan küçük bir grubun rehberliğiyle ülkenin on sekiz tarihsel bölgeye ayrılmasına, ayrı araştırma gruplarının kendi bölgelerine odaklanmasına ve Uludağ Üniversitesi'nde ulusal bir mozaik araştırmaları merkezi kurulmasına karar verilmiştir. Ayrıca Corpus ciltlerinde döşemelerin belgelendirilmesinde bir standart sağlamasının yanında, gelen makalelerin Türkçe çevirileriyle birlikte olması koşuluyla İngilizce, Fransızca, Almanca makalelerle bu basımların çok dilli olması ve böylece genç araştırmacıların daha rahat erişimini sağlamak konusunda görüş birliği sağlanmıştır. Bu araştırma programı Paris'teki AIEMA (Uluslararası Antik Mozaik Araştırma Derneği) tarafından desteklenmektedir.

Türkiye'deki arkeolojik alanlar içerisinde mozaikleri tamamen incelenmiş ve basıma uygun hale getirilmiş olanı Xanthos mozaikleridir. Bu kentte yer alan çeşitli anıtlar, Geç Antik dönemden Erken Bizans dönemi ve sonrasına ait muhteşem döşemelere sahiptir. Bu cilt, Marie-Pat Raynaud tarafından yazılmış ve Xanthos'taki doğu bazilikasını konu almıştır. Bu çalışma bize tüm kilisenin ve bitişik vaftizhanenin mozaik planını Erken Bizans Dönemindeki başlangıcından ve sonrasındaki beş yüzyıllık evrimini inceleme şansını veriyor. Hem *tessellatum* tekniği (küçük ve düzgün kesilmiş taş ya da diğer malzemelerin harç içerisine yerleştirilmesi) hem de *sectile* tekniği (çeşitli şekilde şekillendirilmiş mermer parçaları veya plakaların geometrik bir şekil oluşturacak şekilde yerleştirilmesi) yapıda mevcuttur. Yazar, elde edilen bütün arkeolojik kanıtları, tasarımları yeniden oluşturmak ve döşemelerin kronolojik düzenini göstermek için titizlikle incelemiştir. Bayan Raynaud doğu bazilikasının ve ekini süsleyen mozaikleri yapan çeşitli atölyelerin niteliklerini ayırabilmiş ve ayrıca mozaiklerin mimari oluşumla ilişkisini göstermiştir. Döşemeler, ayinler ve diğer dinsel fonksiyonları yansıtır ve kullanılan dolaşım yollarını görsel olarak vurgular. Az sayıdaki resimli ve figürlü döşemelerde simgesel çağrışımlara sahiptir.

Bu cildin iki kayda değer özelliğini daha belirtmekte yarar vardır, birincisi muhteşem resimlerdir. Birçok renkli fotoğraf, mozaiklerin rekonstrüksiyon çizimleri ve makaleye eşlik eden güzel zemin planları, bu sanat çalışmalarını hayata döndürerek okuyucuya görsel bir zevk vermektedir. Ayrıca Bayan Raynaud mozaikleri ve *sectile* döşemeleri geniş bir sanat tarihi bağlamında ele almakta, diğer Doğu Akdeniz Bölümündeki çağdaş gelişimleri ile derinlemesine karşılaştırma yapmakta ve Xanthos mozaiklerinin bu sanatsal çevrede nasıl geniş bir alana aksettiğini göstermektedir. Sunulan bu çalışma eser kalitesiyle her açıdan "Türkiye Mozaik Corpusu"nda güçlü bir başlangıçtır ve devam edecek monografiler için yüksek bir standart koymaktadır.

Sonuç olarak, bu kitabın basımının Ekim 2009'da Bursa'da yapılacak uluslararası AIEMA sempozyumu hazırlıklarıyla tesadüf ettiğini belirtiriz. Birçok yönden Türkiye, mozaik çalışmalarının modern tarihinde kendini ispatlamaktadır.

Dr. Mustafa ŞAHİN ve Dr. David PARRISH
Türkiye Corpus Projesinin Co-Direktörleri.

I. Introduction

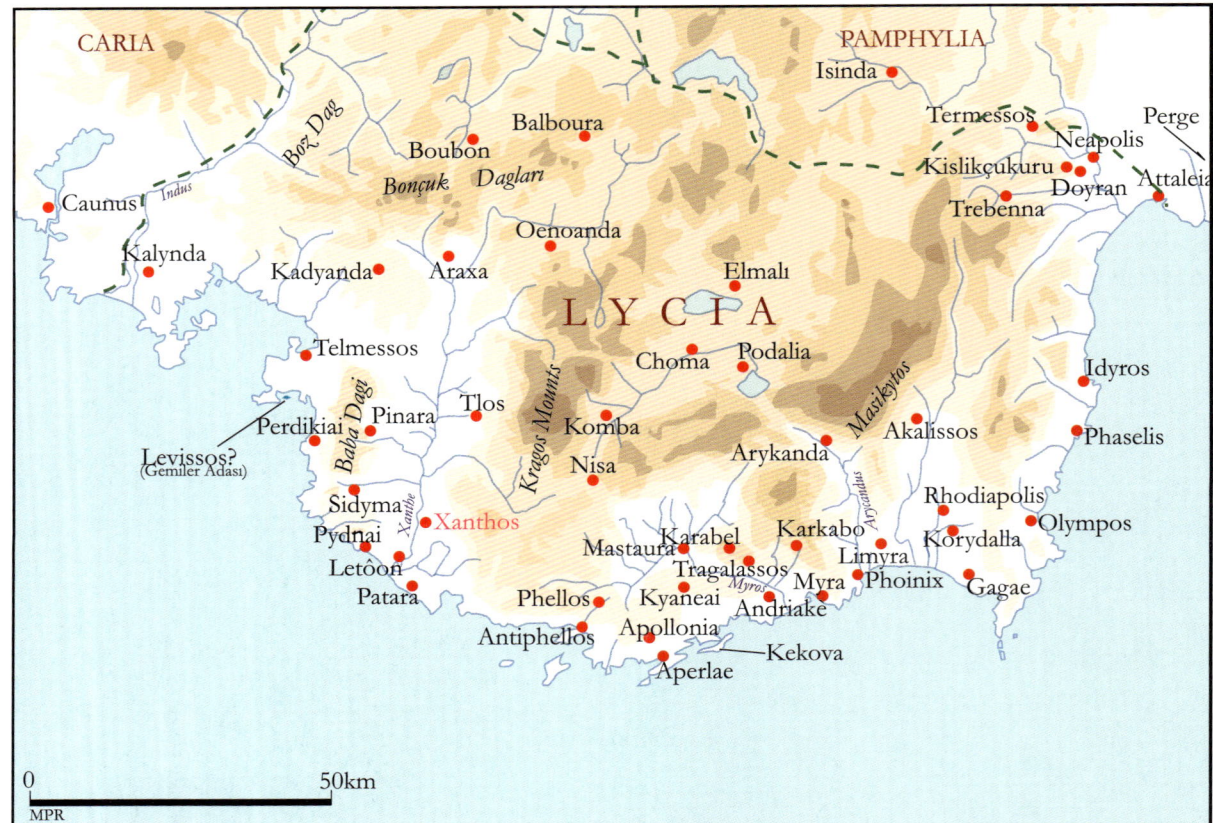

3. Map of Lycia.

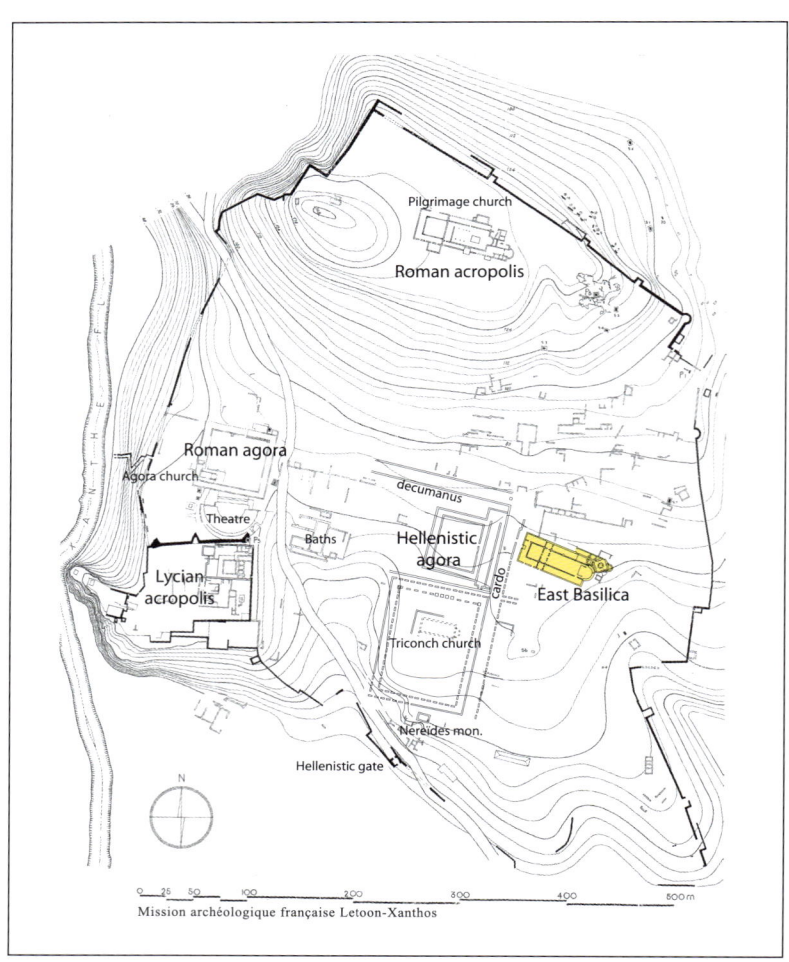

4. Plan of the site of Xanthos.

LA LYCIE BYZANTINE

L'Antiquité tardive
(IVᵉ-VIIᵉ siècles)

La position géographique de la Lycie, en avancée méridionale à l'angle sud-ouest du plateau anatolien, est à la jonction entre la Méditerranée du Levant (ill. 1), – qui comprend la côte sud de l'Anatolie, Chypre, la côte syro-palestinienne et celle de l'Egypte, la ville d'Alexandrie faisant quasiment face à celle de Myra –, et le bassin égéen, verrouillé au sud par la Crète, Karpathos et Rhodes et dont la pointe nord, passées les Dardanelles, est pour cette période Constantinople. Cette situation, tour à tour privilégiée en période de paix mais exposée en période de guerre, favorisa des renversements de fortune brutaux.

Le territoire lycien ne semble pas offrir en lui-même de ressources importantes, même s'il est qualifié d'autosuffisant dans l'*Expositio Totius Mundi et Gentium* (§ XLVI, p. 182-183, éd. J. Rougé, SC 124, Paris, 1966). Il est en effet très montagneux, avec des sommets entre 2500 et 3000 m tombant souvent en à-pic dans la mer. La Lycie (ill. 3) est coupée de la Carie par la chaîne du Boz Dağ qui borde à l'est l'Indos (Dalaman çay) et de la Pamphylie par un autre chaînon qui arrive jusqu'à la mer. À l'intérieur de cet espace, elle est elle-même cloisonnée en une Lycie occidentale, qui comprend la plaine autour de Telmessos (Fethiye) et, séparée par les Monts du Kragos de cette dernière, la vallée du Xanthe (Eşen çay). Celle-ci est jalonnée de diverses bourgades et petites villes. Près de la mer sont implantées les cités de Xanthos, capitale de la Lycie à l'époque antique, et de Patara, port important maintenant ensablé. Plus à l'est, des montagnes élevées (Massikytos, Akdağ : 3024 m) marquent le début de la Lycie centrale où des plaines intérieures permettent l'agriculture et l'implantation de petites cités. Le fleuve Myros, au cours parallèle à la côte, donne sur ces terres un accès plus facile que par la côte à Myra, capitale de la Lycie à l'époque byzantine, et à son port, très actif, Andriakè. La Lycie orientale s'organisait le long du fleuve Arykandeus (Fenike çay) ; Arykanda, Rhodiapolis et surtout Limyra en constituaient les villes principales. La côte orientale offrait deux ports abrités, ceux d'Olympos et de Phaselis. On note l'importance des rivières et de la côte pour l'implantation des villes, l'étroitesse de la zone côtière, qui s'est élargie de nos jours au débouché du Xanthe, du Myros et de l'Arykandus, mais a connu une forte subsidence de la ville actuelle de Kaş à l'île de Kekova, à une époque mal précisée entre le VIIᵉ siècle et aujourd'hui, qui masque la ligne de côte antique. À l'évidence, la communication entre les habitats de la côte était beaucoup plus facile par mer que par terre.

L'organisation politique qui se met en place à partir de la Tétrarchie densifie et superpose les divisions administratives. La Province de Lycie et Pamphylie, attestée en 280, fait partie du Diocèse d'Asie Mineure dès 293. Puis elle est scindée en deux entre 312 et 325, les deux provinces restant dans ce même diocèse. Celui-ci est à son tour intégré à partir de 390 dans la Préfecture du Prétoire d'Orient. La capitale de la province est transférée de Xanthos à Myra, attestée pour la première fois comme capitale de la Lycie sous Théodose II (408-450). Les cités sont au nombre de 34 dans la liste donnée par Synekdèmos d'Hieroclès au milieu du Vᵉ siècle. Elles gèrent un territoire (*chôra*), de même que les bourgades (*kômai*) : l'habitat de base restait le village (*chôrion*). La *Vie de saint Nicolas* qui relate la vie de l'higoumène du monastère de Sainte-Sion montre encore au VIᵉ siècle la force de ces subdivisions et leurs liens de dépendance, notamment lors de l'épisode bien connu où les villageois refusent de descendre à Myra livrer leurs provisions par crainte d'attraper la peste.

Le conflit entre paganisme et christianisme fut, comme partout, violent. Les prédications de l'apôtre Paul à Pergé, puis à Patara, l'importance des communautés juives ont dû introduire le christianisme assez tôt dans la région. Quelques noms d'évêques antérieurs à la paix de l'Eglise sont également conservés dans la tradition hagiographique. Une des premières mentions d'une communauté chrétienne est donnée en 311-312 dans une inscription d'Arykanda, où la cité, suivant la propagande anti-chrétienne de Maximin Daïa en Asie, proteste contre les troubles causés par la folie des chrétiens. Cette opposition païenne correspond à cette date à une majorité qui a à sa tête une élite très soucieuse de culture antique et qui à la fin du IIⁿᵈ ou au début du IIIᵉ siècle faisait tapisser un portique central de la ville d'Oenoanda d'écrits de Diogène. Il est probable que cette nostalgie recoupait aussi une certaine fierté lycienne. Tatianos préfet païen du prétoire d'Orient de 388 à 392 sous Théodose Iᵉʳ, originaire de Sidyma, vit son fils exécuté à Constantinople et fut renvoyé dans sa patrie. Un décret, bientôt rapporté, fut alors pris qui interdisait l'accès de la haute fonction publique aux Lyciens : ceux-ci étaient donc perçus comme un groupe ethnique, au même titre que les Ciliciens, alors qu'ils n'écrivaient plus leur langue depuis longtemps. Du côté des campagnes, un paganisme primaire existe encore au VIe siècle. Nicolas, l'higoumène du monastère de Sainte-Sion, sans doute celui découvert en pleine Lycie centrale, à 5 km au Sud-Ouest de Karabel, évangélise les villages des environs en festoyant avec des paysans affamés et en coupant leurs arbres sacrés.

La hiérarchie religieuse se met en place lentement. L'évêque le plus ancien connu pour la Lycie est Méthode, qui administra sa charge à Olympos à la fin du IIIe siècle ou au début du IVe siècle. Il composa notamment un *Banquet* recourant au dialogue de type platonicien, exaltant la virginité et la charité, mais rejetant la résurrection. Toutefois, seule la cité de Patara envoya un évêque au premier grand concile, celui de Nicée (325). Du grand saint lycien Nicolas de Myra, rien d'historique n'est connu. Son nom n'est ajouté à la liste des Pères de Nicée qu'au début du VIe siècle, date où son culte se répand. Son église est une reconstruction du VIIIe siècle, qui recouvre plusieurs églises antérieures, dont l'une, d'après ses mosaïques, pourrait dater de la fin du Ve siècle.

Les évêchés se développent rapidement ; ils sont au nombre de 37 sous Héraclius. Les églises imposantes se multiplient au centre des villes ou à leur périphérie : quatre à Xanthos et deux chapelles ; deux à Tlos ; deux au moins à Patara ; une à Pinara ; quatre à Gemiler Adası (antique Levissos ?) ; deux au moins à Kyaneai et trois chapelles ; deux au moins à Limyra ; cinq à Andriakè pour nous limiter aux principaux exemples. À l'intérieur de la Lycie centrale, la *kômè* de Tragalassos (Muskar) a livré une intéressante église à transept. Les monastères sont importants dans cette région. Ceux d'Asarlık (sans doute Karkabo), dédiés à saint Gabriel, les deux monastères d'Asarcık (Est et Ouest, ce dernier étant sans doute le monastère de Saint-Jean-Prodrome-le-Baptiste), sur le site antique d'Akalissos, où Nicolas, le futur higoumène de Sainte-Sion, fit ses classes auprès de son oncle avant d'aller fonder, à peu de distance, son propre monastère (site actuel d'Alacahisar) qui est une réplique soignée du précédent. Mais les monastères existaient également près des côtes fortement urbanisées, comme peut-être à Idyros, où une inscription mentionne un moine, et au Letôon.

Cette architecture religieuse est intéressante à plusieurs titres. Tout comme dans la Pamphylie voisine, les plans des cathédrales urbaines sont grandioses, avec recours au transept à Tlos, Patara, Tragalassos, et semblent s'inspirer des grandes basiliques constantinopolitaines. L'un des traits lyciens originaux est l'abondant recours aux triconques, plus rarement aux tétraconques, soit pour l'abside principale, soit pour une chapelle annexe, soit encore pour un martyrium ou un baptistère. L'utilisation des remplois notamment pour les portes, les colonnes, voire les chapiteaux n'a pas empêché le recours à une sculpture importée de Proconnèse (colonnes, chapiteaux, plaques de chancel, ambons), concentrée sur la côte, ni surtout le développement d'une sculpture sur calcaire local très virtuose avec un usage continu du trépan (sur les montants de porte, les architraves, les plaques de chancel, les ambons et les chapiteaux) soit, comme à Limyra, à une sculpture plus douce, à très faible relief et pratiquement en champlevé. Sur les sols alternaient sols en plaque de marbre ou de calcaire, *opus sectile* et mosaïques. Ce premier volume du *Corpus des Mosaïques de Turquie* permettra d'en analyser l'exemple le mieux conservé de la région.

Les églises et les monastères ne sont pas les seules constructions de l'époque, tant s'en faut. Les sites urbains antiques étaient entretenus. Les murailles furent reconstruites à partir de la fin du IIIe siècle et souvent entretenues jusqu'au VIIe siècle, parfois sur un périmètre plus restreint. Les rues, les places publiques étaient dallées, les trottoirs et les portiques mosaïqués. Les maisons étaient aussi remaniées, parfois luxueuses, avec triclinium à abside (*stibadium*). Dans les villages de plateau ou sur la côte, les maisons étaient en revanche composées d'une ou deux pièces parfois surmontées d'un étage. Le développement des bourgs et des villages montre un habitat plus dense qu'on ne l'avait cru. Sur le plateau, se développèrent l'élevage et la production agricole de céréales, mais aussi l'olivier et la vigne, attestés par des pressoirs. Sur les pentes des montagnes lyciennes qui arrivaient jusqu'à la mer poussaient des conifères très recherchés pour les charpentes (Paul le Silentaire évoque les arbres de Patara dans sa *Description de Sainte-Sophie*), mais aussi pour la construction navale. Sur la côte, à ces activités s'ajoutaient la pêche, le cabotage à plus ou moins grande échelle, mais aussi une navigation combinant haute mer et cabotage dont l'exemple le plus clair est la livraison de l'annone d'Égypte à Constantinople et aux armées en campagne, qui faisait escale à Andriaké et sans doute à Patara. L'abondance des installations portuaires le long des côtes et des îles lyciennes est un indice très caractéristique de cette intense activité. L'église avait sa part dans cette richesse et le somptueux trésor enfoui à Kumluca (ancienne cité de Korydalla) vers 560-565 en est la parfaite illustration, quelle que soit l'église de Sainte-Sion à qui sont dédiées la plupart de ces pièces.

5. Drawing of the Harpy Tomb and the "Sarcophagus on a Pillar" (by G. Scharf).

Les tremblements de terre qui affectent Rhodes en 514-516 et Myra en 529-530, la peste de 542 qui atteint Myra et sans doute toute la Lycie ne suffirent sans doute pas à ralentir durablement le dynamisme de cette région.

Les guerres contre les Sassanides et les Arabes

L'avancée sassanide dans les territoires byzantins, commencée depuis 610, jalonnée par la prise de Jérusalem en 614 et celle de l'Egypte en 619, menaçait directement l'approvisionnement en blé de Constantinople et de l'armée byzantine et plus généralement le commerce par les voies maritimes proche-orientales. La conquête de Rhodes en 622/623 dut rendre la menace encore plus concrète. Les attaques arabes qui suivent quelques décennies plus tard eurent le même effet, surtout après la grande victoire navale que la flotte arabe remporta au large de Phoinix (Fenike) en 655. La Lycie eut encore à subir en 672/673 l'hivernage d'une flotte arabe, puis en 678 un débarquement de soldats arabes et le siège d'une ville côtière non précisée (Myra, Fenike ou Patara ?), qui furent repoussés et anéantis par une armée byzantine dirigée par les généraux des thèmes des Anatoliques et des Arméniaques ainsi que par le comte de l'Opsikion.

Cette même année, une autre flotte arabe échouait devant Constantinople. En 715, les Arabes débarquèrent encore à Phoinix pour rechercher du bois de cyprès destiné à l'entretien de leur flotte. Au même moment, l'empereur Anastase II (713-715) restaurait la fortification de Telmessos (l'actuelle Fethiye), rebaptisée Anastasioupolis. En 717, la marine arabe subit un nouvel échec dans sa tentative de s'emparer de Constantinople. Au retour, la flotte subit des pertes importantes au large de la Lycie et de la Pamphylie. Le thème des Kybirrhéotes, créé par Léon III (717-741), renforçait la défense de la Lycie et de la Pamphylie, les protégeant durablement jusqu'au XIe siècle, même si quelques raids sont attestés par des inscriptions arabes à Karacören et Cnide. Chypre (reconquise en 966) et la Crète (occupée de 824 à 960) servirent souvent de base pour des razzias.

La Lycie avait sans doute souffert, notamment dans la seconde moitié du VIIe et dans la première moitié du VIIIe siècle. Toutefois, même à cette période, les pèlerins pouvaient y accéder : l'évêque Willibald d'Eichstätt, en route vers la terre sainte, hiverne en 723-724 à Patara avant de poursuivre vers Kalon Oros (actuelle Alanya, en Pamphylie), site qu'il trouve ravagé par la guerre et dépeuplé. Mais il y avait encore des habitants, une hiérarchie ecclésiastique, attestée notamment par les *Notitiae episcopatuum*, des moines, comme

6. Overall view of the city from the top of the hill (1977).

ce Strategios, « moine de Sainte-Sion » présent au Concile de Nicée en 787. La céramique trouvée dans les fouilles indique une permanence aux VIIe et VIIIe siècles à Xanthos, à Balboura et à Limyra (où l'occupation dans certains secteurs continue jusqu'à l'époque médio-byzantine sans interruption). Il est évident que les villes se contractèrent, que plusieurs furent abandonnées et que dans certains cas leurs habitants se réinstallèrent à proximité (comme ce fut sans doute le cas à Neapolis). Si les nouvelles constructions sont rares durant cette période (et surtout difficiles à dater), on peut ajouter à la réfection des remparts de Telmessos par Anastase II, la reconstruction de l'église actuelle de Myra au VIIIe siècle et la réfection de l'église Saint-Gabriel de Karkabo (Alakilisse) en 812. La construction à Mastaura (actuel Dereağzı) sur le plateau de Lycie centrale, à proximité de la rivière Myros, dans la deuxième moitié du IXe ou au début du Xe siècle, d'une église imposante, d'un style inspiré par celui de Constantinople, souligne qu'en dépit de la menace arabe la prospérité revient.

Le retour de la prospérité
(seconde moitié du Xe-fin du XIIe siècle)

La Lycie, comme l'ensemble de l'Anatolie et du bassin égéen, connaît une intense activité. Celle-ci se marque dans l'architecture et la décoration religieuse. En 1042, Constantin X et Zoe restaurent l'église de Saint-Nicolas de Myra, ajoutant des chapelles, refaisant les dallages en *opus sectile*, les sculptures (notamment celles du *templon*) et les fresques. Vers cette époque, les mêmes réfections sont faites dans les églises de l'île de Levissos (Gemiler Adası), à Cydna (Pydnai), à Kaunos – dans ces deux derniers sites l'ancienne basilique à trois nefs avec charpente est transformée en église à coupole – à Arykanda où deux églises médiobyzantines de taille réduite sont insérées dans une basilique et à Patara où des peintures murales sont introduites dans l'église médiobyzantine située à l'intérieur de l'enceinte médiévale, tandis que deux chapelles byzantines sont construites à l'intérieur des deux grandes basiliques paléochrétiennes. À Xanthos, une nouvelle église et ses annexes s'établissent dans l'ancienne cathédrale publiée dans ce volume. Le baptistère est transformé en sanctuaire par l'ajout d'une nouvelle abside pourvue d'un autel et fermée par un *templon* décoré des médaillons d'une *Deisis*, proche de ceux que l'on trouve en Phrygie. Les dallages en *opus sectile* antérieurs sont complétés et des peintures murales insérées en plusieurs endroits. Ailleurs, les églises de cette époque sont construites sur des espaces libres comme à Islamlar près d'Elmalı (avec fresques), à Sidyma (église au pied de l'acropole) et à Trebenna où les parois sont décorées de peintures attribuées au XIIe siècle. Des monastères sont construits sur des espaces libres leur permettant de s'établir suivant des plans reconnaissables, notamment à Kislikçukuru près de Neapolis en Lycie orientale. Ailleurs ce sont de nouvelles enceintes qui sont bâties, comme le Kastron de Myra, celui de Patara, celui d'Apollonia regroupant autour d'une église à coupole un habitat et une chapelle de même date, ou encore les murailles de Trebenna datées de la première moitié du XIIe siècle. Un petit habitat associé à un monastère occupe un lieu naturellement fortifié à Palamutdüzü près du site de Doyran (Lycie orientale). La sculpture médiobyzantine est rare (un chapiteau à Isinda en Pamphylie, une plaque à Islamlar près d'Elmalı).

Moins dense qu'à l'époque protobyzantine, cette occupation traduit une reprise en main de la région et non une simple occupation éparse. La céramique, insuffisamment étudiée sauf dans certains sites, confirme cette reprise. La défaite des armées byzantines à Mantzikert en 1071 face aux Seldjoukides ébranla l'impression de paix retrouvée. L'insécurité naissante permit à des aventuriers de Bari de s'emparer des reliques de saint Nicolas à Myra (Demre). Toutefois, ce n'est qu'après la défaite de Myriokephalon en 1176 que la situation se dégrada durablement pour le pouvoir byzantin. La prise de Constantinople en 1204 par les Croisés donna le signal de la *partitio imperii* à laquelle échappaient les régions dissidentes de l'empire, notamment celle d'Attaleia, déjà dirigée de façon indépendante par un byzantin d'origine italienne, Aldebrandinos. La prise d'Attaleia (Antalya) par les Seldjoukides en 1207 marquait la fin de la domination byzantine en Lycie et en Pamphylie.

Jean-Pierre SODINI
Professeur émérite, université de Paris I, Panthéon-Sorbonne
Membre de l'Académie des inscriptions et belles-lettres

Bibliographie

AKYÜREK E., "The Bey Dağları in the Byzantine Period: Trebenna, Neapolis and their Territories", in *The IIIrd International Symposium on Lycia, 07-10 November 2005, Antalya*, Akmed (ed.), Antalya, 2006, I, pp. 1-18.

ARMSTRONG P., "Rural Settlement in Lycia in the Eight Century: New Evidence", in *The IIIrd International Symposium on Lycia, 07-10 November 2005, Antalya*, Akmed (ed.), Antalya, 2006, I, pp. 19-30.

FOSS C., "Cities and Villages of Lycia in the Life of St Nicholas of Holy Zion", *Greek Orthodox Theological Review*, 36, 1991, pp. 303-339 (*Cities, Fortresses and Villages of Byzantine Asia Minor*, Variorum, Aldershot, 1996, Study III).

FOSS C., "The Lycian Coast in the Byzantine Age", *DOP*, 48, 1994, pp. 1-52 (*Cities, Fortresses and Villages of Byzantine Asia Minor*, Variorum, Aldershot, 1996, Study II).

HELLENKEMPER H., HILD F., *Lykien und Pamphylien, Tabula Imperii Byzantini* 8, Wien, 2004.

SEVČENKO I., SEVČENKO N. P., *The Life of St. Nicholas of Sion*, Brookline, 1984.

VROOM J., "Limyra in Lycia: Byzantine/Umayyad Pottery Finds from Excavations in the Eastern Part of the City", in *Céramiques antiques en Lycie (VIIe S. a.C. – VIIe S. p.C.), Actes de la table-ronde de Poitiers (21-22 mars 2003)*, S. Lemaître (ed.), Bordeaux, 2007, pp. 262-292 (Ausonius Etudes 16).

7. View of the city of Xanthos in the time of Fellows' travels (by G. Scharf).

LA REDÉCOUVERTE DE XANTHOS

La ville antique de Xanthos est située à quelques kilomètres en retrait du rivage méditerranéen, sur la côte sud de la Turquie, région si belle et riante que les agents du tourisme moderne l'ont appelée la « côte Turquoise ». C'était dans l'antiquité la Lycie, région si prospère qu'elle aurait, au dire d'Homère, fourni aux Troyens leurs meilleurs alliés pendant la guerre fameuse qui les opposa aux Grecs... Ses aimables dispositions naturelles (ill. 6, 7) et les souvenirs de son glorieux passé n'ont pourtant guère attiré les voyageurs avant la période contemporaine, puisqu'il fallut attendre le XVIIIe siècle pour qu'un ambassadeur de France auprès de la Sublime Porte, le comte de Choiseul Gouffier, faisant escale au port de Fethiye, ait l'honneur d'être le premier « antiquaire » à fouler son sol (1776). Plus de soixante ans après, c'est un jeune Britannique fortuné et cultivé, Charles Fellows qui, à l'occasion du « Grand Tour » qu'il fit en Asie Mineure, l'Histoire d'Hérodote à la main, redécouvrit la ville morte de Xanthos le 14 avril 1838. Une journée sur le site lui suffit pour recevoir de telles impressions qu'il y revint deux ans plus tard (ill. 2), tout heureux de se retrouver, écrivit-il dans son journal *« back in my beloved city »*. Deux autres voyages, financés cette fois par les autorités du British Museum que ses descriptions de voyage avaient enthousiasmées, lui permirent d'enrichir ce musée d'une moisson impressionnante de statues, bas-reliefs, morceaux d'architecture qui constituèrent une véritable révélation pour le public du XIXe siècle (ill. 5, 7-10, 183).

Après ces débuts en fanfare, l'archéologie xanthienne retomba dans un sommeil profond, brièvement interrompu à la fin du même siècle, par les prospections d'épigraphistes autrichiens, O. Benndorf, G. Niemann, E. Kalinka et quelques autres en 1881 puis au cours des années suivantes, qui rapportèrent la matière du corpus des inscriptions de Lycie : inscriptions en langue lycienne, grecque et latine.

Il fallut attendre l'année 1950 pour que commencent véritablement les fouilles de Xanthos : cette année là, P. Demargne et P. Devambez obtinrent en effet du gouvernement turc la concession du site archéologique et lancèrent une aventure qui dure encore aujourd'hui et n'a pas fini de donner des résultats.

Les premières fouilles, bientôt reprises par H. Metzger, se concentrèrent sur les monuments les plus visibles du site : les fameux piliers funéraires, mais aussi sur le secteur de « l'acropole lycienne » qui paraissait le plus prometteur, en raison de sa nature d'acropole fortifiée et de la présence évidente de nombreux vestiges. La tâche n'était pas simple car les conditions de l'époque étaient très différentes de celles que l'on trouve de nos jours : pas de route, des conditions de logement et d'alimentation précaires, pas d'outillage, pas de magasins et une main d'œuvre inexpérimentée... C'est avec une ténacité exemplaire que ces premiers explorateurs s'attaquèrent à la tâche. Les résultats viennent très rapidement récompenser leur obstination : des bas-reliefs complétant ceux qui avaient été trouvés au XIXe siècle sortent de terre, l'acropole lycienne révèle la présence de vestiges datant de l'époque paléochrétienne.

L'équipe s'étoffa progressivement par la venue de spécialistes, sollicités en fonction des découvertes qui nécessitaient leur intervention : à partir de 1953, ce fut E. Frézouls qui vint fouiller et étudier le théâtre, à partir de 1954 Ch. Delvoye, dont la présence fut requise pour procéder à l'étude des vestiges byzantins. Les découvertes se succédaient mais posaient autant de problèmes qu'elles offraient de surprises : les archéologues classiques qui dirigeaient la fouille, anciens membres de l'École d'Athènes, étaient rompus à la pratique de l'archéologie grecque mais peu habitués au contact avec les franges du monde grec. Ce fut pour eux, comme pour leurs successeurs, une passionnante aventure intellectuelle et humaine qui leur demanda une grande faculté d'adaptation : la civilisation lycienne présente en effet des particularités nombreuses qui étaient inconnues au début des fouilles et furent parfois la cause de moments de perplexité bientôt surmontée. La céramique locale, les techniques de construction, le style et l'iconographie des sculptures étaient à l'image d'un monde complexe dans lequel les

8. "G. Scharf sketching the Box Tomb" (by himself).

influences extérieures, perse ou grecque, étaient venues habiller un fond culturel indigène qui avait cependant réussi à résister vigoureusement pendant une très longue période.

La découverte de la phase d'occupation protobyzantine fut particulièrement intéressante, et cette dernière continue à fournir aux archéologues des résultats importants. On découvrit alors combien cette région dans son ensemble et la ville de Xanthos en particulier avait été prospère et peuplée du IVe au VIIe siècle. Sur l'acropole lycienne, Ch. Delvoye et H. Metzger fouillèrent plusieurs maisons de cette époque, luxueuses constructions qui, bien que sévèrement détruites, recélaient encore de belles mosaïques. Sur les flancs Est et Sud de l'acropole, des installations balnéaires, appartenant évidemment à ces magnifiques maisons, livrèrent aussi de superbes mosaïques (la mosaïque de Léda, malheureusement victime par la suite de la bêtise humaine) et un véritable petit nymphée avec bassins, niches et fontaines entièrement recouvertes de placages de marbres polychromes.

Les recherches sur les vestiges protobyzantins de l'acropole lycienne furent interrompues après 1961 : l'obtention par H. Metzger de la concession de fouille du Létôon amena le transfert de la mission archéologique française au grand sanctuaire antique, distant de six kilomètres, où les découvertes se succédèrent au cours des années suivantes. Ch. Delvoye ne put mener à bien la publication des travaux qu'il avait menés à Xanthos et qui restèrent en déshérence du fait de son décès quelques années plus tard : ils ont été courageusement repris par A.-M. Manière-Lévêque à partir de 1995.

9. "Raffaelle casting the inscribed stele" (by G. Scharf).

10. Sketch of the archaeological house (by G. Scharf).

En dehors de l'acropole lycienne, les fouilles avaient aussi dégagé en surface une agora d'époque romaine jouxtant le théâtre. Dans l'angle sud-ouest de celle-ci apparut une église paléochrétienne que les fouilles de Ch. Delvoye dégagèrent en partie et que celles d'A.-M. Manière-Lévêque ont achevé de rendre au jour avec la petite nécropole qui était venue l'entourer.

Plus loin, au centre de la grande aire centrale de la ville antique, couverte d'un maquis dense et confus d'où émergeaient çà et là des ruines de maisons modernes et des tronçons de murs antiques, les archéologues identifièrent les restes d'une grande église (ill. 4) dont l'exploration parut s'imposer : aussi, malgré le déplacement des activités au sanctuaire du Létôon, une fouille fut lancée en 1970 par J.-P. Sodini qui a continué pendant plus de vingt ans à en assurer pas à pas les progrès[1]. Ce travail patient et ardu permit la découverte d'un magnifique bâtiment de plus de soixante-dix mètres de long (ill. 11), dont les dimensions mais aussi le luxe des matériaux et la décoration imposèrent l'identification à la cathédrale de la ville. La longue période de fouille fut suivie, au cours des années quatre-vingts et quatre-vingt dix, de missions d'étude et de restauration qui eurent pour but le sauvetage des centaines de mètres carrés

---

[1]. C. Le Roy fut responsable de la Mission archéologique française de Xanthos-Letoon de 1977 à 1994 ; J. des Courtils, actuel responsable de la Mission, lui a succédé en 1996. Interrompus en 1977, les travaux de J.-P. Sodini purent reprendre en 1986.

de mosaïques qui revêtent le sol des portiques de l'atrium et ceux des nefs de la cathédrale.

Enfin, l'extension des fouilles à proximité de la cathédrale a amené, à partir des années quatre-vingt dix, et plus particulièrement depuis 2001 la découverte de nombreux bâtiments officiels d'époque impériale romaine dont la mise au jour a d'abord permis de constater que la ville de Xanthos avait fait l'objet en ce temps-là d'un vaste programme de rénovation urbaine, consistant dans le tracé de grands axes viaires et l'aménagement de deux agoras supplémentaires, appelées agora nord et agora sud, entourées de quadriportiques et dont l'une, l'agora nord, fut flanquée d'une triple stoa de type basilical qui donnait à Xanthos l'illusion de posséder une basilique civile à la romaine.

L'une des observations archéologiques les plus intéressantes qui furent faites au cours de ces travaux récents consista à montrer qu'une grande partie des portiques et autres édifices de l'époque impériale romaine avaient bénéficié, à l'époque paléochrétienne, de travaux d'embellissement à grande échelle : en effet, aux mosaïques dont la présence avait déjà été constatée par les premiers fouilleurs sous les portiques de l'agora ouest, s'ajoutèrent alors d'autres mosaïques dégagées sous un portique bordant le décumanus (portique dont la superficie devait être d'environ 2000 m² à l'origine), mais aussi sous les portiques bordant l'agora nord ainsi que dans les pièces adjacentes, enfin dans la grande salle (180 m²) qui termine au Nord la « basilique civile ». On se trouve là en présence d'un véritable programme de réhabilitation des bâtiments d'époque impériale, programme qui fut mis en œuvre dans cette superbe période de prospérité que connaît Xanthos du IVe au VIe siècle et qui vit aussi la réalisation de la cathédrale et des magnifiques maisons de l'acropole lycienne, tous édifices qui reçurent aussi des tapis de mosaïques et d'autres décorations luxueuses.

Ainsi les fouilles de Xanthos ont-elles permis de ramener au jour la civilisation de la Lycie antique de l'époque où elle apparaît dans l'histoire, mais aussi d'éclairer d'un jour nouveau la période protobyzantine, qui s'avère ici d'un intérêt tout particulier. Quant aux mosaïques, elles occupent assurément une place de tout premier plan dans le bilan de près de soixante ans d'investigations archéologiques…

Jacques des COURTILS
Professeur, université Michel de Montaigne, Bordeaux 3

11. Overall photo of the East Basilica.

12. The East Basilica at twilight.

Captions for the plans in text

◻ Early-Byzantine period, phase 1
◻ Early-Byzantine period, phase 2
◻ Middle Byzantine period
— Early Byzantine painting
— Medio-Byzantine painting
◯ reconstructed column
water pipes
• -0,54   hypsometric level (0,00 in the synthronon)
◻ ◻   tiles (terra cota)
—·—·— excavation limit
12   corpus number of the pavement

THIS first volume of the Corpus concerning Xanthos is the first in a series of publications resulting from international cooperation and collaboration. It is being published in English because work on the volume began before French and German were accepted as alternative languages for the series. The author initially wrote the text in English, which was then carefully and extensively corrected by D. Parrish. The introduction and acknowledgements are presented in French, and a foreword and abstract are provided in Turkish. We hope this mixture is well received by members of the international scholarly community studying mosaics.

The main part of the volume consists of a catalogue of the church pavements, described and analyzed in a format (individual mosaic entry or fiche) established by David Parrish and definitively agreed upon by the General Assembly of AIEMA-Türkiye in its meeting at Bursa in June 2006.

A general discussion of the mosaics and their architectural setting follows.

The Turkish abstract contains a synthesis of the general discussion of the pavements preceded by translations of excerpts from the catalogue. This material contains detailed descriptions of the buildings and their pavements, accompanied by the most important plans.

There has been compiled an index of the sites referred to as comparisons, mentioning their ancient name, the ancient region they belonged to, and the modern name of the country (many ancient sites have the same name today). This index does not pretend to serve as an overall study of mosaics in the Near East.

A bibliography and tables indicating the density of cubes in mosaics come next. The English spelling of site names comes from Barrington 2000.

Three fold-out plans (two phases of the Early Byzantine basilica, and plan of the Medieval church) conclude the volume.

II. Catalogue of the pavements

13. Draft plan of a mosaic of the nave.

The East Basilica is one of the main buildings of the Early Byzantine period, located in the center of ancient Xanthos, near the intersection of the principal *decumanus* and *cardo* (ill.4), both of which probably were flanked by porticoes decorated with Early Byzantine mosaics. An important *dipylon* links the two streets near the façade of the church, and from the *decumanus* leads to the Agora. The building standing opposite the church on the other side of the *cardo* is a major civil basilica with Early Byzantine alterations (floors)[1]. Along the N side of the basilica there probably occurred an episcopal complex, still unexcavated. A secondary entrance leads from the N annex of the baptistery (located E of the church) toward a gate in the city walls, found further S.

The first excavations were conducted by H. Metzger, with soundings made by P. Demargne. J.-P. Sodini undertook a systematic excavation of the large building, from 1970 to 1977. Since 1986, he has made additional soundings, complemented by the restoration of paintings, mosaics and sculpture, and has combined digging with the study of materials (ceramics, tombs) and the completion of the entire architectural and graphic documentation.

---

1. Des Courtils-Cavalier 2001.

BUILDING PRECEDING THE CHURCH

Traces of earlier buildings appeared during the excavations, especially in the deep probe made in the narthex of the Middle Byzantine church erected inside the earlier baptistery. At least one major building occurred on the slope. An important collector basin was located nearby, and it and a few rainspouts may have belonged to a public monument such as a bath building (located N of the center of the N aisle). No evidence of such a structure was actually discovered during the excavations, because it was deeply buried under the terrace supporting the basilica. A mosaic fragment was found in the probe under the Middle Byzantine narthex. This floor continues under the lowest foundations of the Early Byzantine church (ill. 15): the level of the floor in the N aisle and apse occurs ca. 2.20 m above a thick infill. The mosaic also is around 30 cm below the Middle Byzantine floor. As the style and motifs indicate, this pavement probably belonged to a Roman building, perhaps a villa, but nothing remains of its walls.

1. Roman mosaic
Opus tessellatum
Illustrations 14, 15.
Its overall dimensions are unknown, and only a small part of the borders and perhaps of the field is preserved. Fragment's dimensions: 2.60 x 0.70 m.
Density of tesserae/dm^2: 50.

Colors: dark blue, white, red, pink, blue, light yellow and yellow. The dark blue stone outlines the pattern and is used like black; it looks like marble (Aphrodisian marble?).

State of preservation: the fragment is well preserved, with an excellent support and excellent technique in the laying of tesserae, placed very closely together. The pavement was deliberately destroyed by construction of the church. Further W, we found a concrete floor, wich could be an ancient repair of the mosaic pavement, showing it was used for a long time.

Description
Border 1: 88 cm wide. Bichrome latchkey-meander of spaced upright double latchkeys with a square (or rectangle?) in each space (*Décor* I, pl. 40e). The pattern is drawn in red or dark blue triple fillets. A polychrome four-tesserae chessboard pattern adorns the partly preserved square (or rectangle), forming oblique lines of white, dark blue, blue, white, dark blue, yellow. This border is framed on the inner side by a white band six tesserae wide.
Border 2: 39 cm wide. Polychrome tightly braided, round-tongued double guilloche opened to form eyelets (*Décor* I, pl. 75a) on a dark blue ground. The strands are shaded alternately with a dominant red (dark blue, two red, pink, white, dark blue), blue (dark blue, two blue, white, dark blue) or yellow strand (dark blue, yellow, light yellow, white, dark blue). This border is doubled on the inner side by a white band five tesserae wide.
Border 3: 36 cm wide. Red wave pattern (*Décor* I, pl. 101b) on white ground; this border is doubled on the inner side by a red triple fillet and a white triple fillet.
Border 4: 15 cm wide. Simple polychrome guilloche (*Décor* I, pl. 70j) on a dark blue ground. Strands are colored alternately with a dominant red (dark blue, two red, pink, white, dark blue), yellow (dark blue, two yellow, two white, dark blue) or blue (dark blue, two blue, two white, dark blue).
Border 5: 26 cm wide. Polychrome row of tangent juxtaposed bells forming tangent inverted bells and an undulating line, each bell horizontally shaded (*Décor* I, pl. 60 ?) and the undulating line drawn in white. Bell's mouth is marked by a serrated white triangle. Bells are colored alternately blue and dark blue; dark blue, red and pink; dark blue, yellow and light yellow. This border is outlined on the inner edge by a white band three tesserae wide.
Field: dimensions are unknown. Pelta-wheel around a polychrome Solomon knot (*Décor* II, p. 42); it could be part of a repetitive pattern (*Décor* I, pl. 223). Peltae are white, field's corners yellow and red, and resulting spaces between the peltae are red ornamented with a white triangle. Strands of the Solomon knot are alternately shaded blue (dark blue, two blue, white, dark blue) or pink (dark blue, red, two pink, white, dark blue).

Comparisons: among many examples, we cite a mosaic in a bath complex at Sardis (Hanfmann-Detweiler 1962, pl. XXXVII) which shows parallels in the choice of motifs (double guilloche and pelta wheel, Solomon knot).

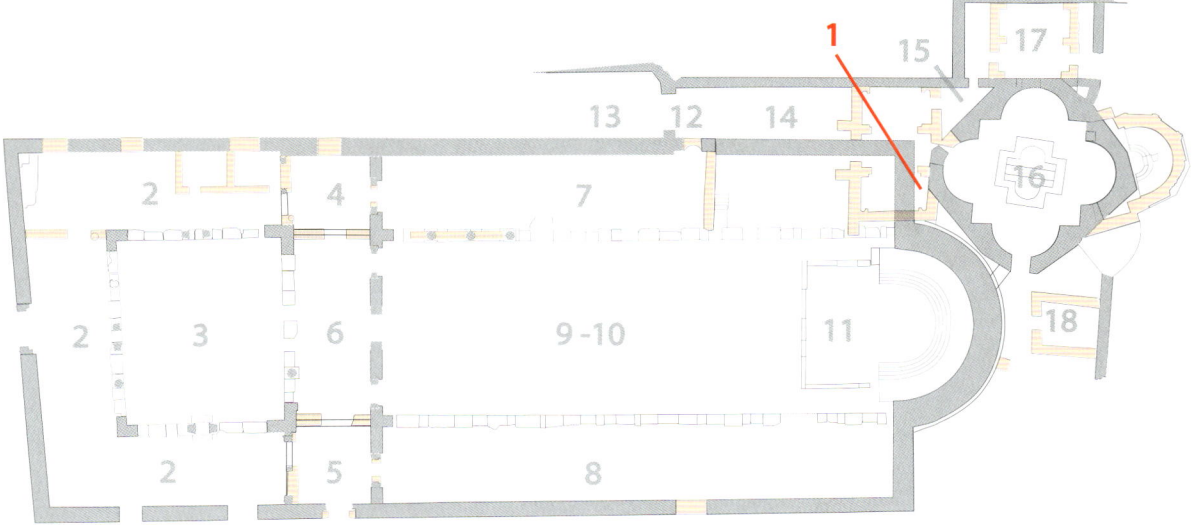

14. Plan showing location of the Roman Mosaic.

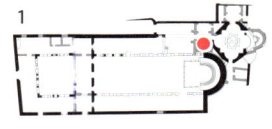

15. Roman pavement.

16. Plans of the two Early Byzantine phases of the floors.

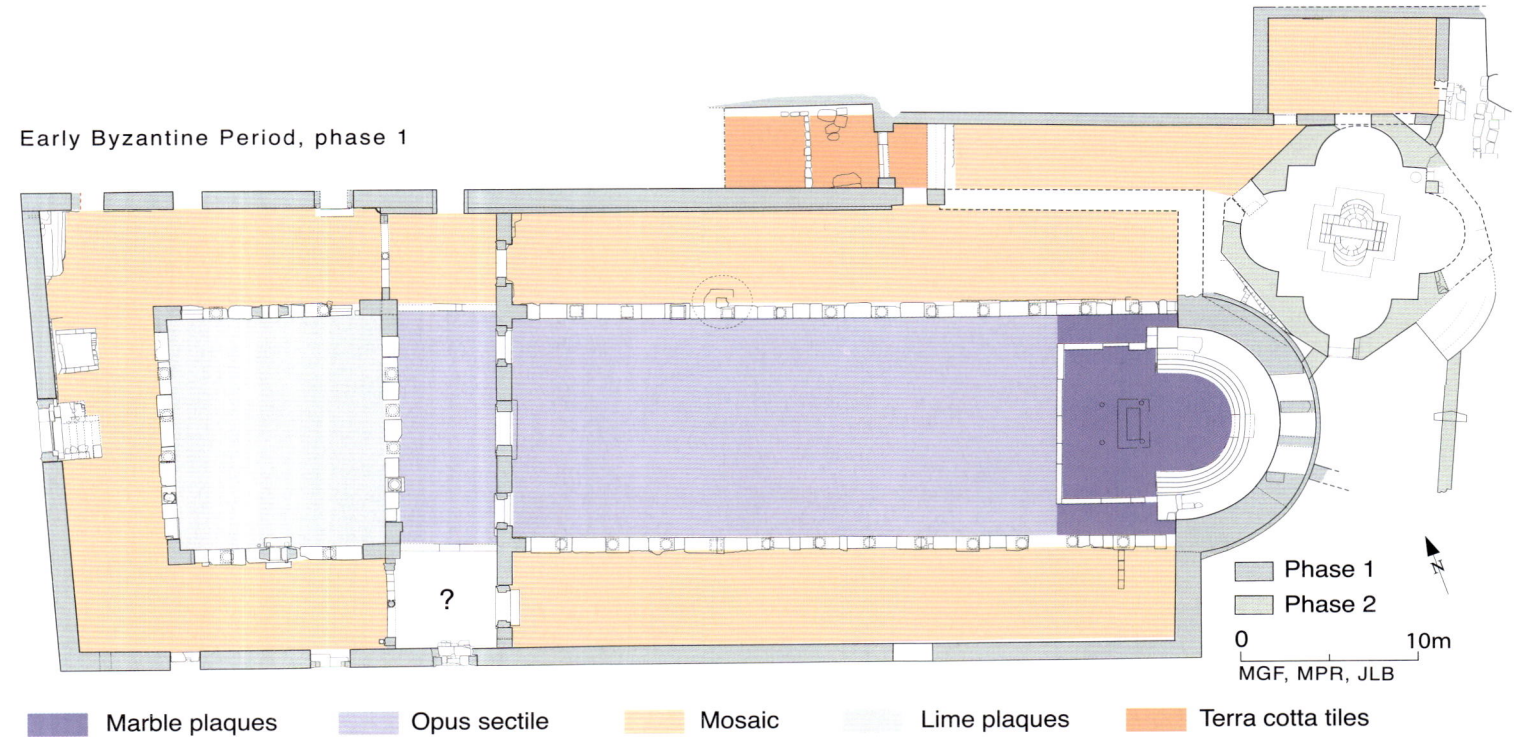

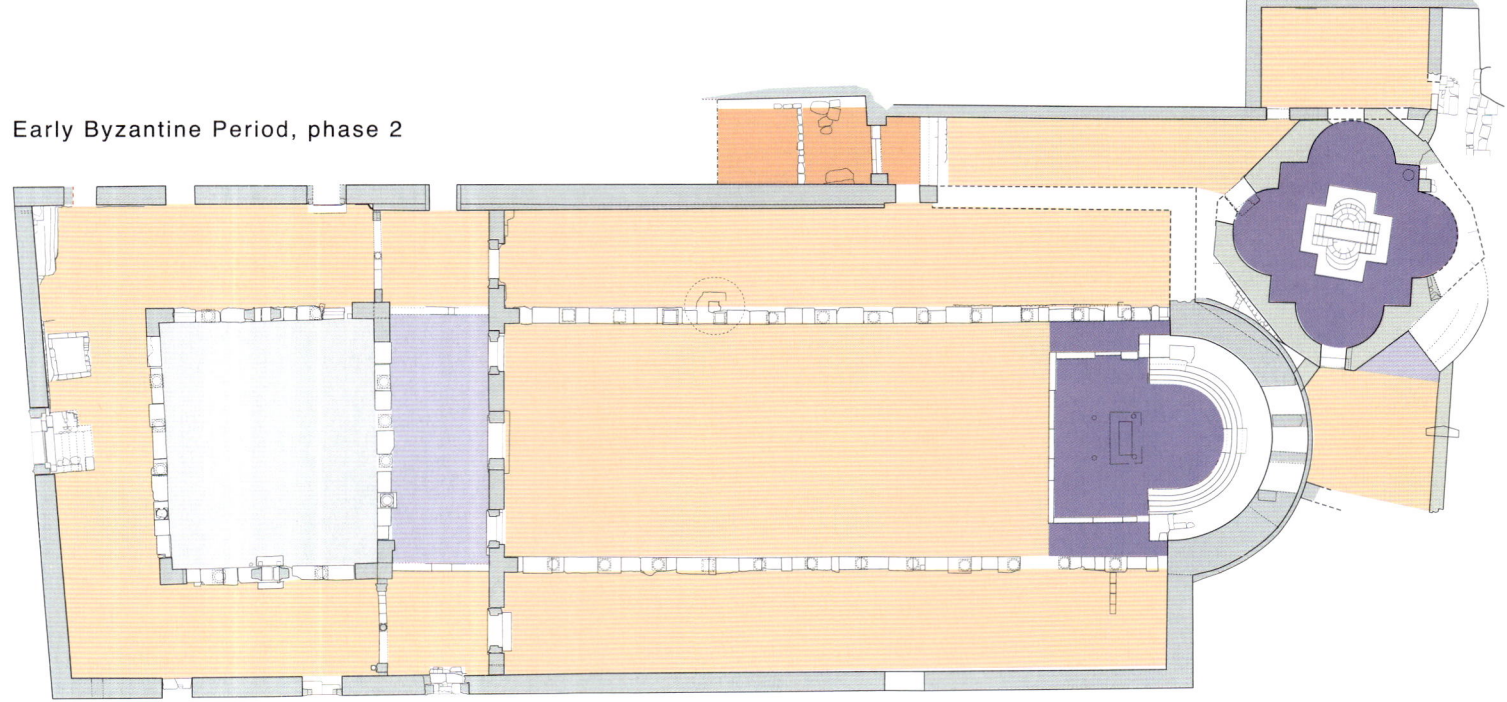

EARLY BYZANTINE BASILICA COMPLEX

The East Basilica (fold-out plans A and B) is a very large building covering ca. 2400 m² (ill. 175). It has a three-portico atrium with a central court below the *cardo*, and the fourth (E) portico forms part of the narthex. The church consists of a nave and two aisles in the proportion of 2/1/1, leading to the sanctuary with its U-shaped chancel screens, and to an apse with a *synthronon* and a central *cathedra* for the bishop. A door occurs in the center of the N aisle, and is connected to a corridor that flanks the church at a lower level; it leads to a baptistery in the form of a tetraconch, located NE of the apse and two meters below it. This wide vaulted space (measuring more than 100 m²) contains central bilobed fonts. N and S annexes complete the ecclesiastical ensemble, and a door in the N annex linked the basilica to a city gate located nearby in a SE direction. The existence of columns, bases and capitals of two different scales proves that there were 2nd-story galleries over the narthex and aisles, although the side-rooms of the narthex, which likely contained stairs, have not yet been excavated. Most of sculptural decoration (made primarily of Proconnesian marble) probably was imported from Proconnessos or Constantinople, with the exception of a few local capitals with gadroons, and *spolia*. The building as a whole recalls in several respects the Church of St John Stoudios in Constantinople, both in its overall form and in many architectural details.

An important episcopal complex probably surrounded the church, mainly on its N side, but this has not yet been excavated.

Atrium

The atrium has three porticoes framing a central court paved with limestone slabs (ill. 18). The mosaics paving the three porticoes (N, W, S sides) appear simply organized, as geometric carpets placed side by side. Upon close observation, we can distinguish the activity of two different workshops, with various characteristics to be defined.

These differences concern the floors' overall arrangement, the presence or not of borders, and the choice of simple patterns versus very complex ones. They also concern the choice of materials and colors and adjustments made to the architectural context.

Two homogeneous ensembles are visible (ill. 19):

- In the N half of the atrium there occur seven carpets decorating the N portico, and the N part of the W portico up to the mosaic carpet located at the foot of the entrance stairs.

- The S half of the atrium contains two long subdivided carpets, one located in the S part of

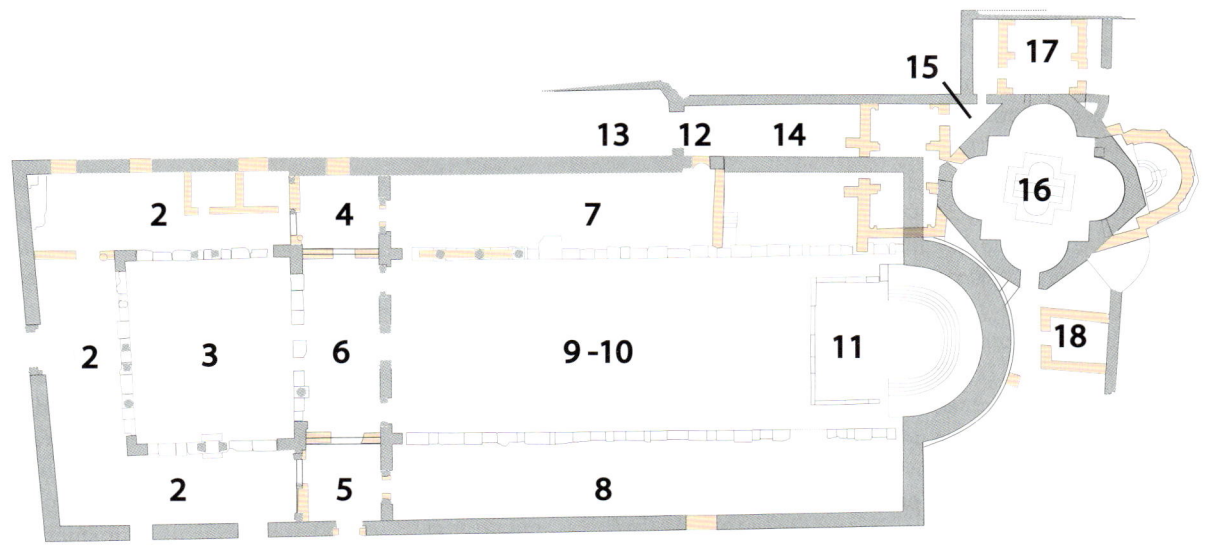

17. Scheme with the numbers of the Early Byzantine pavements.

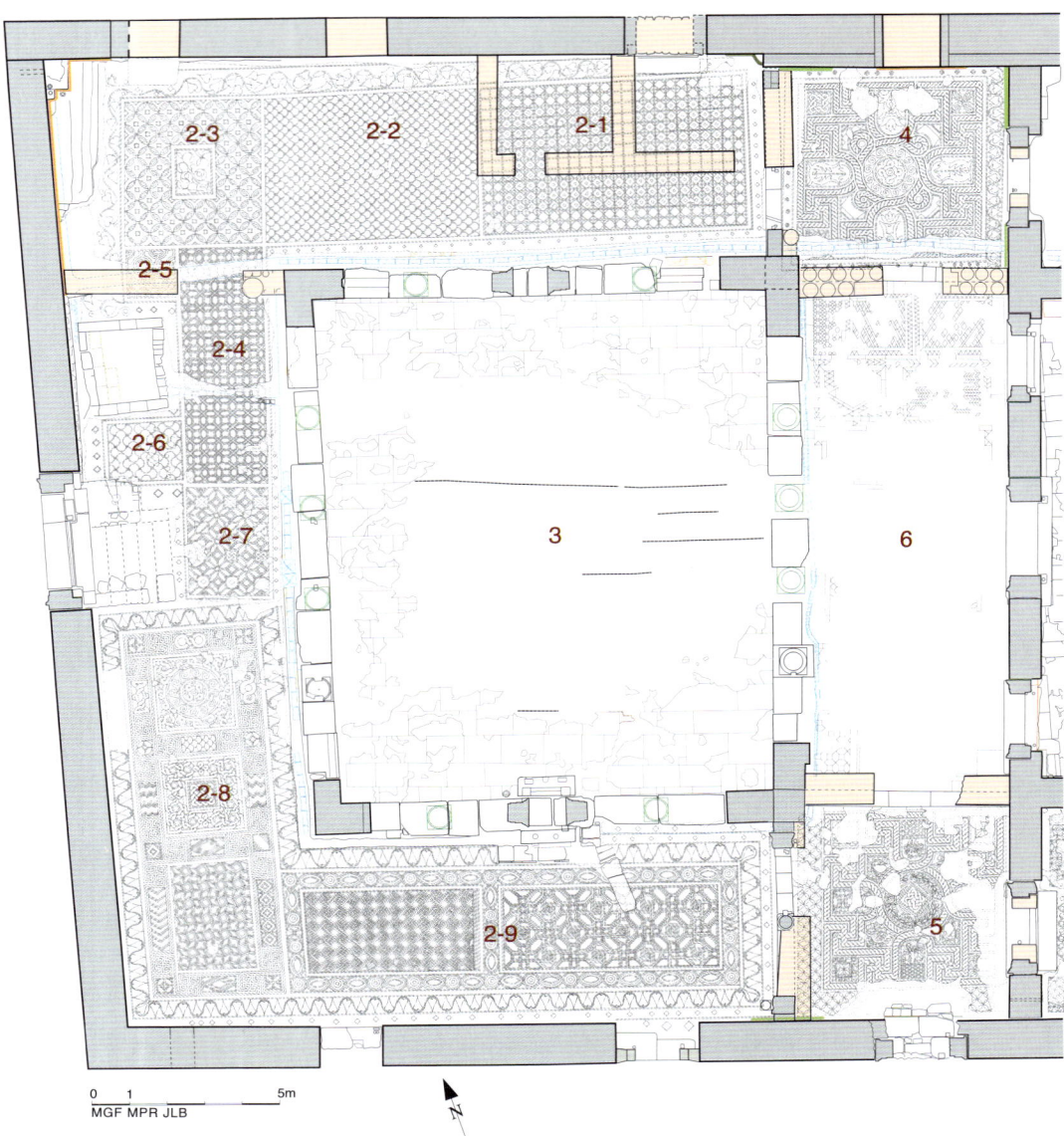

18. Plan of the atrium (pavements 2 and 3) and the narthex (4 to 6).

the W portico (and cut into three sections) and the other found in the S portico (and divided into two sections).

Three doors open toward the N, probably in relation to the episcopal complex; two others open toward the S; and there are three openings toward the central court in the center of the portico stylobates. The lateral part of each of these openings was equipped with chancel screens.

2. Atrium mosaic
Opus tessellatum
Illustrations 18-45, 153-154, 156, 171, 180-181.

N part of the atrium

The mosaics in this sector form an L, including carpets **2**-7. The juxtaposed carpets are separated from each other by a continuous white band six tesserae wide, which frames the ensemble and is separated from the outer margins by a black double fillet.

There are no borders around the carpets (unlike the pavements in the S part of the atrium), and their grouping was complicated by various architectural features located along the wall of the W portico, including a set of stairs, a presumed cleansing basin or *pediluve*, and a masonry around a drainpipe. These architectural features preceded the laying of the mosaics and had to be taken into account by the mosaicist.

The entrance stairs, no longer visible and leaving only traces of their foundations, led down six steps from the street level to the level of the church. The entrance occurs in the middle of the façade wall, and the stairs extend half way across the W portico. We observed two construction phases. The mosaic dates from the widening of the entrance stairs and the main door, and the central opening to the atrium court is aligned with the steps. A large basin (1.25 x 1.10 m), probably used as a *pediluve*, occurs to the N of the stairs, separated from them by a small space (carpet **2**-6). The bottom of the basin, covered by tiles, lies ca. 40-50 cm below the floor level. The roughly square basin has poorly preserved edges, rising 15 cm above the adjacent mosaics, and the basin's placement is slightly oblique.

A vertical waterspout occupies the corner of the N and W porticoes. Originating N of the church (on a higher part of the hill), it extends horizontally 1.00 m above the floor by means of a pipe following the wall and supported by the bedrock mass that encroaches on the portico (up to 0.80 m). It was installed in the Early Byzantine period and restored a few times. It probably was reused early in the Middle Byzantine period and later abandoned and covered over, as demonstrated by a fill with a marble slab found inside the pipe (altar table fragments). A slightly earlier pipe led to the *pediluve*.

Traces of red wall painting appear at various points in the atrium, but they were mostly covered by medieval frescoes. In a few places (NE and SE corners), we can distinguish two layers of painting. In the SE part of the atrium, near the E door, there are represented green grapes on a red ground. The painting on the S wall between the S atrium and S narthex is continuous, indicating that in the first phase, the two spaces were joined (a fact confirmed by study of the architecture, with the mosaic dating to their separation).

All of the atrium mosaics are executed in *opus tessellatum*, preserved *in situ*. They were restored in 2001 and 2007, and verification of their condition is recommended after each tourist season, even though visitors can not walk on the mosaics.

Description
Outer margins
Illustrations 18, 20.

The width of the outer margins surrounding the group of seven carpets in the N atrium varies significantly, following the architectural features and compensating for the obliqueness of certain walls. It measures 30 to 100 cm in width and is adorned with either an ivy scroll or a line of non-contiguous poised squares.

• Ivy scroll: it occurs along the N wall of the church and the W façade as far as the *pediluve*. A double black sinusoid forms the scroll on the N, changing to a red and black double fillet on the W, where the leaf stem linked to the sinusoid is the same color as the fillet from which it rises (alternately red or black) (ill. 20). The leaves, placed obliquely, are colored black along the N wall, and elsewhere appear either blue and red, pink outlined in black, or yellow outlined in red. There occur two leaves in each undulation along the N wall, where the outer margin is framed on both sides by a black double fillet. In front of the door N of carpet **2**-3 (opening in the direction of what probably is the

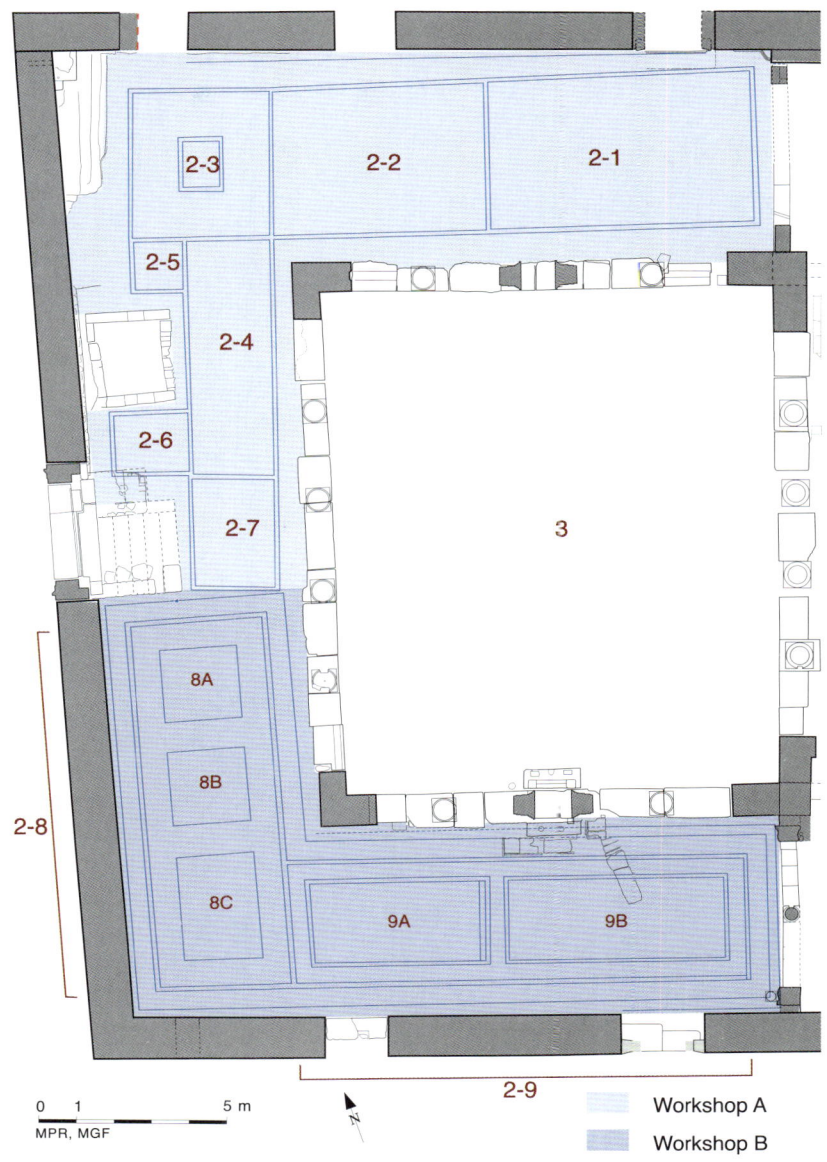

19. Scheme of the atrium, with the numbers of the carpets and panels.

20. Outer margin with *hederae*.

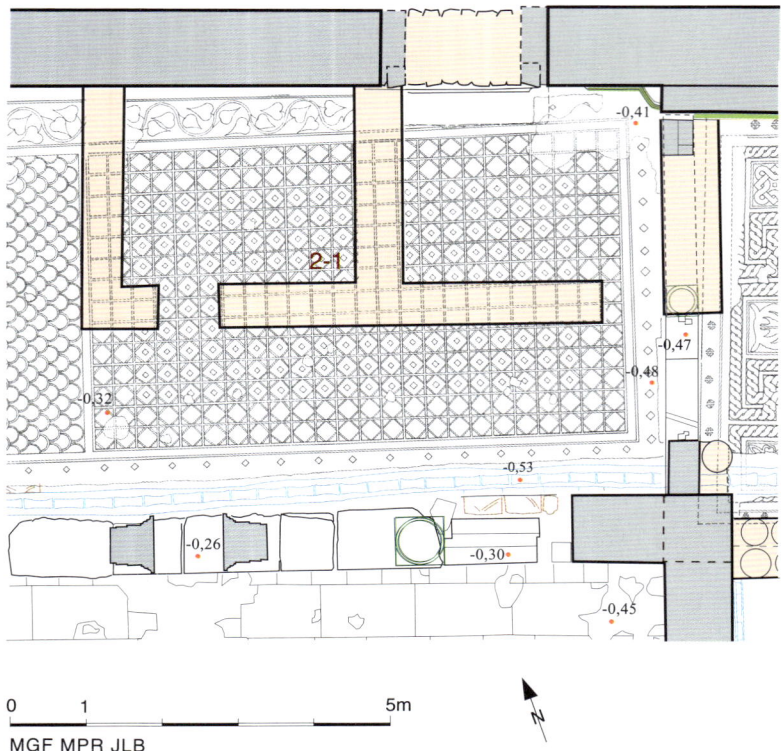

21. Plan of carpet 2-1.

22. Ensemble view of carpet 2-1.

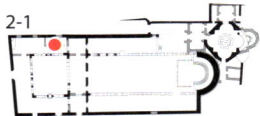

episcopal complex), the outer margin becomes narrower (30 cm) and is adorned with only the stem of the scroll; it has flatter undulations, with each leaf replaced by a small poised serrated square, shaded in black, red, white. Pairs of squares occur in the inner undulations of the scroll. The scroll ends on the E with a bilobed flower laid against a step (now lost), which is located beyond the threshold of the E door of the atrium. Further E, the outer margin becomes plain white.

No black double fillet frames the scroll's outer edge along the W wall. As noted above, a single leaf fills each undulation, sometimes accompanied by a spiral tendril, especially toward the S where the margin is wider. Next to the *pediluve*, the scroll ends in a double volute mostly hidden by a later wall built over the pavement. The undulating stem of the scroll merges at its S end with the black and red double fillet framing carpet **2**-5.

• Lines of non-contiguous serrated poised squares occur in the outer margins of the stylobate of the portico. A later trench damaged these margins when a repair was made to a pipe below the floor (pipe missing in the N part of the W portico). Along the stylobate of the W portico, the squares are colored black and white, whereas along the stylobate of the N portico, they are shaded black, red, white, or only black and red. They are quite regularly spaced near the black double fillet framing the carpets.

The entrance stairs were surrounded by an outer margin of variable width limited by a black fillet. This margin also is punctuated by serrated poised squares, larger on the N, where two of them are visible (one of them black, red, black, and the other black, yellow, red, pink, blue, white). The squares in the E margin are better preserved (black and red). The margin located S of the stairs is plain white. A few other squares of varying dimensions (black, red, white) surround the *pediluve*, placed obliquely. They appear framed by a black double fillet on the S and E, and a red and black double fillet on the N.

Comparisons: a scroll of *hederae* used as an outer margin is so common, particularly in the E Mediterranean, that it does not require us to cite numerous examples. It is worth noting, however, that products of probably the same workshop as the one at Xanthos, occur at nearby Patara, below the so-called Women's Chapel built over a Late Roman structure (Işık 1999, fig. 6; Işık 2000, p. 114, fig. 90), and at Arykanda (Lycia), also with similar mosaics (Akıllı 1988, fig. 4). Closely related scrolls are also visible at Aphrodisias (Bishop's Palace, Rm. 3, Campbell 1991, fig. 52; the Priest's House atrium, Rm. 3 [*ibid.*, figs. 84-85] and especially Rm. 4 [*ibid.*, fig. 88] with a bichrome stem resembling the scroll in the W outer margin in the N atrium at Xanthos. Other examples occur in Greece and the Greek islands, as at Hermione (Sodini 1968, fig. 48), which is stylistically very similar; Nicopolis (Basilica A, S narthex, *ibid.*, fig. 250), and Athens (Tetraconch, Rm. 1, Spiro 1978, fig. 17; Villa, Rm. 5, *ibid.*, fig. 60).

2-1, atrium (N portico)
Illustrations 18, 21-22.
Rectangle at E end of N portico, placed lengthwise. 6.95 x 4.10 m.
Density of tesserae/dm^2: 40.
Colors: black (dark grey), white (limestone), red (terracotta), pink.
State of preservation: good overall, with a few burned spots and small gaps. Middle Byzantine walls (11th c.) were built over the pavement, dividing the surface into small Medieval rooms.

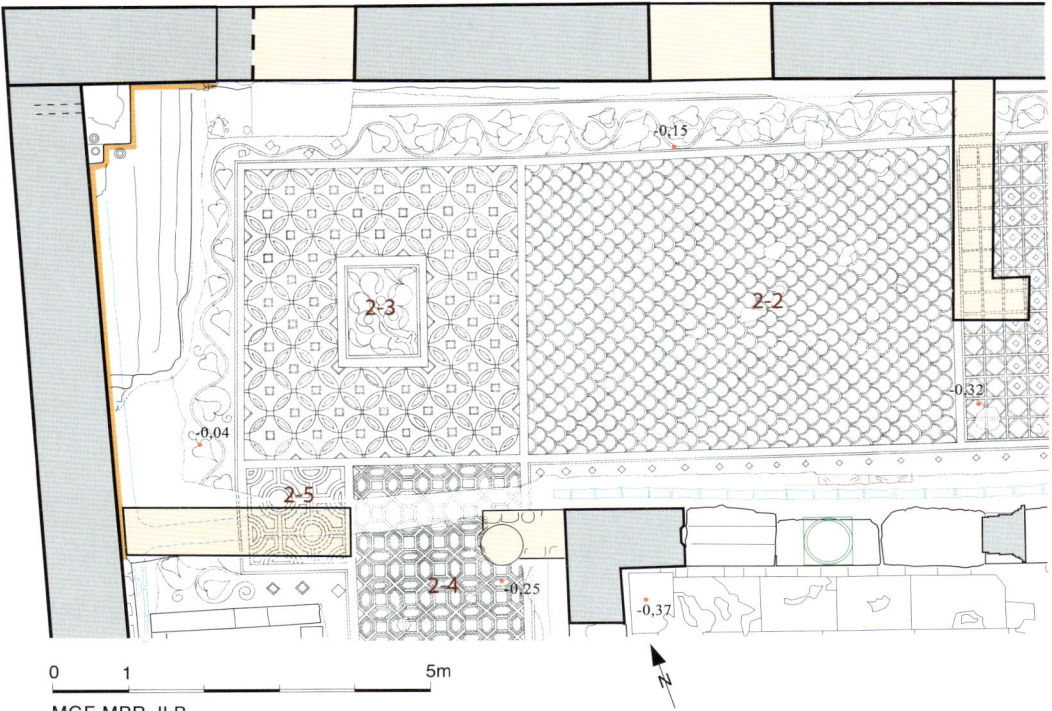
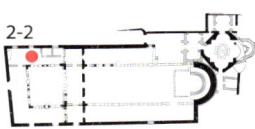

23. Plan of carpets 2-2 and 2-3.

24. Overall view of carpet 2-2.

Description
Border: white band six tesserae wide, framed by black double fillet.
Field: grid of black double fillets (ill. 22), whose intersections overlie polychrome poised serrated squares contiguous to each other (*Décor* I, pl. 123); the poised squares are shaded in color (black, red, rose, with a white center). The grid's compartments contain a small inscribed poised serrated square (black, red, white), except in the outer two rows of the carpet (empty compartments).

Commentary: this pattern was popular in late antiquity, and a few examples occur at Xanthos. The polychrome serrated squares reflect the influence of the rainbow style in this common type of grid, and the design here is very regular. Its originality derives from the superposition of two distinct patterns, one a grid of orthogonal double fillets and the other an oblique chessboard pattern.

Comparisons: probably made by the same workshop is a similar mosaic in neighboring Patara (below the so-called Women's Chapel, built over a Late Roman structure, Işık 1999, p. 171, fig. 6). We also found two examples, not exactly alike in pattern but similar stylistically, in Anemurium, one in the Church of the Holy Apostles (beginning 6th c., atrium, in black-and-white, Campbell 1998, pl. 106), the second in the Central Church ("Treasury" Church, baptistery, beginning 6th c., *ibid.*, pl. 178a). Another example, with superimposed patterns

but a different type of execution, occurs at Sardis (Early Christian Basilica, Hanfmann 1973, fig. 30). On Karpathos, there is a related example (Basilica of Arkaseia, Jacopich 1925, fig. 3).

2-2, atrium (N portico)
Illustrations 18, 23-24, 166.
Rectangle placed lengthwise in N portico. 5.62 x 4.04 m.
   Density of tesserae/dm^2: 43-48.
   Colors: black, white, red, pink, yellow.
   State of preservation: good overall, with a few gaps due to fallen architectural blocks, and a few burned spots.

2-2

25. Overall view of carpet 2-3.

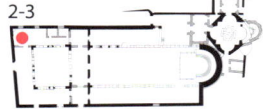

Description
Border: black double fillet and white band six tesserae wide.
Field: the field and border do not seem separated, since white double fillets delineate both the pattern and individual motifs. There is a grid with an orthogonal pattern of adjacent scales (*Décor* I, pl. 215) (ill. 24). The scales (w. 22 cm) are turned eastward and have four different colors, creating the effect of diagonal lines oriented SW-NE. The color sequence is as follows: 2 white, black, with various colors for the center (2 white with a pink center, 2 red with a white center, one yellow with a white center or 2 pink with a white center). There appear a few irregularities mostly along the edge of the field.

Commentary: the originality of this familiar pattern is its white outline, unlike the usual black, making it appear light and airy. The use of color also is unusual and creates a *trompe l'oeil* effect (ill. 166).

Comparisons: this pattern is widespread among mosaics in all periods, and one example closely resembling ours occurs in nearby Arykanda (Lycia) where a few mosaics are similar (Akıllı 1988, figs. 3, 19, 21). We also find close examples twice at Heraklea Lynkestis, Rm. 4 and Refectory (Cveković-Tomašević 2002, figs. 55 and 5) with the same white design and colors creating diagonal lines. Another very similar design occurs in the basilica of Laureotic Olympus (E of the altar, Corpus Greece 2, figs. 127, 224).

2-3, atrium (corner of N and W porticoes)
Illustrations 18, 23, 25-26 and cover image.
Rectangle in corner of N and W porticoes, placed in N-S direction. 3.96 x 3.60 m.

Materials: purple that is a very hard stone, probably marble; its use is rare in this church and limited to a few pavements in the N atrium and N narthex, and also perhaps at the entrance to the N aisle of the church (the mosaic's poor preservation makes this uncertain). Green in the form of a light, bright marble, almost turquoise; its use is quite rare, limited to carpets **2-3**, **2-5** and **2-7** in the atrium and S narthex.

Density of tesserae/dm²: 43 in field, 52 in central panel.

Colors: black, white, red, pink, yellow, purple, green.

State of preservation: the mosaic is intact with a few traces of burning. This carpet, with outer margins of varying width, is not aligned with the W portico's axis, but shifted eastward due to the bedrock and a masonry supporting a drainpipe along the W wall. The design was intended to be viewed from the S, and not from the threshold further N on the axis of the portico, which probably led to the episcopal complex.

Description
Border: black double fillet and white band six rows wide.
Field: a black fillet frames the field, separating it from the outer margin. A small pictorial panel, placed off-center, interrupts the carpet's geometric pattern.

The field has an orthogonal polychrome pattern of intersecting circles (*Décor* I, pl. 237d), forming saltires of quasi-tangent spindles and concave squares, with 4-6 tesserae at the points of tangency (ill. 25). The circles have a diameter of 54 cm, and the spindles are outlined in black. On the NW-SE axis of the pavement, they appear mainly reddish (black, red, pink with a white center), whereas those on the carpet's perpendicular axis are yellow (black, yellow, with a white center). The white concave poised squares contain a small serrated square (black, red, pink, with a white center).

This pattern and its filler motifs are quite regular, and the color arrangement creates a *trompe l'oeil* effect of diagonal lines of spindles of the same color.
Panel: the small off-center panel is rectangular and framed by a white band six tesserae wide, limited by an outer black fillet and an inner black and red double fillet. Without its frame, the panel measures 1.22 x 0.94 m. It contains a diagonally oriented pomegranate tree (ill. 26), whose sinuous trunk is colored red and yellow, with a white center near the base (SE corner). The curved branches have large, spindle-shaped green and yellow leaves outlined in black; in some places, purple replaces black to suggest shading. There appear three easily recognizable pomegranates, colored half red and half yellow, with red and pink in the uppermost fruit.

Commentary: this carpet is significant for the superposition of a floral panel on the center of the field. It was not by accident that mosaicists chose this location for special decoration: its position

26. Detail of carpet 2-3, pomegranate tree.

in one corner of the atrium drew the viewer's attention, leading him to the N aisle and beyond it to the baptistery. The pomegranate tree, found in many churches in the Near East, often symbolizes resurrection and accordingly leads to the baptistery in this building. It is the only pictorial panel in the church's atrium and can be seen from the building's entrance. The closest door on the N probably was a secondary entrance to the episcopal complex and was approached by (at least) one step raised above the level of the pavement.

Comparisons: the field's pattern is very common, with only two examples cited from Asia Minor, respectively at Aphrodisias (Campbell 1991, Bishop's Palace, Rm. 3, pl. 49) where the pattern displays the same polychrome diagonals as at Xanthos; and at Anemurium (Necropolis Church, Russell 1988, fig. 6).

The pomegranate tree is a frequent symbol in Early Christian mosaics. We cite a mosaic at the nearby site of Gemiler Ada (Island of St. Nicholas, Lycia) where there is preserved a very similar pomegranate tree, perhaps made by the same workshop (Church 3, Asano 1998 without numbered pages) ; also at Aphrodisias (the Priest' House, Rm. 4, Campbell 1991, pls. 88-90) where the double scroll of laurel displays leaves very similar to those in the Xanthos pomegranate tree. In Thessaloniki too, a pomegranate tree offers parallels with ours (intersection of Moreas and Mouson Streets, Corpus Greece 3, pl. XLII).

2-3 field

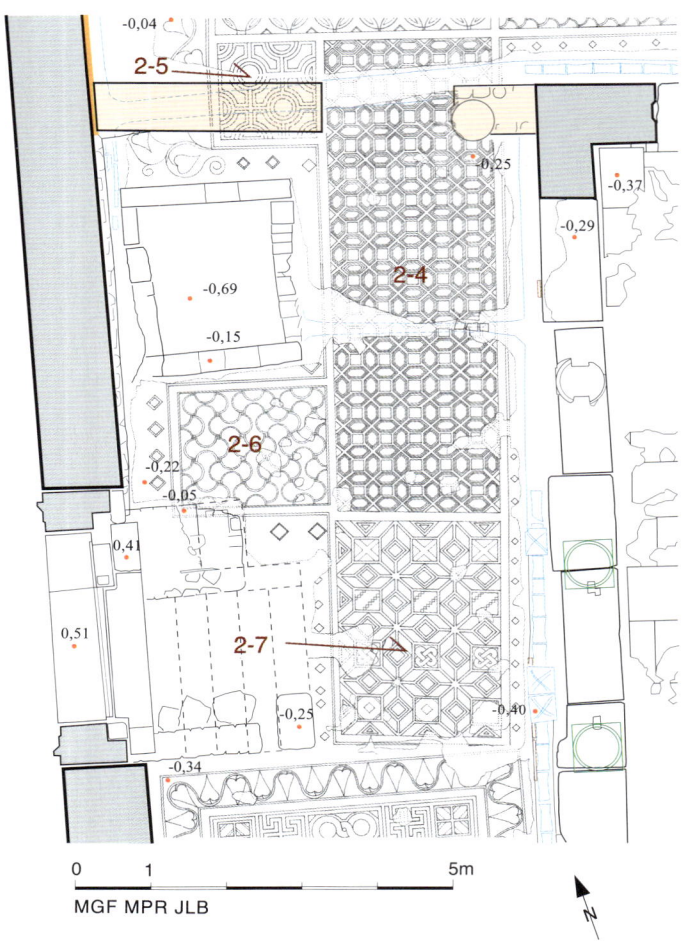

27. Plan of carpets 2-4 to 2-7.

28. Overall view of carpet 2-4 to 2-6.

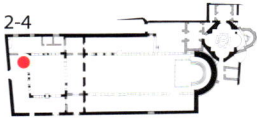

2-4

2-4, atrium (W portico)
Illustrations 18, 27-28.

Rectangular carpet, flanking the stylobate of the W portico (but not centered in the portico, nor aligned with the panel showing a pomegranate tree in carpet **2**-3). 6.52 x 2.20 m (slightly irregular). It forms a corridor linking carpet **2**-3 in the corner with the pavement at the foot of the entrance stairs (carpet **2**-7) and it has the same width as the latter. One can see the masonry foundation constructed between this carpet and the W wall, which occurs halfway along the pavement and originally formed a basin for ablutions, as its placement near the entrance indicates (cf. the architectural description). N of this basin is small carpet **2**-5, and to the S is carpet **2**-6. The orthogonal arrangement of the carpets gives the ensemble a structured appearance, despite the grouping of several variously shaped units. The present corridor indicates the path of circulation.

Density of tesserae/dm^2: 40-45.

Colors: black, white, yellow, pink.

State of preservation: the S part of the carpet was damaged by many heavy, fallen architectural fragments (lintel of the main entrance) and there are traces of burning. The NE corner of the mosaic is covered by a wall (with a reused column) added during the Middle Byzantine period, when the atrium was divided.

A few trenches were dug through the mosaic to repair the drains underneath. This was done both at the end of the Early Byzantine period and in Middle Byzantine times, but the trenches were made before the space was divided by walls (the pipes probably were clogged after years of disuse and abandonment). The first N-S trench was opened in the E outer margin of the mosaic along the stylobate, to uncover the terracotta drainpipes placed around the atrium. This trench was randomly filled with fragments of stone slabs. Two other narrow trenches divided the carpet from E to W, probably also to uncover drainpipes, with one of them passing through the center of the carpet and the other appearing N of it (evacuation of the *pediluve* and a feeder pipe); all of these features relate to the masonry located next to carpet **2**-3 (water transport). The N transverse underground drainage is an extension of that occurring along the stylobate of the N portico and probably is connected to it.

Description: orthogonal pattern of irregular octagons (ill. 28), intersecting and adjacent on the long sides, forming squares and oblong hexagons (*Décor* I, pl. 170a). A white double fillet forms the grid, which is five octagons wide and seventeen octagons long. The oblong hexagons are outlined by a black fillet, doubled on the long sides. On the N-S axis, the hexagons are colored pink (two rows) with a white center; on the perpendicular axis they are yellow (double fillet) with a white center. There are no irregularities in the polychromy. The squares (12 cm/side) are outlined in black and have a white center. The field is framed by a white band six tesserae wide. The color scheme creates the effect of an orthogonal grid of rows of hexagons.

Comparisons: it is a very common pattern, and we find it twice elsewhere in the East Basilica (N aisle inv. **7**-2, and S aisle inv. **8**-4). We cite only a few examples in Asia Minor and others that are closely related stylistically, as at Arykanda (Lycia) (Akıllı 1988, figs. 1, 20A-20B). Also at Aphrodisias (Campbell 1991, Priest's House, Rm. 6, figs. 94-95) where the pattern is very similar to Xanthos, N atrium, with the same chromatic arrangement and design executed in white; at Knidos (in Church V of the 6th c., Love 1972, fig. 35), at Kelkit (near Erzincan, Sevim 1991, fig. 1). We also found numerous examples in Greece, as in churches at Amphipolis (Basilica Gamma, Rm. 12, Spiro 1978, fig. 705) with a white design, or Laureotic Olympus (Corpus Greece 2, fig. 225), Epidauros (nave, Sodini 1968, fig. 17), Daphnous (N transept, *ibid.*, figs. 123-124) on a dark ground, and Philippi (Basilica beneath the Octagon, Rm. 1, Spiro 1968, fig. 706). On the islands, see Rhodes (Basilica of Hatjiandreas grounds, Corpus Greece 1, fig. 58c), very close in style; Astypalaia (Basilica Kareklè, Corpus Greece 1, fig. 3) and Kos (Basilica St. John, baptistery, Di Matteis 2004, pl. LXXXVIII-1).

2-5, atrium (W portico)

Illustrations 18, 25 (top right), 27.

Rectangle (almost square) located in portico margin W of N end of carpet **2**-4, slightly trapezoidal. 1.32 x 1.28 m. This small carpet occurs between the W wall of the atrium, carpet **2**-3 on the N, carpet **2**-4 on the E, and the *pediluve* on the S. It fills an empty space but does not follow the path of circulation. Two-thirds of this carpet is covered by a Middle Byzantine wall built over the pavement. The N trench cutting carpet **2**-4 occurs just in front of this carpet and probably continues through it, although the later wall conceals this part.

Density of tesserae/dm^2: 40-46.
Colors: black, white, pink, yellow, green, red.
State of preservation: visible part is in good condition.

Description: orthogonal pattern of irregular octagons with four concave sides, forming circles and concave-sided oblong hexagons (*Décor* I, pl. 171a). A white double fillet creates the grid (ill. 25, top right). The circles (diam. 40 cm) are variously colored (black, red, yellow, two white, black with a white center). The oblong hexagons have varied colors along the diagonal axes: black, pink, yellow with a white center on the NE-SW axis; and black, green, pink with a white center on the perpendicular axis. A white band six tesserae wide frames the carpet, and is limited by a black double fillet. The pattern's module is very large compared to the modest size of the carpet, and the motif is repeated only one and a half times within the field.

Comparisons: this very common pattern can be observed a few times in the city of Xanthos: in the S portico of the main *decumanus* (larger scale of the pattern) and in the N annex of the Church of the Agora, Rm. N. We cite an example at Knidos (Love 1973, pl. 73, fig. 5).

2-6, atrium (W portico)

Illustrations 18, 27-28.

Rectangle located in portico's peripheral space. 1.95 x 1.60 m. The carpet decorates a narrow space between the *pediluve*, the stairs and carpet **2**-4.

Density of tesserae/dm^2: 42.
Colors: black, white, red, yellow, pink, green.
State of preservation: covered by a layer of calcite, the grid design and colors of this mosaic are not easily legible. These deposits can be related to the basin located immediately to the N. A few gaps are due to fallen blocks, and traces of burning are visible.

Description: orthogonal pattern of alternately vertical and horizontal adjacent pairs of opposed scales (*Décor* I, pl. 220), polychrome with four white tesserae at the point of intersection. The scales running in a N-S direction have the same colors as the perpendicular ones (black, pink, two white, green), except for the center, where they appear yellow for the former, and red for the latter. The scales cut by the border are somewhat irregular: all of the half-scales are colored yellow without a green fillet. The carpet, outlined by a black double fillet, is framed by a white band six tesserae wide, like the other pavements in the N part of the atrium.

Comparisons: it is unnecessary to give comparisons for this common pattern.

2-7, atrium (W portico)

Illustrations 18, 27, 29-30.

Rectangle placed lengthwise in W portico along the path of circulation and appearing slightly trapezoidal. This carpet lies between the main entrance stairs (of six steps) and the stylobate, on the axis of the church and at the center of the portico.

Dimensions: 2.14 x (2.94 to 3.00 m).

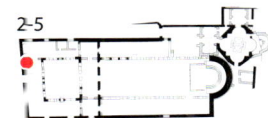

2-5

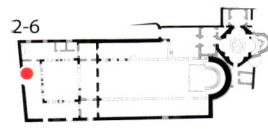

2-6

29. Ensemble view of carpet 2-7, with the location of the main stairs on the left.

30. Detail with rainbow style filler motif.

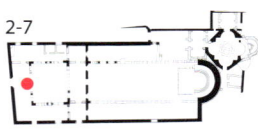

2-7

Density of tesserae/dm^2: 45 to 48.
Materials: purple, green, blue (light blue) that are all marble; red tesserae are terracotta.
Colors: black, white, red, pink, blue, green, yellow, purple.
State of preservation: two principal gaps and other smaller ones resulting from fallen superstructure, entrance sills, and columns in the atrium; surface buckles.

Description: a white double fillet forms the mosaic pattern and the border, which measures six tesserae wide and is framed by a black double fillet. An orthogonal pattern of tangent eight-parallelogram stars forms squares and smaller poised squares (ill. 29) (*Décor* I, pl. 173b). Parallelograms are alternately yellow and pink, outlined in black. The large squares, in four rows of three squares each from N to S, also are outlined in black and their content varies by row.
Row 1 (N): poised serrated cross, created by two white fillets that form lateral triangles, shaded black, purple, pink, green, blue, white.
Row 2: chessboard pattern of four tesserae (ill. 30), with diagonal lines of polychromy in no precise order; purple and white dominate over other colors.
Row 3: squares enclosing Solomon knot on a white ground, with black band outlined by green, yellow or purple as principal colors.
Row 4 (S): each square contains an inscribed octagon, with a small poised serrated central square shaded in black, purple, red, green, and having a white center. Small poised squares in the interstices of the design have shaded colors in various combinations.

Commentary: the treatment of motifs in this carpet, especially the use of color, accentuates the large squares.

Comparisons: this type of grid is common to many countries and periods from Roman Republican times to the Byzantine era. In Asia Minor, an early example occurs in the *impluvium* of the Villa of Oceanus at Zeugma (Zeugma 2007, pp. 91-93), another in Adana, Mosaic of Orpheus (Budde 1972, fig. 26), Tarsus (*ibid.*, fig. 233), and many others in Antioch, as in the House of the Drinking Contest (Rm. 1, Levi 1947, pl. 30); in Ephesus, in the Alytarchenstoa (S stoa or portico of Curetes Street, Jobst 1977, fig. 41). Particularly close stylistically are mosaics from sites in Greece and on the Greek islands: a few examples at Kos, Basilica of St. Paul (Corpus Greece 1, fig. 35b), St. Stephanos, main Basilica (N aisle, Parrish 2001, fig. 20), portico O of the baptistery (Di Matteis 2004, pl. XXXI-1) and Area of the Western Baths (Bas. A, *ibid.*, pl. XXIII-3). Also Euboea at Chalkis (Corpus Greece 1, figs. 70a, 71b; Sodini 1968, fig. 330), with the same filler motifs and design module, all shaped by a white double fillet; Paleopyrga of Argos (W of the apse, Sodini 1968, fig. 5); Astypalaia (Corpus Greece 1, fig. 1a) or Hermione, narthex of Bas. A (Sodini 1968, fig. 39). In Athens there are two examples, in a villa (Rm. VII, Spiro 1978, fig. 57) and in the Thucydides Street Baths (Corpus Greece 2, fig. 217). In Thessaloniki, there is a close example in the Church of the Acheiropoietos (Corpus Greece 3, pl. XXVII); in Macedonia at Heraklea Lynkestis, a close example in the small basilica (exonarthex, Tomašević 1975, pl. CLXXXVIII-1); in Jordan, an example comes from Shunah al-Janubiyah (near Livias, Piccirillo 1993, p. 322, fig. 665) where the overall execution closely resembles that of the Xanthos floor.

S part of atrium

The S part of the atrium has no architectural features encroaching on the portico corridors, making the carpets' arrangement simpler. The mosaics form a homogeneous ensemble composed of two groups of panels: in the W portico (**2**-8), the corner included, there is a long surface divided into three panels (**2**-8A, **2**-8B, **2**-8C) and in the S portico a group of two panels (**2**-9A, **2**-9B). Each group has its own wide border that also separates individual panels. The two long carpets 8 and 9 are parallel to the walls, and are linked to them by an outer margin and a single external border with a continuous ivy scroll, grouping all of the mosaics in the S part in a large L, clearly distinguished from the N atrium.

Outer margins
Outer margins framing this suite of carpets (**2**-8 and **2**-9) are quite narrow and regular (20-50 cm), with the carpets placed parallel to the walls. In their narrowest section, along the W wall, they appear plain white in rows nine tesserae wide set parallel to the wall. Elsewhere, poised serrated squares punctuate the margin (in the S portico, along the stylobate of the court, at the E threshold, and along the S wall) and in some places this line of squares is doubled, with a red double fillet separating the rows (S portico: NE and SE parts). Squares are colored black, red, yellow, with a pink center, or black, red, pink. Number of tesserae varies according to size of the motif.

Outer margins were partly destroyed along the stylobate of the court by a late trench, made to repair or reinstall an underground pipe; elsewhere, they are well preserved.

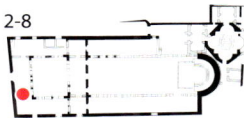

31. Plan of carpet 2-8, with panels A, B and C.

32. Scheme of carpet 2-8, with numbers of the panels and compartments of the border.

2- South overall border

Overall border
This border (ill. 31) frames all of the mosaics in the S half of the atrium and consists of an ivy scroll (*Décor* I, pl. 64d) limited by a black double fillet (48-52 cm wide). Dense and regular, it unwinds in a sinusoid made of a black double fillet. A vertical ivy leaf fills each undulation and is linked to it by a black stem. The leaves, outlined by a black double fillet, are colored primarily red or yellow with a pink or blue center, except for a single white leaf located near the N stylobate of the S portico.

State of preservation: this border, like the outer margins, was partly destroyed by a trench dug in the middle of the S portico, in front of the fountain; reused slabs covered by a layer of calcite fill the oblique trench.

Commentary: the regularity of the scroll and rigid position of its vertical leaves make the border appear geometric rather than floral.

2-8, atrium (W portico)
Illustrations 18, 31-40, 154, 156, 180-181.
This mosaic is a large rectangle covering the entire space between the stairs and S wall of the atrium. A single internal border surrounds the space and divides it into three panels, **2**-8A, **2**-8B, and **2**-8C. 11.70 x 5.40 m.

Border
The border (ill. 31-36) is limited by a white band five or six tesserae wide on all sides.
Width: 84 cm with white bands, 64 cm without.
Density of tesserae/dm^2: 41.

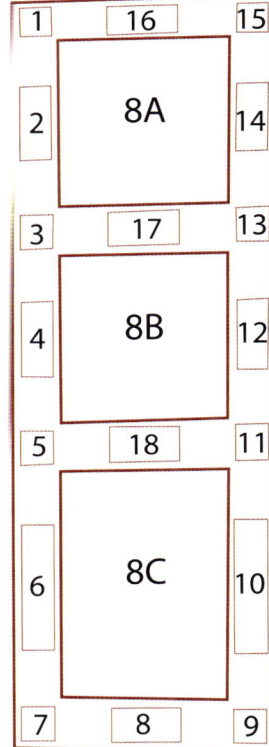

33. Detail of the border, rectangle 2.

Colors: black, white, yellow (stone), red (terracotta), pink (terracotta), blue (light blue Proconnesian marble) and a single purple tessera (marble).

State of preservation: fractured by fallen architectural elements (mainly from the nearby basilica entrance) in NE corner of the border. There are a few gaps and traces of burning, but overall condition is good.

Description: swastika-meander of spaced recessed reverse-returned swastikas with alternately a horizontal rectangle and a square in each space (*Décor* I, pl. 39e, f, g). Squares (44 cm/side) occur at corners and rectangles (90 x 44 cm for small sides, 175 x 44 cm for longer sides) appear in center of panel's sides. A triple fillet (black, red, black) forms the meander.

Filler motifs of squares and rectangles vary, often paired on opposite sides of the panel. Squares are usually outlined by a black double fillet, rectangles by a single black fillet.

Square 1: grid of double fillets forming four squares superimposed on a serrated octagon in shaded colors (black, red, yellow, pink, blue, white). Resulting triangles have same colors and create the effect of four oblong hexagons surrounding a central poised square.

Rectangle 2 (ill. 33): shaded bands (black, yellow, blue, white; and black, red, pink, white) form a central spindle and two semicircles, interlaced with loops. Lateral spaces contain a blue or pink enclosed motif.

Square 3: circle of four spindles (black, red, with a pink or yellow center). Center consists of a concave enclosed square, black outlined in blue. Corners contain a black included motif.

Rectangle 4: zigzag rainbow pattern of double fillets (*Décor* I, pl. 199b); the chromatic sequence (black, blue, white, pink, red) is repeated four times over the rectangle's length.

Square 5: poised inscribed square shaded in color (two red, two black, six white, black, red, pink, blue, white) creating the effect of two concentric squares. Corners also are shaded in color (white, blue, pink, yellow, black).

Rectangle 6: long rectangle filled by a band of superimposed chevrons (*Décor* I, pl. 7g). The chevrons, formed by serrated fillets of four tesserae, create a sequence of colors (pink, red, black, yellow, blue, white) repeated 9 times over the rectangle's length.

Square 7: the square is outlined by a double fillet on three sides and a single fillet on the fourth (W). The pattern is similar to square 1, with a grid of double fillets forming four squares. The serrated

octagon below is shaded in color (black, red, pink, blue, white). The corner triangles have the same colors, creating the effect of white hexagons placed around a central square.

Rectangle 8 (ill. 34): inscribed lozenge, shaded in color (two black, yellow, red, pink, two blue, with a white center). Corners contain inscribed motifs, either black or red outlined in blue.

Square 9: grid made by a black double fillet, forming four squares superimposed on a white poised cross. Lateral serrated triangles are shaded in color (black, red, pink, blue, white) (cf. square 13).

Rectangle 10 (ill. 35): very large rectangle made by a black double fillet (opposite 6). It is divided into five squares, each filled with a serrated poised square, shaded with four tesserae (black, yellow, red, white). Corners also are shaded in color (black, red, pink, white, black).

Square 11: two opposite corners (SW and NE) contain a serrated triangle, shaded with four tesserae (black, yellow, red, pink, white, blue) and creating the effect of a white diagonal band.

Rectangle 12: zigzag pattern formed by a double fillet with a color sequence (black, yellow, four or five red, blue, white) repeated three times. This décor closely resembles rectangle 4 on opposite side of the panel.

Square 13: grid made by a black double fillet forming four squares superimposed on a white poised cross. Lateral triangles are shaded in color (black, white, pink, red, yellow with a black center).

34. Detail of the border, rectangle 8.

2-8 border

Rectangle 14: three circles interlaced by a serrated band (black, yellow, red, pink, white, blue, black). Central circle is colored blue and white; lateral circles have a black center; corners contain an inscribed blue motif.

Square 15: circle of four spindles colored red or yellow and outlined in black. A black concave square fills the center.

Rectangle 16 (ill. 36): two large circles interlaced with a small central loop, formed by a serrated band (black, white, red, yellow, blue, black). Circles contain a central serrated poised square (black, red, blue, with a white center). Resulting spaces contain an inscribed motif (blue, black, red, yellow, pink, white).

Rectangle 17: it divides panels **2**-8A and **2**-8B. Orthogonal pattern of polychrome adjacent scales (Décor I, pl. 215) whose colored interiors create diagonal lines of scales with a red or yellow center. The pattern measures four and a half scales long and two scales wide.

Rectangle 18: it divides panels **2**-8B and **2**-8C. Inscribed lozenge made by double fillet shaded in color (black, yellow, red, pink, blue, white). Corners contain a red triangle outlined in black.

There occurs a single purple tessera in the middle of a swastika in the N part of the border. The proximity of panel **2**-7, where such purple marble also is used, helps explain its presence here, as a borrowing from the workshop laboring nearby in the N part of the atrium.

Comparisons: it is a common border in the rainbow style, adopted everywhere. We shall mention only nearby sites: Gemiler Ada (Church 3, Asano 2000, fig. 7), Aphrodisias (Priest's House, Rm. 5, Campbell 1991, pls. 92-93) with similar filler motifs (knots, lozenge inscribed in a rectangle, circle with loops, circle of four spindles, guilloche mat, square and curvilinear square interlooped, shaded chessboard patterns), and another close example in Perge (Mansel 1974, fig. 7). Also at Anemurium (Church of the Holy Apostles, S aisle, Campbell 1998, pl. 118) with similar filler motifs in rainbow style in a different overall pattern (chessboards, circle of spindles, looped spindle or square serrated, rosette, chevrons, looped square or lozenge in a gradation of colors). Many other examples exist in Syria, Greece and throughout the Near East, as well as in N Africa, Spain, Italy and Gaul.

Panel 2-8A, S atrium (W portico)
Illustrations 18, 31, 37, 156, 180-181.
Square located S of the main stairs and panel **2**-7. Ca. 2.00 x 2.00 m.
  Density of tesserae/dm^2: 43-45.
  Colors: black, white, red, pink, yellow, blue (light blue Proconnesian marble).
  State of preservation: good, except in NE corner where there are a few gaps.

Description: centralized design of concentric motifs (ill. 37, 156), in the following order from outside inward:
• Interlaced circle in a square, with loops all around the circle, and small circles with three loops in each corner. A shaded band forms the design, with the dominant color alternating among red (black, two red, blue, white, black), pink (black, two pink, blue, white, black), blue (black, three blue, white, black) and yellow (black, two yellow, blue, white, black). Resulting spaces contain inscribed black motifs, and corner circles have a small central black circle.
• Order of concentric circular borders: white band three tesserae wide; polychrome wave pattern (*Décor* I, pl. 101) with inward-facing waves shaded black and red with a pink center, and outward-facing waves colored white with a blue center; black double fillet; white band three tesserae wide.
• Central looped cross with eyelets inscribed in a circle; a shaded band forms a saltire cross (black, yellow, pink, white, blue, black). Resulting spaces have an inscribed motif, colored pink with a black or red center (ill. 156). Center of design is red with a white point.

35. Detail of the border, rectangle 10.

36. Detail of the border, rectangle 16.

37. Overall view of panel 2-8A.

38. Overall view of panel 2-8B.

Commentary: this carpet, typical of the rainbow style, has the same central feature as the U-cross in the N compartment of the narthex (inv. **4**), clearly produced by the same workshop. We found an example with the same taste for complex interlacing at Ephesus (S stoa or portico of Curetes Street, Miltner 1958, pl. XXII, fig. 9, Jobst 1977, fig. 49).

Panel 2-8B, S atrium (W portico)
Illustrations 18, 31, 38, 180-181.
Square panel placed in middle of carpet **2-8**. 2.04 x 2.04 m.
  Density of tesserae/dm^2: 44 to 49.
  Colors: black, white, yellow, red, pink, blue (light blue Proconnesian marble).
  State of preservation: NE corner is fractured, probably from fallen architectural elements; scattered gaps in N part of panel (ill. 180).

Description: concentric design of a square enclosed within a square (ill. 38) (*Décor* II, pl. 292d) having a wide border. The border (60 cm wide) contains a strapwork of circles and crosses of loops interlooped tangentially, in shaded bands (*Décor* I, pl. 82h). The crosses of loops occur in the center of the panel's sides. The circles, grouped by threes in the corners, are interlaced with both the external and internal bands framing the border. Each circle is framed by three or four loops joined by an elliptical ring made of a shaded band. The shaded bands are formed by four main colors (blue, red, yellow, pink) and the circles have a red, yellow or pink center outlined in black. This border seems dense and confusing but is perfectly executed. After a white band four tesserae wide, the central square, outlined by a black double fillet, contains a polychrome guilloche mat (*Décor* I, pl. 140e). The mat has four loops on a side, formed by a shaded band with the same colors as the preceding border, and it appears against a pink ground.

Comparisons: the border is very similar to the border of the nave mosaic in nearby Gemiler Ada (Church 3, Asano 1998, without page numbering) where this kind of strapwork appears fragmentary. In Syria we can cite a parallel at Qumhane (Balty 1989, fig. 182b).

Panel 2-8C, S atrium (corner of W and S porticoes)
Illustrations 18, 31, 39-40.
Rectangle placed lengthwise in W portico. This panel occupies the corner between the W and S atrium porticoes. 1.46 x 1.02 m.
  Density of tesserae/dm^2: 42.
  Colors: black, white, yellow, red, blue.
  State of preservation: very good, with one small gap and a few traces of burning.

Description: orthogonal polychrome pattern of adjacent lozenges and squares (*Décor* I, pl. 161a) arranged diagonally (ill. 39). A white double fillet creates the pattern, which is surrounded by a white band five tesserae wide. The lozenges appear yellow on the SE-NW axis and red on the perpendicular axis, all outlined by a black double fillet (ill. 40). The squares are colored blue, outlined in white and black.

Comparisons: we note two examples in Asia Minor at Gördes (*Platea Petra*, Dedeoğlu 1993, fig. 3) where this pattern is used in the nave, but at a larger scale and with geometric filler motifs, creating a different overall effect, and at Ephesus (Hanghaus 2, Rm. 22, Jobst 1977, fig. 101) ; also an example on Kos (annex, Bas. A, Di Matteis 2004, pl. XXV-1) with filler motifs of knots and scales; and one in Zeugma (Oceanus Villa, Zeugma 2007, pp. 95-97). But we have closer parallels in Thessaloniki (in the peristyle portico of the complex situated N of the Palace of Galerius (Corpus Greece 3, pl. VIII), and at the intersection of Gounari and Prinkipos Nikolaou Streets (*ibid.*, fig. 53).

2-9, atrium (S portico)
Illustrations 18, 41-44.
It is divided into two panels, A and B, framed and separated by a common border. Total dimensions: 3.30 x 12.00 m.

In a secondary phase of the Early Byzantine period, probably close to the time of the original construction, the central door opening into the court was blocked by the creation of a fountain. Its overflow poured onto the paved court through a pipe covered by a circular limestone grate (now destroyed). The wastewater channel was connected, at the base of the fountain on the S side, to an underground drainpipe skirting the entire portico. The latter pipe, dating to the atrium's construction, was laid before the mosaic covering it. A trench was later opened, probably for repair, during the Early Byzantine period and randomly filled with reused slabs. The pipe heads SE, but the trench stops after encroaching on the first third of the pavement. Its further extension underground is detected through a continuous depression in the mosaic surface.

Border: it surrounds and divides the two panels, extending over the S portico of the atrium. The border alone is 40 cm wide, and 64 cm with white bands added.
Density of tesserae/dm^2: 43.
State of preservation: the border is intact, except in center of N section flanking the stylobate, near the trench mentioned above.

39. Overall view of panel 2-8C.

40. Detail of panel 2-8C.

Description: polychrome row of tangent circles and horizontal spindles (*Décor* I, pl. 22i) outlined by a black double fillet and seen against a pink ground. Spindles and circles contain a black and yellow enclosed motif with a black center. A pair of small vertical spindles punctuates the center of the panel's short sides (there was no space for a horizontal spindle); they are colored pink and joined by a short white dash. The border is framed on all sides by white band five or six tesserae wide.

Comparisons: we cite three nearby examples of this common type of border, one at Gemiler Ada (nave, Church 3, Asano 1998, without page numbering), the second in Arykanda (Akıllı 1988, figs. 2, 21b) and the last at Limyra (Cathedral, Rm. N of the apse, Borchardt 1997, figs. 10-11, 14). Another close comparison is the mosaic border of the *vestibulum* of the civil Basilica at Xanthos, on

2-8C

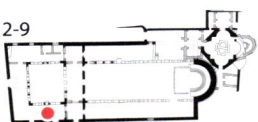

41. Plan of carpet 2-9, panels A and B.

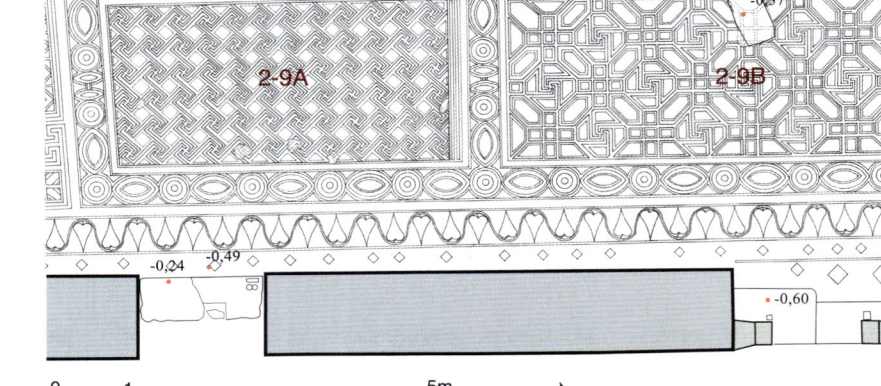

42. Overall view of panel 2-9A.

2-9A

the other side of the *cardo* passing in front of the East Basilica. Still in Turkey, at Ephesus (S stoa or portico of Curetes Street, Jobst 1977, figs. 49-50). A further comparison exists is Syria at Apamea (House of the Pilasters, Balty 1984, pls. 1-2). Similar vertical spindles dividing ordinary ones exist in the tetraconch of the Hadrian's Librairy, Athens (Sodini 1968, fig. 86).

Panel 2-9A, atrium (S portico)
Illustrations 18, 41-42.
Rectangle placed lengthwise in S portico, E of corner panel 8C. 4.56 x 2.22 m.
 Density of tesserae/dm^2: 42-45.
 Colors: black, white, red, pink, blue (light blue Proconnesian marble), yellow.
 State of preservation: panel is nearly intact, with only three small gaps and large traces of burning (S half and NE corner).

Description:
Supplementary panel: (2.22 x 0.17 m) a black double fillet frames this narrow panel, which doubles the width of the border on the mosaic's short E side. It is a band of polychrome fillets: two black, white, blue and pink in the center, arranged symmetrically; the pink fillet is doubled on the N and appears single on the S. This panel was added to maintain a strict symmetry in the mosaic's design.
Panel: orthogonal pattern of spaced swastika meander with single returns made of double fillets (ill. 42), the spaces staggered and containing a square (*Décor* I, pl. 191a). The squares of the diagonally set pattern are variously colored, forming parallel rows of the same color; from N to S, they successively appear blue, red, yellow, blue, pink. The squares cut by the border form black triangles.

Commentary and comparisons: the originality of this very common pattern of the rainbow style is its diagonal placement within the frame, and the colors of the squares which form lines of squares of similar hue. A close example occurs at Antioch (Cruciform Church of Yakto, baptistery, Lassus 1938–2, fig. 30). Yet another close parallel is in Hama, N Syria (Metropolitanate excavations, Donceel-Voûte 1988, fig. 439). A more sophisticated meander, diagonally disposed as at Xanthos, was found at Misis (Budde 1969, pls. 116-119).

Panel 2-9B, atrium (S portico)
Illustrations 18, 41, 43-44.
Long rectangle placed on portico's long axis, E of 9A, and occurring in front of the fountain described above. 5.66 x 2.22 m.

Density of tesserae/dm^2: 39-43.

Colors: black, white, pink, blue (light blue Proconnesian marble), yellow.

State of preservation: repair trench cuts into one third of the panel toward SE (see above) and contains reused limestone slabs and flat tiles. This Early Byzantine trench seems to stop where the repair occurs; however, as the mosaic surface continues in the same direction, it sinks down, suggesting the presence of a pipe underground extending toward the S. Otherwise, the pavement is in good condition, with a few gaps and light traces of burning. The surface as a whole has a slight depression in the center.

Description:
Outlined polychrome pattern of adjacent crosses and irregular octagons, forming oblong hexagons; a black double fillet composes the pattern. The crosses consist of five squares, and a swastika is inscribed in the octagon (ill. 43) (*Décor* I, pl. 180f). Each of the five squares of the crosses contains a small blue square outlined in black, while the spaces around the swastikas are filled with small trapezoids, also blue outlined in black. The hexagons contain an inscribed motif outlined by a black double fillet and are variously colored: yellow for those slanted NE-SW, pink for those slanted in the opposite direction. The half-hexagons on the S side (shaped as trapezoids) appear white.

In this panel, the hexagons predominate because of their strong coloring, and the overall pattern of the mosaic is obscured by the dense network of lines (ill. 44). Initially there appears an oblique grid of hexagons, with other motifs seeming secondary.

Comparisons: a very common pattern throughout the Mediterranean in all periods, found in Africa, Britain or Gaul and also in the eastern regions, and here characterized by a linear treatment, with colors applied selectively. Its fragmentary appearance is due to the subdivision of all motifs: crosses made of four squares surrounding a central square; octagons with a swastika surrounded by four trapezoids. In Greece this pattern was particularly favored and often is linear in appearance, as at Laureotic Olympus, with filler motifs of a knot and palm tree (sanctuary, Corpus Greece 2, fig. 225); Delphi (Basilica in the museum court, Sodini 1968, figs. 109-110); Megalopolis (House, Corpus

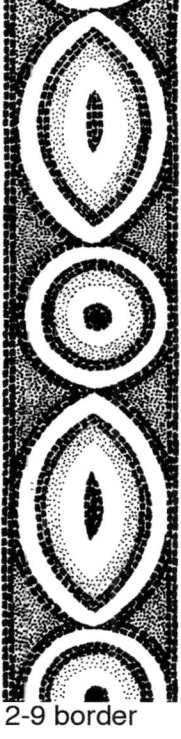

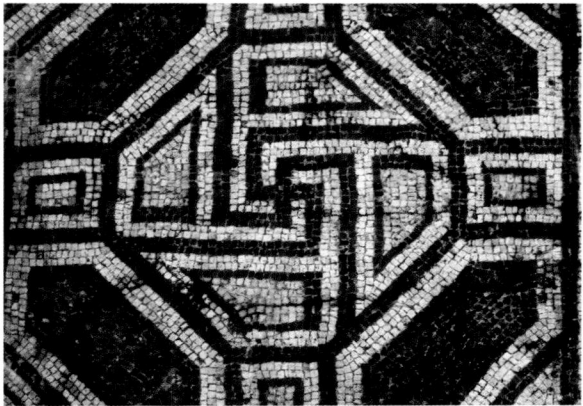

43. Detail of panel 2-9B.

44. Overall view of panel 2-9B.

Greece 2, figs. 77-86) and Thessaloniki (complex N of Galerius's Palace, Corpus Greece 3, pl. VII) with swastikas in the crosses, and figural motifs in the octagons; Klapsi (triconch Basilica, Sodini 1968, figs. 174, 178-180), and Nea Anchialos (Basilica Gamma, Spiro 1978, fig. 367) with figural filler motifs. Both Echinos (building in Achilles Road, Corpus Greece 2, fig. 287b) and Daphnous (Basilica, Sodini 1968, fig. 131; Spiro 1978, figs. 319-320) present a different pattern but show the same unusual way of filling the octagons as at Xanthos. In Turkey, Meriamlik offers an example of this pattern (Theklabasilika, Herzfeld-Guyer 1930, fig. 35) with geometric filler motifs.

Commentary about the atrium

Examination of the atrium reveals the presence of two different mosaic workshops that contrast in various respects: their sense of space, adaptation to the surrounding architecture, materials, repertory of motifs, and style. Some materials and basic colors are shared, such as local limestone used for white and black (actually dark grey), and a hard red stone. Pink seems to be a lighter variety of the latter stone. Yellow is a dark ochre stone, sometimes with a slightly greenish shade. Blue tesserae are very light and bright and made of reused Proconnesian marble of the same type seen everywhere on the site (columns, pavements, revetments, etc.). The repertory of motifs of both workshops shows Syrian influence, but in different ways.

Stylistic conclusions

The atrium mosaics are characteristic of Near Eastern style of the 5th-6th centuries, particularly as seen in northern Syria. Carpet **2**-7 reflects the rainbow style[2], including its range of colors, chessboard pattern, and effect of modeling. In the S part of the atrium at Xanthos, carpet **2**-8 represents another trend, namely, a preference for interlacing and centralized designs. This trend is contemporary with the first in Syria (beginning of the 5th c.) and continues later. Meanders and multiple filler motifs make the décor seem dense and displays a distinct *horror vacui*. Division of the surface into smaller units, the concentric arrangement of motifs, and large and numerous borders become common in Syria ca. 415 CE. Another feature of eastern mosaics encountered in both parts of the atrium is the systematic decoration of outer margins.

Overall, we can detect the presence of two workshops influenced by the rainbow style, distinguishable mainly in their sense of overall design and conception of space, disparities that would not exist within the same workshop (see *infra* chapter entitled "Synthesis", ill. 152).

3. Atrium court

Pavement of slabs
Illustrations 18, 45.
The open air court of the atrium is almost square (13.70 x11.80 m). Its floor is a flagstone pavement, made of limestone slabs.

State of conservation: the central part of the court is lost, with a few traces of slabs in the partly preserved mortar. The edges are better preserved, especially on the N and S sides.

Description
The slabs are placed with their longer side oriented E-W, in 18 parallel rows. Along the N and S stylobates, the width of the slabs varies and depends on the empty space remaining (ill. 45). Typical slabs measure 0.60 to 0.80 m wide, and 0.40 to 1.20 m long (average: 1.10 x 0.70 m).

Support
There were found few traces of the plaques' imprints on the exposed mortar of the court, but the upper layer (setting bed) is lost. Instead, a careful cleaning of the surface of the lower mortar layer revealed a few parallel rows of tiles sherds, set on edge and end to end along the E-W axis. They served as wedging for the plaques. It is the only example of this technique used for plaque pavements in the church. The more common method for setting large plaques at the proper level is to insert small flat fragments (terracotta sherds and marble pieces) under the center and corners. The technique used here seems an innovation and recalls the lines observed in the support of the mosaic in the S narthex compartment (inv. **5**). Between the lines appeared tiles or bricks fragments set on edge, but arranged in a loose manner (different from the S narthex generally). It seemingly remained in poor condition for a long time: the plaques probably disappeared in the medieval era, and this might explain the fact that the mortar is very worn.

---

2. On the "rainbow style," see the works by D. Levi, J. Lassus, J. Balty, P. Donceel-Voûte, L. Budde, J.-P. Sodini...

45. Plan of the atrium court, pavement 3.

Narthex

The narthex occupies the entire E portico of the atrium between the N and S walls of the church (27 x 5.20 m). It is divided into three parts (ill. 18), clearly separated at ground level by two stylobates: two square compartments, one at each end of the narthex, flank a large rectangular central space. This tripartite division of space has the same proportions as the atrium and the church proper. A 2nd-story gallery covered this E portico, a feature that did not exist in the three other porticoes of the atrium.

Both the N and S compartments are paved with mosaics (inv. **4** and **5**) of Early Byzantine date. The twin compartments are open on all sides with doors, one leading to exterior spaces, i.e. spaces flanking the church symmetrically and perhaps containing stairs that led to the level of the 2nd-story galleries. On the side of the atrium, the opening at first was very wide and then was narrowed by the addition of lateral piers and two arches supported by a central column. The S example was partly preserved and can be reconstructed from elements found nearby; the N portico threshold probably was similar. A simple stylobate divides the side compartments from the central section of the narthex. During the Middle Byzantine period, most of the thresholds were narrowed or partly closed by the construction of walls.

The central space is the same width as the court and the church nave. It was framed on the W by four tall columns supporting an architrave and 2nd-story gallery, with an opening in the center of the stylobate; chancel screens sealed off the lateral spaces between columns. To the E, three doors lead into the nave (ill. 18), which is framed by huge, reused Roman architraves, creating a majestic effect paralleled in other large basilicas of the same period, such as S. Sofia and S. John Studios in Istanbul or S. John at Ephesus. The central door is especially large (3.76 x 1.85 m), whereas the smaller lateral openings stood around 2 m high. These imposing doors of the church were visible from the entrance stairs and were framed by the tall columns resting on the E stylobate of the court and the 2nd-story gallery surmounting the narthex. The pavement in the central part of the narthex consists of a very fine *opus sectile* floor (inv. **6**), preserved over one third of its surface. This pavement was partially restored during the Middle Byzantine re-occupation, mostly on its N side.

The underground pipe skirting the N portico of the atrium continues into the N compartment of the narthex in the direction of the N aisle. The S outer margin of the mosaic was damaged during a repair of this pipe. A small pipe that was just under the surface follows the stylobate in the central part of the narthex and served to clean the pavement surface.

Traces of red Byzantine painting still appear in a few places. Many fragments of painted and moulded stuccoes were found during the excavation in the N compartment, and a fragment of it is still *in situ* on the N part of the E wall, forming a sort of plinth with a triple moulding.

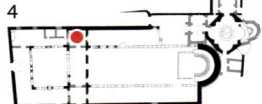

4. narthex (N compartment)
Opus tessellatum.
Illustrations 18, 46-48, 155, 164a.
Square mosaic paving N compartment of narthex. Stylobates of marble or limestone steps form the thresholds. Reconstructed dimensions: 6.00 x 5.50 m. This space, placed symmetrically in relation to S compartment, is a vestibule preceding the N aisle of the church and ultimately the baptistery.

Materials: dark blue marble of Aphrodisias (?), also used in the nave and N aisle, but not in the atrium. Red is terracotta.

Density of tesserae/dm^2: 41-45.

Colors: black, white, red, pink, yellow, dark blue.

State of preservation: the S outer margin was later destroyed in digging a trench to restore a pipe below ground (cf. the atrium). There are three gaps near the N wall, where a huge, reused Roman lintel fell.

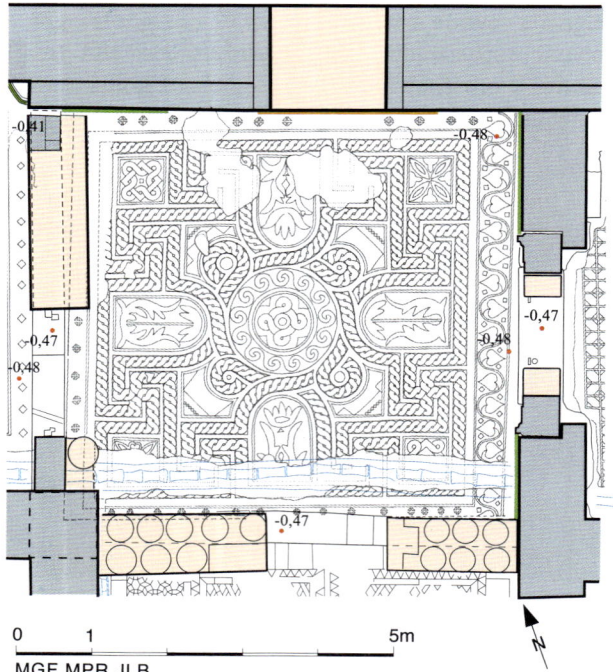

46. Plan of the N compartment of narthex, pavement 4.

Description

Outer margins: White outer margins surround the mosaic and are 10 to 34 cm wide. On three sides (N, W, S) the white ground is ornamented with black florets spaced irregularly. On the E side is an ivy scroll (48 cm wide) following the wall and framed by a black double fillet (a sort of supplementary panel). Vertical black ivy leaves are flanked by black and pink florets.

Field (5.80 x 5.60 m): almost square, the field contains a circumcentric pattern formed by a continuous guilloche that also surrounds the field, forming a border. Circumcentric pattern, in a square and around a circle with loops, of four lateral arches interlaced tangentially with the circle, and of four chevrons in the corners placed adjacent to the arches (sometimes called a "cross of four U's"). A simple guilloche delineates the pattern, the chevrons organized as two swastika-meanders flanking a corner square (*Décor* II, pl. 367b). The guilloche has three dominant colors: red (black, two red, white, black), yellow (black, two yellow, white, black) and pink (black, pink, yellow, white, black). This guilloche appears on a black ground and is framed on both sides by a white triple fillet, interrupting the design at the intersections.

The arch-shaped panels are filled with stylized floral motifs, arranged in pairs. On the E-W axis, these are a plant with acanthus leaves having a rounded base; the leaves are colored red outlined in black (ill. 48). From this base rises a straight stem colored black with a red center and supporting a large, rounded flower on top - a sort of umbellifer ? -, colored dark blue and outlined in black, with four large lanceolate petals curving downward.

On the N-S axis, leaves of a similar acanthus type flank the plant, and are colored red and pink. A short central stem ends in a bud or rounded fruit supported by two small black sepals. A large calyx with five points blossoms above the leaves, outlined in black and with the points colored red and pink or red and yellow; the center appears white. A small black triangle occurs immediately below the calyx.

The central medallion (ill. 155) is surrounded by a wavy line (*Décor* I, pl. 101) colored black and blue outside and pink and red inside. Following a black

47. Overall view of the room.

48. Detail of an arch.

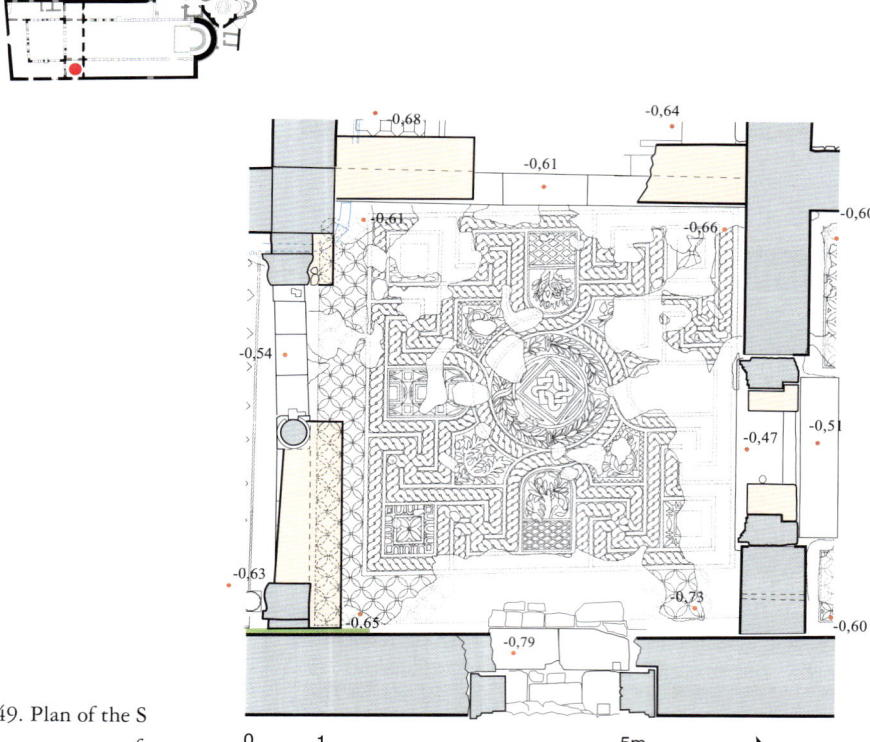

49. Plan of the S compartment of narthex, pavement 5.

double fillet, the central medallion contains a circle of four loops in shaded bands, successively colored black, dark blue, red, pink, white, black. The center is a blue point outlined in black. Four small triangles ornament the edge of the medallion (black, red, white) making a white quadrilobe appear around the circle with four loops.

The spaces placed diagonally around the central circle each contain a loop with a black center, and the corners have triangles shaded in varied colors (black, red, white, pink, yellow).

Squares in the corners of the field are occupied by various motifs:

NW square: poised square and curvilinear square (cushion) interlooped, the first with predominant yellow color, and the cushion with principal red color. A small black square punctuates the center.

SE square: poised square with four lateral loops, in shaded bands (black, two red, white, black). A small square is enclosed in the center and decorated with a four-tesserae chessboard pattern. The sequence of colors from W to E is as follows: pink, yellow, black, red, white, pink, black, yellow. This square, partially preserved twenty years ago, is now lost (it was crushed in the pipe trench).

SW square: compound rosette of eight noncontiguous elements, four as heart-shaped leaf and four as spindle-shaped petal (*Décor* II, pl. 269); the first are colored red, outlined in white and black, the second are white and framed by a black double fillet.

NE square: unitary rosette of four non-contiguous elements as spindles; lateral half circles resting on the square frame adorn the spaces between petals; they are colored red and black, with a small lanceolate petal on top (today lost).

Commentary: this pavement has stylistic parallels with the mosaic in the N atrium (white bands and no borders) but it is better attributed to workshop B (Chapter "Synthesis"): it more closely resembles the S atrium, stylistically, with its taste for interlacing and centralized patterns. The similarity between the central panel of the atrium (inv. **2**-8A) and the N compartment in the N narthex (inv. **4**) must be emphasized, for it shows the effect of the same hand.

Comparisons: *infra* inv. **5,** *infra* inv. **10**-7B; see also *infra* the chapter "Synthesis"; the motif of "cross of U's" has been studied in Raynaud 1996.

5. narthex (S compartment)

Opus tessellatum, removed, restored and reset *in situ.*
Illustrations 18, 49-58, 161-162, 164c.
Square paving S compartment of the narthex. Space primitively largely open toward W (atrium),

S (leading to the exterior of the church, supposed location [unexcavated] of a staircase giving access to the upper gallery level, E (S aisle) and N (central part of narthex). Stylobates or steps of marble or limestone form the thresholds. Dimensions 5.85 x 5.72 m. This space, symmetrical to the N compartment, is a vestibule preceding the S aisle.

Materials: presence of glass tesserae, unique among all of the basilica pavements; green marble in leaves of laurel garland, similar to those in N part of atrium, carpets **2**-3, **2**-5 and **2**-7.

Density of tesserae/dm^2: 51-57, greatest for glass tesserae (5-6 mm/side).

Colors: black, white, red, pink, yellow, blue, green, light green.

State of preservation: pavement was found in poor condition, with buckled surface, large damaged areas and traces of burning. In 1986, it was decided to remove the mosaic, restore it, excavate underneath and reset it. It was laid on a new lime mortar bed, with a sufficient slope for drainage. It remained for years covered by a thick glue and canvas sheet, while awaiting cleaning. Because the restorer J.-M. Dupage[1] did not return, P. Blanc and L. Krougly finished the work in 2001. I never saw the mosaic, since my first season at Xanthos began just after the pavement was lifted, and I was not present during its final cleaning. However, I had occasion to participate in the excavations of the mosaic's support and foundations, which was a very gratifying experience.

Only two thirds of this pavement is preserved. The E and S sides are mostly missing, and large gaps occur in the NE corner. The collapse of heavy architectural elements must have contributed to this damage. Many traces of burning have darkened or transformed the colors, with glass tesserae affected more than stone by the heat. These tesserae are often crumbled, leaving only their imprint. Some antique restorations are visible, having been made before the burning and abandonment.

Support (or foundation)
(ill. 50-54, 161)

Lifting the mosaic allowed excavation of the pavement's support, found to be very original and indeed unique in this building.

It displays an unusual technique rarely attested in other Early Byzantine mosaics, with a few exceptions found in Albania[2]. The two-layer support

(foundation) is directly deposited on level, packed earth. The lower layer consists of tiles and bricks fragments of more or less square shape, set on edge, and using almost no mortar (ill. 50). As a first step, mosaicists divided the surface, beginning by the N wall, into 8 bands (62 to 68 cm wide) using parallel E-W lines of brick and tile sherds, set on edge and end-to-end (ill. 52)[3]. They then filled the bands with other terracotta sherds set on edge and laid

50. Support on which the mosaic was laid.

51. Photo showing removal of the support.

---

1. Atelier de Restauration de la Pierre et du Bois.
2. See *infra* chapter "Synthesis", note 20. Cf. Vrina (Butrint plain) and the apse of Basilica E at Byllis, where this technique seems linked to a problem of soil stability, respectively the presence of damp soils, or a steep slope. Other examples probably exist in Early Byzantine construction, and there is needed further study of the subject, something difficult to achieve because of a general lack of technical precision in mosaic research. By contrast, we found much more evidence from Roman times, especially in the open air spaces of public buildings.
3. The lines were interrupted at 80 cm from the E wall and 30 cm from the primitive W limit and these spaces are filled with perpendicularly set up tile sherds.

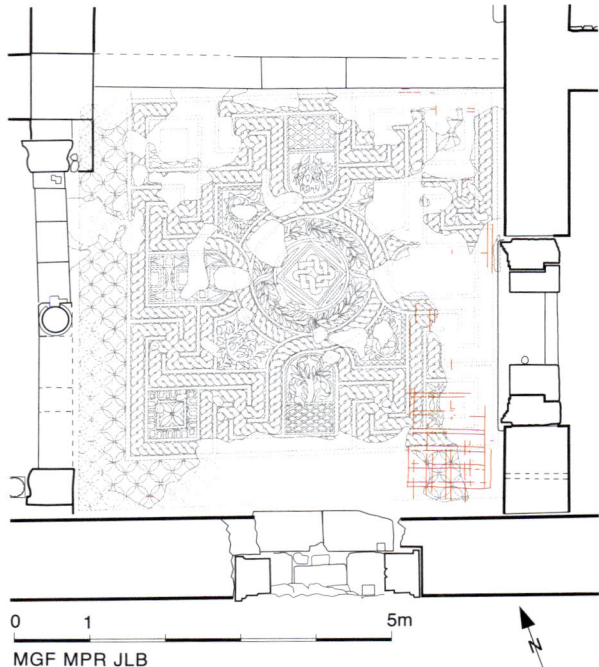

52. Lines of tile and brick sherds shown after removal of the dividing bands.

53. Preparatory sketch on the mortar, below the mosaic: plan.

54. Preparatory sketch: detail.

perpendicular to the lines and tightly joined (ill. 51). A thin uniform layer of mortar was spread over the ensemble and showed traces of a preparatory sketch on the surface. There were engraved lines forming a simple grid and demonstrating how much care was taken to make this mosaic, which has a very sophisticated pattern. Then was added the final delicate setting bed for the tesserae ("lit de pose"). In other words, here we did not find the traditional three layers of *statumen*, *rudus* and *nucleus* used almost everywhere else for the foundations of mosaic pavements to provide a solid and uniform support[4]. The special support found a Xanthos is in excellent condition and probably resisted earth tremors very well (see *infra* chapter "Synthesis").

Preparatory sketch
Remains of the preparatory sketch (ill. 53, 54) are preserved in the SE corner of the room and along the NE edge, on the surface of the foundation. They show a tight grid of lightly engraved bands (each band is ca. 5 cm wide and formed by two parallel lines, not very straight); these bands form squares (ill. 53) (ca. 18 cm/side). This drawing probably was very useful in tracing the supplementary border of intersecting circles, and in elaborating the complex U-cross pattern and its meanders[5].

---

4. The traditional layering of *rudus* and *nucleus* is here replaced by the single layer of tile and brick sherds.
5. About preparatory sketch, see Prudhomme 1975; a good document of the well known example of Stabia, in Italy (Madrid 2001, p. 103 and bibliography about this pavement). See also the works of E. Chantriaux on this subject, especially a communication at ICCM Symposium, 18-25 October 2008, Palermo, forthcoming.

Description
Supplementary border (instead of outer margins)
A supplementary border frames the pavement only on the S (84 cm wide) and W sides (76 cm wide), and on the W this border is partly covered by a Middle Byzantine wall that blocks half of the original entrance (the visible part of the border is 32 cm wide). These two large border sections have an orthogonal pattern of intersecting circles (*Décor* I, pl. 237): the polychrome concave squares are shaded black, white, black, yellow, with a black central crosslet, whereas the outlined spindles appear white. The S threshold encroaches on this border.

Field (5.80 x 5.40 m)
The almost square field is shifted toward the N and E, and a thin white band no more than two or three

tesserae wide occurs along the walls on these sides. The centralized pattern is similar to the décor of the N compartment (inv. **4**), with differences of details and filler motifs that radically change the overall effect. The design is formed by a continuous simple guilloche that also frames the field, creating the appearance of a border.

Circumcentric pattern (ill. 55-56), in a square and around a circle, of four lateral arches, interlaced tangentially with the circle, and four large chevrons posted in the corners, adjacent to the arches (pattern sometimes called a "cross of four U's"). The chevrons are organized as two swastika-meanders flanking a square (*Décor* II, pl. 367a). The guilloche strands present three dominant colors, red (black, three red, white, black), yellow (black, three yellow, white, black) and blue (black, three blue, white, black).

A garland of laurel leaves frames the central circle, and is ornamented with obliquely entwined ribbons and small elliptical links, all of this outlined by white triple fillets. The pairs of ribbons on the E-W axis are colored red and yellow with a blue center. Two elliptical links on the N-S axis are shaded red, white, pink, black (the colors in this area are badly burned and hardly legible). The garland itself is divided into four sections by the ribbons and links, and it is composed of leaves whose colors change from one quarter to the other: green leaves with a white head shown against a black ground, and yellow leaves with a white top shown against a red ground. The central black circle has an inscribed poised square framed by both a black double fillet and a white one. Within the circle, a square and a poised curvilinear square (cushion), interlaced, fill the space and appear against a yellow ground. The shaded band forming the cushion is white, blue, green. The resulting spaces shaped as portions of circles flanking the posed square are shaded green and blue or yellow with a green center.

Three of the arches are preserved, and all four must have appeared as opposing pairs. In the N-S axis, a fence occupies the lower part of the arch, and has a diagonal lattice pattern, forming lozenges of alternating colors: yellow and blue in the S arch, pink and blue in the N arch. To suggest volume and shading, the lozenges are outlined in white on one side and red on the other. Above this small fence emerges a fruit tree, whose form fits the rounded shape of the arch. In the N arch (ill. 57), the leaves are made with green glass outlined in black; in the S (ill. 58), they are colored black and framed by green glass tesserae. The fruits resemble yellow and pink pears. Tesserae forming leaves and fruits are smaller than elsewhere.

The W arch is entirely decorated by a geometric pattern, a grid of bands with intersecting squares forming square compartments inscribed in a circle, and creating the effect of bobbins (*Décor* I, pl. 144e). Smaller intersecting squares are colored yellow, framed by red and white lines. The bobbins are shaded blue, and the portions of circles include red and blue motifs. The larger squares have an included motif in shaded colors (white, red, black, blue, white… destroyed part). A white ground is barely visible in this pattern.

The squares in the corners of the field form similar pairs along the diagonals:

55. Reconstruction of the design of the centralized pattern.

56. Overall view of the pavement.

57. Detail of the N arch, with a fruit tree behind a garden fence.

58. Detail of the S arch.

NW square: very damaged, it is surrounded by a small border of tangent white spindles, one horizontal and two vertical, shown against a red ground on the outer half and a black ground on the inner half. Center part is lost.

SE square: same border. The spindles are bichrome, white outside and blue inside to suggest relief. Center is lost.

SW square: border of arcades (arches) and darts, drawn in white on a colored ground (black and blue outside, red and white inside). The small arcades (arches) contain a white egg on a black ground and the corners contain a square (red, black and blue), and the center consists of a black quatrefoil surrounded by lateral white and red crosslets on a dark ground.

NE square: hardly visible, its border is similar to the previous one; the center contains a white quatrefoil on a colored ground, pink, yellow, blue.

Four trapezoidal spaces flank the central circle, and are ornamented with floral motifs, largely destroyed on the NE.

SW trapezoid: leafy stem with green leaves, supporting a fruit, colored red, yellow, blue, and framed by a rounded calyx of branches, seen against a red ground; blue lanceolate leaves are outlined in white, or appear yellow with a white top.

NW and SE trapezoids: calyx formed by two leafy branches, the leaves blue or green outlined in black toward exterior of calyx, and yellow and white on red ground within the motif. Two round fruits appear in the empty center of the calyx, in bad condition, with red as the dominant color.

Commentary: the unusual support, the preparatory sketch and the original style of the mosaic, different from every other pavement in the building, give this mosaic a very prominent position among the basilica's floors. It is clearly the product of a different workshop from that encountered in the basilica proper. It also is worth underscoring the use of glass as a material within this pavement.

Comparison: for examples of the same pattern, see Raynaud 1996, and inv. **4** and inv. **10**-7B; see also *infra* the chapter "Synthesis". The closest example concerning the repertory of this mosaic is in Aphrodisias (Bishop Palace, Rm. 3, Campbell 1991, pl. 52): we observe a tight centralized pattern built on guilloche meanders and squares, close in style but with geometric filler motifs. The supplementary border is very similar (intersecting circles) and disposed also on two sides of the room.

6. narthex (central compartment)

Since the original construction of the church, the floor of the central compartment of the narthex was adorned with a pavement made of *opus sectile*. It is clearly separated from the flanking mosaic compartments by a low and narrow stylobate. Moreover, the eastern wall of the central compartment in the narthex leading to the nave, with its three doors, had a revetment combining white marble with dark schist.

A reconstruction of the pavement's overall design can be suggested. This pavement belongs to a category of floors characterized as "geometrico a piccoli elementi entro pannelli"[6], in other words, "*opus sectile* floors with the panels composed of geometric patterns of small-scale units". This type of pavement was very popular in the Near East, especially during the entire 6th c., first in North Syria and soon afterward spreading to Cyprus and the south coast of Turkey, as well as to Greece and the Balkans. However, it was less common in the West, for example in Italy and France[7].

Opus sectile floor.
Illustrations 18, 59-62.
Rectangle placed lengthwise on N-S axis in center of narthex, flanked on N and S by two square compartments discussed above.

Dimensions: 14,10 x 5,30 m.

Materials: black schist, white limestone, local gray-green marl stone, terracotta (brown and red).

Various marbles: light colored, such as white marbles (of unknown origin)[8], grey marbles, Pentelic (white with thin pink veins), Chemtou (giallo antico from Tunisia), light blue or light grey Proconnesian (or "Marmara"), "flowering peach" from Iasos (white with orange veins), pavonazzetto or Skyrian (white with purple veins), biggio antico (beige), coralline breccia (pink) from Bithynia, nero scritto marble.

The dark marbles are represented by rosso antico and rare dense coralline breccia (red), red and green porphyry, green breccia from Thessaly ("verde antico"), green cipollino from Karystos, dark grey marbles, dark blue (perhaps from Aphrodisias), blue-gray, greco scritto (from Algeria?).

Colors: various, with a chromatic palette emphasizing the contrast between light and dark types of stone.

State of preservation: this meticulously and precisely made pavement is destroyed to a significant degree, with only a portion of the N zone and a smaller

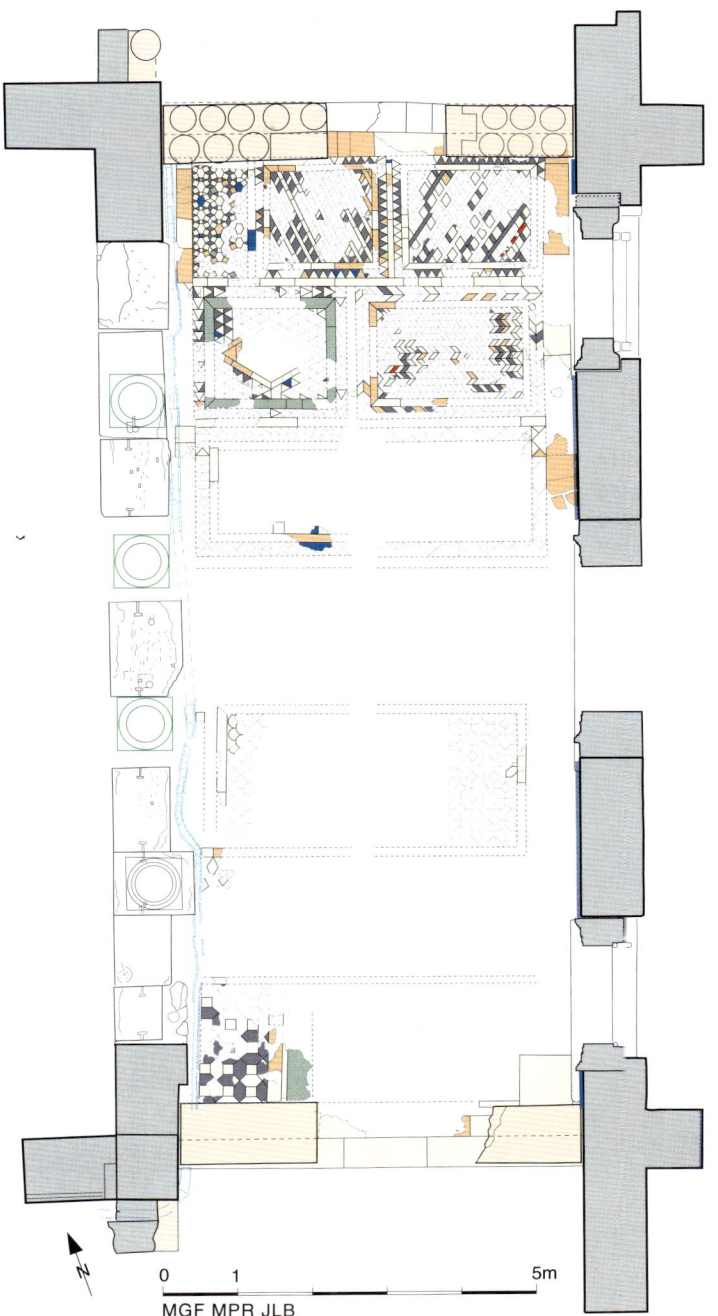

---

6. Guidobaldi-Guiglia Guidobaldi 1983, especially p. 319. See Froidevaux-Raynaud 2005, "pavement de petit module à panneaux" for an overall survey of the success of this type of pavement. See also *infra* chapter "Synthesis".
7. See *supra* note 6.
8. M.-G. Froidevaux, J.-P. Sodini and M.-P. Raynaud participated with a poster in the 7th International Asmosia Conference (Association for the Study of Marble and other Stones used in Antiquity), in Thassos in September 2003. The aim of the presentation was to have the opportunity to meet specialists of ancient marble. It was important to verify and confirm our own identifications of the stones' provenance. We hoped that it also would be possible to recognize a few white and light-colored marbles, but L. Lazzarini, who kindly helped us and answered our questions, explained that even with sophisticated methods, the certain identification of white marbles was often impossible. For marble identification, see Lazzarini 2004, Lazzarini 2007, Gnoli 1971, De Nuccio-Ungaro 2002, Fant 1988, Pensabene 1998, Del Bufalo 2004, etc.

amount of the SW sector remaining. It was damaged by earthquakes, as pavement fragments deeply buried under the stone lintels and door jambs show, with these huge blocks lying in the places where they fell. Unfortunately, the central part of the floor located in front of the main door is lost, and it may have received special attention due to its privileged setting. The pavement has been restored (N part) in 2008 by S. Yeşil Erdek (see chapter "Synthesis").

Support (foundation): the mortar does not include leveling pieces, usually made of terracotta or marble fragments[9]. This is a common characteristic

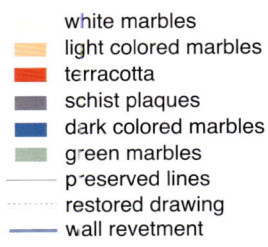

9. This use is reserved for large plaques that required perfect leveling, but in the case of small units, they were adjusted "by sight".

59. Plan of the central compartment of narthex, pavement 6.

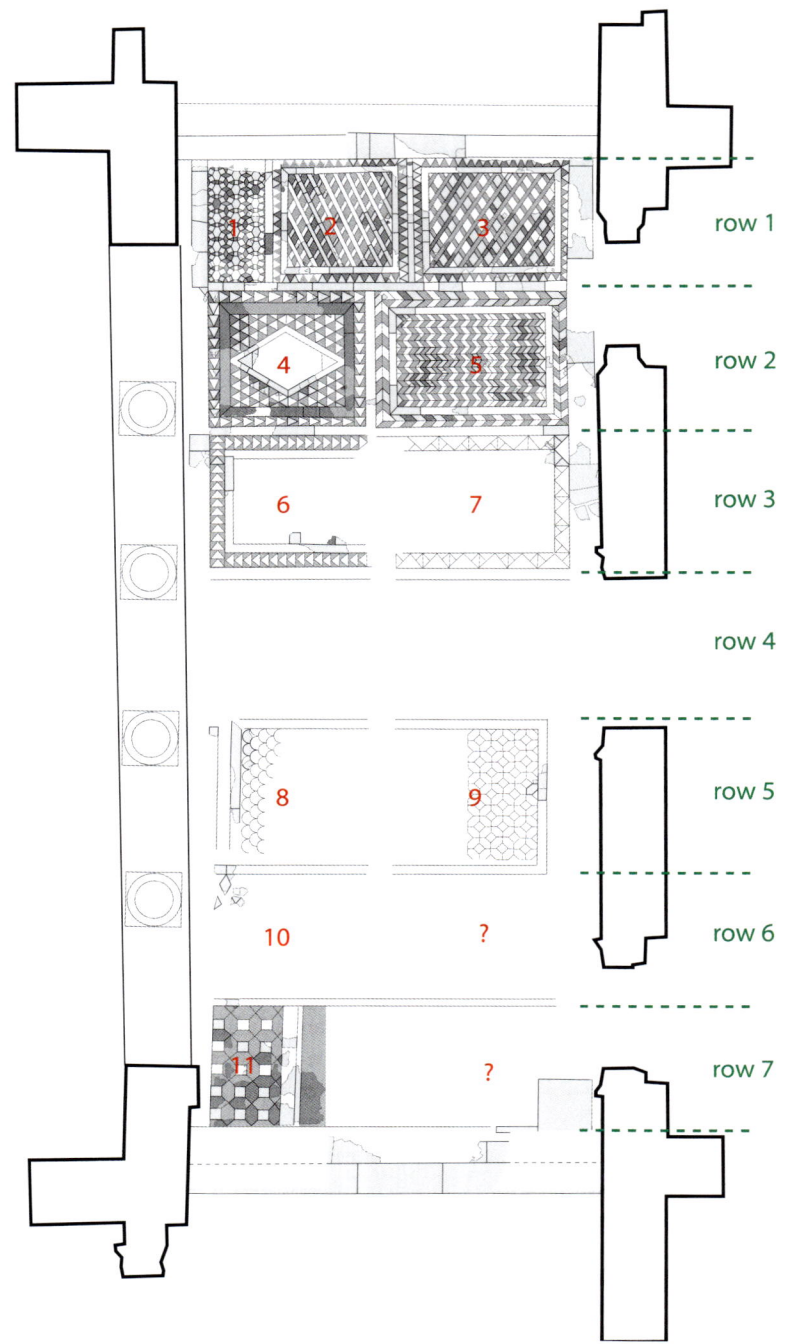

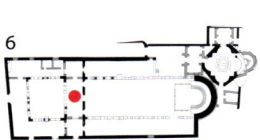

60. Scheme with the numbers of the panels of pavement 6.

of "*opus sectile* floors with panels made of small-scale units". The units are small enough to be wedged by the thick mortar, which can easily absorb the differences in thickness of the various materials. Many traces left in the mortar helped complete the overall design of individual pavements.

Description

The design of the central narthex pavement (ill. 59-60) faithfully reflects a special type of *opus sectile* floor in which the surface is divided into rectangular panels of modest, somewhat varied dimensions, all of them separated by plain bands (8 to 14 cm wide) made of light-colored marble (white, light grey or light blue Proconnesian). The field of each panel contains its own geometric pattern, made of small pre-fabricated units of different stones, i.e., marbles, limestone and schist. The originality of this pavement is the presence, rarely attested elsewhere, of a decorated border (10 to 20 cm wide) inside most of the panels[10]; these borders are separated from the field by a narrow band of plain light marble (7 to 12 cm wide). We may suppose that the organization of the mosaics in the church influenced the *opus sectile* workers to adopt these internal borders. The panels are arranged in groups of two or three within the width of the narthex, most of them aligned on the E-W axis and forming bands or rows of panels. We can further reconstruct seven parallel rows in the entire room. The patterns of the borders are simple and the patterns of the fields are mainly isotropic, with only one centralized design preserved.

A wide border of slabs surrounds the pavement, separating it from the walls. These slabs are made mainly of light-colored or Proconnesian marbles.

A narrow channel used for wastewater skirts the W edge of the pavement, heading southward and following the stylobate's blocs, which are irregular on this side (ill. 59). Of shallow depth, this channel was partly recovered in the S compartment (NW corner) and probably ended into the pipe running South under the carpet 2-9B in S atrium.

Rows are described beginning on the N, and within each row from W to E (ill. 60).

First row
It is composed of three panels, of unequal dimensions (ca. 1.65 m wide).

• *Panel 1*
Located in the NW corner, this panel is flanked on the W by the pipe mentioned above.
Dimensions: 1.65 x 0.75 m; it is the smallest panel in the room, arranged in a N-S direction, showing a degree of symmetry with panel 11 in the SW corner, also placed on the N-S axis.

State of preservation: preserved over more than half its surface.

Description: honeycomb-pattern of squares, contiguous by a corner and forming oblong hexagons and equilateral triangles, little squares and lozenges, creating the effect of tangent irregular dodecagons. This rare pattern is complex and difficult to analyze (ill. 62a), and the scale of the units is very small. Oblong hexagons are made mainly of

---

10. We observed borders in six panels in the N part of the pavement, and in panel 8, but not in the smallest ones, panel 1 or SW panel 11.

light-colored marbles, white, light grey, two pieces of light blue Proconnesian, a few of limestone, one of Pentelic marble, two of dark blue marble (Aphrodisias?), one of local green stone (schist?); triangles and lozenges consist of dark schist, and squares are mostly made of light-colored marbles. There are visible one square of rosso antico, a few made of pavonazetto or Skyrian marble, limestone, white marble, three green marble squares and two dark blue marble hexagons. The units are extremely small with the triangles barely measuring 7 cm on a side.

• *Panel 2*
Dimensions: 1.78 x 1.65 m.
Preserved over one third of its surface.

Description: its border is 10-11 cm wide, decorated in a saw-tooth pattern, with the triangles on the outer edge made of light marble (two rosso antico triangles, one of white marble, one of pavonazetto or Skyrian marble, one of coralline breccia and perhaps one piece of Iasos marble) and the other made of dark materials, mostly schist. After a narrow (7 cm) light colored band (Proconnesian and white marbles, limestone, nero scritto), the field displays a lozenge lattice-pattern of intersecting bands (*Décor* I, pl. 201). Lozenges are made of schist, separated by narrow bands of light-colored marble, mainly white (bands ca. 5 cm wide), continuously from NW to SE, with those running on the opposite direction fragmented into small parallelograms. There appear a few irregularities among the materials, such as a small fragment of terracotta in the W border of the field, and a few dark marble triangles in the S border.

• *Panel 3*
Dimensions: 2.06 x 1.65 m, somewhat longer than previous panel.

Less than half is preserved. Border and field patterns are identical to panel 2, except that the continuous bands separating the lozenges run from SW to NE (ill. 61). One of them consists of terracotta units. This panel presents the opposite tonal range, with a dark lattice (schist and terracotta bands) seen against light-colored lozenges (white and Proconnesian marble, and a rare white marble with pink veins).

Second row
This row contains panels 4 and 5, and is a little wider than the first one.

• *Panel 4*
Dimensions: 2.05 x 1.83 m.
Preserved over roughly one fourth of its surface, this panel shows a few original characteristics.

The border, ca. 15 cm wide, is a row of superposed isosceles triangles (*Décor* I, pl. 1a), the triangles turned southward in E and W parts, eastward in N and S parts. Triangles are made of white marble against a dark schist ground. A green marble band separates the border from the field (15 cm wide) and contains cipollino from Karistos, of two different shades. The field (1.50 x 1.25 m) displays a concentric pattern, a large lozenge within the plain rectangular border, its acute angles tangent to the border. The spaces around the lozenge contain triangular chessboards (ill. 62b), showing a contrast of dark and light colors (schist and dark marble pieces versus white marble; two of the dark triangles consist of local dark green stone). The central lozenge is framed by a narrow band of light-colored and white marbles. The lozenge itself is almost lost, except for the W corner, made of an equilateral grey triangle (marble from nearby Muğla?) and a band along its inner edge. A few fragments of the plain bands are made of nero scritto marble.

• *Panel 5*
Dimensions: 2.52 x 1.83 m.

It is partly preserved. The border shows a bichrome double row of lozenges forming superposed chevrons, the chevrons in alternating colors and turned in various directions (N for the W border, E for the N and S borders, and S for the E border). Its width varies slightly, becoming

6-1

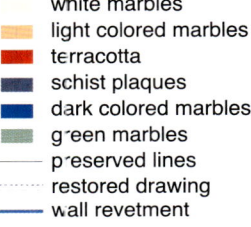
white marbles
light colored marbles
terracotta
schist plaques
dark colored marbles
green marbles
preserved lines
restored drawing
wall revetment

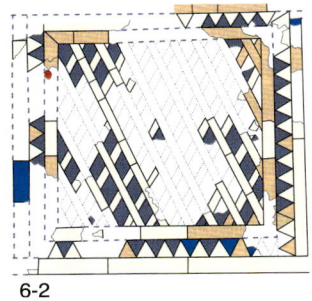
6-2

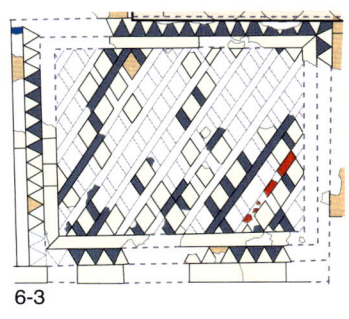
6-3

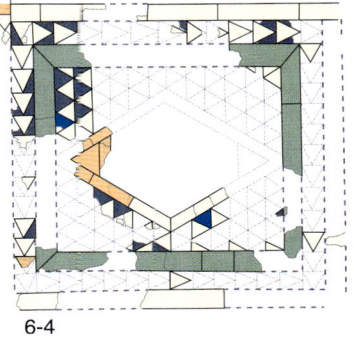
6-4

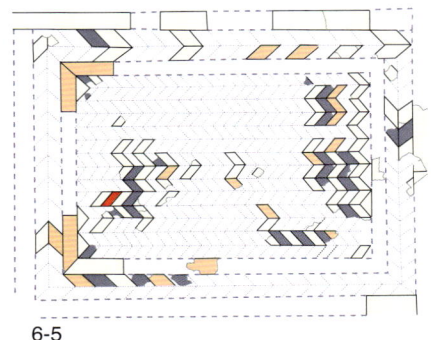

6-5

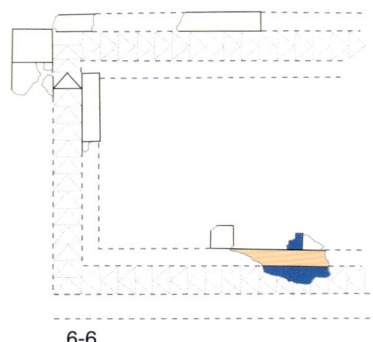

6-6

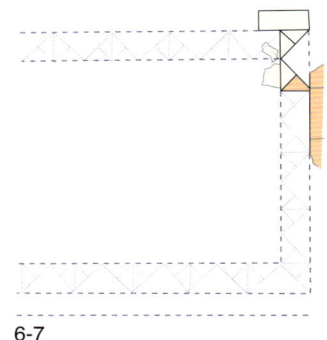

6-7

white marbles
light colored marbles
terracotta
schist plaques
dark colored marbles
green marbles
preserved lines
restored drawing
wall revetment

narrower on the S side (from 20 to 16 cm wide). The use of materials causes the dark chevrons to contrast with the light chevrons (various marbles). The field contains an isotropic pattern of chevrons made of parallelograms (*Décor* I, pl. 203f) smaller in scale than units in the border, with dark lines of chevrons (schist and terracotta) contrasting with light ones (light-colored and white marbles among which we distinguished pavonazzetto or Skyrian, Proconnesian and nero scritto). One parallelogram is made of terracotta rather than schist, one consists of Pentelic marble, one is of pavonazzetto.

Third row
This row, containing panels 6 and 7, is 1.80 m wide; the panel's length can not be determined.

• *Panel 6*
Mostly missing, with only small pieces of its frames (plain and decorated) and few elements of the field remaining. The border (19 cm wide) probably showed a linear pattern of a row of superposed right-angled triangles (*Décor* I, pl. 11d), although only one white marble triangle is preserved. The internal band of plain light-colored marble is represented by two fragments (white or light marble). The field is known only from a square unit of white marble, and two pieces of dark marble laid against a white one. The pattern can not be reconstructed.

• *Panel 7*
It is almost completely destroyed. Only the border pattern is partly legible, as small fragments in the NE corner show: it may have formed a line of large triangles, with the inner ones subdivided into four triangles. A second possibility is that there was a line of squares, with individual squares subdivided into two triangles.

Fourth row
Central part of the row is completely lost. This row was probably as wide as the others, ca. 1.80 m.

Fifth row
ca. 1.80 cm wide.

• *Panel 8*
E-W dimensions unknown, N-S ca. 1.80 cm.

If the border once existed, as traces in the mortar indicate, it is not preserved. After a narrow white band, a small fragment containing a few tangent scales in white marble, probably part of an isotropic pattern, is all that remains of the field's decoration.

• *Panel 9*
Dimensions unknown, probably 1.80 m wide.

Inside narrow white band, two fragments of oblong hexagons are visible. They could have been part of an orthogonal pattern of intersecting and tangent octagons, determining oblong hexagons and poised squares (same pattern as Panel 11 below).

Sixth row
ca. 1.70 m wide.

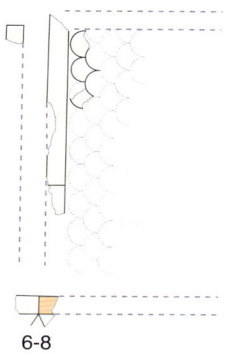

6-8

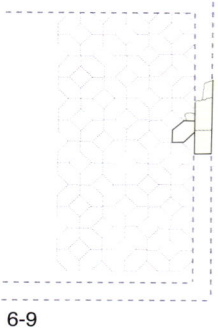

6-9

6-11

• *Panel 10*
A single lozenge plaque (border ?) and a few tiny fragments are insufficient to allow an interpretation of this row's panels.

Seventh row
(South): 1.65 m wide.

• *Panel 11*
Dimensions: 1.65 x 0.90 m.

Preserved over half of its surface, it contains an isotropic orthogonal pattern of intersecting and adjacent octagons, forming squares and oblong hexagons (*Décor* I, pl. 169d). This panel has no internal border, like Panel 1, and is symmetrically placed in relation to the latter. Hexagons are made of schist, and squares of white marble (with also one of Proconnesian). Behind the E end of this panel, after two light-colored bands of marble (a wide and a narrow one, together 25 cm wide) occurs a large slab of green marble from Thessaly (34 cm wide). Nothing is preserved of the pavement further E, except for a large white marble slab laid against the E wall (S of the church's S door), and encroaching on the row's surface. Two rows of wide light-colored slabs separate the panel from the S stylobate.

Commentary: the main aesthetic interest of this kind of pavement is the striking contrast it creates between light and dark elements, making the patterns easily legible (ill. 61), and it is worth noting the various types of polychrome materials used. All of the marbles were re-used and originally extracted at sites all around the Mediterranean[11].
Patterns in the panels' fields are simple and common, faithful to the repertory of this kind of pavement and not noteworthy for the originality of the pattern chosen; more surprising here is the presence of borders, very rare in this type of floor. The technical precision in cutting very small pieces also is significant, for they are sawn with straight edges, sharp angles, and regular shapes (prefabricated pieces) and have narrow joins (ill. 62).

Comparisons: two examples in Xanthos, respectively in the Residence of the Lycian Acropolis (inv. **32** of the anticipated next volume of the Corpus of the mosaics of Xanthos[12]), and in the Agora Church sanctuary (*ibid.*, inv. **47**); also one in Letoon Byzantine complex, (Metzger 1966,

61 View of the first row of the *opus sectile* floor 6.

figs. 9-10). For comparisons with this kind of *opus sectile* floor, see Froidevaux-Raynaud 2005, and chapter "Synthesis". In Turkey, one of the best known pavements of this kind occurs in the Gymnasium of Sardis (Ramage 1972, figs. 14-16; Hanfmann 1973, figs. 11-12). At Elaioussa Sebaste there are three groups of close examples: all of the pavements in the North Church (Equini Schneider 1997, figs. 5-6, 14; Equini Schneider 2008, p. 93), in the Byzantine complex on the Roman Agora, (Equini Schneider 1998, figs. 11-12 and 16; Equini Schneider 2008, p. 55-57), and in the church on the island (Equini Schneider 1998, fig. 18) are typical of this kind of *opus sectile* floor. At Ephesus, the Basilica of St. John (Hörmann 1951, pls. XL5, LXVI, LXXIV). In Ankyra (Roman house, Kadıoğlu 1997, figs. 1-2, 11). In Kelenderis (basilica, Zoroğlu 2003, fig. 7). In Sagalassos, the sanctuary of the church (Waelkens 2000, fig. 4) and the baths (Waelkens 2005, fig. 8). In Korykos, various examples (Herzfeld-Guyer 1930, Klosterkirche, fig. 168; Grabeskirche fig. 158; Basilica extra-muros, fig. 118; Kathedrale, fig. 102). It also is well attested in Constantinople (see Guidobaldi-Guiglia Guidobaldi 1983, n. 658), for which we mention examples in Hagia Sophia, Kalenderhane Camii, Saraçhane Camii. In Cyprus, the magnificent example of the Basilica of Ayios Philon at Karpasia (Michaelides 1992, p. 113, no. 65), the Basilica of

---

11. On the increasing taste for marble during all of the Byzantine era, see Sodini 1994, pp. 177-201; Sodini 2002, pp. 129-146.
12. Corpus Xanthos 2, forthcoming.

62. Details of the *opus sectile* 6;
a, panel 1;
b, panel 4.

Campanopetra at Salamis (in East Baths, Roux 1998, figs. 309-311), in the church apse, narthex, S corridor and N aisle, E atrium, (*ibid.*, fig. 248, plans III and IV). At Amathous, in the Acropolis Basilica we find a floor of this design with a central corridor (Pralong 1994, figs. 5-7, 10). On Crete, at Gortyna in a 6th c. church (Basilica of Mitropolis, sanctuary, Farioli-Borboudakis 2005, fig. 2). Other examples exist in the Aegean Islands, on Samos, on Lesbos at Mytilene and on Rhodes. Many such pavements have been recently excavated in Thessaloniki (Vitti 2005, pp. 695-711), the major examples being at the intersection of Prasakaki and Koukouphle Streets, (Corpus Greece 3, pls. 262-263), in the Octagon (Vitti 2005, fig. 2), and we also know many other examples in Macedonia (Philippi, Octagon; Edessa, Stobi and Veria). In Syria, the beautiful example of Qala'at Seman (East Basilica, Donceel-Voûte 1988, pp. 225-240), the cathedral of Apamea (Balty 1972, pls. LXXVII-LXXIX) and a parallel at Seleuceia Pieria (Campbell 1941, pl. II). In Jordan, Umm Qeis Gadara (Picirillo 1993, figs. 691-692, 694), Gerasa, St. John the Baptist and St. Theodore (Donceel-Voûte 1988, p. 29); the Petra Cathedral nave (Petra Church 2001, figs. 21-24, 27). A few examples occur in Palestine (Church of St. John, Jerusalem) and in North Africa (Cyrene, Atrun, Ptolemais in Libya; Utica and Thuburbo Majus in Tunisia). In Europe, the examples are less numerous and less typical: we note pavements in the Basilica Emiliana in Rome and Arles (Verrerie) in France.

North Aisle

The N aisle of the church is preserved in its Early Byzantine state over a little more than half of its original length. The E part was deliberately destroyed and excavated in Middle Byzantine times to a depth of ca. 2 m, in order to create additional space in front of the new church erected in the original baptistery. Perhaps also this part of the church had suffered more than others from successive earthquakes, because of its position on a thick artificial terrace, which was easier to destroy than to reconstruct. The base of the N wall in this area reaches far below the level of the other foundations of the church. A crude Middle Byzantine staircase was then constructed at the intentional break in carpet **7**-3, leading down to the level of the new church (situated ca. 2 m below the floors of the Early Byzantine building). Probably another carpet **7**-4, once decorated the E part of the aisle that was destroyed. During the same extensive renovation, the Early Byzantine stairs leading to the baptistery were almost completely removed, and the door near the center of the N wall, which communicated with the stairs and led to a NW annex and corridor, was closed by a Middle Byzantine niche. Another, symmetrically placed door in the S aisle also was blocked, probably at the same time.

The N aisle is separated from the nave by a stylobate made of reused blocks carefully aligned on the nave side and appearing irregular on the N side. The stylobate blocks supported columns (or socles plus shorter, reused columns), which in turn upheld a 2nd-story gallery; chancel screens filled the intervals between the vertical supports.

Wall paintings: a few red fragments occur on the N part of the W wall; a narrow space once filled by wall painting separates the mosaic from the masonry, attesting the presence of a presumed painted layer.

An important bottle-shaped cistern is located under the N aisle. Its well-head occurs between the stylobate and the Early Byzantine mosaic, immediately S of carpet **7**-2. Since the mosaic partly covers the cistern and the stylobate does too, we may suppose that the cistern was constructed before the church or, more likely, made for the church's use. The cistern well-head was probably reconstructed during the Middle Byzantine period, when the pipe coming from the NW corner of the atrium and ending at the cistern was repaired.

As stated earlier, the preserved N part of the Early Byzantine building and its floors remained in use during the Middle Byzantine period even though the rest of the church was partly ruined; a new roof was erected over the preserved part of the N aisle during the latter era. Modern excavations found this zone cluttered with architectural elements (columns, large blocks) which had fallen after the building's complete abandonment, and in some places the structure was adapted to form a crude pen for cattle, directly above the Early Byzantine floor (late mediaeval occupation).

7. N aisle
Opus tessellatum.
Illustrations 63-76, 165.

Originally covering the entire aisle, this mosaic was later reduced in size; it was restored in modern times and is in good condition. It is remarkably homogeneous in style and certainly was completed in a single phase. Three juxtaposed rectangular carpets survive, numbered **7**-1 to **7**-3 from W to E. They primarily present geometric patterns, and a common border separates and surrounds these carpets, unifying the ensemble. The first carpet

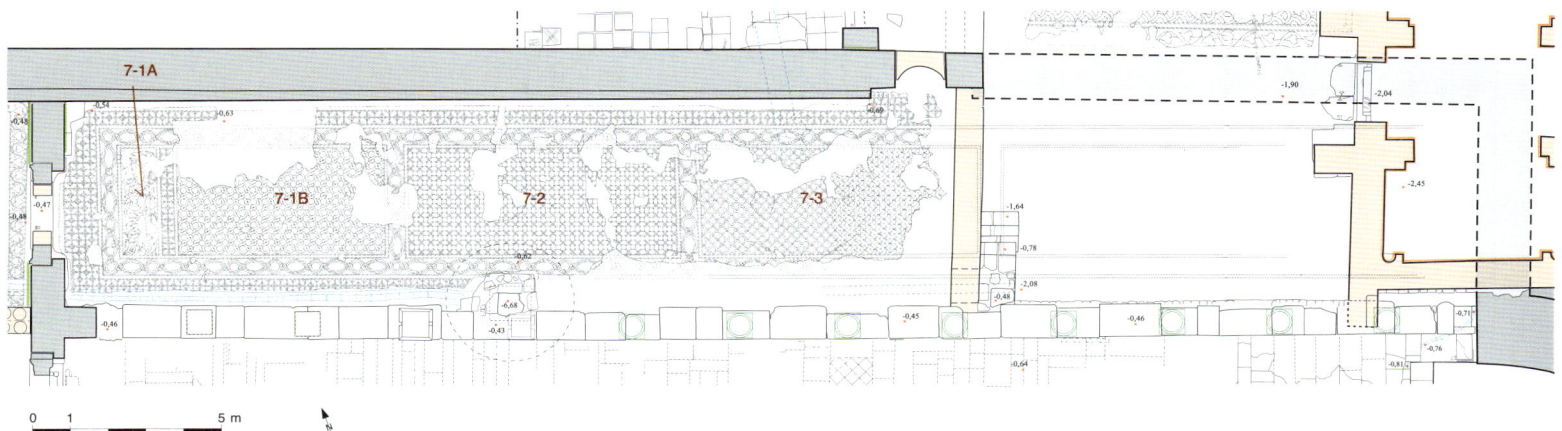

63. Plan of the N aisle, pavement 7, with the numbers of carpets and panels.

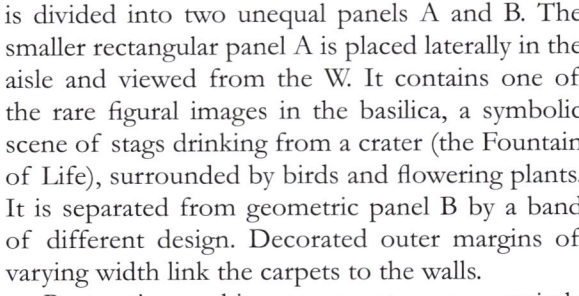

64. Outer margins, border and band between panels 7-1A and 7-1B.

7- border

is divided into two unequal panels A and B. The smaller rectangular panel A is placed laterally in the aisle and viewed from the W. It contains one of the rare figural images in the basilica, a symbolic scene of stags drinking from a crater (the Fountain of Life), surrounded by birds and flowering plants. It is separated from geometric panel B by a band of different design. Decorated outer margins of varying width link the carpets to the walls.

Restoration: this pavement was entirely consolidated[1] *in situ* and the gaps carefully cleaned and filled with lime mortar, with better water drainage also provided. A thick protective cover was placed over the mosaic (layers of river gravel and large pebbles, plastic and river sand).

Outer margins
Around the three preserved sides of the aisle, the margin's width (ill. 63, 64) varies from 9 to 38 cm. It is divided into two parts: 1) a narrow white band found along the base of the walls, and connected to an inner decorated part (three to six tesserae wide); 2) a wider decorated part having a geometric pattern and taking the form of either a single band (N and S), or enlarged to form an isotropic pattern both at the W end (two bands wide, changing to two and a half in front of the door leading to the narthex), and in front of the door at the center of the N wall (two bands wide).

Colors: black, white, red.
State of preservation: the outer margins of the N aisle are well preserved on the N and W sides, but only partially intact on the S (for less than half the

1. P. Blanc and L. Krougly, September 1994 and 1995.

length of the mosaic) where the digging of a trench to repair an underground pipe damaged it, as can be seen in front of the stylobate up to the entrance of the cistern. Further E, the margin is lost. In front of the N door, the white band is ornamented with small poised squares in a line. Some gaps punctuate the outer margins, especially at the W end, with its burned spots.

Description: grid of black double fillets with alternate intersections superimposed on a poised serrated polychrome square (forming a pattern of adjacent and intersecting octagons) (*Décor* I, pl. 123f). The serrated squares are colored black, red (one or two fillets) with a white center. This motif used as a band is also found between panels A and B of carpet **7**-1.

Commentary: this pattern is used here both as a linear design and an isotropic pattern (in larger areas); it is close in style to carpet **2**-1 (N atrium) but its overall appearance is different, because of the alternation of the squares that here makes octagons appear.

Border
It develops as a continous band around the N aisle and also separates it into carpets **7**-1, **7**-2 and **7**-3 (ill. 63-67); a probable fourth carpet (**7**-4) was later destroyed at the E end.

Dimensions: 33 cm wide with the white bands, 23 without.
Materials: light blue Proconnesian marble gives the blue color, a type of marble found frequently in the building.
Density of tesserae/dm^2: 62.
Colors: black, white, red, light blue.
State of preservation: this border is mostly preserved, except for a large gap on the NW, and in the SE half of the preserved pavement. There are some traces of burning especially at the W end.

Description
Line of circles and spindles (*Décor* I, pl. 22), interlooped tangentially in shaded bands, alternately with blue (black, two blue, two white, black) or red as the dominant color (black, two red, two white, black). Within each motif is an inscribed polychrome motif, made of black and red double fillets enclosing a white center. Resulting spaces contain a small black trapezoid. This border is outlined by black double fillets, and framed on each side by a white band five tesserae wide.

Comparisons: this type of border has numerous comparisons in the rainbow style: one may cite examples in Asia Minor: Dağpazarı (Koropissos), basilica narthex (Gough 1958, pl. IX, fig. 13), very similar in style; and Ephesus (S portico of Curetes street, Miltner 1958, pl. XXIII, fig. 9; Jobst 1977, figs. 49-50).

7-1, N aisle, W carpet
Illustrations 63, 65-68, 165.
The first to be seen upon entering the W end of the nave, it is composed of two panels, A and B, separated by a geometric band.

Overall dimensions: ca. 7.05 x 2.92 m.

Panel 7-1A
Occurring at the W end of the nave (ill. 66-68), it is placed laterally within the aisle, facing W. 2.92 x 0.96 m.

Materials: a few special tesserae appear in this panel, such as dark blue (marble?) and perhaps purple (in a very bad state of preservation because of large burned spots, as in carpets **2**-3, **2**-5 and **2**-7 of the atrium).

Density of tesserae/dm^2: 61 to 69 (stags).

Colors: black, white, red, yellow, dark blue, purple (?).

State of preservation: a low row of blocks was found lying on the mosaic, probably put there to divide the space during the late period, even after the Middle Byzantine occupation.

The panel was badly damaged by fire, probably when the church collapsed, as gaps formed by fallen architectural elements near the door suggest (the aisles were covered by 2nd-story galleries). Large gray spot surround the gaps, making some colors barely legible.

Description
A symbolic scene common to the entire Byzantine world fills this rectangular panel. Two inward-turned stags flank a large central crater, drinking water pouring from the vase. They are depicted in a landscape with floral elements and various birds. The design is not skillful, but the animals are easily recognizable. A black double fillet outlines the panel.

The crater is drawn with black double fillets. Rounded and lacking handles (ill. 67-68b), it stands on a small conical black foot, marked in its center by two white tesserae. The belly is ornamented with five colored gadroons, outlined in black, whose polychromy accentuates the three-dimensional effect: the large outer gadroons are colored red, outlined in white toward the interior, and the next inner ones appear purple (?), framed in blue and white; finally, the damaged central gadroon is colored blue and white. The neck also is seen in perspective through shading with vertical lines of double fillets (from left to right: black, purple?, blue, white, red, blue, yellow, black), which suggest modeling and reflected light. The open mouth is emphasized by blue tesserae framed by a white fillet. Two small streams, formed by a blue triple fillet, flow from the mouth on both sides and curve up toward the stags' heads.

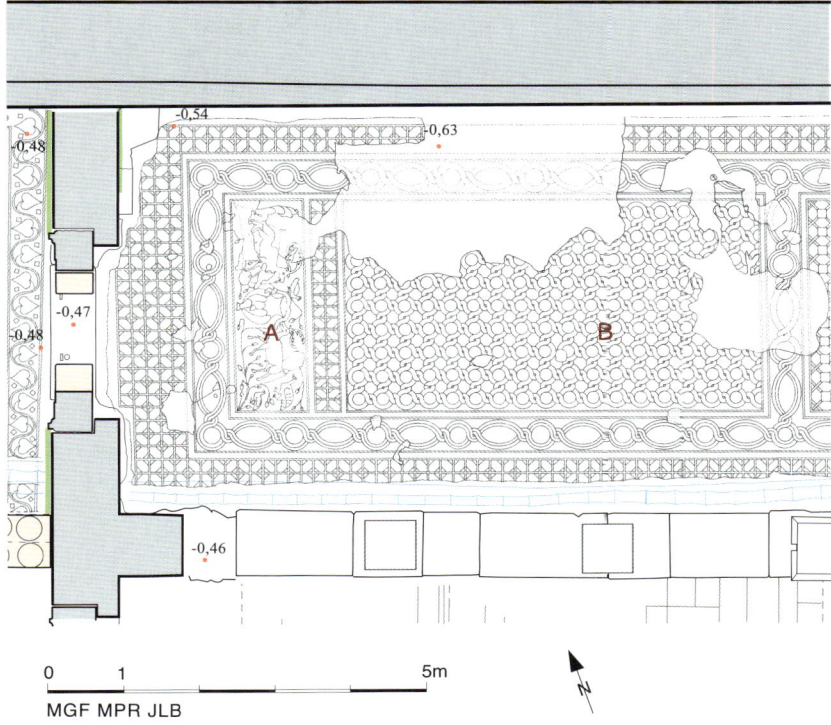

65. Plan of carpet 7-1.

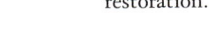

66. Ensemble view after restoration.

67. Panel 7-1A before restoration.

68. Details of the panel 7-1A, before (a) and after restoration (b).

a

b

The right stag (S) is well preserved (ill. 68b), as it is seen in profile and outlined in black. He moves forward, walking toward the spring. His antlers are quite thin and white ears are drawn on each side of the yellow head. The mouth is open toward the streaming water, and some blue tesserae are visible within it. The spindle-shaped eye is formed by a white tessera outlined in black. The animal's spine and back are colored yellow sprinkled with black, and then comes a serrated double fillet, black and dark blue. The rear of the thigh is purple (?) dotted with black tesserae. The belly, breast and thigh are colored dark blue with a white center, while the tail is curled up and colored black like his genitals and right back leg. The front left leg is bent, colored blue at the shoulder and then shaded black. The yellow rear left leg appears stiffly bent as the animal moves forward.

The left stag (N) is badly damaged and although placed symmetrically in relation to the first, the effect of movement is stronger. The antlers, partly preserved, are more prominent. The head appears yellow and dark blue, the belly white, dark blue, black, and the rump is dark blue dotted with red, while the back is yellow sprinkled with black like a chessboard, and the shoulder is dark blue and the legs black.

Above the crater, on the left (N side), a bird in profile faces right, outlined in black. The wing is red, underscored in white and black, with a white dotted line in the middle. The belly is dark blue, the neck black and red, and the head appears black with a red eye and has a red open short beak. The legs are roughly drawn in red.

Behind the right stag (S side), at the top of the panel, is a bird with a heavy broad tail, colored blue with white stripes; its beak, long, red and curved, and its long yellow neck with black stripes could indicate a duck (ill. 68a). The eye is white; the wing yellow dappled with black lines and outlined in white; the breast purple (?); and the belly and legs are blue with red extremities.

Below the previous bird, and facing the crater is a third bird, colored dark blue and blue. Its wing is outlined in yellow and dotted white and purple (?); the thin short neck appears blue and red; and the head and beak are tiny, while the legs and eye are colored red. It could be a partridge.

The landscape elements consist of sinuous plant vines with multiple stems spreading over both halves of the panel. Black lines delineate these stylized floral shapes and their secondary stems. Rosebuds, composed of a black and white trifid corolla with a red point, embellish them. The vines originate in the lower corners and fill the empty spaces of the scene.

The panel is very incomplete on the N side, and we do not know if other birds were present. The scene as a whole appears somewhat naïve and formal, as if made by a mosaicist not used to depicting animals and realistic figures, but rather well executed geometric patterns.

Comparisons: there are a few comparisons for this scene in Turkey: we mention a church near Çağlayanköy of Gördes (Manisa, Lydia), shown in a talk presenting this theme (Tok 2008), with a panel representing two stags around a crater containing vine scrolls (Dedeoğlu 1993, fig. 8; Tok 2008, fig. 6). A few examples of the type of scene are encountered in Cilicia, at Dağpazarı (sanctuary of the South Church, Gough 1961, fig. 5), with two lambs on either side of a crater with plant shoots; at Anemurium, Korykos, Karlık and Misis, the iconography is somewhat different, showing a literal respect for holy texts in the representation of a Peaceful Paradise.

This kind of scene is well attested in Greece, at Hermione (Meïdani House, Sodini 1968, figs. 74-75), with ivy scrolls emerging from a crater and especially in Macedonia, at Amphipolis, Bas. A, in a medallion (S aisle, Zikos 1989, fig. 7); at Heraklea Lynkestis, Martyrium 2, (Cveković-Tomašević 2002, figs. 31-33), Bishop's Palace, triclinium (*ibid.*, fig. 56a), refectory (*ibid.*, fig. 23); at Stobi (Polycharmos Palace, triclinium, *ibid.*, fig. 57; Petrova 2007, without page numbering);

69. View of carpet 7-1B, before removal of the fallen columns and the later structures built over the mosaics.

7-1B

70. Detail of carpet 7-1B.

71. Detail of carpet 7-2.

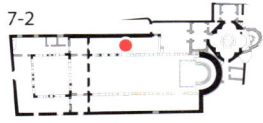

7-2

72. Plan of carpet 7-2.

Baptistery of the Episcopal Basilica (Mikulćik 2003, pp. 123, 126). It also is found in Epirus, for example at Salona (Salona Christiana 1994, p. 99), at Saranda (Onchesmos, Albania), in a late church that replaced a synagogue (Nallbani-Raynaud, forthcoming).

Band separating panels **7-1A** and **7-1B**
Illustrations 64-67.
Dimensions: 36 cm wide.

Description: grid of black double fillets with alternate intersections superimposed on poised serrated polychrome squares (forming a band of adjacent and intersecting octagons) (*Décor* I, pl. 123f). The serrated squares are shaded black and red (one or two fillets) with a white center. It is the same décor as that in the outer margins, with the same colors, materials and module.

Panel 7-1B
Illustrations 63, 65, 69-70.
Long rectangle (slightly irregular) placed lengthwise in the aisle. 5.50 x 2.92 m.
    Density of tesserae/dm^2: 68.
    Colors: black, white, red, blue.
    State of preservation: the late line of blocks resting on panel **7-1A** continued over the entire panel **7-1B**. The mosaic is partly destroyed in the NW zone (outer margins, border and field), and somewhat fragmentary on the E side. It was necessary to restore this fragile area. Heavy elements of the superstructure fell on the pavement, piercing it deeply (beams?).

Description
Polychrome orthogonal pattern of circles in shaded bands interlooped tangentially, forming irregular concave octagons (*Décor* I, pl. 235a). The shaded bands have blue (black, two blue, two white, black) or red as the dominant color (black, two red, two white, black). Both the relatively small concave octagons and the large circles have inscribed black motifs that appear more or less regular. Overall, this geometric carpet resembles a tightly woven mat.

Comparisons: very common pattern for the mosaic field (see in the same building, nave mosaic *infra* inv. **10**-5). In Asia Minor, visible at Miletus (Church, Müller-Wiener 1977-78, pl. 33-2); at Anemurium, (Church of the Holy Apostles, narthex, Campbell 1998, pl. 108) with small inscribed motifs; at Aphrodisias, Priest's House (Rm. 3, atrium, Campbell 1991, pl. 84; Rm. 4, *ibid.*, pls. 88-89), with central quadrants in circles, but in a larger scale; Iasos (Basilica on the Acropolis, Levi 1966, fig. 74; Basilica near gate E, *ibid.*, figs. 19-20); Küçük Tavşan Adası (basilica, Andaloro 2005, fig. 4). On Kos, this pattern is very frequent in Early Byzantine times, and there are many examples, as in the entrance to one baptistery (Di Matteis 2004, pl. XXVIII-3, or *ibid.*, pl. LI-3), or in Mastichari, Church of St John (Parrish 2001, fig. 3). In Greece, very close in style

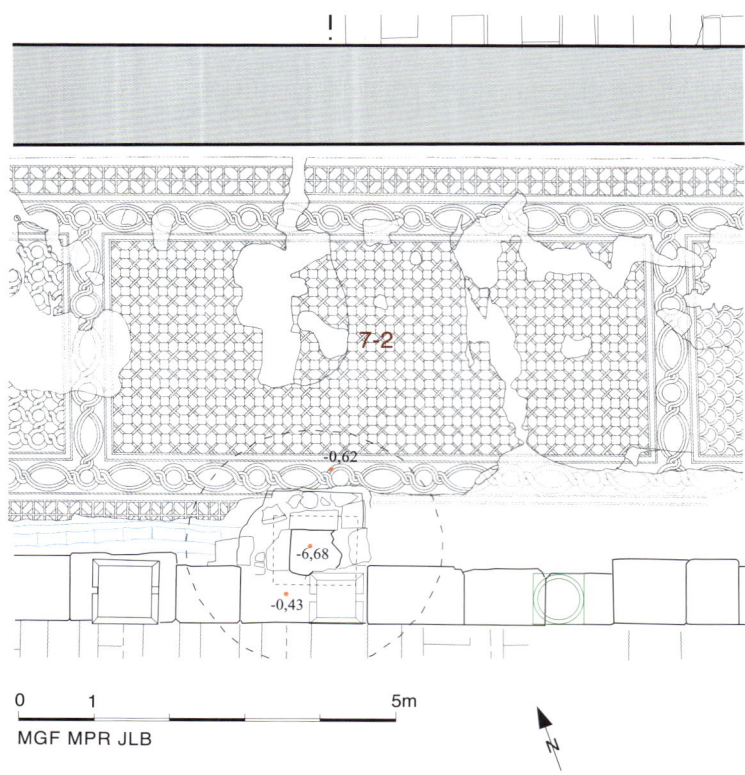

7-2.

73. Overall view of carpet 7-2.

are mosaics at Hermione (Bas. A, Rm. 1, Spiro 1978, fig. 158); Nicopolis, Bas. A (N and S annexes of narthex, nave, Sodini 1968, figs. 252-256) with figural filler motifs; Athens (Hadrian's Library, N ambulatory, *ibid.*, fig. 12) with geometric motifs.

7-2, N aisle (central carpet)

Illustrations 63, 71-73.

Second rectangle placed lengthwise in the aisle, E of previous panel.

Dimensions: 7.13 to 7.08 long, 2.92 m wide.
Density of tesserae/dm^2: 66.
Colors: black, white, red, blue.

State of preservation: the line of blocks previously observed on carpet 7-1 continued over the entire length of carpet 7-2; a few large gaps pierce the carpet, perhaps caused by large burning beams fallen from the 2nd-story gallery, since they spread across the entire width of the mosaic. Large burned spots frame the gaps.

Description
Outlined orthogonal pattern of irregular octagons adjacent and intersecting on the longer sides, forming squares and oblong hexagons (*Décor* I, pl. 169c). This pattern is very dense and composed with a small module (square 12 cm/side). A black double fillet forms the pattern. The small squares have four blue tesserae in the center. The oblong hexagons contain an inscribed motif, alternately red or white, outlined by a black single fillet: the polychromy of these hexagons creates the effect of a grid of hexagons, alternately appearing dark and light.

Comparisons: same very common pattern as in *supra* Atrium inv. 2-5, and *infra* S aisle carpet 8-4. We also note a similar example at Arykanda (Akıllı 1988, figs. 1, 20A-20B).

7-3, N aisle (central carpet)

Illustrations 63, 74-76.

Third rectangle placed lengthwise in the aisle, E of the previous panel. 6.54 x 2.92 m. Its original complete length is estimated to be ca. 7.05 to 7.15 m, like the two other carpets.

Density of tesserae/dm^2: 56.
Colors: black, white, red.

State of preservation: the line of blocks continued over a third of this carpet's length. The N half is largely ruined and the pavement is fractured in its S part. Restoration and consolidation helped prevent this mosaic from crumbling, as did the creation of efficient drainage. Major areas of burning frame the deep holes.

The E end of this pavement was destroyed during the Middle Byzantine remodeling of the church, when two meters of earth were removed from that sector. The restorers made a modern support to stabilize the pavement in its precarious state.

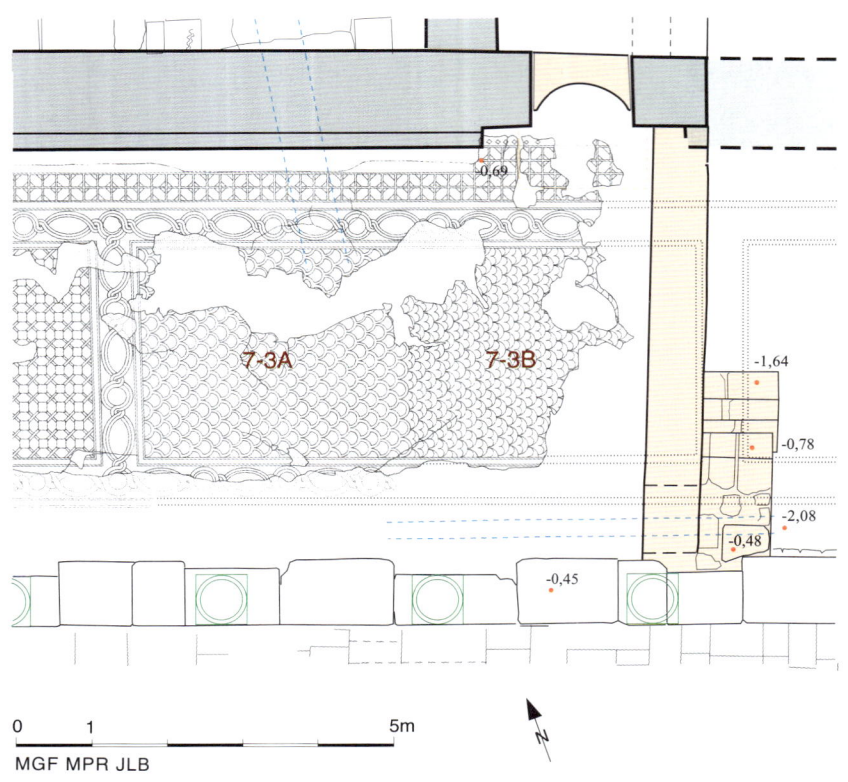

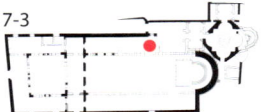

74. Plan of carpet 7-3.

Description

This carpet is decorated with a geometric pattern that probably was divided into two equal parts of different appearance. This difference does not result from a change of pattern, but from the way in which the same pattern was treated. There is no break between the two sections; instead, the transition is smooth and unbroken.

The W part (3.50 m long) is decorated with an outlined orthogonal pattern of adjacent three-color scales (*Décor* I, pl. 215). A white triple fillet traces the design, accented on its inner edge by a black double fillet, with the center alternately appearing red and white. Each sort of colored filler motif is repeated along the diagonals (14 scales SW to NE).

The E half (only preserved for 3 m) has a polychrome orthogonal pattern of tangent peltae creating the effect of scales (*Décor* I, pl. 222a). The peltae are colored red outlined in black, and have a triangular serrated black apex pointing downward.

The module used for elements in both parts of the pavement is the same. The transition between them is discreetly achieved by a line of tangent half-circles traced by a black single fillet.

Commentary: this contrast between two different ways of employing the same pattern is rare (ill. 76). It is another example of the local mosaicists' fascination with creating "*trompe l'oeil*" effects and a witness of the virtuosity of this workshop.

75. Overall view of carpet 7-3 before restoration.

7-3, A and B

76. Detail of carpet 7-3 after restoration, with a subtle change of pattern.

7-4, N aisle (eastern destroyed carpet)

Totally destroyed, this carpet probably covered part of the same surface area as the preceding carpets (ca. 7.00 x 2.90 m): it most likely contained a geometric pattern in a small module, conforming to the very homogeneous style of the preserved mosaics in this aisle (ill. 63).

Commentary: a rapid calculation shows that, judging from the length of the two W carpets (ca. 7 m), two others of similar dimensions could have filled the space estimated for the third and fourth carpets. If carpet **7**-3 was 7 m long, the change of pattern would occur exactly in its center, making the overall hypothesis plausible. The organization of the entire N aisle would have been done by a mathematical division into four equal parts, occupied by tight geometric patterns. The exception is the small entrance panel, intended to draw the viewer's attention and perhaps to guide people toward the baptistery, not visible from the church, because it occurred at a lower level behind the apse.

Conclusion for the N aisle mosaics: the overall organization, enclosing all of the carpets within a single border made of a line of circles and spindles interlooped tangentially, recalls mosaics at Anemurium, in the Church of the Holy Apostles (S aisle, Campbell 1998, pl. X, figs. 116-118), having a yellow ground (in the nave) with animals as filler motifs; mosaics in the central Church, S aisle (*ibid.*, pl. 185) and N aisle (*ibid.*, pl. 187) are closer in style to the mosaics of Xanthos. Another parallel is in Dağpazarı, Cilicia (narthex, Gough 1958, p. 46).

South Aisle

The door from the narthex was narrowed in a second phase. A second door opens near the center of the S wall, paralleling the door in the N aisle. This entrance was later blocked. As in the N aisle, the S aisle is separated from the nave by a stylobate, whose reused blocks are aligned on the nave's inner edge and appear irregular on the side of the S aisle.

A low stylobate, preserved only in a single course, cut the mosaic 2.80 m before the E end of the aisle. It was built just after the pavement of the first phase was laid, and it probably served as a partition separating the nave from an E annex, perhaps forming a *diakonikon* (with a low chancel?). A late bench was also placed against one part of the S wall in a secondary phase (dismantled by archaeologists to expose the mosaics underneath).

The mosaics of the S aisle are more difficult to read and interpret than those in the N, for they are badly preserved. From close observation there appear discontinuities in the patterns; in a few instances, the same motif is rendered in different ways even within nearby fragments, attesting to the presence of various "hands" and phases. We also observe some late and randomly executed ancient repairs.

77. Plans of the S aisle, pavement 8, phase 1 (carpets 1 to 3); phase 2 (carpets 4 and 5).

Recent restorations in the S aisle[1] afforded several significant discoveries: we found traces of a preparatory sketch and identified two principal phases of mosaics, helping to explain the archaeological history of the church. They also confirm that there was a hasty re-decoration of this area (*infra* nave floor inv. **10**): the pavements were rapidly repaired, by filling in the gaps with a design roughly imitating the previous décor. The collaboration between archaeologists and restorers in this sector allowed soundings to be made under mosaics that needed reinforcement of their support, and the study of the supports themselves provided valuable information.

Observation of the mosaics also helped us understand their chronology better, when the architectural context and sculptural decoration could not be easily interpreted[2].

"Open area" excavation of the E part further allowed us to locate the graves created after the destruction of the Early Byzantine church and its abandonment as a place of worship. Artifacts from the tombs date this cemetery to the second half of the 7th c.[3].

The relative chronology of the building for the Early Byzantine period relies to a large extent on study of this area in the S aisle.

---

1. Patrick Blanc and Laurence Krougly, 1994-1995.
2. Raynaud-Sodini 1998.
3. Buckle and two crosses, cross-dated with other sites (Corinth, Cyprus) to the second half of the 7th c., more precisely to the 3rd quarter (Constantius II, 641-668).

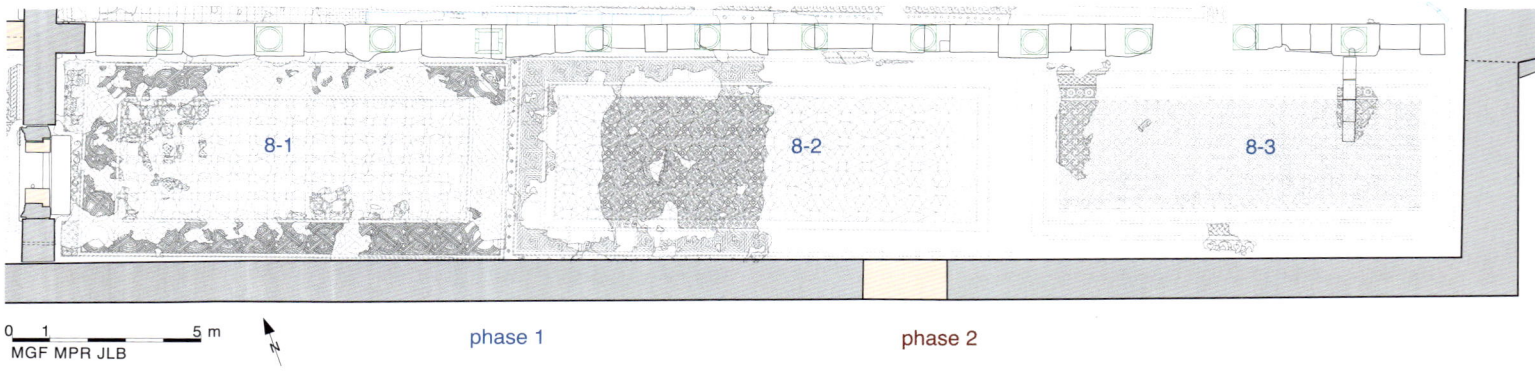

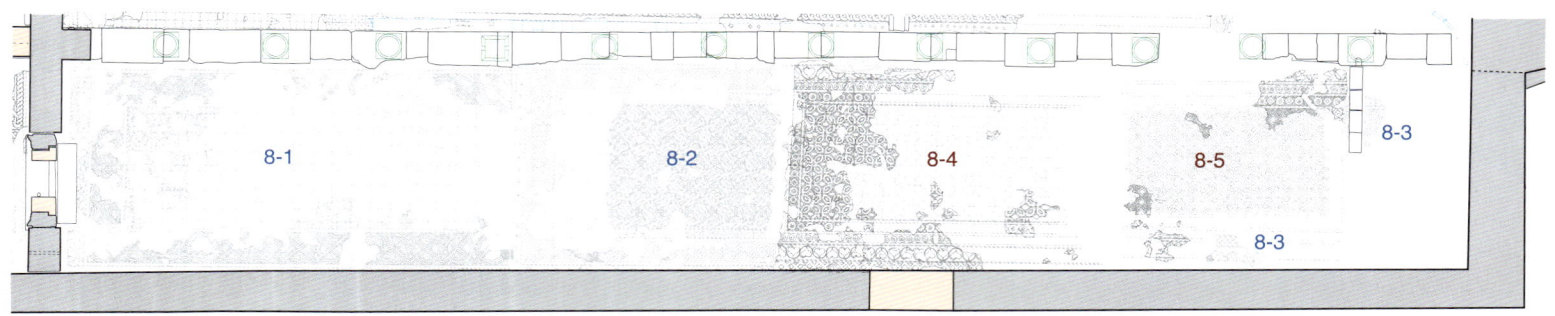

8. S aisle

Illustrations 77-91, 157, 168-169, 174.

We distinguish two main phases of floors in this aisle: the first includes mosaics made at the time of the building's construction and comprising three juxtaposed carpets (**8**-1 to **8**-3). A second period of decoration consists of the repair and filling of gaps and disturbances made to the previous floor by the insertion of carpet **8**-4 and the associated repairs (**8**-5) (ill. 77). The meticulous excavation of the gaps yielded clear evidence of a disastrous earthquake that occurred between the two phases, causing a large part of the decoration to be destroyed.

Organization of the décor: most of the mosaics in this building form ensembles, which are divided into carpets that are clearly grouped within a single border or a common outer margin. This is a coherent arrangement and unifies each space: the atrium (divided into two separate areas) and the N aisle show this, and as we shall see below the mosaics of the nave also form an identifiable ensemble. By contrast, the floors in the S aisle in the first decorative phase composed three independent units, each having its own outer margins and wide borders that vary in proportions. This new fashion, linked to the choice of particular complex patterns, seemingly reflects the activity of a single workshop. Today these designs are barely visible because of the mosaic's physical condition and disturbances caused in the second repair phase, which complicate reading of the ensemble. A few reconstruction drawings help visualize the appearance of both phases. Each carpet will be studied in relation to its own outer margins and borders.

Phase 1 (South Aisle)

8-1 S aisle, first phase
Illustrations 77-79, 168.
Overall dimensions: 11 x 5.20 m.

Outer margins
The outer margins of this W carpet are narrow (8-40 cm) and adjust the carpet to the irregularities of the architecture, especially to the blocks of the stylobate, unaligned on the S side. They also follow the S wall. These outer margins are white.

On the W side, they skirt the step that precedes the threshold of the door and encroaches on the S aisle.

The outer margin in front of the step is decorated by a simple scroll 28 cm wide (*Décor* I, pl. 64). Drawn in black double fillets, the scroll has volutes containing a rounded fruit (?), red outlined in black.

Two small rectangular panels fill the space on either side of the step.

• N panel (1.90 x 0.50 m) is placed laterally in the aisle. It contains a polychrome orthogonal pattern of intersecting circles (*Décor* I, pl. 237g), forming quatrefoils and concave poised squares. A

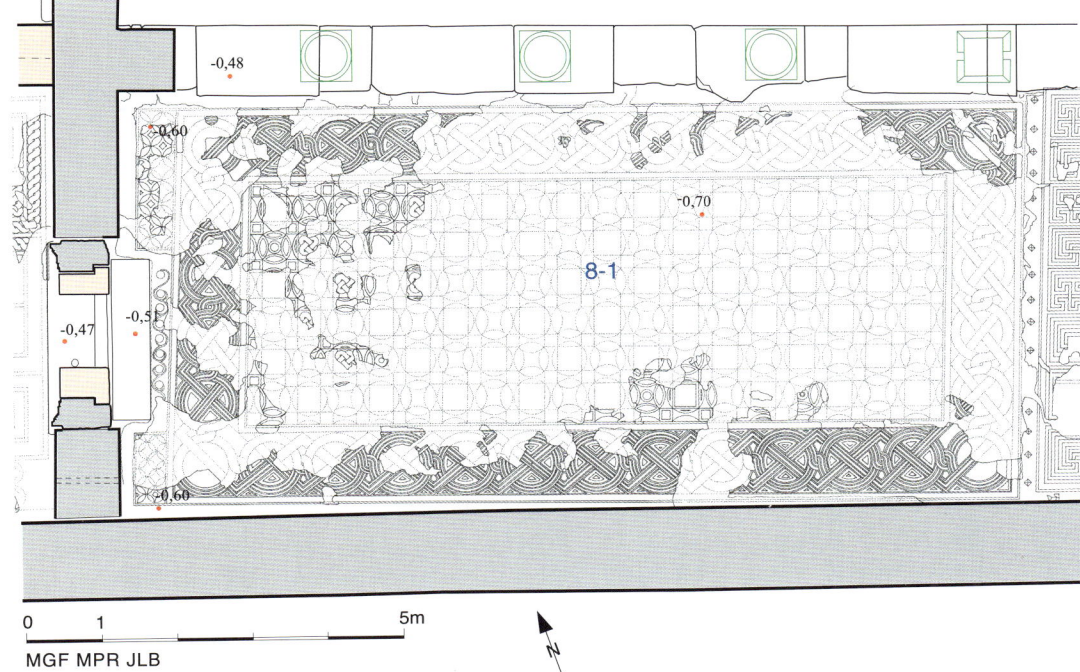

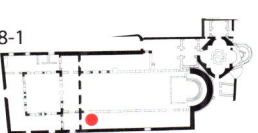

78. Plan of carpet **8**-1.

79. Overall view of carpet 8-1.

8-1 border

white double fillet creates the design. The spindles of the quatrefoils are colored white, outlined in red and black. The concave squares are shaded black and red with a white center. The pavement displays a few gaps.

• S panel (0.98 x 0.44 m) also is disposed laterally in the aisle. Because the step is not centered in the wall but displaced S of the entrance, the space between it and the S wall is shorter than on the N. This smaller panel presents the same pattern as the latter. The concave squares contain an inscribed motif, colored red outlined in black. It is largely destroyed.

Border

A large border surrounds carpet **8**-1, 1 m wide with white bands, 0.82 m without them.

Colors: black, white, red, Proconnesian light blue marble.

State of preservation: about half of the border is preserved. It is very fragmentary, showing many traces of burning and a small repairs.

Description

Strapwork of circles interlooped tangentially (*Décor* I, pl. 82g) and interlaced with a band of two interlaced and crossed zigzag patterns forming tangent poised squares (ill. 79). A single black fillet frames the border, followed by a white band five tesserae wide and a black double fillet. Shaded bands form the pattern, with the circles having a dominant red color (black, white, two red, black) and the zigzags shaded predominantly blue (black, white, two blue, black). These bands are framed on both sides by a white double fillet that interrupts the motif at each intersection, breaking up the continuity of the lines. The four quadrants created by the pattern within each circle are shaded in color (two red, two white, with a red or black center). Residual spaces have black or red inscribed motifs, outlined in black.

This border appears very complex and fragmented, but quite regular.

Field

Rectangle placed lengthwise in the aisle at its W end. 9.20 x 3.30 m.

Density of tesserae/dm^2: 55.

Colors: black, white, red, blue.

State of preservation: very poor. Only small scraps of the field are preserved, with many tesserae missing (about one tenth of the ensemble is preserved). Some places have only a "negative" impression. In other places, the first mortar layer has disappeared (setting bed for tesserae), revealing traces of a preparatory sketch underneath. We observed long lines lightly engraved and extending as far as we could see in the area covered by the carpet: a sort of grid to help complete the pattern of the field, which is particularly complex and sophisticated.

Description

Grid of rows of tangent circles, with small squares in the intervals (ill. 78-79), (absent from *Décor* I, combining elements of 144e and 147b). The circles are filled with an inscribed square alternately concave or straight-sided. In the first case the circles appear made of spindles, in the latter they dont. The pattern makes bobbins appear between the circles, and it is drawn by a white double fillet.

The circles with an inscribed, straight-sided square outlined in black contain a Solomon knot in shaded bands, with either red (black, two red, one or two white, black) or blue as the dominant color (black, two blue, one or two white, black).

The circles of four spindles have spindles outlined by white double fillets and a filler motif colored black, red and blue. They shape a concave square alternately filled with an inscribed circle (black, two white, black, red or black, two red, blue) or an inscribed poised square (black, two white, black, red). Similarly colored motifs create diagonal lines running NW-SE.

The small squares in the intervals are shaded in color (black, two red, with a white center); the bobbins, outlined in black, white, two red, contain two white or blue triangles. Portions of circles surrounding inscribed squares contain a short red line.

Commentary: this pattern is very complex, and we know no exact comparisons. The mosaic's poor state of preservation complicates the reading. The pattern's lines appear untidy and its overall organization does not emerge clearly. The linear aspect of the pattern and border is underscored by the light, rather bland use of color.

Comparisons
Border: at Pisidian Antioch, Church of St. Paul (mosaic dated by an inscription to the end of the 4th c.), where the outer border of the nave presents a similar pattern, executed in guilloche and striped band (Mitchell-Waelkens 1998, pl. 141). In Greece, at Megalopolis (House, Corpus Greece 2, fig. 90). Not exactly similar is the border of the nave of the Church of Shavei Zion (Israel, 5th c., Ovadiah 1987, pl. CXLV).
Field: the pattern is rarely found in a similar form, except perhaps in Ephesus (Basilica im Ostgymnasium, S nave, Vetters 1984, fig. 6). A simplified version of it exists, in Turkey, on Gemiler Ada, (Church 1, Ölüdeniz Area 1995, fig. 18). See also a mosaic from Çomlekşaz (Phrygia) near Denizli (Yıldız 1992, figs. 11-12) where the pattern, simplified and laid out obliquely, is the same but in contrasting colors; on Rhodes, the example of Arkaseia (Karpathos), in the Church of Alypos (atrium of S. Anastasia, Maiuri-Jacopich 1928, fig. 85; Jacopi 1932-33, fig. 2); at Sardis, in the Synagogue (Hanfmann-Detweiler 1968, fig. 25); at Antioch (Villa of Yakto, Rm. 46, Lassus 1938-2, fig. 4). In Syria, Church of Hama (Balty 1995, pl. 20-1), and in Jordan, at Yasilah Church (Piccirillo 1993, p. 341, fig. 757), in contrasting colors. In Greece with a different treatment, at Elis, central carpet of the Church (Peloponnese, Corpus Greece 2, fig. 127); Daphnous (Boeotia, Basilica, *ibid.*, fig. 296); Antikyra (Basilica narthex, *ibid.*, fig. 239b); at Philippi, Macedonia (House at the intersection of Philippou 16 and Zaliki Streets, Corpus Greece 3, pl. 164). Cf. also in N Cyprus, at Sipahi (Ayia Trias Church, N narthex, 6th c., Chypre du Nord 1995, p. 105), mosaics with a repertory very similar to those in Xanthos, East Basilica.

8-2, S aisle, first phase
Illustrations 77, 80-81, 89, 157, 168-169, 174.
This rectangular carpet is in the center of the aisle. Reconstructed dimensions: 11-12 m long x 5.40 m wide.

Outer margins
The N outer margin is white, varying from 2 to 22 cm wide. Along the S wall it is regular (18 cm wide) and dotted with small black serrated poised squares. A triangular flower (tassel-shaped) replaces the first motif on the W end, flanked by two white "leaves" with stiff black contours, a curious, fantasy-like element of a type rarely encountered in Xanthos (*infra* chapter "Synthesis").

The outer margin separating carpets **8**-1 and **8**-2 on the W side belongs to carpet **8**-2, since the edge between the two carpets shows that carpet **8**-2

8-1 field

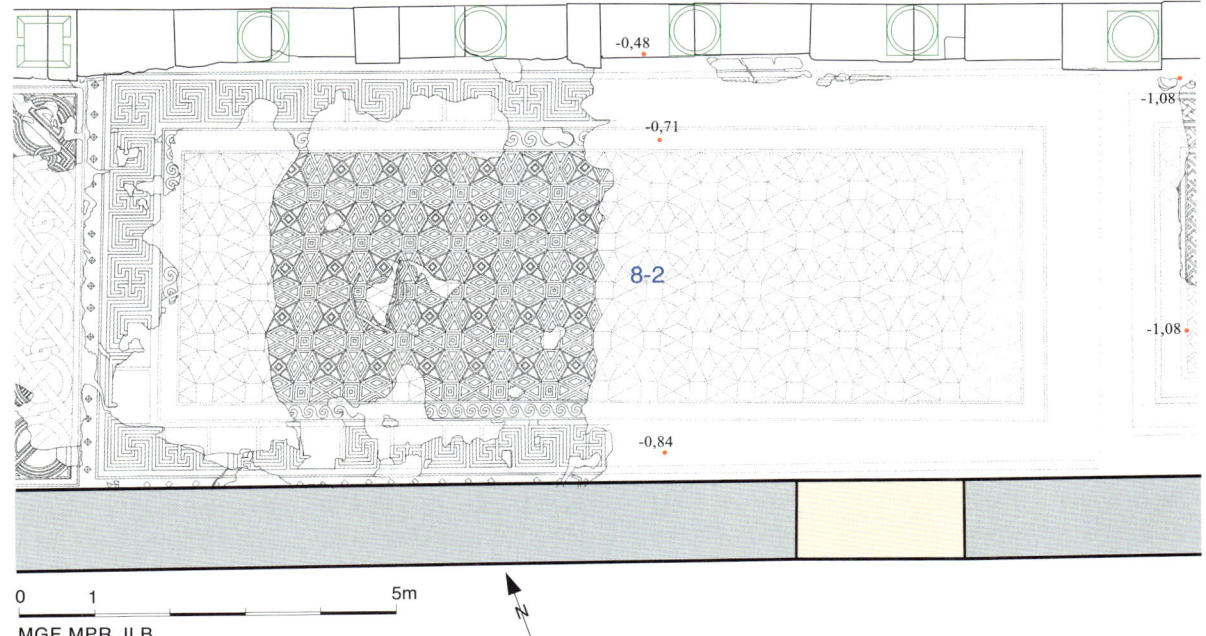

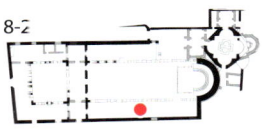

80. Plan of carpet 8-2.

8-2 field

81. Overall view of carpet 8-2.

8-2 borders

came after carpet **8**-1. The margin is decorated with serrated poised squares, shaded in color (two black, red, with a white floret center).

The E part of carpet **8**-2 was destroyed, and its outer margins and borders have disappeared.

Border 1
Preserved on only three sides (W, N and S). 78 cm wide.
  Density of tesserae/dm^2: 53-55.
  Colors: black, white, red.
  State of preservation: many gaps have damaged this border, and a repair is seen in the S border.
  Description: swastika-meander of alternate doubled-turned and recessed reversed-returned swastikas (*Décor* I, pl. 36c). The design is drawn by a triple fillet, alternately red or black on a white ground (ill. 168). A band of five white tesserae flanks the border on both sides, within an outer black double fillet.

Border 2
Only three sides are preserved (W, N, S). 32 cm wide; it is decorated by a simple wave pattern (*Décor* I, pl. 101b), black on a white ground, with the black waves turned outward. A band of five tesserae and a black double fillet frame this border on the inside.

Field
Rectangle disposed lengthwise in the aisle. Preserved over 5.76 x 3.40 m. The original complete length probably exceeded 9.50 m (ca. 11 m).
  Density of tesserae/dm^2: 58.
  Colors: black, white, blue, red.
  State of preservation: a large band more than 1 m wide spanning the carpet on the W is destroyed (resulting from the fall of a large beam?) and a few other gaps are scattered in the field. The carpet and its borders are abruptly interrupted on the E in a jagged line. We only can surmise the carpet's original dimensions, since its E limit is unknown.

Description: orthogonal pattern of irregular hexagons and squares, forming four-pointed stars (*Décor* I, pl. 186b, c). The field is framed by a black double fillet, whereas a white double fillet traces the pattern (ill. 81). The pattern creates the illusion of intersecting 16-sided polygons. The hexagons are organized as pairs of lozenges framing a central hourglass. Each lozenge contains a filler motif (black, two red, with a blue center). The squares are ornamented with an enclosed square (two black fillets, two red, with a blue center), and the triangles forming an hourglass are colored black (two fillets) and white. The four-pointed stars are divided into four triangles (white outlined in black) surrounding a poised square (black, two white, black, red, with a blue center).

Commentary: this pattern is complex and rare, and its very linear treatment here underscores its originality. At first glance, the motifs that stand out are the four-pointed stars, heavily outlined in black. Each motif is fragmented into small-scale pieces (lozenges, squares and triangles) making the pattern barely legible and forming a network of short lines. The lines are much more important than the color as in carpet **8**-1, and this contrasts noticeably with the mosaics in the rest of the church (ill. 157). If this carpet is slightly later than carpet **8**-1, both probably represent related phases of the same campaign.

Comparisons: in Turkey, there is an example at Yılı Phokaia (Phocaea, Özyiğit 1999, fig. 58) in contrasting colors, and one at Hierapolis in Phrygia dating to the 5th c. in contrasting colors, in which the hexagons are not subdivided into pairs of lozenges but contain figures (House with Ionic Capitals near the Theater, De Bernardi Ferrero 1995, fig. 3); at Ephesus (Hanghaus 2, Rm. 11, Jobst 1977, fig. 88). There is another stylistically close example, but a little different in construction, at Aphrodisias (Bishop's Palace, Rm. 2, Campbell 1991, pls. 50-51). Also at Anemurium (N Parados, Smith 1969, p. 184). A centralized example in contrasting colors occurs at Antioch, House of the Evil Eye (Antioch Mosaics 2000, p. 40), and another on a colored ground was found at Apamea (Balty 1995, pl. 18-2). Further southward, we know an example at Caesarea Maritima (Room in the building W of the Theater, Ovadiah 1987, pl. XXXVII-2). On Kos, Northern Baths (Gymnasium, Di Matteis 2004, pl. XCII-3). In Greece, this type of grid seems very popular, especially in the region of Thessaloniki (Kassandrou Street, Corpus Greece 3, pls. 119, 244-245, and XXXII; Athena Street, building, *ibid.*, pl. XXIII). Also at Demetrias (Bas. Alpha, Spiro 1978, fig. 437, a black and white mosaic), Amphipolis (Bas. Gamma, Spiro 1978, fig. 687), and Chios (S. Isidoros, nave, Corpus Greece 1, pls. 118, 120). In Philippopolis (Plovdiv, Bulgaria, beg. 5th c., Room of the Marine Scene, Valeva 1995, fig. 15). The best parallel remains the two mosaics from Amphissa (Phocis, Greece), with different filler motifs (in the baptistery and an apsidal room, Corpus Greece 2, figs 7, 320-324); we shall see below (baptistery) that the fonts at Amphissa offer the only close comparisons to the Xanthos baptistery.

8-3, S aisle, first phase
Illustrations 77, 82-85, 90-91.

Rectangle disposed lengthwise at the E end of the aisle in the first phase. Reconstructed dimensions: ca. 11 m long. Only three small groups of fragments are preserved.

The biggest one (A) was found during excavations conducted when consolidating the pavement, and was sunk far below its original level. The new pavement made during the second phase completely covered it. This fragment indicates the

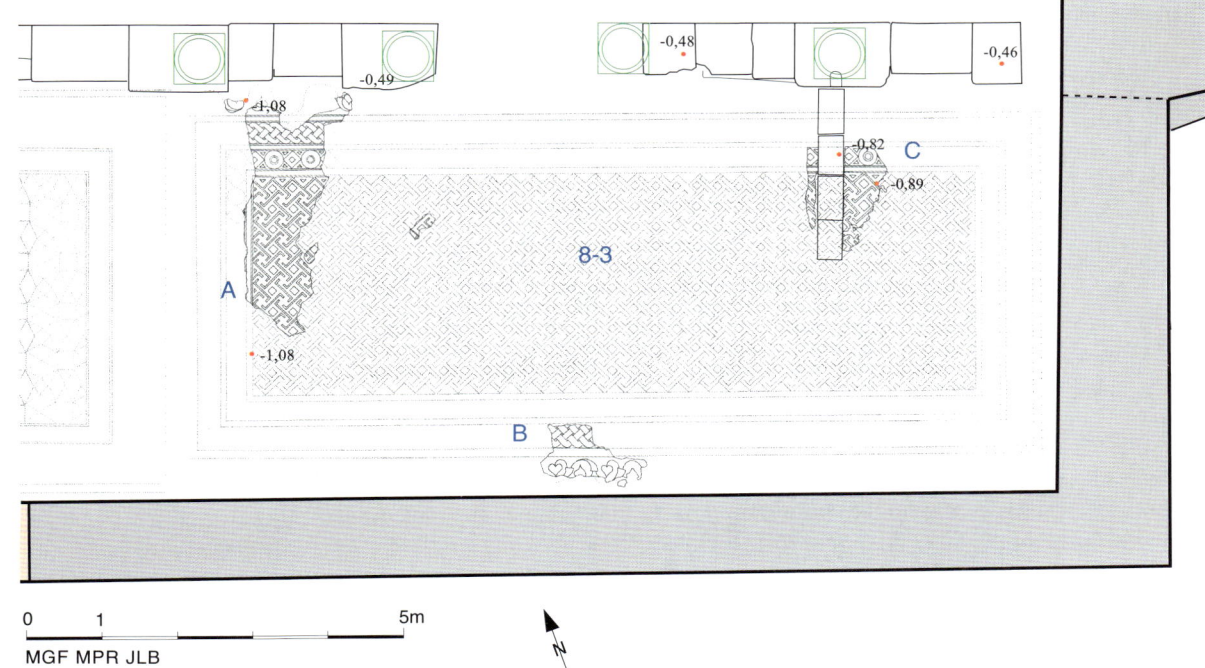

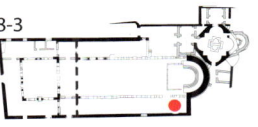

82. Plan of carpet **8**-3.

83. Deeply sunk fragment A of carpet 8-3, covered after an earthquake by the repairs 8-5.

84. Detail of the different levels of the phases of the two floors.

8-3

W limit of the field, with the return of the border. It also confirms the two phases of this aisle.

The second fragment (B) located along the S wall more clearly shows the outer margins' décor.

The third group (C), composed of two fragments, is the part running along both sides of the partition wall of the E annex. It demonstrates that this wall carefully partitions the earlier mosaic probably in the first phase of the floors, perhaps just after the floors were laid: the two fragments of the first phase mosaic are linked to it. The narrow stylobate separates a small eastern room from the aisle, and it supported a chancel screen over which it was possible to see the same pattern continuing further E.

Density of tesserae/dm^2: 45 to 47.
Colors: black, white, red, blue.
State of preservation: luckily, these three scattered fragments allowed reconstruction of the entire floor design.

Outer margins
Visible both in fragments A and B, they are decorated with a *cornucopia* scroll sprouting ivy leaves (*Décor* I, pl. 64). A black double fillet outlines the *cornucopia*, colored red, with the opening framed by a black fillet (ill. 91). The leaves are outlined in black and alternately colored red and blue, and the stems are black. The link to the wall is lost in both fragments, and we can only suppose that the narrow space between the scroll and the wall was plain white.

Border 1
Visible in fragments A and B, it is framed on both sides by a black double fillet and a white band five tesserae wide; 35 cm wide without white bands. It is a polychrome shaded four-strand guilloche (ill. 83) on a black ground framed by a black double fillet (*Décor* I, pl. 73d). Strands are shaded alternately with dominant blue color (black, two blue, two white, black) or red (black, two red, two white, black).

Border 2
Visible in fragments A and C, it is decorated with a row of tangent outlined circles and poised squares, shown on a red ground (ill. 83). The motifs are outlined by a black double fillet, and have an enclosed motif (black, two red, with a center white). The border is outlined by a single black fillet and broadened on its inner edge by a white band four tesserae wide, separating the border from the field.

Field
Visible in fragments A and C, and in a tiny piece of the panel's center. Dim. ca. 9.50 m long.
Density of tesserae/dm^2: 47.
Colors: black, white, red.

Description
The field is framed by a black double fillet. It contains a three-color orthogonal pattern of spaced swastika-meander with a single return, drawn by white double fillets and creating squares (*Décor* I, pl. 190a) on a black ground. The composition is placed diagonally within the frame. The squares are red outlined in black. Since the meander lines are traced in white (ill. 83, 85 on right), this "negative" design makes the pattern appear airy and somewhat difficult to read. It seems very regular.

Commentary: the very graphic, linear style of these three carpets is characteristic of a particular workshop (workshop C, see *infra* chapter "Synthesis") of the first phase, whose designs are traced in white. Black is made by a stone that dissolved with exposure to the air (a sort of marl, or calcareous clay): most tesserae are perceived through "negative" impressions in the mortar, as we also observed in the nave and baptistery annexes.

Comparisons: a very similar example of this common pattern exists in the church at Tegea but is not laid obliquely (it occurs in a supplementary panel, Sodini 1968, fig. 70).

Phase 2 (South Aisle)

Two types of restorations were made to fill gaps resulting from the earthquake (ill. 77).
 - The first consisted of laying an entirely new carpet, carpet **8**-4, between the remnants of the earlier carpets **8**-2 and **8**-3 after cleaning and leveling. The field of carpet **8**-4 completely differs from the former, but its borders imitate those of carpet **8**-3. It is treated like an independent carpet, and probably abutted vestiges of the earlier carpet **8**-2, to prevent any further destruction of the latter.
 - The second type of antique restoration consisted of filling gaps, known from three fragments (repairs in zone **8**-5) that existed in the earlier carpet **8**-3, which probably was better preserved than carpet **8**-2. The restorers roughly imitated the original pattern with differences of detail.

8-4, S aisle, second phase
Illustrations 77, 86-89, 157.

This carpet was made to fill the empty space resulting from destruction in this part of the aisle. An outer margin and three borders surround it on the N and S sides; only an outer margin and a single border frame its W end. The E part of the carpet is lost.

Outer margins

The only decorated margin occurs on the S side of the carpet where it follows the wall. 25-35 cm wide.
 Row of tangent outlined poised serrated squares, flanked by triangles (grid of squares disposed obliquely). Squares and triangles are colored black.
 The N outer margin is a plain white band (14 cm wide), preserved for only 80 cm of its original length. It stops against an intentionally preserved fragment of the original outer margin (from first phase's carpet **8**-2) still linked to the stylobate, but placed at a higher level and sloping downward. For unknown reasons, the new pavement incorporated this remaining fragment, but did not follow the original lines.
 On the W side, a large white band (preserved up to 18 cm in width) connected carpet **8**-2 to the new one. The link between them is lost, as always happens with two carpets of different phases because of the different composition of their mortars. The four white fillets of tesserae framing the border are regular, but further W, the join with carpet **8**-2 is irregular.

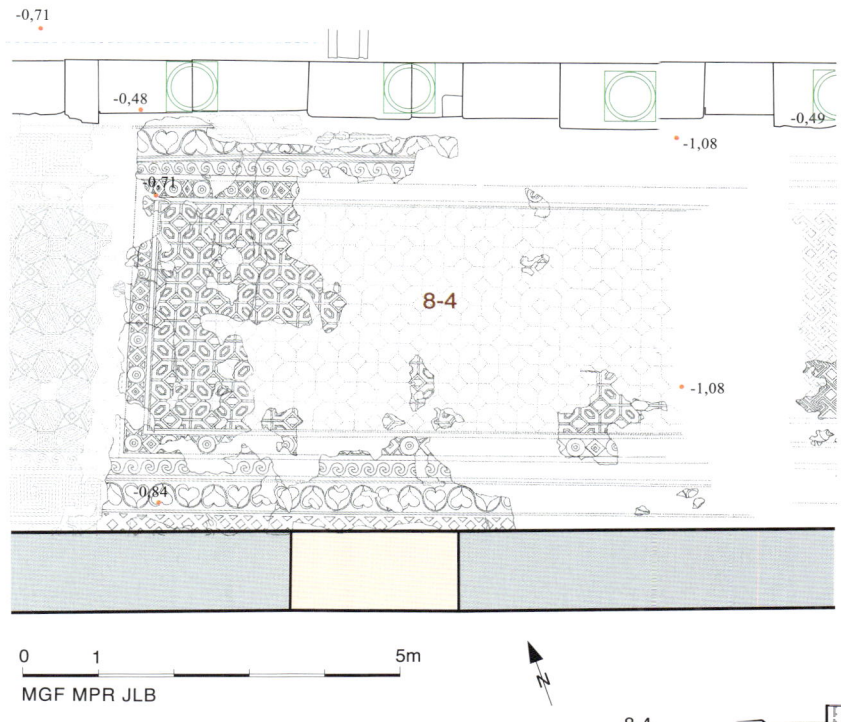

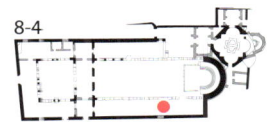

85. Overall view of carpet 8-3 and repair 8-5 (at left).

86. Plan of carpet 8-4, phase 2.

87. Photo of carpet **8-4**.

Border 1

Dimensions: 42-44 cm wide. Preserved on S side, and partly on N, it never existed on W.

Ivy scroll (*Décor* I, pl. 64d), drawn with a black double fillet, and with each leaf's stem indicated by a single black fillet. Leaves point vertically up or down, outlined by a black double fillet and alternately colored black and red. An irregularity occurs in the N border where two sinusoids are shorter than the others, and a small black and red heart-shaped leaf replaces the usual type. It occurs near the earlier preserved fragment, and it probably indicates where the work of making the new border ended. This border is tightly framed by a black double fillet, and a white band four tesserae wide broadens it on the inner side.

Border 2

23 cm wide without white bands.

Simple wave pattern, black on a white ground (*Décor* I, pl. 101b), with the black waves pointing inward. A single black fillet frames this border, and a white band five tesserae wide broadens it on the inner side.

The N border varies in width, becoming narrower toward the W (down to 14.5 cm), in a slightly curved line.

Border 3

26 cm wide without white bands.

This border surrounds the field on its three preserved sides. It is decorated with a polychrome line of tangent circles and poised squares (*Décor* I, pl. 22c), framed by a black double fillet (ill. 87). The design is drawn by a white triple fillet on an alternately pink or red ground. Both circles and squares bear an enclosed motif outlined by a black double fillet and colored red with a white center. Some squares are replaced by lozenges to fit the shorter space available (especially in the NW corner, where the units contain a simple black inscribed lozenge).

8-4 border

88. Carpet **8-4** during restoration: many fragments of the first phase mosaic were reused as foundation blocks for a second phase floor (at right).

Field
Rectangular and disposed lengthwise, only the preserved dimensions are known: 6.80 x 3.14 m.
Density of tesserae/dm²: 57-61.

State of preservation: precarious. At its discovery, this carpet seemed to have been ground up and broken into small pieces, fractured in many places by heavy elements. The preserved part represents one fourth of the total surface. Its profile is wavy with the tesserae no longer attached to the support. Although the E limit is not preserved, the proximity of the preserved fragment B from the earlier carpet **8**-3 allowed us to estimate the original length at ca. 7 m maximum. The restoration of this pavement has been very delicate due to the poor condition of its support.

Description
Orthogonal outlined pattern of irregular octagons adjacent and intersecting on the longer sides, forming squares and oblong hexagons (*Décor* I, pl. 169c). The pattern is formed by a black double fillet (ill. 87-88). The hexagons bear a polychrome enclosed motif on a white ground, alternately with two black and four red rows of tesserae on the NE-SW axis, and two black, one red with a white center on the opposite axis. The poised squares contain horizontal serrated lines, colored black and red on a white ground.

Comparisons: we recall the same pattern used in Atrium, *supra* inv. **2**-4, or in N aisle carpet, *supra* inv. **7**-2.

8-5, S aisle, ancient repairs, second phase
Illustrations 77, 85, 90-91.
A few fragments consist of repairs made to the damaged carpet **8**-3, filling in gaps that mostly occurred in the W part as the result of an earthquake. Two factors help explain the relative chronology among the fragments of carpets **8**-3, **8**-4 and the repairs in zone **8**-5. The repairs present slight differences in their décor, and examination of their foundations showed that they were laid above the debris of the earlier carpet **8**-3, which was turned upside down or reversed to provide a new support for the repairs[4].

The borders and boundary of the field in zone **8**-5 are not aligned with the corresponding parts of carpet **8**-4. It proves that the borders between carpet **8**-4 and zone **8**-5 were made separately, with a space in between.

---
4. About the earthquake, its destruction and the restoration of the floors, see Raynaud-Sodini 1998 and *infra* chapter "Synthesis".

Small fragments were found to the S and a larger one to the N, in positions W of the annex wall; they present three borders similar to the borders of carpet **8**-4.

When the Early Byzantine restoration of this E part of the aisle occurred, the stylobate separating the aisle from the E annex still existed; it perhaps then became an actual wall. The floor of the aisle was repaired with a border making a new return along the stylobate (in the first phase, there was no border along this stylobate, and the mosaic design continued uninterrupted up to the E wall of the basilica). This arrangement shows a deliberate decorative choice.
Border 1: ivy scroll.
Border 2: wave pattern.
Border 3: line of tangent circles and poised squares.

These fragments do not conform to the original border of carpet **8**-3, which consisted of a four-strand guilloche, roughly replaced by the row of waves.
Field: 5.50 x 2.90 m.
Density of tesserae/dm²: 56-57.

Description
Orthogonal pattern of spaced swastika-meander with single return in black double fillets, the spaces staggered and containing a square (*Décor* I, pl. 190a). The composition is placed diagonally within the frame. It is very similar to the pattern of the previous carpet **8**-3, indeed almost an exact imitation, except for the fact that the design is drawn by a black double fillet on a white ground, instead of a white double fillet on a black ground (ill. 85). Filler motifs in both sections are the same. The minor differences help clarify what was restored.

89. Detail of an ancient part (from carpet **8**-2), inexplicably preserved in the new carpet **8**-4.

8-4 field

CORPUS OF THE MOSAICS OF TURKEY   LYCIA

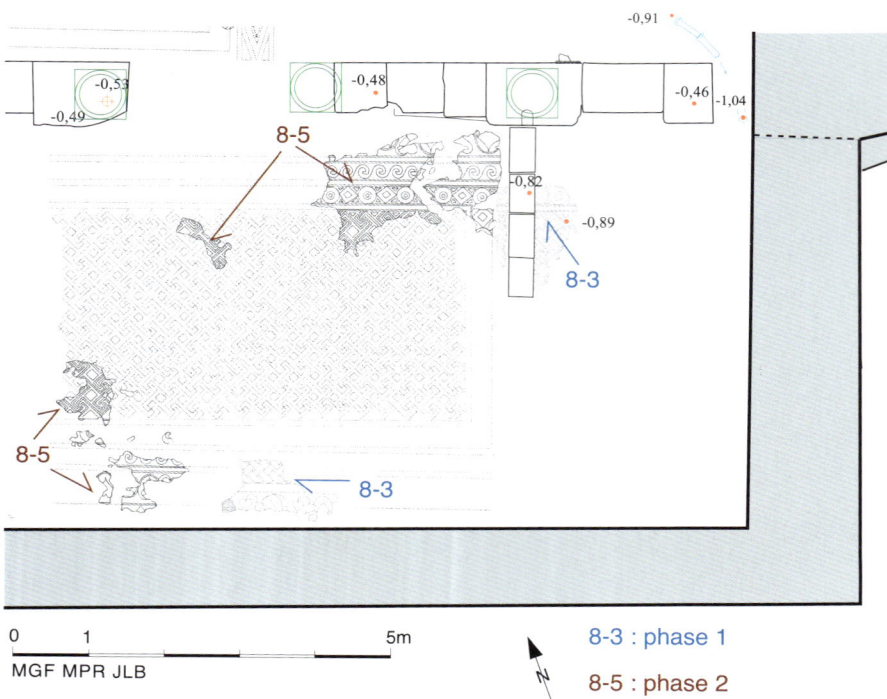

90. Plan of repairs 8-5, bordering fragments of phase 1 (8-3).

Commentary: it is difficult to attribute this restoration to an already identified workshop. We link the destruction of the first floor in the S aisle to the ruin of the nave during the earthquake, even if it is hard to find precise connections between pavements in both areas.

Other, miscellaneous repairs

Several patches spread over the S aisle, forming crude restorations of small dimensions. Usually, they do not imitate the missing pattern (or do so badly) and were not made by professional mosaicists.

One occurs at the E end of carpet **8**-1 (SE corner), a crudely made patch (32 x 29 cm): the exterior double fillet follows the previous pattern, but two other black stripes do not conform to the original design and its colors (ill. 168). A second repair occurs in the S border of carpet **8**-2, next to the wall, and it clumsily imitates the complex meander design. Another very small repair occurs further E along the same border. The last repair is a small patch adhering to fragment B of carpet **8**-3 on its W side.

The chronology of these repairs is difficult to determine, and they seem to be linked to mosaics of the first phase, but it is difficult to ascertain their date. They could be restorations of the first phase, made before the earthquake, or they might come after the second phase. Since we have not noticed any restorations of mosaics belonging to the second phase (including in the nave), we prefer the first hypothesis. They obviously were not made by trained mosaicists but by craftsmen not specialized in this type of work.

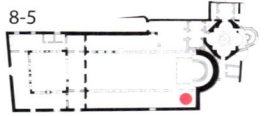

91. Fragments of the two phases, the ancient parts (at right) are preserved inside the new pavement.

Nave

The nave of the church is very spacious, measuring 30.70 x 13.20 m from the entrance on the W to the enclosed sanctuary. A stylobate separates the nave from the two aisles and originally supported columns and 2nd-story galleries located above the aisles. Tall windows and three large bays in the apse illuminated the nave. Three doors led from the central compartment of the narthex to the nave, with the central opening having wide proportions and the other two being smaller. Huge reused Roman blocks framed the doors, and the thresholds consist of stone steps. The nave floor is joined to the sanctuary's stylobate which supports a chancel screen.

The nave was roofed and used for worship only during the Early Byzantine era, but even in this relatively short time, the floor had two very different kinds of paving, laid within a period of a century and a half, between the 5th and end of the 6th centuries, probably due to earthquakes (see chapter "Synthesis"). The first pavement, inv. **9**, dating from the building's construction, was a mixture of stone plaques and sections of *opus sectile*. It was destroyed suddenly, and after all of the ruined elements' removal, it was quickly replaced by a new pavement of mosaic, inv. **10**, laid directly on the preserved support of the earlier floor. Traces of the plaques are visible in gaps within the mosaic, and they allow a partial reconstruction of the lost *opus sectile* pavement.

A final abandonment probably occurred at the beginning of the 7th c., after the basilica roof collapsed in a fresh disaster. The creation of a cemetery within this sacred space near the ancient sanctuary caused the pavement to be damaged due to the digging of graves. A few artifacts[1] found in the graves can be dated to the middle of the 7th c.

The pavements in the nave dating to both the first and second periods cover the entire space between the two stylobates, and extend from the W wall to the sanctuary screen. The sanctuary's stylobate encloses a rectangular space of 9.00 x 5.40 m, in front of the apse and *synthronon*. It is flanked on the N and S by narrow corridors paved with marble plaques (inv. **11**), giving access to the sanctuary through lateral entrances and separated from the nave pavement by a sort of threshold[2]. The axial door of the sanctuary facing the nave perhaps led to a central *ambo*, although nothing remains from this zone: the entire eastern part of the nave is badly destroyed by the later installation of many graves[3], removing any traces of an *ambo* base. However we found many carved limestone fragments belonging to two different ambos, and a fragment of a third made of marble.

1. First phase, *opus sectile*

9. Nave, *opus sectile* floor

The first pavement in the nave, contemporary with the building's construction, was an *opus sectile* floor, the most luxurious type of pavement. This floor did not last very long and was destroyed by a violent event identified for the S aisle as an earthquake[4]. The mortar support for this earlier pavement remained *in situ*, and it shows many cracks and small fissures. The plaques and units of *opus sectile* were loosened by motion of the earth, and they probably were carefully salvaged to be recycled, for we know how highly prized marble was during both the Early and Middle Byzantine periods. During the Byzantine era generally, there was no fresh quarrying of marble and this material instead was reused.

This kind of pavement, vulnerable to earthquakes, was replaced by a mosaic laid directly on the mortar of the previous pavement[5], and soon enough to save the plaques' imprint from disappearing due to the surface's being walked upon. Reusing the previous mortar also saved time. Another advantage of this procedure was that the two floors could be laid evenly. After a short pause following the natural catastrophe, the chief priority most likely was to restore worship in the cathedral.

No plaques were left *in situ*, except for a row of plaques located along the W side and a few fragmentary pieces thrust deeply into the soil by fallen architectural features, and subsequently covered by the new mosaic. Tiny fissures were observed in all parts of the *opus sectile* mortar. They explain the poor preservation of the mosaic laid directly over it, caused by the slow seepage of water and plant growth in the fissures.

---

1. Cross and buckles, Raynaud-Sodini 1998, p. 469, figs. 12-14; for the anthropologic and demographic study of the site at this period, see Buchet-Manière Lévêque 2006, pp. 133-147.
2. A small mosaic panel, from the second floor, is partly preserved at the entrance to the S corridor. It is likely that a marble plaque occurred in the original floor, separating the nave from both flanking corridors, as we can still observe on the N. Once destroyed, it was replaced by a mosaic during the restoration phase.
3. Sodini-Buchet 1996.
4. It is mainly the study of the S aisle's mosaics that confirmed this suggestion, previously based on observations made of the setting bed in the nave.
5. This mortar was reused as the *statumen* of the mosaic.

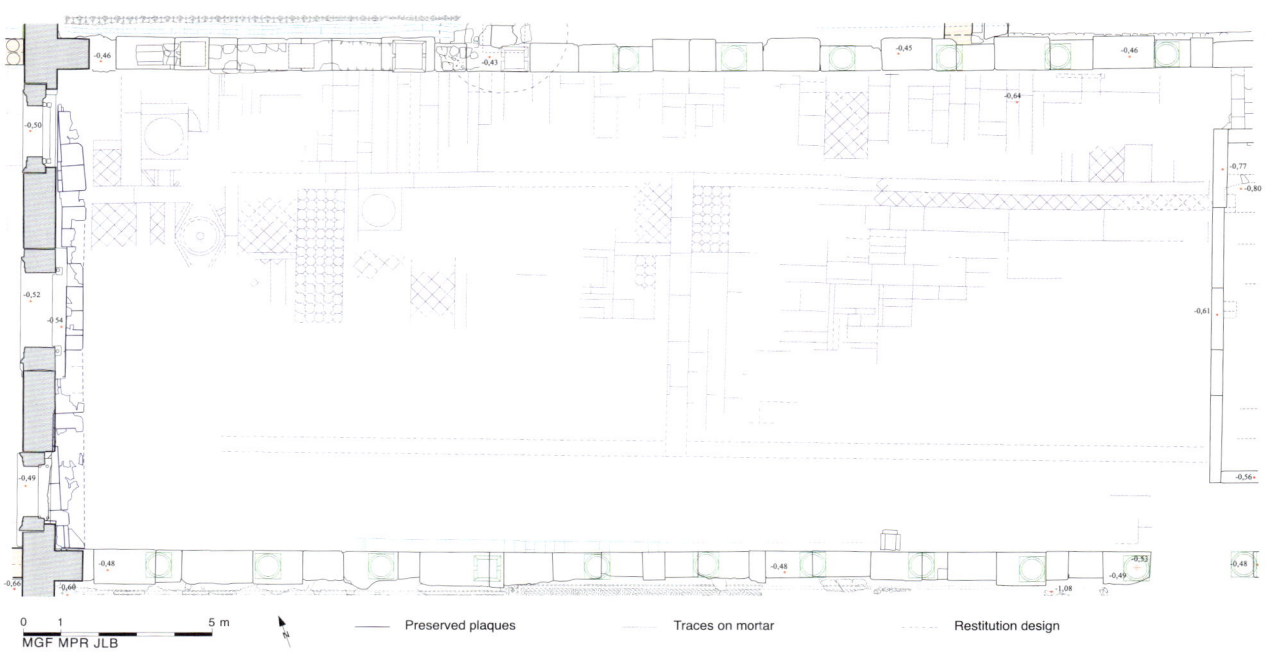

92. Plan of the *opus sectile* pavement 9 (first phase of the nave).

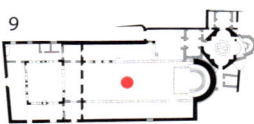

93. Detail of the surface mortar, showing the prints of the plaques.

94. Support of the *opus sectile* floor, mainly composed of pebbles.

Opus sectile floor: destroyed.
Illustrations 92-94.

Situation: rectangular pavement, covering the entire nave from the entrance doors to the sanctuary.

Dimensions: 30.70 x 13.20 m.

Materials and colors: the pavement stones are lost, but we assume there was an alternation of dark schist with light marble or limestone, displaying patterns in contrasting colors.

State of preservation: preserved almost exclusively in negative form, since most of the pieces of stone had been removed. The only preserved part, found along the W wall, is an irregular large band (0.70-1.00 m wide), made of marble plaques, becoming narrower on the N. These plaques are badly preserved and broken in pieces, but probably were saved and remained relatively intact because of their location at the base of the wall (ill. 92).

In the rest of the nave, only traces are visible in some areas. In the N part, most of the later mosaics also have vanished, presumably from the collapse of many architectural features, such as 2nd-story galleries and ground-level colonnades. In this area the mortar was exposed and many traces are visible (ill. 93). There is less evidence from the S part of the nave where the mosaics of the later floor are better preserved, concealing the *opus sectile* mortar.

The later *opus tessellatum* (inv. **10**) needed modern restoration, and removal of a few mosaic sections[6] revealed, during restoration and before excavation,

---

6. One large section was removed with a large roll (by J.-M. Dupage, 1988), whereas some other pieces were removed in sheets (by P. Blanc and L. Krougly, 1993-1995).

the mortar of the lower pavement. We could observe and draw traces of it before the preserved mosaic was reset *in situ*. In all places where the setting bed was visible, we could see clear traces of the *opus sectile* plaques. The design of all of these traces, projected southward symmetrically, suggests the general layout of the floor design.

In a sounding under the floor, the upper layer of the support was found to contain the plaques' imprints, below which could be seen a layer of pebbles alternating with flat stones set on edge (ill. 94), and carefully set in mortar. Below this occurred a more roughly made layer of stones and mortar.

Description

The nave floor is a combination of two types of pavements, called a "mixed technique"[7] and showing an alternation of panels of *opus sectile* of small-scale elements[8] (as we observed in the central compartment of the narthex) with a paving of plaques and strips, as we see in the baptistery. This mixed fashion has an aesthetic purpose, perhaps linked to the liturgy, rather than being purely coincidental. The nave pavement is roughly divided into three parallel channels, forming "corridors" that correspond to the entrance doors. The division is unequal (ill. 92), with less than one fourth of the nave's width reserved for the N and (probably also) S corridor respectively, and more than half belonging to the central zone. A long plain marble band separates the three "corridors," except at the W end where it seems to be interrupted 5-6 m from the W wall. We shall describe the preserved impressions of the pavement, and then speculate on its overall arrangement.

North corridor

The marble band separating this N sector from the central one seems slightly curved, but this probably resulted from the ground's disturbance by the earthquake. Narrow plaques of varying width, laid in a N-S direction, cover the rest of the surface. The slabs had two main thicknesses, determined from the depth of the "prints;" they alternated between very thin schist plaques and thicker marble ones, as can also be seen in other pavements of the church. Two panels with an *opus sectile* of small scale were observed (oblique black and white chessboard pattern).

At the W end near the entrance to the nave, the layout becomes less regular and is a somewhat disorderly combination of *opus sectile* panels and bands. One square panel contains a circular medallion.

Central corridor

Not fully visible, it seems to be divided into two main fields. The W half is composed of many modestly proportioned panels of *opus sectile* of varying size and pattern, featuring small-scale units separated by plain bands running N-S. This is quite similar to the pavement in the narthex, but here the scale of the panels and their elements is nearly twice as large. The E half of the nave's central corridor seems to have been composed of large marble plaques and plain bands running E-W, with almost no *opus sectile* panels included; it was perhaps surrounded by a border of poised squares, preserved on the N side. Between the two halves of this central corridor is a wide band of plain marble running N-S. In the W sector, we noticed that most of the plaques ran N-S. There were two panels with centralized designs, one of them a lozenge in a rectangle, and the other a circular medallion in a square. The isotropic patterns of the *opus sectile* panels are either patterns of contiguous octagons creating small poised squares or oblique chessboards, both done in contrasting materials.

South corridor pavement is unknown, mainly hidden under preserved mosaics, or destroyed by later tombs.

Commentary: the organization of the nave is tripartite, reflecting the three-part division of the W wall and suggesting lateral passageways flanking a central corridor. This arrangement is especially important to the church liturgy and is here emphasized by a hierarchical decoration of the floor[9]. After an initial impression of disorder, the pavement design in fact seems systematic enough to respond to specific needs. The contrast between dark schist and light-colored plaques (mainly Proconnesian marble as elsewhere in the church) is the main decorative effect of this pavement, similar to the effect observed in the floor of the baptistery and in the marble wall revetment of the narthex and baptistery. Some colored marbles also may have been employed in the nave floor, comparable to the central compartment of the narthex. The clarity of the negative impressions indicates that the plaques were very well cut (by sawing) and had

---

7. Donceel-Voûte 1988, p. 450. See also Froidevaux-Raynaud 2005, especially note 14.
8. Froidevaux-Raynaud 2005, Guidobaldi-Guiglia Guidobaldi 1983.

9. This special point will be studied in the overall publication of the East Basilica excavations, in relation to the walls and paths of circulation. The relationship between liturgy and decoration needs to be examined in studying the entire building (publication in progress under J.-P. Sodini's direction).

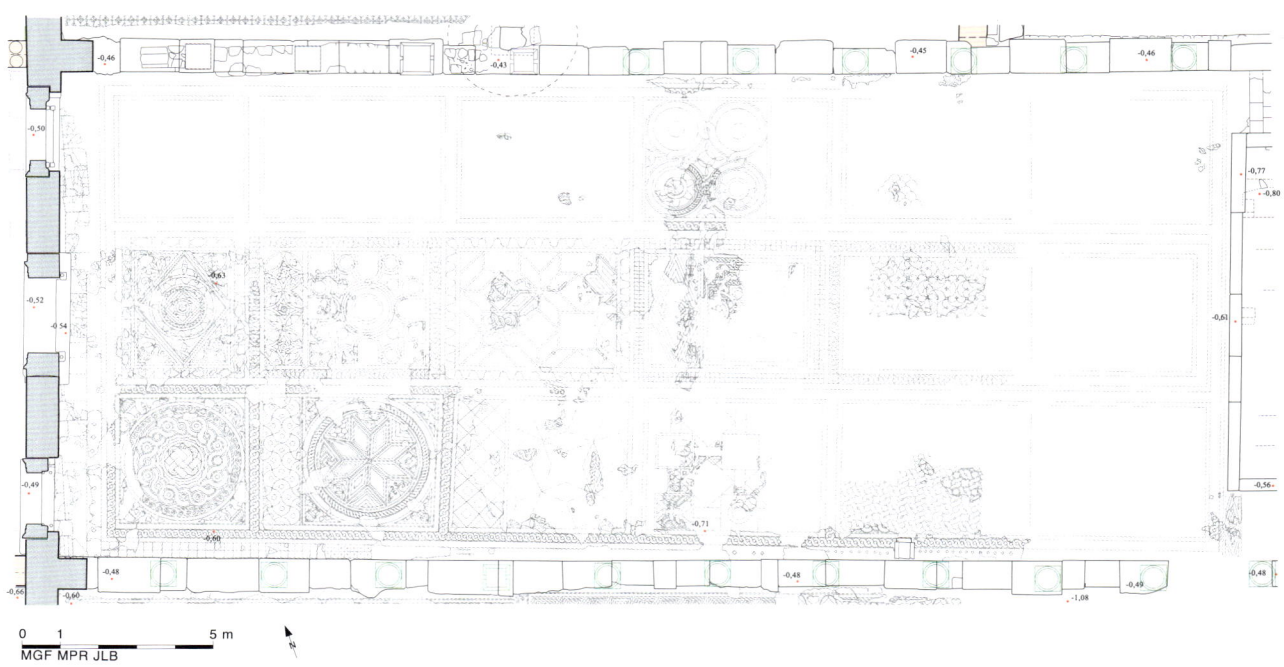

95. Plan of the mosaic 10 (phase 2 of the nave).

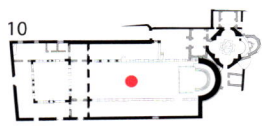

96. Scheme of the nave mosaic with the numbers of carpets, from 10-1 to 10-13.

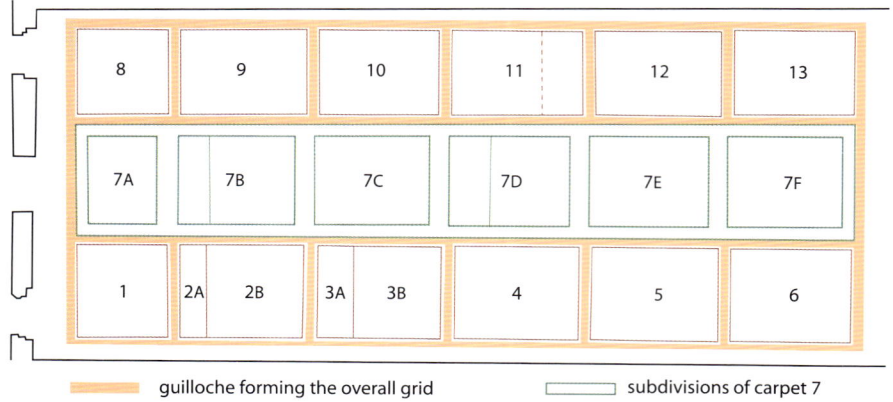

sharp angles. The design of the *opus sectile* patterns is regular and of good quality. In the nave there were no secondary borders framing the *opus sectile* panels, unlike the narthex floor.

Comparisons: we refer to the bibliography cited in Froidevaux-Raynaud 2005 and Donceel-Voûte 1988. Examples at Sagalassos (Apoditerium, Waelkens 2003, fig. 8), Ephesus (portico at S of the Varius Baths, Jobst 1977, fig. 51), Resafa, Church of the Holy Cross; in Seleucia Pieria, the Martyrion; in the Baptistery of S. Epiphanios at Salamis (Cyprus) where the disposition of the veins in the marble plaques plays a major decorative role, with the latter placed symmetrically (mirror illusion) as in stone marquetry.

In conclusion, it is worth noting that at other sites mosaics are generally replaced by *opus sectile* floors, more highly valued during the Early Byzantine period. The unusual (and opposite) choice at Xanthos probably was influenced by three factors: the fact that mosaics are more resistant to earthquakes; the desire for a hasty renovation after the disaster; and finally the lower cost of a pavement of *opus tessellatum* compared to one made of marble plaques.

2. Second phase, mosaic

10. Nave, second phase mosaic

The W wall is separated from the mosaic by an irregular band (70-80 cm wide), made of marble plaques: the fractured appearance of these plaques suggests that they belonged to the first floor, shattered by the earthquake. These fragments probably were kept because they were better preserved than the rest of the pavement.

The mosaic design shows similarities to the earlier *opus sectile* floor: it is decorated with an orthogonal grid of bands, dividing the nave into three nearly equal "corridors" (3.90-4.00 m wide for the lateral corridors, a little wider for the central corridor: 4.40 m). In the new floor, each corridor is composed of various juxtaposed carpets or panels. This design is formed by a wide two-strand guilloche, which also divides the lateral corridors into carpets and helps unify the ensemble.

According to the floor's layout, the two lateral corridors seem to have contained six carpets each (the E zone of the nave is partly destroyed) including one almost square carpet on the W end, and five rectangular ones filling the rest of the corridor. The central corridor is not subdivided by the guilloche: rather, it forms a single very long

97. Detail of the band and the S outer margin.

pavement section, composed of six juxtaposed panels, each framed by its own border and with the W panel appearing almost square. The long central corridor is emphasized by this arrangement, and by the rich borders of the various panels, leading probably to the *ambo* and to the sanctuary's axial entrance (ill. 95-96).

The rectangular-shaped carpets are, for the most part, composed of a square panel joined to a smaller rectangular panel.

In the SE corner, just before the lateral pavement of plaques connecting the sanctuary with the S stylobate, there is a partly preserved supplementary panel paved in mosaic, used as a threshold.

The carpet numbers begin in the SE corner of the nave (ill. 96) and continue in each of the three corridors toward the NE corner, going from **10**-1 to **10**-13. A few carpets are completely missing.

Opus tessellatum, a few fragments removed and then reset *in situ*.
Illustrations 13, 95-117, 159, 164b, 170, 172, 182.
Dimensions: 30.70 x 13.20 m.
Density of tesserae/dm^2: between 49 and 56.
State of preservation: very little of this large mosaic is preserved, about one fifth of its surface, but many fragments scattered within the W and S sectors allowed reconstruction of the patterns in several cases. The N part is almost entirely lost, and the E sector, laid against the sanctuary, is damaged by many later graves.

Restoration campaigns were necessary to reinforce the pavement preserved *in situ*, in the SW corner of the nave. Some parts were in danger of disappearing because the tesserae were loosened from the mortar (due to infiltrations of soil and roots in the mortar cracks resulting from earth tremors). The whole pavement has been restored between 1982 and 1988.

Materials and colors: black, white, red, pink, light blue Proconnesian marble (called blue), yellow, light yellow, dark blue marble, a few orange stones. *Outer margins* of the nave have varying widths (ill. 95, 97).

• N, it is barely preserved in a few fragments. It is 20-25 cm wide, with the rows of tesserae arranged perpendicular to the stylobate and appearing plain white. A small fragment, around carpet **10**-11's level, obviously belongs to another phase, probably later than this mosaic: it is a quite wide fragment (ca. 30-80 cm), colored white, but the tesserae create oblique and curved lines (motif impossible to reconstruct). It is a unique example in this church of a decorative use of monochromatic tesserae. Could it be a repair made at the end of the Early Byzantine occupation of the nave?

• W, as we saw above, the three thresholds from the narthex are marble steps. A large band of Proconnesian marble plaques follows the W wall across the nave's entire width (70-80 cm wide). The mosaic begins beyond these plaques, which are filled with cracks, sometimes ground into small pieces, in a generally poor state of preservation. The outer margin of the mosaic on this side is badly deteriorated, very fragmentary, and of quite regular width (ca. 37 cm). It is punctuated by small serrated poised squares, outlined by a single red fillet. The simple black fillet that limits this outer margin is augmented on the inner edge by a red fillet and a white band 15 cm wide.

• S, outer margin has a very inconsistent appearance. It gets narrower toward the E (50 to 20 cm wide), and it covers a pipe, visible through a gap. Its decoration varies: at the W end, along carpet **10**-1 and part of carpet **10**-2, after a white band a few centimeters wide near the stylobate, it displays an orthogonal grid made by a single red fillet, forming two rows of squares whose dimensions narrow toward the E (band 43-37 cm wide). The eight last pairs of squares contain a small

10 border

red crosslet. An area of *opus signinum* ca. 2 m long then extends the outer margin toward the E (old repair of the pipe?). Its level is slightly higher than that of the mosaic. After a gap of 1.5 m, the margin changes into square or octagonal plaques (next to carpet **10**-3), half of which have disappeared. This part is supplemented by a white band of mosaic 15 cm wide. Around the middle of carpet **10**-4, the mosaic's outer margin reappears, very wide and with the white ground made of perpendicular rows of tesserae, punctuated by small red serrated poised squares, irregularly spaced (ill. 97). This margin is interrupted by a marble and terracotta hole for inspecting the pipe and resumes beyond it for a few meters. The E extremity is lost.

• E, along the sanctuary's stylobate, the margin is a narrow white band a few fillets wide, preserved in only a small fragment.

There is no border between the margins and the decorative band forming the grid of the field.

Field (carpets **10**-1 to **10**-13)
The grid divides the rectangular nave into three unequal corridors, slightly wider in the middle (ill. 95-96). The band forming this grid is ca. 23 cm wide, and it surrounds the entire field from one stylobate to the other, and from the W wall to the sanctuary stylobate. It also subdivides the N and S corridors into six carpets each, and frames the entire central carpet (covering all of the central corridor). The design of the band is regular and rectilinear, skillfully bridging intersections.

Description of the band.
Polychrome tightly braided simple guilloche, opened to form eyelets (*Décor* I, pl. 71e) on a black ground (ill. 97). The strands show alternately blue, dark blue or red as the dominant color, in varying combinations of colors (black, white, red, pink, blue, yellow, dark blue). This band is framed on both sides by a white band 9 or 10 tesserae wide (laid in parallel rows). A red fillet broadens the guilloche on one side.

Comparisons: an example at Phocaea (Yılı Phokaia, Özyiğit 1999, p. 58).

10-1, nave, S corridor
Illustrations 95, 98-99, 159b, 172.
Almost square, it occurs in the SW corner of the field. 3.50 x 3.70 m.

Density of tesserae/dm^2: 53-55.

Colors: black, white, red, blue, light yellow, yellow, Aphrodisian dark blue marble.

State of preservation: this carpet is almost intact. A few deep gaps occur in the W part, center and SE corner (now restored, ill. 161), due to the collapse of heavy architectural elements, which also penetrated the pavement's support. Calcite covers the N part of the carpet, especially the border, evidence of the formation of a large puddle of water after the roof's destruction. To some extent, this calcite layer helped preserve the mosaic and gave it waterproof protection; elsewhere it suffered more without the calcite.

Description
The field contains a centralized design of concentric motifs (ill. 99), notably a circle-in-a-square. The circle contains a few other concentric circles.

• Corners are diagonally similar. NW and SE corners each contain a rounded crater without handles and with gadroons alternately colored red or blue; the small foot of the vase is black. Between the belly and neck are horizontal lines (black, white, light yellow, blue, red, black in the SE corner; black, white, blue, yellow in the NW corner). The neck is high, and vertical serrated bands suggest shading (successively red, light yellow, blue, with a white center, shown symmetrically). The vase mouth is blue outlined in black: on both sides, and there emerges a stem (red or black) which ends in spiral tendrils and two red heart-shaped leaves, one turned toward the crater's foot and the other toward the acute angle of the corner. The NW motif is sprinkled with dark blue tesserae.

The NE and SW corners contain a semi-circular cluster (ill. 159b), with a scalloped inner edge. A pair of three-lobed sheaths emerges from the cluster ends, with black fillets supporting a few ivy leaves and tendrils. The clusters are colored red and yellow, outlined in black; the sheaths are yellow, whereas the ivy leaves appear red in the SW corner, blue in the NE corner, outlined in black. The two clusters are not identical, showing differences due mainly to an uncertain design.

• The central circle contains a few enclosed borders framing the central design: red double fillet; white band four tesserae wide; wave pattern (*Décor* I, pl. 101b) shown red on a white ground and pointing inward; black double fillet; white double fillet.

• Centralized wreath-like pattern, around an enclosed circle and within the previous borders, of 16 large and smaller circles, interlaced in a shaded band and forming a central concave polygon (ill. 99), the large circles tangent to the outer circle (*Décor* II, pl. 311a). Rather regular, the pattern is delineated by a white double fillet. The shaded band's width varies; one section is mainly reddish (two white, black, four to eight red, two yellow), the other blue (two white, black, four to ten blue).

Filler motifs in the resulting spaces are outlined in black and alternately shaded blue, or dark blue with a red center. Space between the concave polygon and the inner circle is polychrome (red, blue, red, two white, blue, two dark blue). Filler motifs of the circles are colored in black, white, yellow, red, with the number of rows varying according to the size of the circle.

• A dark blue double fillet forms the central circle.

• The central motif is a square interlooped with a Solomon knot. Shaded bands of the knot are colored black, two white, three yellow, three red, black. The square is mainly blue (black, two white, seven blue, black) and the resulting spaces are white outlined in red.

Comparisons: we commonly find wreaths of 8 circles all around Mediterranean, N Africa, Spain, Italy, Greece and Near East: we cite only two comparisons, at Torba Manastır (palestra, Özet 2001, fig. 9 and a panel of the nave, with the same centralized wreath-like pattern of circles); of the same period, at Khirbet Muqa, (Donceel-Voute 1988, 1, fig. 132). Two examples with 16 large and small circles that are close stylistically occur at Sparta (Corpus Greece 2, fig. 149) and Pisidian Antioch, Church of St. Paul, (Kitzinger 1974, fig. 59; Taşlıalan 1996, drawing I, p. 243) where the mosaic is dated by an inscription to the end of the 4th c.

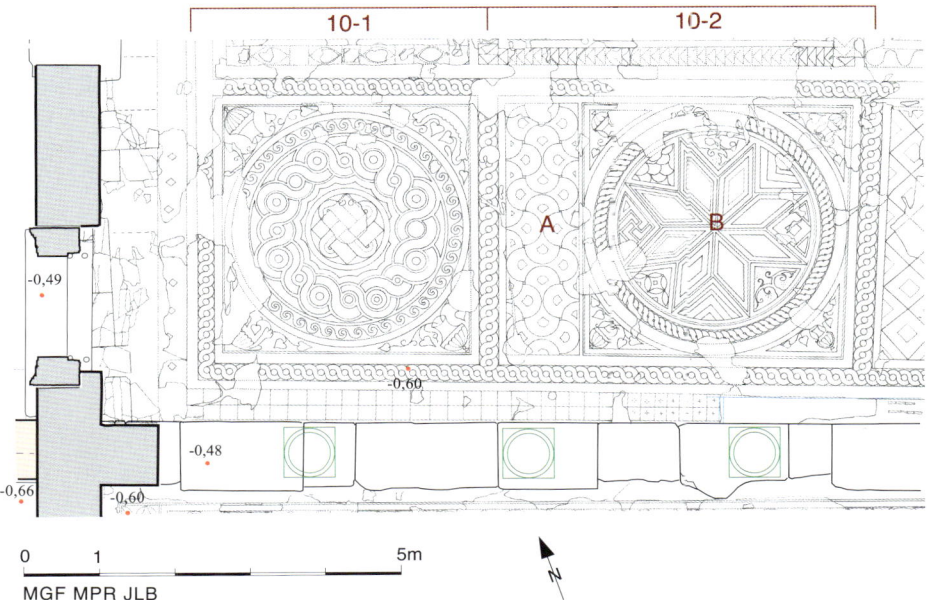

98. Plan of carpets 10-1 and 10-2.

99. Orthogonal view of carpet 10-1.

10-2a

10-2, nave, S corridor
Illustrations 13, 95, 99-102, 159a.

This carpet consists of two juxtaposed panels: the first (panel A on the W) is of rectangular shape and disposed laterally in the nave; the second (panel B) is square-shaped. Total dimensions: 4.70 x 3.70 m.

Density of tesserae/dm^2: 56.

Panel 10-2A
3.47 x 0.95 m. Framed by a red fillet.

Orthogonal pattern of adjacent alternately vertical and horizontal pairs of opposed scales (*Décor* I, pl. 220a), here polychrome, delineated by a black fillet (ill. 100-101). They present the following chromatic sequences: pairs of scales pointing N-S are shaded black, red, two white, three blue, two red, with a white center; pairs disposed E-W are black, two red, two white, three yellow, two red, with a white center. There are a few variations of these colors. The motif is reproduced only once in the panel's width, and three times in its length, in a large scale.

Panel 10-2B
3.55 x 3.50 m. This slightly irregular square panel is a little longer than wide.

Colors: black, white, red, pink, blue, yellow.

State of preservation: almost complete, this carpet shows many little cracks, and its support is in a poor state (lack of cohesion). A sinking line or depression follows a N-S line, parallel to a second line located between carpets **10-1** and **10-2**.

Description
Centralized design of concentric motifs, a circle enclosed in a square (*Décor* II, pl. 292a). The panel is outlined by a red fillet doubled in black. The circle is made of a sequence of narrow borders, and the center is filled with a large inscribed star of eight lozenges (ill. 13, 100).

A shaded band surrounds the corners and appears mostly blue, outlined in white and framed in black. The corners enclose small craters with stiff handles and gadroons (ill. 102). In form and color, they are similar to the craters in carpet **10-1** and are colored pink, red, black, white, blue, yellow. Stems, ivy leaves and tendrils emerge from the vases.

A sequence of borders surrounds the main circle: a large white band ten tesserae wide, forming the perimeter of the circle; a shaded simple guilloche on a black ground (*Décor* I, pl. 70j), the shaded strands predominantly reddish or blue (respectively black, red, yellow, white, black and black, two blue, white, black); a black double fillet; a white band three tesserae wide.

In the middle is a centralized design of concentric motifs consisting of a polychrome star of eight lozenges inscribed in a circle (*Décor* II, pl. 289b). A black double fillet forms the pattern.

100. Orthogonal view of carpet 10-2.

Filler motifs in the lozenges are concentric lozenges of varied color on a white ground (ill. 13). Portions of circles between points of the star (triangles with a convex side) have an enclosed motif with various filler motifs: pattern of intersecting circles made of blue or red spindles outlined in black and with a central red floret; four-tesserae chevrons colored in a sequence (red, blue, white, yellow) repeated three times; red stylized tree, with tendrils as branches (ill. 159a); poised square containing a serrated enclosed poised square shaded in color (black, white, two red, two yellow, black, white) with corners colored black, white, with a blue center; serrated chevrons on a white ground shaded in a chromatic sequence (black, white, blue, yellow, red) repeated twice; an almost destroyed tree whose red tendrils can be distinguished; pattern of adjacent scales outlined in black and white, with a blue, yellow or red center (peripheral motifs are irregular in color and design); swastika meander with returns delineated by a black double fillet and red triangles in the resulting spaces.

Comparisons: this pattern is very common in all areas with the rainbow style; in Cilicia, at Narli Kuyu, we have a good comparison inside a square (Budde 1969, pl. 166) and another at Adana (nave, Budde 1972, p. 60, fig. 51). We also cite in Greece an example at Thessaloniki (Olympiados Street, Corpus Greece 3, pl. 132) and in Syria, at Apamea (Maison aux Pilastres, Balty 1984, pls. 1-2).

10-3, nave, S corridor
Illustrations 95, 103-105.
Rectangular carpet composed of two panels, a rectangular one on the W side, disposed laterally (panel A) and a more or less square one (panel B). 4.65 x 3.70 m. The two panels are framed and separated by a white band 8 or 10 tesserae wide (narrower between the panels).

State of preservation: panel A is less than half preserved (SW part primarily). Panel B is almost entirely destroyed: a few fragments of burned tesserae are still visible. Its preservation is precarious because of the poor condition of the support, filled with lacunae and fractures.

Density of tesserae/dm^2: 56.
Colors: black, white, red, yellow, blue.

Panel 10-3A
3.50 x 1.25 (to 1. 32).

Oblique grid of black double serrated fillets, forming poised squares (*Décor* I, pl. 124b). Poised squares (ill. 104-105) contain a serrated polychrome poised motif (black, three blue, two red, three yellow, with a white center surrounded by four black tesserae). Along the border, the chromatic sequence can be different (black, blue, red, pink, with a central crosslet). Lines and proportions are irregular and the scale varies; the design is two squares wide and five and a half squares long.

Panel 10-3B
Nearly square rectangle, a little wider than long. 3.45 x 3.10 m.

Close study of the scanty fragments allowed us to recognize the limits of the panel and propose a reconstruction of the overall pattern (ill. 103). It is a centralized circumcentric pattern, in a square and around a poised octagon, of eight small lateral squares adjacent to the octagon and four lozenges in the corners, forming lateral triangles (pattern also called "starred octagon"); the poised octagon has an inscribed four-pointed star (or star of four lozenges) forming lateral lozenges

101. Detail of carpet 10-2a.

102. Detail of a vase (carpet 10-2b).

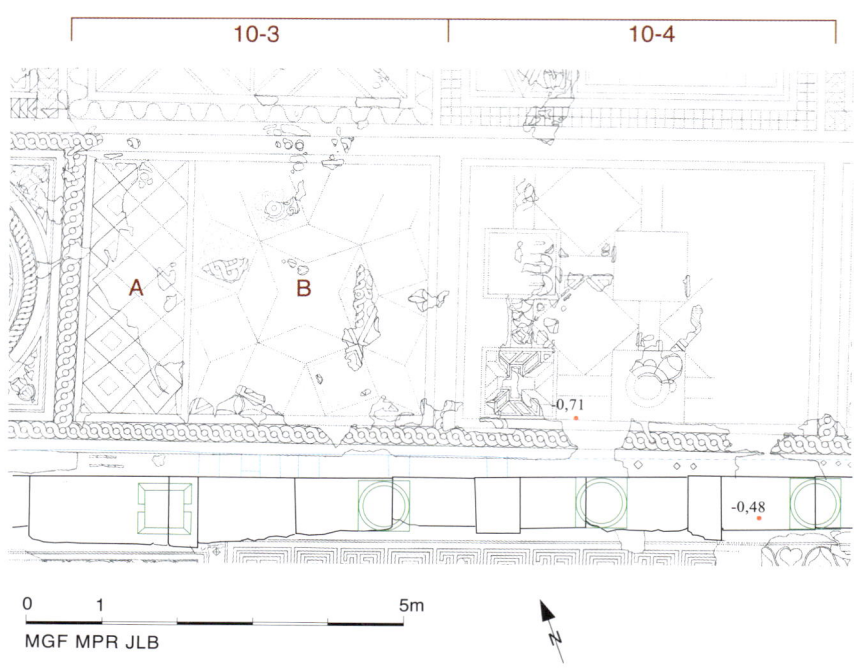

103. Plan of carpets 10-3 and 10-4.

(*Décor* II, pl. 373b). Since the edges are lost, we can not determine exactly how the mosaicist managed to insert this complex geometric pattern into the irregular main square; some motifs probably were distorted, as individual fragments suggest.

Some filler motifs in the squares are legible: one contained a black and white circle of waves, surrounding a circle with a red and black center and forming red corners; a second one encloses a cushion and a poised square interlooped in a shaded band colored alternately red (black, red, yellow, white, black) or blue (black, two blue, white, black), forming a small concave square filled by a red square with white central point. Other squares are lost, but a few scattered tesserae and traces in the support indicate that they were all surrounded by a white band two tesserae wide framed in black. Lateral triangles are alternately acute (center of the sides) and obtuse. Two of them show the same filler motif: a vertical spindle between two horizontal half spindles, with a red or yellow center. Filler motifs of the lozenges remain unknown. The central star is lost, and there remains part of a lateral lozenge, filled with a cross of guilloche (strands with red or blue as the dominant color) flanked by lateral semi-circles of the same colors.

Comparisons: very common centralized pattern in Ancient Syria, for example, Apamea and Antioch, House of Ge and the Seasons (Antioch Mosaics 2000, p. 282); Yakto Complex (Lassus 1938-2, fig. 22) and Deir esh-Sharqi (Balty 1995, pls. 19, 1-2); it is one of the favorite patterns in the "rainbow style"[10]. In Cyprus, at Salamis, Church of Campanopetra, (Roux 1998, fig. 252). Less

---

10. See Balty 1984 and the examples cited: Antioch (House of the Buffet Supper, pl. V-2), Apamea (Synagogue, pl. VI) and Deir esh-Sharqi (nave, pl. V-3).

104. Orthogonal view of carpet 10-3.

common in Jordan and Palestine, where we can cite the example of Madaba, (Church of the Salyata Family, N aisle, Piccirillo 1993, figs. 158-159). On the contrary, it is very frequent in Greece, for example in the Churches of Nea Anchialos (Bas. Gamma, N Rm., Spiro 1978, fig. 408; Bas. Delta, Sodini 1968, fig. 201) with filler motifs such as rosettes and knots; Epidauros (villa, N Rm., Spiro 1978, fig. 115).

10-4, nave, S corridor
Illustrations 95, 103.
Rectangle placed lengthwise. 4.80 x 3.70 m.
Colors: black, white, dark blue, blue, red, yellow.
Density of tesserae/dm^2: 53.

State of preservation: very poor, with only a few fragments and isolated tesserae preserved and scattered over its surface. The E part is totally lost, and we do not know if this carpet was composed of a single rectangular pattern (like carpets 10-5, -7C, -7E) or two separate panels (as in carpets 10-2, -3, -7B, -7D, -11), namely, a square one on the W side, and a rectangular one on the E side. Continued preservation of these fragments is uncertain.

Description
Polychrome grid of bands, with squares surimposed and exceeding the intersections (ill. 103), forming poised squares in the compartments (*Décor* I, pl. 146c). The module of the pattern here is very large (two poised squares on a side), and the design is not centered but cut by the outer frame and not very skillfully disposed within this frame. Three squares' filler motifs are legible: the SW square encloses a small cross, surrounded by pairs of parallelograms, lateral triangles and small squares in the corners. The cross is made by a shaded band (black, white, red). The parallelograms are alternately pink and red, or yellow and blue, always framed in black and white; the triangles are colored red and yellow, and the corner squares black, red, with a white center. A knot of interlooped motifs fills the NW square (we see two loops with dominant blue or red that could be part of a mat). The SE square, very incomplete, contains a centralized motif: around a central circle occur four ogives and four small semi-circles, forming a sort of rosette; the central circle is black, white, red, yellow but the center is lost. A single ogive is preserved, shaded black, dark blue, blue, white, and the small semi-circles are yellow outlined in black. One preserved rectangle forming the grid band contains a fragment of a guilloche, and a second one a row of three scales. The poised squares are not legible, except for one perhaps filled with an eight-pointed star inscribed in a circle.

10-3a

105. Detail of carpet 10-3a.

Comparisons: Perge, Güney Baths (Inan 1985, figs. 26-27), and Anemurium, Church of the Holy Apostles, (beg. 6th c., atrium, with filler motifs of various checkerboards and knots, Campbell 1998, pl. 111); Central Church (apse and S aisle, *ibid.*, pls. 183-184), where the pattern is oblique, with rainbow-style filler motifs; Limyra, Room N of apse of the Cathedral, almost linear (Borchardt 1977, fig. 39). We also mention in Cilicia the Church of Alacami (Kadırlı, narthex). In Cyprus, Kourion, Basilica near the sea (first phase mosaic, beg. 5th c., Hadjichristophi 2005, fig. 7). There is a beautiful example in Rhodes, in the nave of the Basilica of Bishop Eucharisto (Jacopi 1932-33, pl. LII).

10-5, nave, S corridor
Illustrations 95, 97, 106.
Probably rectangular, hypothetical dimensions: 4.80 x 3.70 m.
Colors: black, white, red, blue, yellow.
Density of tesserae/dm^2: 55.

State of preservation: almost entirely destroyed, with a narrow scrap present along the S border and a small fragment to the N.

Description
Polychrome orthogonal pattern of circles in asymmetrically shaded bands interlooped tangentially (ill. 97, 106), forming irregular concave octagons (*Décor* I, pl. 235a). The shaded bands alternately appear predominantly yellow (two black, two white, three yellow, red, two black), blue (two black, four or five blue, two white, two black) or

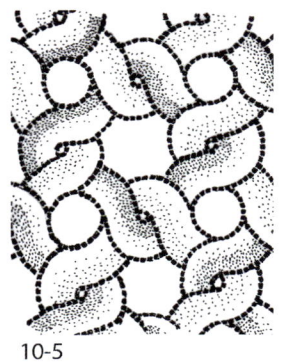

106. Plan of the panel 10-5.

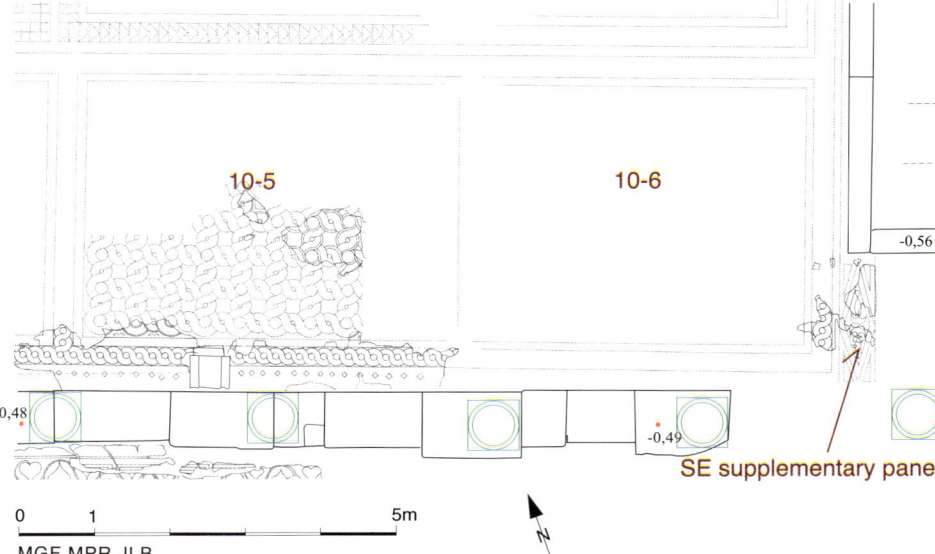

red (two black, three or four red, two white, two black). Center of the large circles is white; concave octagons (one partly legible) contain a square; and concave lateral trapezoids (along the edges of the panel) enclose a red line.

Comparisons: very common pattern; Anemurium (Church of the Holy Apostles, narthex, Campbell 1998, pl. 108, with small inscribed motifs); Iasos (Levi 1966, fig. 74); Aphrodisias, (Priest's House, Rm. 3, E atrium, Campbell 1991, fig. 84; Rm. 4, atrium, *ibid.*, fig. 88) with larger module; Oylum Höyük (Basilica Alanı, Özgen 2000, fig. 6). On Kos, where this pattern is very typical of Early Byzantine times, there are many examples, as in Mastichari, entrance to the Baptistery of St. John (Di Matteis 2004, pl. XXVIII-3), E of the baptistery (*ibid.*, pl. LI-3), or Church of St. John (Parrish 2001, fig. 3). In Crete, at Gortyna, Church of St. Michael (Farioli-Borboudakis 2005, pl. 33-2). Many examples in Greece, among which Hermione (6th c., Bas. A, SW corridor, Spiro 1978, fig. 158; Corpus Greece 2, fig. 66) very similar stylistically; Nicopolis (Bas. Alpha, N and S annexes, S narthex, nave, Spiro 1978, fig. 483); and Hadrian's Library in Athens (tetraconch, N ambulatory, *ibid.*, figs. 15-16).

10-6, nave, S corridor
Illustrations 95, 106.
Completely destroyed by later tombs, very densely arranged in E part of the nave.

10-7, nave, central corridor
Illustrations 95-96, 107-115, 164b, 182.
This carpet, surrounded by the usual guilloche border, occupies all of the central corridor of the nave, covering its entire length (dimensions: ca. 28.40 m long x 3.80 m wide). It looks like a central continuous corridor, isolated from the lateral parts and leading without interruption from the nave's axial entrance to the sanctuary. It is divided into six panels (ill. 96), each with its own wide border and sometimes composed of two smaller panels, one rectangular and the other square, as observed in the S corridor. They will be described from the W, and called panels A-E.

Density of tesserae/dm^2: 49-55.

Panel 10-7A
Illustrations 95, 107-108.
Rectangular, the long side disposed laterally in the nave and aligned with the central door.
Dimensions: 3.80 x 3.20 m.
Colors: black, white, dark blue, blue, red, yellow, orange.
Density of tesserae/dm^2: 53.
State of preservation: this W part is covered by a calcite layer (cf. carpet **10**-1), which keeps the tesserae together. Colors are barely legible through this opaque film. Many gaps and traces of burning dot the surface. The patterns are delineated by black tesserae made of a stone that disappeared almost systematically (effect of fire and water), as it dissolved and is only legible in the "negative". The border is incomplete.

Border: 22-23 cm wide. Polychrome jeweled band of tangent squares and horizontal spindles (*Décor* I, pl. 24c). Squares are outlined in black and orange, and contain a diagonal blue stripe framed in orange and yellow on a white ground. Spindles are colored blue and surrounded by black and orange fillets.

The border has a red ground, with tiny four-tesserae ornaments, arranged in pairs between the motifs.

Field: rectangle placed laterally in the nave. 3.12 x 2.50 m.

Centralized design of concentric motifs, formed by a lozenge inscribed in a rectangle, the lozenge enclosing concentric circles and a central poised square. The panel is framed by a white band outlined in red.

The lozenge is traced by a white band framed in red and black (ill. 108). Triangular corners are framed by a shaded band (red, two orange, white, two black, red); their filler motifs form similar pairs on the diagonal:

NW and SE corners enclose a jar without a foot, from whose straight mouth emerge two crossed stems that intersect, ending in volutes and tendrils. Jar is colored blue, outlined in black, with orange and red stripes at the top of the belly. Stems are made of red and black fillets. NW motif is very damaged.

NE and SW corners contain a crater with gadroons lacking handles. Gadroons are alternately of dominant blue (blue and white), or red color (black, white, yellow, with a red center). Top of the belly is outlined with horizontal stripes (black, red, yellow) below a narrow blue neck. Two stems (black and red) emerge from the vase and have spiral ends.

The enclosed circle in the lozenge has a series of concentric borders: - a shaded band (black, red, two white); - an undulating row of three-color inverted bells (*Décor* I, pl. 60d), delineated by a white double fillet, framed in dark blue. Outer bells are colored orange and red, inner bells blue and dark blue. In the mouth of the bells a white serrated triangle touches the frame; - a red serrated saw-tooth pattern, pointing inward (*Décor* I, pl. 10g) and framed on both sides by a white band three tesserae wide.

The central circle is outlined in dark blue. It contains a poised square interlaced with loops and with an inscribed circle, in shaded bands alternately with blue or red as the dominant color. The center is colored red and outlined by a black double fillet with a white central tessera. Residual spaces of the motif are colored red or framed by a dark blue fillet.

The points of the lozenge are similar in opposing pairs: N and S, they contain a large striped spindle (blue, white, yellow, black, red, black, white and symmetrically the reverse), flanked by a curved stem on both sides. E and W, the corners contain a chessboard pattern of single tesserae, black and white on the E, and red and white on the W.

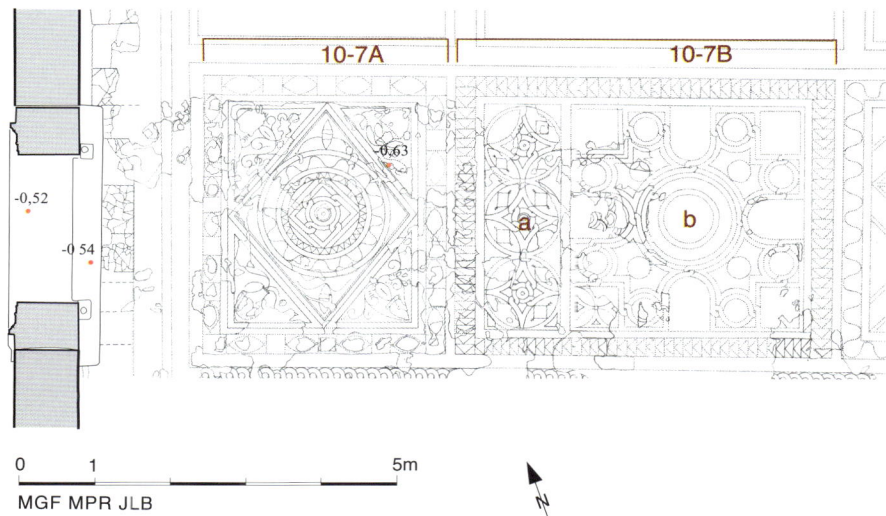

Panel 10-7B
Illustrations 95, 107, 109-110.
Rectangle disposed lengthwise in the nave. Total dimensions: 5.06 x 3.80 m.

Panel **10**-7B is framed by its own border, and the field is divided into two unequal parts, a rectangular W panel disposed laterally in the nave, and a square E panel.

Colors: black, white, blue, red, pink, orange, yellow.

Density of tesserae/dm^2: 49.

State of preservation: half preserved in the W third, it gradually deteriorates toward the E. In the W panel the tesserae are held together by calcite; black tesserae are dissolved and preserved in the "negative", making neighboring parts unstable. Preserved parts are riddled with tiny cracks. The E square panel is almost completely lost, with

107. Plan of the W part of carpet 7: panels 10-7A and 10-7B.

108. Panel 10-7A, before restoration.

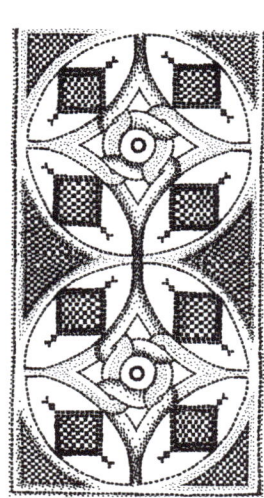

109. Reconstruction of design of the panel 10-7Bb.

110. Panel 10-7Bb, in great danger of disintegration.

10-7B-a

a few bunches of tesserae distributed over the surface and often dissociated from the support, itself crumbled: the preservation of this panel is very dubious as natural deterioration is difficult to stop (due to a poor support) We were fortunate to have recognized the pattern before it totally disintegrated. The badly damaged fragments have nevertheless been reinforced.

Border: width 28 cm. Row of superposed white right-angled triangles on black ground (*Décor* I, pl. 11d).

Supplementary panel a: rectangle placed laterally in the nave. 3.10 x 1.02 m.
Wide row of three tangent circles of four spindles, forming poised quatrefoils (ill. scheme 10-7B-a). The concave poised square in the center of each circle is interlaced with loops to a small central circle. Shaded bands delineate all of these motifs, alternately having a dominant red (black, red, orange, white, black) or blue color (black, two blue, white, black).

The panel is framed by black and red fillets. The corners are outlined by a polychrome band (white, pink, red, black). The spindles enclose a poised inscribed square filled with a chessboard pattern of black and white tesserae, with black tassels and black four-tesserae ornaments. The central circles are colored white. The resulting lateral triangles are filled with a black and white four-tesserae chessboard pattern.

Main square panel b: 3.08 x 3.10 m. It is lost for the most part (ca. 90%). By some miracle, the poor small fragments (ill. 110) were sufficiently well arranged to permit reconstruction of the pattern.

It is a centralized circumcentric pattern, in a square and around a circle, of four lateral arches tangent to the central circle, and four squares in the corners, the arches linked to the squares by small circles, all points of tangency interlooped, here in a shaded band (*Décor* I, pl. 368a); this motif (ill. 109) has also been called a "cross of four U's"[11]. The dominant color of the shaded bands is alternately black (black, white, three black) and red (black, two red, white, black). The corner squares have an inscribed black and white square with a quatrefoil, blue and orange, surrounded by serrated lateral triangles of the same colors, or simply blue. The arches are short, shorter than those in both compartments of the narthex where we find a very similar design. Only one arch's filler pattern is preserved: it consists of a pattern of scales, formed by a white double fillet outlined in black, the scales colored red, pink or yellow. The intermediate circles are lost, except for part of one, framed by serrated fillets. The central circle (diam. 1.40 m) is framed by a triple fillet (black, red, white). There follows an undulating row (*Décor* I, pl. 60d) delineated in white, with alternating chromatic

---

11. Raynaud 1996, fig. 14.

accents, the outer bells red and orange, the inner ones blue; this border is framed on both sides by a white band four tesserae wide. The center of the circle is lost. One of the resulting spaces around the central circle is partly preserved, framed by a band shaded red (black, red, yellow, white, black) or blue (black, two blue, white, black) with a central circle of four black spindles, delineated in red and having a white center. Small serrated yellow triangles, outlined in black and pointing toward the corners, adorn the circle.

Commentary: the proximity of two other examples of the rare pattern of a "cross of four U" helps assure its identity here, despite noticeable differences in detail.

Comparisons: the pattern of the supplementary panel is common during the 6th c. It also exists in the field of the N annex of the Baptistery of the same East Basilica, with interlaced shaded bands (*infra* inv. **17**, see the comparisons). We can cite elsewhere in Turkey the examples of Arykanda (Basilica, nave phase 1, Bayburtluoğlu 2004, p. 143) and Anemurium, Necropolis Church (under the sanctuary, Russell 1988, fig. 6). This motif is especially prized in Near Eastern mosaics (Syria, Jordan and Israel) among which we note an example at Ma'ale Adomin, St Martyrius Monastery (Israel, Bar Shay 1995, pp. 119-120).

For the examples of the cross of U's pattern panel **10-7B**, see Raynaud 1996; in Xanthos, *supra* inv. **4** and inv. **5**, and *infra* the chapter "Synthesis".

Panel 10-7C
Illustrations 95, 111-112, 182.
Rectangle disposed lengthwise in the nave. 4.80 x 3.80 m. It is composed of a single field framed by its own border.
  Colors: black, white, red, yellow, blue.
  Density of tesserae/dm^2: 54.
  State of preservation: two fragments are preserved, one near the middle of the field and another in the E part, bridging panels **10-7C** and **10-7D** (ill. 112) and permitting reconstruction of the pattern. A N-S depression crosses the panel, and the support is in very poor condition. The fragments have been reinforced (the E panel was removed and its support consolidated) but their durability is questionable, since the support is in precarious condition, often powdery.

Border: 26 cm wide. The border is outlined in red. Undulating row of polychrome inverted bells (*Décor* I, pl. 60d), delineated by a white double fillet. Outer bells are colored yellow, red, black, inner

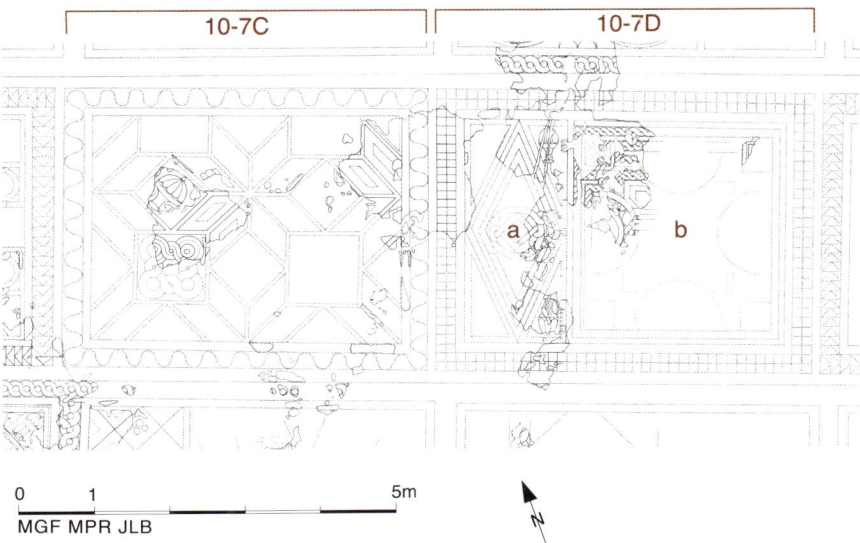

111. Plan of the central part of carpet 10-7: panels 10-7C and 10-7D.

112. Overall view of the panel 10-7C.

bells are blue, black. The bells' mouth is adorned with a red serrated triangle.

Field: rectangle placed laterally in the nave. 4.06 x 3.12 m.
Orthogonal pattern of stars of eight parallelograms, tangent by the points (ill. 111), forming squares and smaller poised squares (*Décor* I, pl. 173b). The scale of the pattern is very large (one and a half stars in width, one and two half-stars in length). A white triple fillet forms the pattern. The parallelograms alternate between a dominant red color (black, two red, two yellow, two red, black, with a blue center) and a blue one (two black, four blue, two white, black, with a red center). Of the large squares, only one is partially preserved, with a centralized filler motif of a poised cushion and a quadrilobe, interlooped in shaded bands, colored

113. Deep depression between panels 10-7C and 10-7D, before the temporary removal, leveling and restoration.

red (black, three red, yellow, two white, black) or blue (black, two blue, four white, black); the center of the corner circles is black. The central concave octagon is incomplete, but contains a black inscribed motif. A few small poised squares are preserved: one contains a fine rounded crater with gadroons and a round black foot (ill. 182). The gadroons are alternately colored with a dominant red or blue. The base of the neck is emphasized by horizontal stripes (black, red, yellow, white, black). The neck is blue with a white center, and the mouth black, red, yellow. The black handles are S-shaped and adorned by small black and red heart motifs. An ivy leaf (black, red, yellow) and a tendril fill the resulting spaces. Another poised square, barely visible, seems to contain a square of four serrated triangles.

Comparisons: see Atrium 2-7, here in a larger scale. Among others, we can cite the close example of Argos, Paleopyrga (Sodini 1968, pl. 1) or an example in Zeugma (Mainad Villa, mosaic of the "Gypsy Girl", Zeugma 2007, p. 75).

Panel 10-7D
Illustrations 95, 111, 113.
Rectangular panel placed lengthwise in the nave, composed of a border, a rectangular W panel (a) and a square E panel (b). 4.95 x 3.85 m.

Colors: black, white, red, yellow, blue.
Density of tesserae/dm^2: 53.

State or preservation: this panel was disturbed by a deep depression crossing the mosaic in a NE-SW direction. Only half of rectangular panel a. and the NW corner of panel b. are preserved, split by many tiny cracks. The support is in very poor condition. This mosaic was removed (M. Dupage in 1988) with a roll, and a drawing was made of the earlier *opus sectile* pavement (traces of which were still visible under the mosaic); a surface sounding also was conducted. The mosaic has been reset on a new support and consolidated, but it is still very fragile and vulnerable. Thus, despite the restoration, the mosaic's preservation is problematic like most of the nave pavement.

Border: width 26 cm. Band of chessboard pattern on two rows (*Décor* I, pl. 14a), black and white framed by red and black fillets.

Rectangular panel a: rectangle placed laterally in the nave. 3.08 x 1.34 m.

Centralized design of concentric motifs, formed by a lozenge inscribed in a rectangle (*Décor* II, pl. 299e). The lozenge encloses concentric lozenges (ill. 113), and is interlooped with a central circle. It is drawn by a white band four tesserae wide framed in black and outlined on the inner side by a shaded band (five blue, white, black). The central circle is interlooped with an inscribed poised square, in shaded bands with an alternately dominant blue (black, two blue, white, black) or yellow color (black, white, yellow, white, black). The corners are framed by a yellow band outlined in white and black. Two of them are preserved (NE and SE) and enclose a tall vase, sort of amphora with a triangular black foot, gadroons on the belly (alternately red and yellow, blue), and horizontal polychrome stripes on top (blue, red, yellow, white). Blue tesserae encircling the neck suggest modeling. The mouth is yellow, framed in black and red, and the small handles are thin and colored black. An ivy stem emerges from the vase, adorned with red or yellow leaves outlined in black.

Main square panel b: almost rectangular, its longer sides are on the E and W. 3.08 x 2.85 m. A complete reconstruction of the pattern was impossible. We recognize a centralized circumcentric pattern, with four lateral semi-circles and four small corner squares (*Décor* II, pl. 357), all combined around a lost central motif. These elements seem to be drawn by a guilloche meander, whose logic and complex design could not be determined (ill. 111).

The asymmetry of this nearly square panel poses difficulties, since links to the central motif seem to be created by loops in the broader area (N-S) and segments in the narrower part (E-W). The guilloche contains strands of an alternating dominant color (black, two blue, white, black; or black, red, yellow, white, black). One corner square is partly preserved and shaded in colors. Part of the semi-circles is framed by a dominant red color, and the center is blue with a white point.

Commentary: it is an original complex pattern, uncommon and in the same style as the "cross of U's" found in carpet **10**-7B; we greatly regret its loss.

Panel 10-7E:
Illustrations 95, 114-115.

Hypothetical dimensions 5.00 x 3.85 m, to maintain a degree of symmetry with the S part of the nave, as occurs elsewhere in preserved areas.

Density of tesserae/dm²: 55.

Colors: black, white, blue, dark blue, red, yellow.

State of preservation: a small fragment of the border is preserved on the N, as is a large fragment of the field in the center. The latter fragment was removed at the same time as neighboring panel **10**-7D, and reset on a new support after the design of the *opus sectile* impressions below was recorded. It was then consolidated.

Border: width 26 cm. It is a row of superposed right-angled triangles (*Décor* I, pl. 14d), black on a white ground.

Field: orthogonal pattern of tangent polychrome peltae in alternately upright and recumbent confronted pairs (ill. 114-115) ("running-pelta pattern"), forming cordiform interspaces (*Décor* I, pl. 222e). Peltae are all delineated by a black double fillet. In a N-S direction, they have a predominantly red color (two red, with a yellow center), while in an E-O direction they are colored blue (two dark blue, with a blue center). The apexes are formed by black serrated triangles.

Comparisons: the pattern of peltae is rather common, for example at Çiftlik (Sinop, Early Christian Church, narthex, Parcel 194, Tatlican 1996, figs. 21-22) on a dark ground. We found many examples in Greece of the same period: among them, Demetrias, Bas. B (nave, Sodini 1968, fig. 173), Hermione, Bas. A (nave, *ibid.*, fig. 43), Aigosthena, narthex, (*ibid.*, figs. 104, 97).

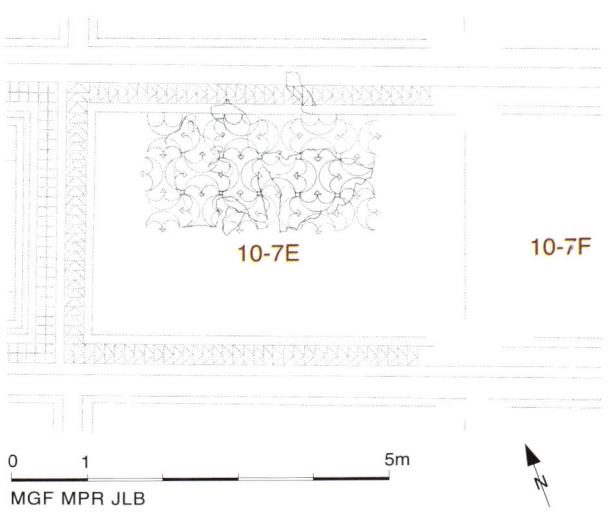

114. Plan of the panel 10-7E.

115. Overall view of the fragment 10-7E, before temporary removal.

Panel 10-7F
Illustration 95.

This part of the nave corridor, near the sanctuary, is completely lost, having been destroyed by later tombs. Nothing remains of the mosaics or the impressions of the earlier *opus sectile* floor. We only can suppose that this panel was square.

10-8 and 10-9, nave, N corridor
Illustration 95.

These western carpets of the N corridor of the nave are lost, and we can only speculate that they had the same proportions as the neighboring panels (**10**-1, **10**-2, **10**-7A and **10**-7B).

10-10, nave, N corridor
Illustration 95, 116.

Two isolated fragments show a loop in a shaded band (pattern of squares with loops in the corners?).

10-7E

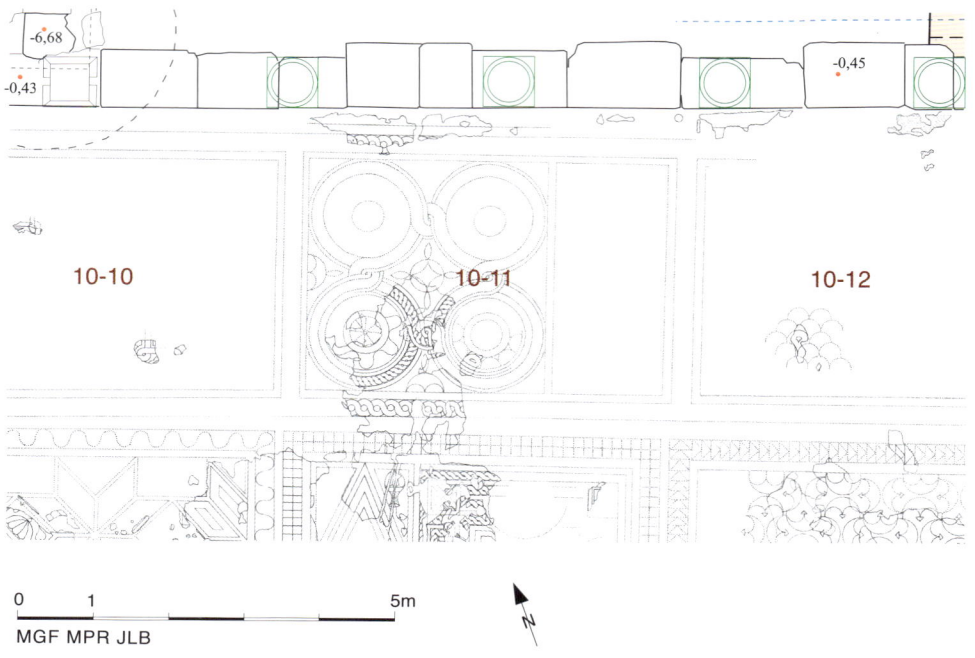

116. Plan of carpets 10-10 to 10-12.

10-11, nave, N corridor
Illustrations 95, 116-117.
Unknown dimensions, perhaps similar to the panel located to the immediate S (4.95 x 3.20 m) but it might instead have been square (as suggested in the drawing) with a supplementary panel.

117. Detail of carpet 10-11.

Colors: black, white, red, yellow, blue.
Density of tesserae/dm^2: 56.
State of preservation: a fragment is preserved on the S, as is a small piece of the overall guilloche (border on the N). This panel displays the same depression as that observed in neighboring panel 10-7D to the immediate S.

Description
Polychrome orthogonal pattern of circles in guilloche bands interlooped tangentially, forming irregular concave octagons (*Décor* I, pl. 235a). The module of the pattern is very large (ill. 116): it is only two circles wide, and two or three long (in the first case it is a centralized pattern, in the second it is an isotropic one). The guilloche strands alternate a dominant blue hue (black, two blue, white, black) with a red one (black, red, yellow, white, black).

The SW circle encloses the following order of inscribed circles (ill. 117): a shaded band (black, red, yellow, black); an undulating row (*Décor* I, pl. 60d) with outer bells colored red and yellow, and inner ones blue, the mouth of the bells marked by a white triangle; a shaded band (black, red, yellow, four white, black, red). The central circle has a radial centralized pattern of eight *radii* (*Décor* II, pl. 345a), colored black on a white ground.

The SE circle is largely destroyed. It is surrounded by the same shaded band, supplemented by a row of tangent semi-circles resting upon an outer line. The semi-circles are shaded black, white, with a red center.

The central irregular octagon, appearing as a concave square is almost lost, but it probably contained a circle of four blue spindles, prolonged by blue lanceolate petals pointing toward the corners of the space.

The only preserved lateral triangle contains a blue pelta surmounted by a blue lanceolate petal.

Comparisons: Gemiler Ada (Church 3, Asano 2000, fig. 4); Ephesus (Bas. im Ostgymnasium, N nave, Vetters 1984, fig. 6), Pisidian Antioch, church (nave, Taşlıalan 1996, plan 2). In Greece, Nicopolis, Bas. A (nave, Sodini 1968, figs. 252-254). This pattern has a particularly impressive isotropic example in Carthage (Complex of Bir Ftouha, Stevens-Kalinowski-Vandeleest 2005, figs. 6-1 to 6-5).

10-12, nave, N corridor
Illustration 95, 116.
Only one small fragment was found *in situ*, showing a scale that can either be part of an orthogonal pattern of scales, or an isolated filler motif.

10-13, nave, N corridor
Illustration 95.
A very small, insignificant fragment is visible on the E, allowing no reconstruction of the pattern.

10, nave, SE supplementary panel
Illustration 95.
Perpendicular to the S stylobate, it occurs between the nave and the narrow corridor flanking the sanctuary chancel screen on the S. 1.60 x 0.50 m. It is situated at the transition between mosaic and plaques pavement

Colors: black, white, red, yellow, blue.

State of preservation: very poorly preserved, its pattern can nevertheless be reconstructed. It is a centralized design of concentric motifs of a stretched lozenge within a rectangle. A white band outlined in red delineates the lozenge. A pair of outward-facing peltae (black, red, yellow, with a white center) fills the center of the motif. Their apex consists of a short horizontal black double fillet, four poised black tesserae, and a black spindle with a blue center adorned with two black dots in the corners. Interspaces are colored blue with a black center.

Commentary: this threshold panel is the only preserved one in the building not made of stone. Its design, very traditional, is typical of carpets in a similar location: a lozenge in a rectangle.
Commentary about nave: the black color is a stone which melted with exposure to outside heat (sort of marl, or calcareous clay); tesserae are visible "in the negative", as we also observed in the S aisle, and N and S baptistery annexes. Yellow is very light, as in N annex of baptistery. Orange is a rare color in the church; the dark blue stone appears in some areas, N narthex and N annex. The entire pavement exhibits a strong aesthetic unity, the product of a single workshop with a taste for very inventive use of various patterns and multiple filler motifs.

Comparisons for overall organization: Gemiler Ada, Church 3 (Asano 2000, fig. 7), "décor multiple" in a grid of guilloche. Anemurium, Church of the Holy Apostles (S aisle, Campbell 1998, figs. 117-118), "décor multiple" with filler motifs in rainbow style. In Greece, Church at Epidauros (corridor leading to the "baptistery", Sodini 1968, fig. 20); at Nea Anchialos (S portico of atrium, *ibid.*, fig. 196); at Aigosthena in Athens (nave, *ibid.*, fig. 97), with a central corridor surrounded by lateral ones divided into a sequence of panels by a grid of guilloche.

11. Nave, sanctuary
Pavement of marble plaques.
Illustration 118.
This pavement of marble plaques[12] reveals two phases of floors, in a few locations where they were superposed. This succession perhaps corresponds to the two phases of the Early Byzantine nave's floors.

Description
The pavement can be divided into four sections: the floors in the N and S corridors flanking the sanctuary enclosure, the rectangular sanctuary floor, and the apse pavement.
• The N corridor opens both on the W toward the nave and on the S toward the sanctuary (4.50 x 1.70 m); a narrow section also extends further E along the base of the synthronon (1.75 x 0.75 m). Half of the floor is preserved and consists of plaques of Proconnesian marble placed in parallel N-S rows. The westernmost row is narrow (35 cm wide) but the others are broader and have a quite regular width (ca. 55-60 cm). The length of the preserved plaques varies considerably. A fragmentary plaque suggests that a slab marks the entrance of the fisrt phase floor.

---

12. "Plaques pavement": elaborate stone pavement, mixing large plaques with narrow bands. The plaques and bands do not create intricate geometric patterns like an *opus sectile* floor but are arranged in a simple form of overall decoration. This kind of pavement sometimes alternates materials (large plaques of marble and narrow bands of schist), as a few examples in Xanthos show (East Bas.: inv. **9**, inv. **16**; in the forthcoming Corpus Xanthos 2, Acropolis Residence inv. **32**, Agora Church inv **47**).

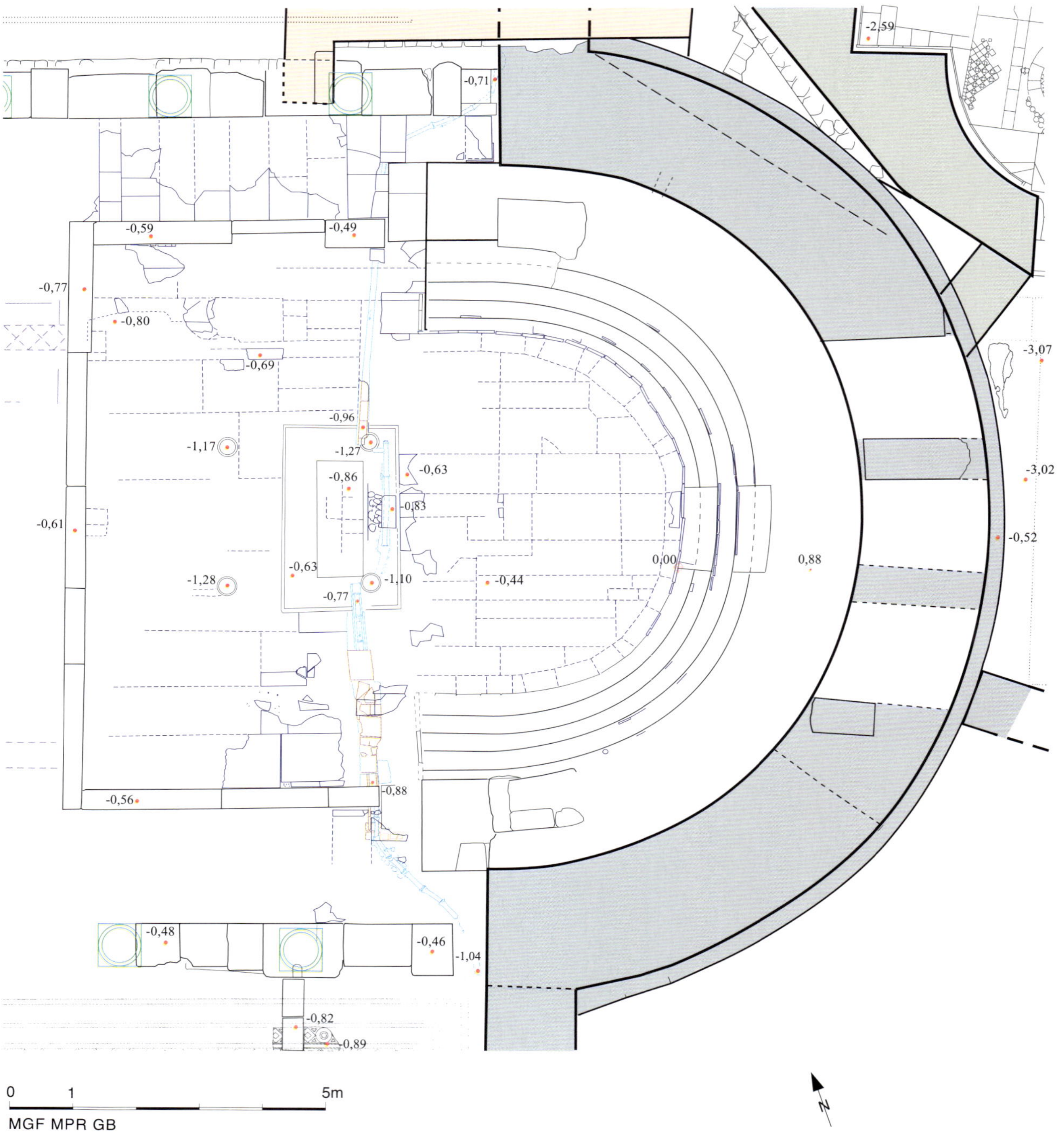

118. Plan of the sanctuary and the apse (*synthronon* and altar socle). Pavement 11.

• The S corridor pavement is almost completely lost, and there remain small fragments of plaques, demonstrating the symmetry of the layout. Its entrance, leading to the nave, is partly preserved and paved in mosaic in substitution of the probable previous plaque, destroyed, (*supra* inv. **10**).

• The rectangular part of the sanctuary floor is covered by rectangular plaques oriented E-W and surrounding the altar table on three sides. These marble plaques are almost entirely lost (they probably were reused elsewhere), but traces on the support allow a reconstruction. The units have wider dimensions than those in the N corridor (ca. 85-1.00 m wide, and of varying length) and formed ten rows of plaques. This part of the pavement surrounds the slightly buried rectangular base of the altar table on three sides. Four holes forming a rectangle are visible in the floor, two of them placed in front of the altar and two others at the corners of the altar base. In the NE corner of the sanctuary, the paving seems more irregular and has narrower plaques.

• The apse pavement continues the sanctuary floor at the same level but with plaques of different size and of less regular proportions; they could hardly have been seen from the nave. For the most part there remain only traces. The *synthronon* and its steps also were covered with white marble revetment.

Commentary: the placement of the plaques clearly is not random: the same arrangement was adopted both for the first *opus sectile* floor of the nave (inv. **9**) and for the sanctuary pavement. In both cases, the plaques were placed in a N-S direction in the N and S parts, but oriented E-W in the axial part. This choice of materials and pattern was deliberate, and it generated a visual movement in the central part of the nave toward the sacred E end. This observation leads us to believe that the sanctuary pavement belongs to the first phase of the church and survived the earthquake with limited restorations.

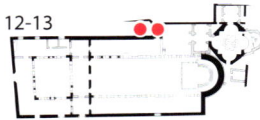

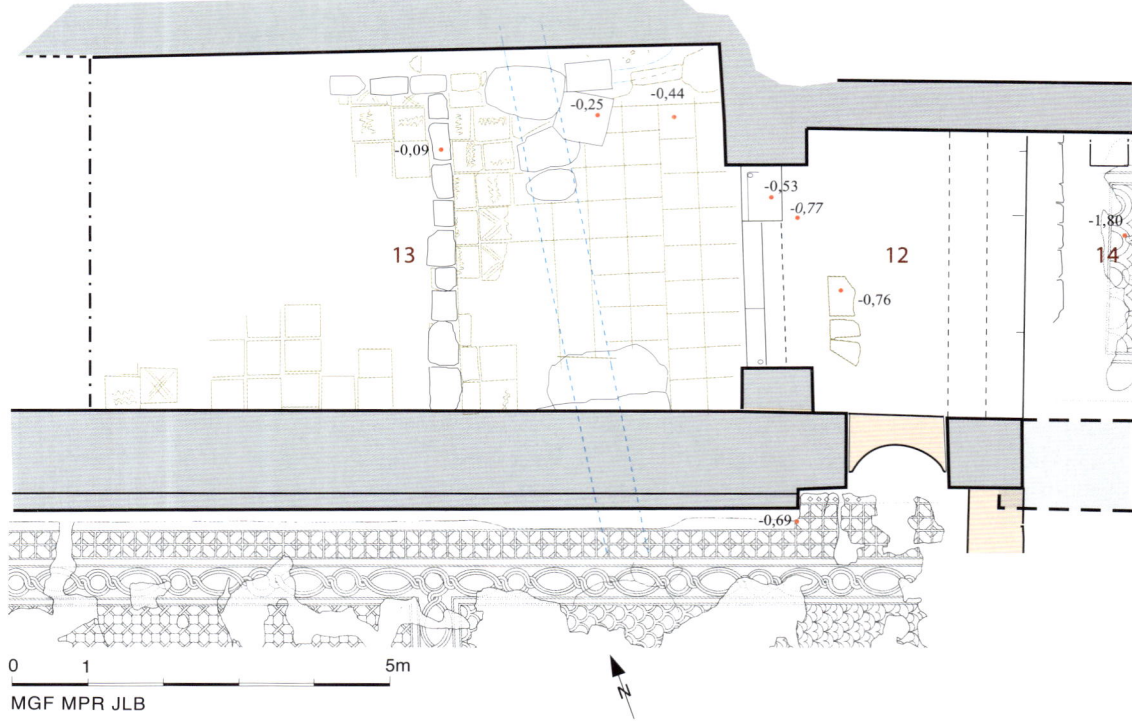

119. Plan of the access to the baptistery situated N of the N aisle: pavements 12-13.

Access to the Baptistery

A sort of vestibule (inv. **12**) is located N of the church's N aisle door. It gave access both to a room on the left (inv. **13**) and a corridor on the right (inv. **14**), which occurs three steps below and leads to the baptistery. Both the vestibule and the room on the left (forming the NW annex) were paved with terracotta tiles.

12. N half landing
Pavement of terracotta tiles
Illustration 119.
Only three fragments of the terracotta tiles are preserved, ca. 8 cm below the level of the church.

120. Pavement of tiles 13.

13. NW annex
Pavement of terracotta tiles.
Illustration 119, 120.
The W limit of the space is unknown but the excavated area is ca. 5 m wide x 8 m long. The room is divided into two sections of different levels by a rough step leading to the higher W part. This space may have been a room for ablutions (or latrines?) on the way to the baptistery. A wide underground drainpipe crosses the room obliquely, covered by wide plaques and coming from further N in the building to evacuate wastewater. A smaller pipe lies along the N wall and empties into this main sewer pipe.
The pavement (located 25 cm above the floor level of the church and 30 cm above the vestibule) is well preserved and made of terracotta tiles. The square tiles measure ca. 50 cm on a side, and show multiple impressions of fingers drawing diagonals or zigzag lines.

The corridor leading to the baptistery (ca. 19.50 m max. length) probably contained two carpets of similar length, inv. 14 and 15.

14. Corridor, W carpet
Opus tessellatum
Illustrations 121-122.
It decorates the floor of a long corridor situated N of the church and 1,10 m below its level (a few broad steps were used to reach this corridor),

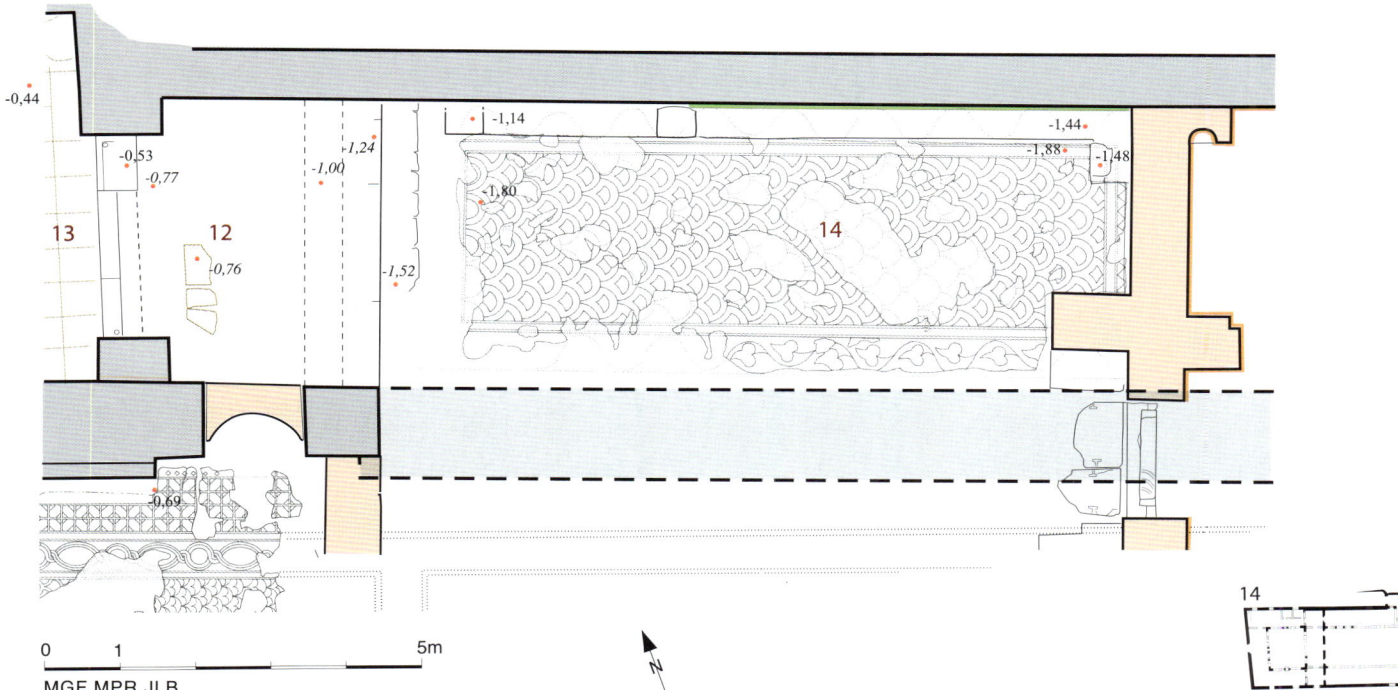

121. Plan of the corridor leading to the baptistery, mosaic 14.

122. View of the mosaic 14.

14 field and border

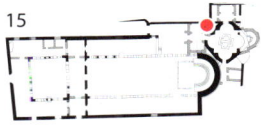

123. Only preserved fragment of mosaic 15, in front of the door of the baptistery's N annex.

specifically between the limit of the N aisle and a retaining wall built 3,90 m N of it. The latter wall seems to pre-date the church complex, and perhaps played a major role in determining the overall orientation of the building. This corridor gave access to the baptistery further E. All of this area was later modified greatly to create the Middle Byzantine building. The corridor's retaining wall was supplemented inside by a Middle Byzantine bench resting on the floor, and the space expanded southward to form an open air court (*infra* "Middle Byzantine building").

Rectangular carpet. ca. 9.00 x 3.70 m.

Density of tesserae/dm^2: 25-27, with large-scale tesserae.

Colors: black, white, red (terracotta).

State of preservation: the S wall was destroyed in Middle Byzantine times. Many traces of burning punctuate the pavement and there are many gaps, probably due to fallen, burning architectural elements. The fire that destroyed this area might be the same disaster (13th c.) that ruined the church erected in the baptistery and the whole Middle Byzantine building, an event followed by abandonment of the site as a place of worship.

Outer margins: N and S, they are adorned with an ivy scroll having a horizontal leaf in each undulation. A black fillet traces the pattern; leaves are colored red. The E outer margin is decorated by a saw-tooth pattern (*Décor* I, pl. 10a); the saw-teeth are

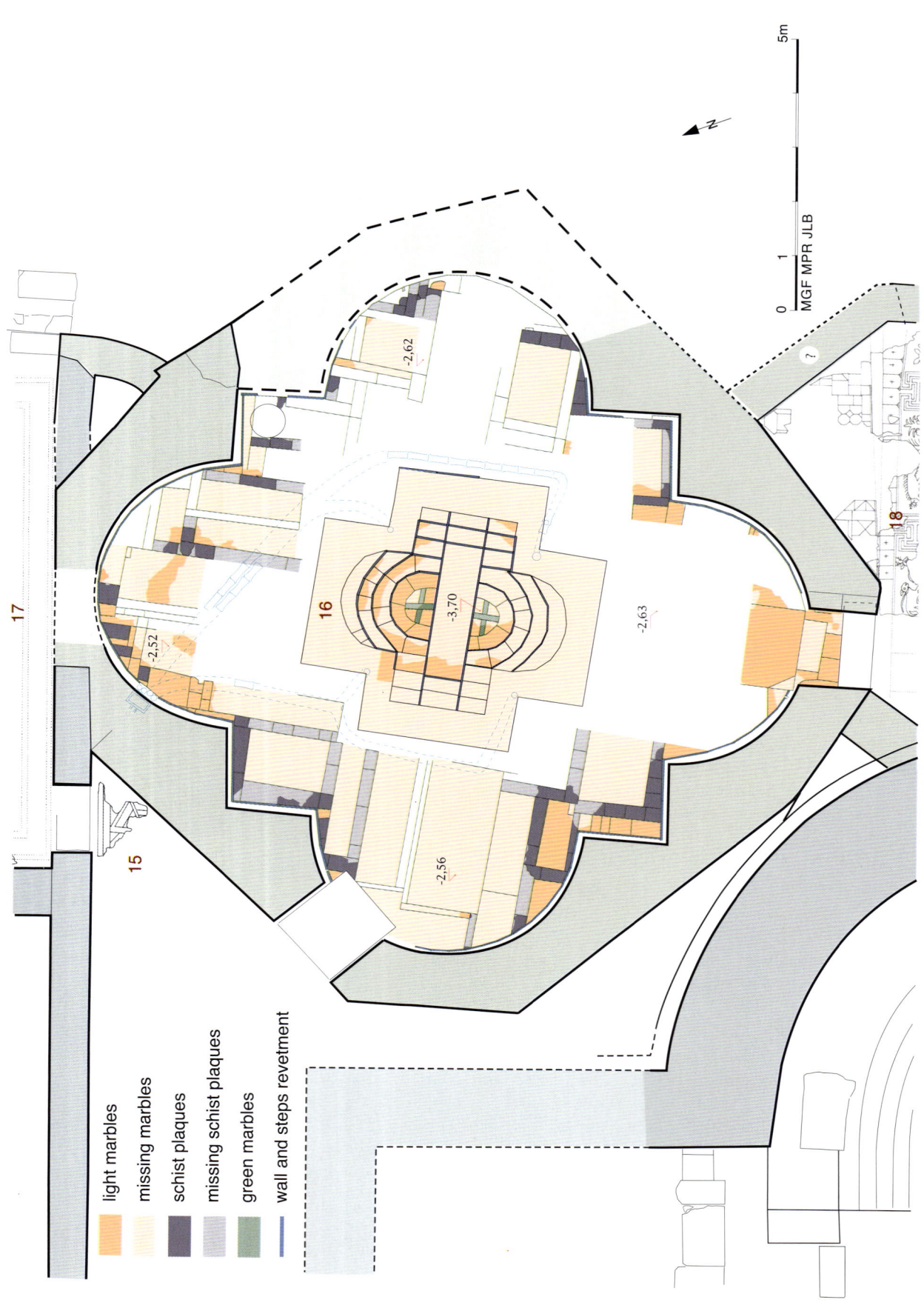

124. Plan of the Early Byzantine Baptistery, pavement 16.

colored red, outlined in black. The W outer margin is plain white.

There is *no border* but a simple white band five tesserae wide.

Field: polychrome orthogonal pattern of adjacent scales (*Décor* I, pl. 215). A black fillet framed by four white fillets forms the scales (ill. 122). The included motif is red outlined in black.

Commentary: the tesserae are poorly shaped and unpolished, and mortar covers part of the tesserae in some places. The mosaic was laid with a somewhat uncertain design and restricted colors, quite different from the mosaics found elsewhere. The large size of the tesserae is unique in this church and is more characteristic of a service room floor. However, this corridor had genuine significance in the liturgy, leading to the baptistery. The rough and solid work in this location might be explained both by the presence of a team inexperienced in mosaic work, and by the hypothesis that this floor covered an area exposed to the open air. The simple pattern, traced by white fillets, and the use of white bands recall the production of the workshop A, active in the N atrium. (*infra* chapter "Synthesis").

15. Corridor, E carpet
Opus tessellatum
Illustrations 123, 128.

A very small fragment of mosaic is preserved S of the threshold (SW side) leading to the N annex. A mosaic probably covered the floor of this long trapezoidal space, located between mosaic **14** and the baptistery entrance. This sector was completely transformed during the Middle Byzantine period, with the construction of a court and a large vaulted narthex in front of the new church installed in the baptistery. The main entrance of the tetraconch was later moved further S, approximately on the axis of the building. The previous Early Byzantine mosaic also was destroyed.

The pattern of this tiny fragment can not be reconstructed (ill. 123). We only observe a shaded band flanking the threshold and the beginning of another shaded band. Better in quality and colors than inv. **14**, its appearance (size and colors of tesserae) is close to that of the N annex floor. The pattern of this geometric mosaic was very likely adapted to fit the trapezoidal shape of the room it adorned (ill. 128). The presence of an equilateral triangle in the mosaic, and the treatment of the angles, suggest a hexagon formed of six equilateral triangles, in shaded colors (red, yellow, black, white). The design seems quite irregular.

Baptistery

125. Detail of the fonts.

The Early Byzantine baptistery was built below the church's E end. It was constructed after the completion of the church and its apse. The baptistery's plan is that of a tetraconch placed within a square, the diameter of the four conchs appearing smaller than the sides of the square, forming corners. The external shape of the baptistery is that of a poised square, with some irregularities that resulted from adapting it to the pre-existing church and N limit. The vault over the fonts was covered with mosaics, destroyed by the same catastrophic fire that destroyed the entire Middle Byzantine complex during the 13th c. The vault mosaic was partially found broken into small pieces in the destruction layer covering the floor. The entrance door opens obliquely

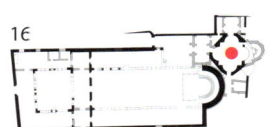

126. Overall view of the baptistery from the apse, showing pavement 16 at the periphery and Middle Byzantine *opus sectile* floor 19 in the center.

in the W conch[1], and gives onto the vestibule-corridor connecting the N aisle (at a lower level) with the tetraconch. Another door on the axis of the S conch leads to the baptistery's S annex. The baptistery walls were covered with stone revetment. Originally, there was no direct access to the N annex, space that only opened onto mosaic **15** (E part of the corridor).

16. Baptistery pavement
Pavement of plaques[2]
Illustrations 124-127.

The Early Byzantine pavement of the baptistery is organized around the fonts' contours, shaped as a cross. These fonts are not aligned exactly with the N-S axis of the tetraconch, but diverge slightly in a NW-SE direction, to accommodate the oblique placement of the baptistery entrance. The pavement plaques are disposed perpendicular and

---
1. The oblique placement of the door was necessary to allow circulation around the corner of the N aisle.
2. See definition *supra*, note 12, p. 105 (sanctuary).

parallel to the edges of the fonts, and laid from the center toward the edges. Near the walls, residual spaces are filled with irregularly shaped plaques.

The pavement is best preserved along the periphery (ill. 124), for the central fonts were later sealed by a new pavement in the Middle Byzantine period (inv. **19**). Some lost plaques left imprints in the mortar, and these traces permitted reconstruction of most of the design. The pavement blends large marble plaques with narrow bands. The bands, sometimes doubled, consist primarily of schist, thinner than marble and consequently less deeply sunk into the mortar. A few bands are made of light-colored marble. The large plaques are disposed in a cross-shape around the fonts (ill. 126). The overall appearance of the pavement is that of a dark grid filled with irregular light-colored plaques. Can we classify this pavement as an example of *opus sectile*, or is it simply a bichrome pavement of plaques, a term that seem more in accordance with this plain type of floor? Attention is clearly focused on the fonts.

Comparisons: there are close comparisons of pavements of schist and marble in Xanthos, such as the pavement of the *triclinium* of the NE Residence of the Acropolis, in the forthcoming Xanthos Corpus 2, inv. **32**, in a grid of bands with *opus sectile* panels. The apse of the Church on the Xanthos Agora, *ibid.*, inv. **47**, and the apse of the Byzantine Church in the Letoon (Metzger 1966, figs. 9-10) both present a fan-shaped composition (semi-circular radial pattern, *Décor* II, pl. 350). A regional example of the same type occurs in the apse of Church 3 of Gemiler Ada, Island of St. Nicolas (Asano 1997, figs. 10-11, 16) showing an orthogonal grid of bands.

Fonts
The cross-shaped borders of the fonts were deliberately destroyed in creating the new Middle Byzantine church within the walls of the baptistery. The fonts themselves, filled in and sealed by a new pavement laid over them, are quite well preserved. They are composed of two semi-circular basins of stepped form, separated by a narrow E-W axial passageway (ill. 124-125), having three steps at each end. This passageway was shielded from water in the adjacent basins by thin vertical marble panels on its sides, which kept the officiating priest dry when the pools were filled to the brim. On either side of the central passageway, a narrow, five-step stair allowed access to the basin from either the E or W, and provided an exit on the opposite side. The two semi-circular basins rise through three steps[3]. The fonts were adorned by a rich revetment, composed of various kinds of marble. The bottom of each basin displays a rough green cross (ill. 127) (cipollino from Karystos or breccia from Thessaly) on a clear ground (pavonazetto, Proconnesian marble). The steps are embellished primarily with light-colored marble (white, grey, Proconnesian, pavonazetto), while the curved risers are covered by light-colored marble and green cipollino. The only close comparison to these double fonts occurs in the Peloponnese at Amphissa (Themelis 1977, pp. 242-250, Corpus Greece 2, fig. 323, Ristow 1998, n° 233, pp. 152-153).

Mortar (foundation)
The setting mortar of this pavement is a common, recognizable type. It is smooth and pink with much crushed terracotta, and appears solid and well preserved. It is very different from Middle Byzantine mortar (white and powdery), and this fact helped to distinguish the impressions of each period. The upper layer is ca. 20 cm thick, over a solid stone foundation.

127. Detail of the floor of the font showing a rough cross.

Wall revetment
The wall revetment of the tetraconch is partly preserved in the lower zone. It is made of white marbles, and during the excavations we found large fluted pilasters that probably decorated the corners of the baptistery, and perhaps framed the doors. Fragments of wall painting (red and green) were also excavated in the baptistery, and probably came primarily from the medieval narthex.

Vault
The vault was covered with mosaics, found crushed after an intense fire. The study of many boxes of fragments gathered during excavation did not allow us to make a graphic reconstruction of the vault decoration[4]. However, we recognized a large inscription (ca. 20 cm high), a few geometric borders, a large area occupied by a vine scroll, and some pieces probably belonging to human figures (flesh tints). Unfortunately we can not describe this vault mosaic more precisely, noting that it contained many glass tesserae of bright colors and employed a sophisticated technique of painted joins, colored like the surrounding tesserae.

It is worth noting that within the medieval infill of the fonts were found fragments of the vault mosaic, proving that this vault was already in a bad state of preservation before the medieval occupation. This was confirmed by the presence of other fragments inside the pipes of the fonts, and still other pieces were reused in the medieval walls. Nevertheless, an important part of the vault

---

3. For the fonts study, see Sodini 1980, p. 122, note 1, and Ristow 1998.

4. Jolivet-Raynaud 2000, this study will be developed in the publication of the excavations under J.-P. Sodini direction, forthcoming.

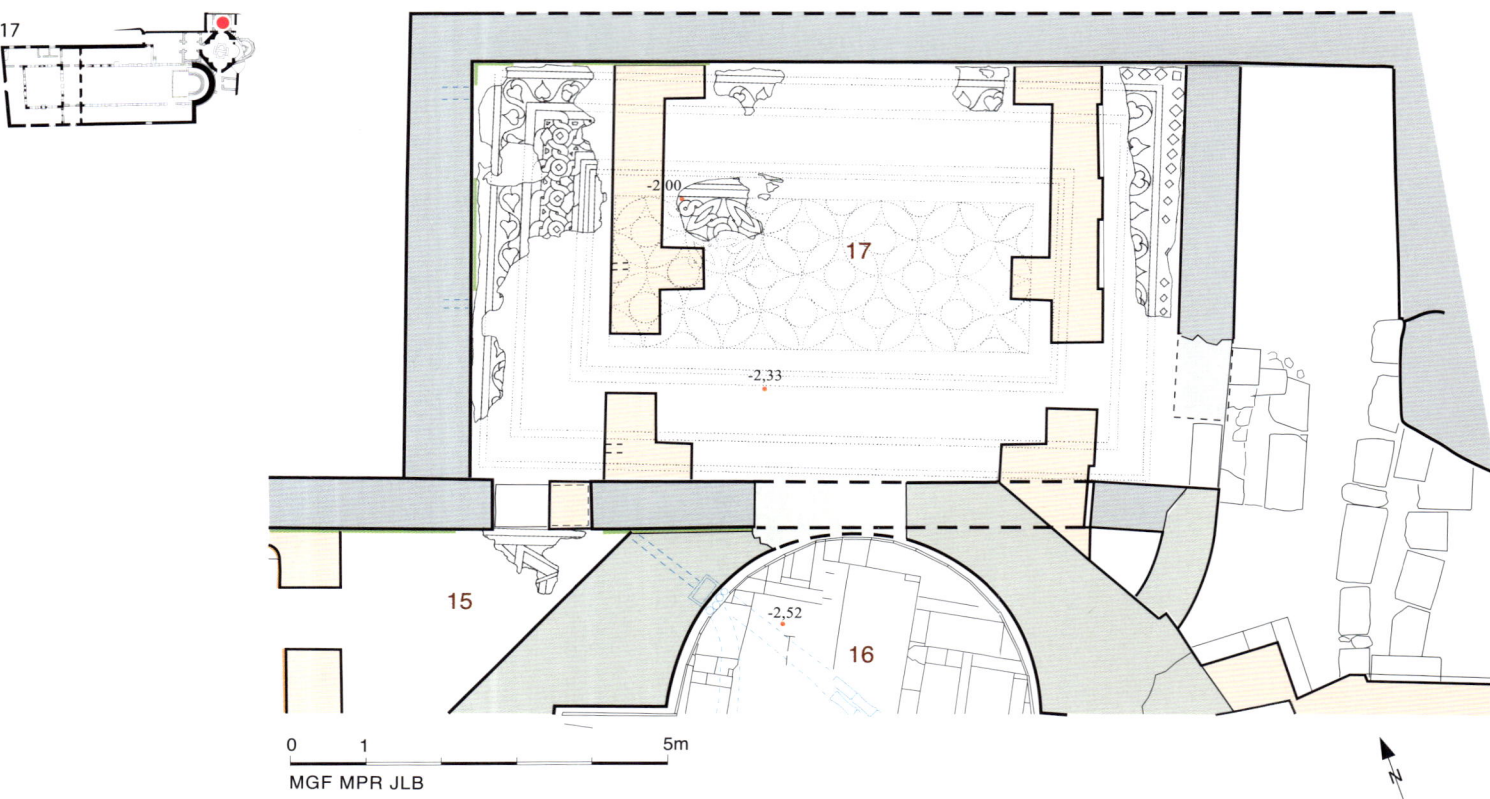

128. Plan of the N annex of the baptistery, pavement 17, and mosaic 15 at lower left.

mosaic remained *in situ* until the total destruction by a huge fire during the 13th c. Indeed, most of the vault fragments were excavated from the destruction layer of the medieval Church, above its late pavement.

Commentary: the example of Xanthos follows an overall fashion in the style of vault mosaics of the 5th and 6th c. in the Early Byzantine world, as at Thessaloniki or in Italy, particularly at Rome and Ravenna[5]. We are here in an early stage, before the gradual abandonment of scrolls and floral elements in favor of tall figures, shown in frontal view and with elongated proportions. There already exist bright colors and probably figures, but organized in superimposed registers and combined with geometric borders, placed above a large mosaic inscription (now lost).

Comparisons: for examples of nearby vault mosaics, see Gemiler Ada, Church 3 (Asano 1997, figs. 22-23) where small fragments of the apse ceiling were decorated with figures. At Anemurium, in the Central Church (Treasury Church, beg. 6th c., Campbell 1998, pls. 173, 175-176), there are fragments of human figures and an inscription likely coming from the *ciborium*. At Çiftlik, Early Byzantine Church (5th c.), were found remains of wall and vault mosaics (molten glass tesserae, Tatlican 1996, fig. 15), and at Kartmin, in the sanctuary vault, dating to 512 CE (Hawkins-Mundell-Mango 1973, figs. 5-12); the decoration combines scrolls and geometric borders.

17. Baptistery - North annex
Opus tessellatum
Illustrations 128-129.

A large rectangular room (dim: 9.50 x 5.60 m) seems contemporary with the first phase of the church in its Early Byzantine period. It is located N of the baptistery. Its main axis runs E-W; access to the annex was through a door at the W end of the S wall, opening to the end of the corridor (inv. **15**) and forming an acute angle with the baptistery wall. Originally, the N annex did not open directly into the tetraconch. Its E wall was pierced by a crude narrow door communicating with the exterior, a door modified and widened in the Middle Byzantine period.

Fresco fragments were still in situ on the N wall, and many fragments were found during excavations.

Mainly rectangular, but with the W wall at a slightly oblique angle. 9.50 x 5.30 m.
Density of tesserae/dm²: 54 in the field.

---
5. Ling 1998, pp. 98-112; Dunbabin 1999, pp. 236-253.

Colors: black, white, red, yellow, blue, dark blue, brown. Yellow is very light, as in the nave. Brown, a new color, is made of hard stone, a sort of very dense green. Black tesserae are preserved "negatively" in hollow spaces, as in the S annex.

State of preservation: the mosaic is preserved in the NW corner, and along the walls (N, W and E). A small patch also is preserved in the center. Although only a small fragment of the field remains, the overall decoration of this room can be reconstructed.

Outer margins
On the W and N, they are white, with the rows of tesserae arranged parallel to the wall. On the E and in the NE corner, they are punctuated by serrated poised squares (dark blue and red, with a yellow center). The square placed in the corner is not poised but parallel to the walls. A shaded band limits the margin and separates it from the first border. It is colored black, red, three white, yellow, black.

Border 1
Dimension: 35 cm wide. Ivy scroll (*Décor* I, pl. 64), with a single vertical leaf in each undulation as in the S Atrium, alternately red or yellow, outlined in black. In the W border of variable width, the leaves are set horizontally after the third undulation (ill. 129). S border is lost. Corner leaf is oblique.

Border 2
Dimension: 90 cm wide. Strapwork of tangent circles in asymmetrically shaded bands (*Décor* I, pl. 82e). The shaded bands are colored either with red as the dominant color (black, blue, two red, white, black) or yellow (black, brown, two yellow, white, black) (ill. 129). Circles are adorned with a polychrome serrated poised square (brown, blue, red, yellow, the center as a white crosslet sometimes outlined in black). Lateral residual motifs contain an inscribed black motif. This border is framed on both sides by another shaded band (two black, red, five white, red, two black).

Border 3
Dimension: 20 cm wide. Large symmetrically shaded band (*Décor* I, pl. 6b) with following sequence of colors: black, two brown, two red, two yellow, two white and symmetrically the reverse. Toward the center of the room, a black double fillet and a white triple fillet underline this border.

Field
There is only a small fragment left, but the field dimensions can be reconstructed. 5.60 x 2.05 m.

129. Detail of the NW fragment of mosaic 17.

There remains half of a circle of four spindles around a circle. The field probably was decorated with an isotropic pattern covering all of the free space within the borders. The pattern very likely is a polychrome grid pattern of tangent circles and recumbent spindles formed by interlooped asymmetrically shaded bands (the circles representing the intersections), creating the effect of a pattern of large intersecting circles (ill. 128) (*Décor* I, pl. 244f). Circles of four spindles are non-contiguous. Colors are barely legible because of burned patches. The shaded band seems formed by a fillet successively black, white, blue, two red, black.

Comparisons: the overall organization of the small field framed by multiple borders (such as guilloche, saw-tooth line, varied kinds of linear strapwork, circles and spindles) recalls many mosaics of Antioch (ex. House of Aion); Misis-Mopsuestia; Dağpazarı (6th c.) or Zeugma and Anemurium (Church of the Holy Apostles); influence confirmed by the choice of patterns.

Field pattern: there is another example in the nave of the East Basilica (*supra* carpet **10**-7B); in Turkey, at Anemurium, (Necropolis Church, under the sanctuary, 6th c., Russell 1988, fig. 6). Also Çiftlik, 5th c., parcel 194 (Tatlican 1996, fig. 25; Hill 1995, fig. 1, pls. 29b, 30a-b) where the same taste for large and multiple borders is noticed. On Karpathos Island, the Basilica of Arkaseia (Jacopich 1925, fig. 4). In Syria, Church of Suhmata (Balty

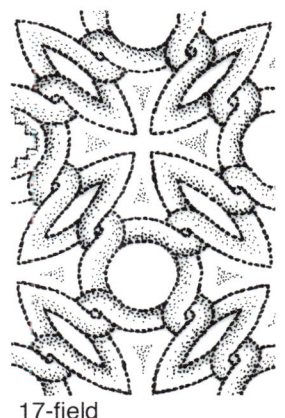

17-field

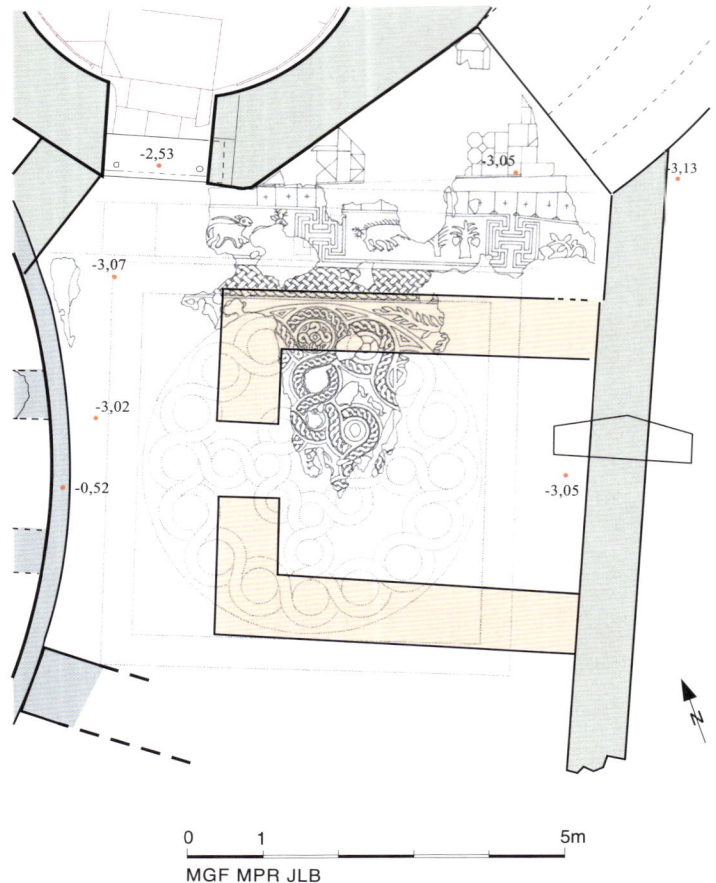

1995, pl. 31-1), Deir el'Adas (N aisle, Donceel-Voûte 1988, fig. 26), Byblos Villa (*ibid.*, fig. 6). In Jordan, this pattern is very popular: Rihab, Church of St. Mary (Piccirillo 1993, p. 310, fig. 622), Church of St. Paul (*ibid.*, p. 312, fig. 627), Madaba, the Bacchus Procession mosaic (*ibid.*, p. 76, figs. 40, 45). We have already cited the parallel in Israel of Ma'ale Adomin, Monastery of St. Martyrius (Bar Shay 1995, pp. 119-120, fig. 9) to which we can add Sephoris (Netzer-Weiss 1994, p. 54) and Jerusalem (St. Marie de la Probatique, Dauphin 2005, p. 249, figs. 1-2a).

Scroll of hederae: Aphrodisias (Priest's House, Rm. 3, atrium, Campbell 1991, fig. 82).

Strapwork of tangent circles: many examples in the rainbow-style area. We cite nearby Gemiler Ada (Church 3, Asano 2000, fig. 7) and Kos (Bas. St. John, Di Matteis 2004, pl. LXV-3). In Greece and Macedonia, at Nicopolis (Bas. Delta, diakonikon, Sodini 1968, figs. 280-282); at Thessaloniki (intersection of Moreas and Mouson Streets, Corpus Greece 3, pls. 180-181); Heraklea Lynkestis (Rm. 4, Cveković-Tomašević 2002, p. 62, figs. 45-46) or Stobi (Episcopal Basilica, first phase mosaic, beg. of 5th c., Mikulčik 2003, p. 122, and narthex, *ibid.*, p. 123).

130. Plan of the S annex, pavement **18**, mixing mosaic and *opus sectile* floor.

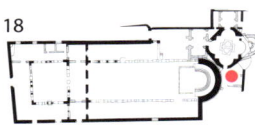

131. Remains of pavement **18**, view from the apse. Medieval walls have destroyed part of the mosaic.

18. Baptistery South annex

This space occurs immediately below the church apse and leads directly to the baptistery (S door in the S conch). Its floor is at the same level as the baptistery. The shape of this room is complex, since it is squeezed between the curvature of the church apse on the W, the small S conch of the baptistery on the N (its polygonal outer wall), and an E limit forming an angle (probably due to the natural slope of the terrain); the S limit was not found, having fallen down the slope. Some rebuilding occurred in the Middle Byzantine period, in order to create a separate rectangular room within this space (its walls were built directly over the mosaic).

It was decided to make a large square pavement in this area, and they filled the corners and surrounding spaces with *opus sectile* and marble plaques on the N, linked to the mosaic by an outer margin; a large mosaic outer band on the irregular and curved W side. Part of this mosaic was deliberately destroyed on both the E and W sides when new structures were built during the medieval era. These remains cover the NE part of the pavement, within the small Middle Byzantine room, and the floor's pattern can be reconstructed.

Mosaic 18A, Main carpet
Opus tessellatum
Illustrations 130-136, 160, 163.
Probably square, ca. 5.00 x 5.00 m.
Density of tesserae/dm^2: 60.

Colors: black, white, red, yellow, pink, gray. Black is a stone that melted with exposure to heat and moisture (sort of marl, or calcareous clay): tesserae are visible "negatively", as we also observed in the S aisle, nave and baptistery's N annex.

State of preservation: this mosaic is preserved over approximately one eighth of its surface, with small gaps. The existing fragment is solid, and its preservation is not a problem. It has been reinforced in situ. Part of the N border also is preserved, allowing complete reconstruction of the pavement.

Outer margins
North: 24-46 cm. East: 16 cm.

• N margin: a marble string course separates the mosaic from the *opus sectile* pavement. The margin itself is of triangular shape, becoming wider toward the E and appearing plain white. It is broadened by a line of adjacent squares (or rectangles) drawn by a black fillet (*Décor* I, pl. 9), with a black crosslet in the center of each motif. A small serrated triangle at their base accentuates the divisions between squares and rectangles. The E compartment is divided in two by a horizontal black line.

• E margin: only a small fragment is legible and appears plain white, with the tesserae laid parallel to the wall and without a clear limit for the adjacent border.

• On the W side, we note a small white fragment with a curved black fillet. It could be a scroll stem, a type of motif often chosen to fill an irregular space in this church. The white tesserae around the fillet are placed irregularly, in parallel or perpendicular fashion.

Border 1
This border is preserved only in the N part of the mosaic, but there is enough room to assume a return on the E side. On the W and S sides, the irregular spaces did not make room for a regular motif like this border.
Dimensions: 80 cm wide.

Description
Latchkey-meander of spaced upright double latchkeys with a long rectangle in each space (*Décor* I, pl. 40e). A black triple fillet forms the meander. The rectangles contain figural scenes, with animals and plants, which can be read from the center of the room (ill. 131, 163).

• W rectangle: hunting scene with a hound held on a leash (ill. 132). The hound is white outlined in black, and the leash red. No one holds the leash. The hound is turned rightward, its red eye outlined in black, and its open mouth colored red. The tail, ears and head are colored black. A short yellow line emphasizes the jaw, and a few colored tesserae dot the hound's body. At first glance, this animal looks like a hare because of his long ears. It runs after a stag (ill. 133), whose antlers are visible, yellowish branches with red tips.

• Central rectangle: it contains a quadruped and trees. The animal is black and gray (burned white stone ?), turned rightward. The legs end in three-part hoofs. The body is bristling with long black hairs: these features and its short corkscrew tail suggest a wild boar (ill. 134). What remains of the head could be the end of the snout, with an oblique line of gray tesserae, perhaps a tusk. It is bent down toward a sort of palm tree, drawn as a simple black trunk from which emerge stiff branches. In the right part of the compartment is another, red tree outlined in black. The branches are made by a triple fillet (black, red, black). Heart-shaped red fruits hang on both sides, outlined in black (spot of burning).

• E rectangle (or square) forming the corner of the border: half of a tree is preserved, with curved red branches outlined in black and adorned with pink, yellow and red leaves (ill. 135). The down-

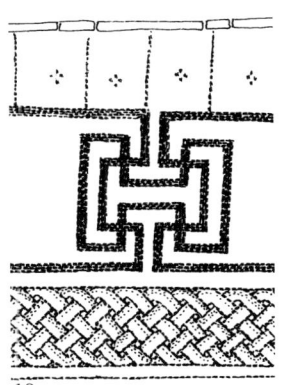

132. Detail of the dog.

133. Detail of the stag.

turned end of a branch bears a heart-shaped red and pink fruit, outlined in black. The branch's extension toward the S implies that the border probably turned and wrapped around the corner of the field on both the N and E sides.

Border 2
Dimensions: 45 cm wide.

Description
Shaded six-strand guilloche (*Décor* I, pl. 73f) on a black ground (ill. 131). The shaded bands are alternately colored with a dominant blue (black, two yellow, two blue, black), yellow ((black, two white, two yellow, black) or red hue (black, two white, two red, black). The border is framed by white bands five tesserae wide on the N, and three tesserae wide on the S. This border probably wrapped around all four sides of the field.

Field
Square, ca. 2.30 x 2.30 m.

Description: centralized design of concentric motifs, a circle inscribed in a square (ill. 130). The large circle itself displays a wreath-like pattern, in a circle and around a square of eight circles, of 16 circles linked to the square by 4 circles arranged as a cross, interlaced in simple guilloche (*Décor* II, pl. 311c). A white triple fillet traces this complex pattern (ill.136), framing the guilloche and forming interruptions at the crossings. The guilloche alternates dominant red bands (black, two red, white, black) with yellow ones (black, two yellow, white, black). The circles diminish in diameter from the edges to the center (outer circles: 76 cm; intermediate circles: 66 cm; inner circles: 60 cm).

Filler motifs of the outer circles vary, and three are partially legible. The circle at the N is intact and encloses a circle with four loops, traced with shaded bands alternately with red or yellow as the dominant color; the resulting spaces have inscribed motifs of the same colors. The second contains a small black circle prolonged by a nub (a pear?). The last one, very damaged, bears a circle of four spindles forming a concave square divided into two triangles, as far as can be determined.

Among the intermediate circles, only one is visible but its center is lost.

The inner circles contain a small circle colored red or yellow. One of them encloses a flower, a sort of red tulip with a serrated opening, linked to a red stem; this circle is outlined in red. Among the resulting spaces formed by the pattern, only one is incompletely preserved. It contains two stiff black birds with heads turned toward the center of the room, each having a black and white eye and beak. Geometric and red floral elements surround them: a circle with a white center framed by barbs, a heart-shaped leaf and a fragmentary stem that is barely legible.

The center of the composition forms a concave octagon enclosing a small ibex or goat, with backward-curving red horns, and a yellow body framed in black. Its head turned to the N, this animal is bent over two flowers, red and yellow. The octagon is outlined in red or yellow.

The corners of the main square contain an inscribed triangle colored black, white, with a red or yellow center. In the E corner appears part of a sinuous branch, red and yellow, covered by blue leaves outlined in black (ill. 160). It could be part of an acanthus spray. A small fragment of another curved stem is visible. In the NW corner there is a fruit resembling a grapefruit: it perhaps emerged from a vase (or crater) set diagonally in the corner.

Commentary: we note some stylistic parallels between this mosaic and the nave mosaic, especially in the rendering of floral elements as in the corner motifs of carpets 10-1, 10-2 or 10-7A, in addition to similarities in the drawing of the patterns.

134. Detail of the boar.

135. Detail of trees.

Comparisons: *Border*: very common, in Cilicia at Dağpazarı, South Church (Gough 1961, figs. 4-7). The palm tree looks like the same motif in Gemiler Ada, Church of St. Nicholas (Church 3, Asano 1998, without numbering of pages), but there it is larger and more detailed. We found some similarity in a fruit tree used as a filler motif in a geometric mosaic of Kos, Basilica at Mastichari (near the Harbor Baths, Di Matteis 2004, pl. LXIV; Corpus Greece 1, fig. 49). See also this motif in Laureotic Olympus, Greece (in the sanctuary, end of 5th c., Spiro 1978, fig. 87; Corpus Greece 2, fig. 225b), with hederae-shaped fruits; in the nave of Klapsi a boar and a hound run around a shield of triangles (Sodini 1968, figs. 188-189). The association of a hound, a stag, and a boar separated by trees recalls the organization and repertory found at Heraklea Lynkestis (Chancellery, Rm. 4, Cveković-Tomašević 2002, figs. 45-46), in a large free panel instead of the border with multiple filler motifs (as at Xanthos).

Field: the pattern is very elaborate and rare (I do not know an example exactly the same), and this unusual choice contrasts with the somewhat unsure lines and stiffly drawn animals. It is likely that most filler motifs were figural (animals) or floral, and this is a rare enough feature in the church to merit emphasis. The sophisticated pattern reflects a taste for complex and unusual centralized designs, also encountered in the nave. Many other stylistic similarities (trees, colors, style of draftsmanship, accumulation of varied motifs, impression of randomness...) link the S annex mosaic with the nave floor. The multiplication of small compartments filled with figural motifs also parallels the evolution of mosaic style in Syria. The closest comparison for the centralized wreath pattern occurs in the Agora of Thessaloniki (E part, Corpus Greece 3, pp. 68-69, 77b).

Opus sectile floor 18B

Illustration 130.

An *opus sectile* pavement decorates the NE corner of this annex.

Dimensions of the preserved triangular section: 4.70 x 2.80 x 3.60m.

Materials: white limestone, black schist, terracotta (one green fragment), light colored marbles (Proconnesian, pavonazzetto, grey and white marbles), cipollino, and dark blue marble.

Description: the decoration of this part of the floor begins alongside the mosaic's N outer margin (irregular line of adjacent squares) and a thin, drawn-out white band (0 cm at W to 30 cm wide at E).

The decoration of the triangular field seems to be divided into small panels, with a geometric pattern of small-scale units, as we also observed in the central narthex. It is destroyed over most of its surface, and the overall design is unknown. On the W one barely distinguishes a band of half-hexagons and triangles (two half-hexagons in width). A second fragment on the E shows a pattern of octagons and poised squares. Yet another piece in the N corner appears to be part of a pattern of octagons and squares. These small panels are separated by plain bands of stone.

136. Reconstruction design of the centralized pattern.

MIDDLE BYZANTINE CHURCH AND ANNEXES

Illustrations 137-150, fold-out plan C.

Probably at the beginning of the 11th c., a new church and its annexes were installed in the better preserved parts of the original East Basilica, and many of the older floors were reused at this time. After a general cleaning of the ruins, the new establishment occupied the older atrium, narthex, N aisle and baptistery.

The most important physical changes converted the vaulted baptistery into a new church. An *opus sectile*[1] pavement covered the former fonts, and a large E apse with a *synthronon* replaced the previous E conch (and had a different orientation), all of this preceded by a *templon* decorated with an image of the *Deisis*[2]. A door also was cut through the N conch toward the N annex. Both the N and S annexes were divided into smaller spaces by walls (built directly over the mosaics in the S annex; foundations were dug under the mosaic level in the N annex), with the entrances covered by rough slabs (inv. **21**c and **21**d).

The position of the W entrance to the new church was significantly changed from the past. The new church required a more impressive approach from the W, created by removing earth to a depth of 1.85 m below the original Early Byzantine building (thereby destroying half of its N aisle) and for a distance of 14.50 m in front of the converted tetraconch. At the same time, the adjacent, earlier corridor (inv. **14**) was extended toward the S, and all of this area became an open-air atrium (ca. 10 x 11 m); the rest of the floor probably consisted of beaten earth. Further E, a completely new narthex was created after the existing structures in this area were razed. The narthex is a rectangular room, covered by three parallel barrel vaults, and the walls displayed figural paintings representing hierarchs, bishops, saints, holy women, deacons and martyrs. A pavement of rough limestone plaques precedes the W axial door of the narthex (inv. **21**a), but the floor in this place is now lost (inv. **21**b). The door in the E wall of the narthex, leading to the new church's interior, was rebuilt and shifted to the main axis of the building.

---

1. Large marble slabs partly covering the fonts were removed during excavation; old photographs helped reconstruct the design.
2. Sodini 1980.

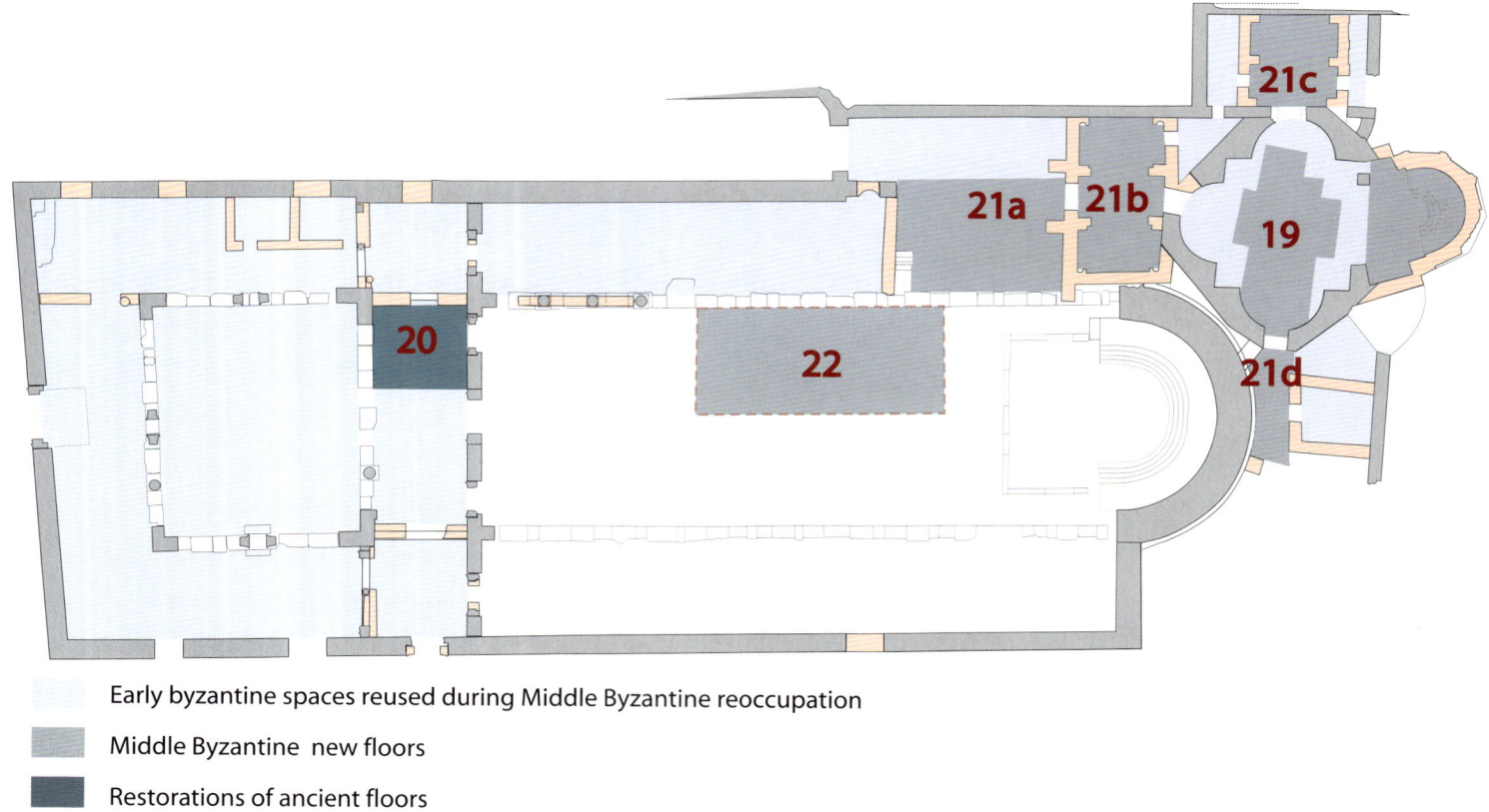

137. Plan of the Middle Byzantine complex with numbers of the floors.

- Early byzantine spaces reused during Middle Byzantine reoccupation
- Middle Byzantine new floors
- Restorations of ancient floors

The atrium, narthex and W half of the N aisle of the Early Byzantine church now served as a circulation route between the city's *cardo* and the new church, with a few of the flanking spaces subdivided to form small rooms. The atrium probably was well preserved, as we can judge by the good condition of the mosaics, which were laid on bedrock and not on an artificial terrace. By this time, the original narthex and N aisle probably had lost their 2nd-story galleries and roofs, but were roofed over anew during the Middle Byzantine period. The N aisle was shortened, with a transverse staircase leading downward (from S to N) to the new atrium court. The old door giving access to the Early Byzantine corridor and baptistery was then sealed by a semicircular niche, preceded by a chancel screen (traces in the mosaic).

The walls dividing the new spaces were laid over the earlier mosaics and were sometimes built entirely of reused blocks, occasionally consisting of reemployed sawn columns. In addition, the walls in the N part of the original atrium and narthex were decorated with fine Middle Byzantine frescoes representing standing militant saints[3].

Mosaics in a good state of preservation were reused without any restorations. By contrast, the *opus sectile* pavement in the central compartment of the narthex had suffered a great deal from earthquakes and was roughly restored. It also is true that the nave and S aisle of the Early Byzantine building remained unused, because of their ruinous condition and the fact that they had been transformed into a cemetery several centuries earlier.

---
3. Catherine Jolivet dated the wall paintings to ca. the first half of the 11th c.: Jolivet 1981.

Church

19. Middle Byzantine Church
Opus sectile floor
Illustrations 137-144, 151.

The transformation of the baptistery into a church in the 11th c. necessitated important modifications, especially regarding the floor. The abandoned fonts were filled and covered by a new pavement. Following the contemporary fashion for *opus sectile* floors, the Middle Byzantine planners at Xanthos chose this type of pavement. The peripheral parts of the earlier pavement, which were well preserved, remained in use and were sometimes restored or added to. However, the central part of the floor

138. Detail of a shield of triangles, from the Middle Byzantine *opus sectile* floor.

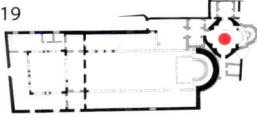

139. The original fonts were entirely covered by the medieval floor, seen here partly preserved at the time of excavation; later these plaques were removed to study the fonts.

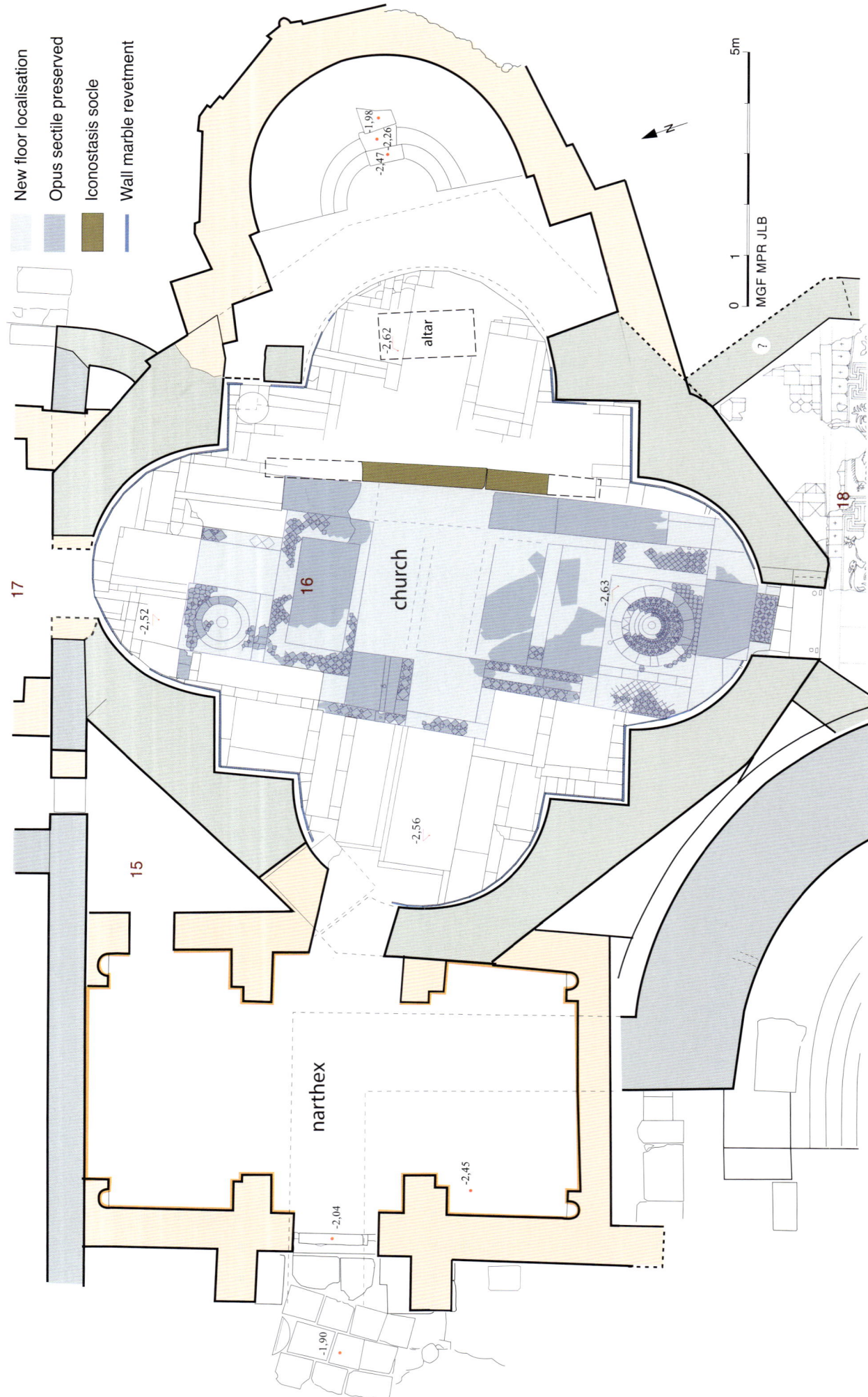

140. Plan of the new church built within the old baptistery, pavement 19.

was a completely new creation (ill. 139-140). The pieces of marble probably were salvaged from the earlier pavement, namely, the borders of the fonts and surrounding plaques. Stylistically, this surface is typical of Middle Byzantine floors of *opus sectile*[4]. Dimensions: the part newly paved is ca. 11.00 x 5.50 m.

State or preservation: it is preserved over one third of its surface; the central part covering the fonts consisted of large marble plaques, still partly preserved in 1976 (during excavation, ill. 139) and removed in 1977 by the archaeologists exploring the fonts.

Materials and colors: exclusively marble; light-colored, such as unidentified white marbles, grey marbles, Pentelic (white with thin pink veins), light blue or light grey Proconnesian (or "Marmara"), Skyrian (white with purple veins), coralline breccia (pink and red from Bithynia), nero scritto marble. The dark marbles are represented by green cipollino from Karystos, dark grey marbles, dark blue (perhaps from Aphrodisias), blue-grey, and greco scritto (from Algeria?).

Description
The overall organization is well planned, incorporating the previous remains. The part in front of a new *iconostasis* is covered by a wide plain band (probably from the edges of the fonts, very thick and strong). Bands divide the rest of the surface into panels; the bands are plain or decorated with geometric patterns (mainly lines of poised squares, *Décor* I, pl. 15). The panels themselves are square or rectangular, and the two preserved squares contain a centralized pattern. It shows a medallion enclosed in a plain circular frame, the inner pattern taking the form of a shield of triangles (ill. 138) (*Décor* II, pl. 327b) or a

141. Field detail.

142. Panel with a circular medallion; notice a medieval restoration at top left, with two reused colored marble plaques.

143. Example of field pattern.

shield of poised squares (ill. 142) (*Décor* II, pl. 335a). The rectangular carpets are filled with isotropic patterns: a chessboard of squares (ill. 143); a pattern of adjacent octagons forming small poised squares (ill. 144); intersecting and tangent octagons forming small poised squares (ill. 142). A small rectangular panel was inserted into the older pavement in the

144. Detail showing the cutting technique of the marble units.

---
4. We refer to the recent study of the East Basilica's *opus sectile* in Froidevaux-Raynaud 2005, and its bibliography. We supplement this with a publication unavailable for our study: Demiriz 2002, which offers an inventory of medieval *opus sectile* in Turkey.

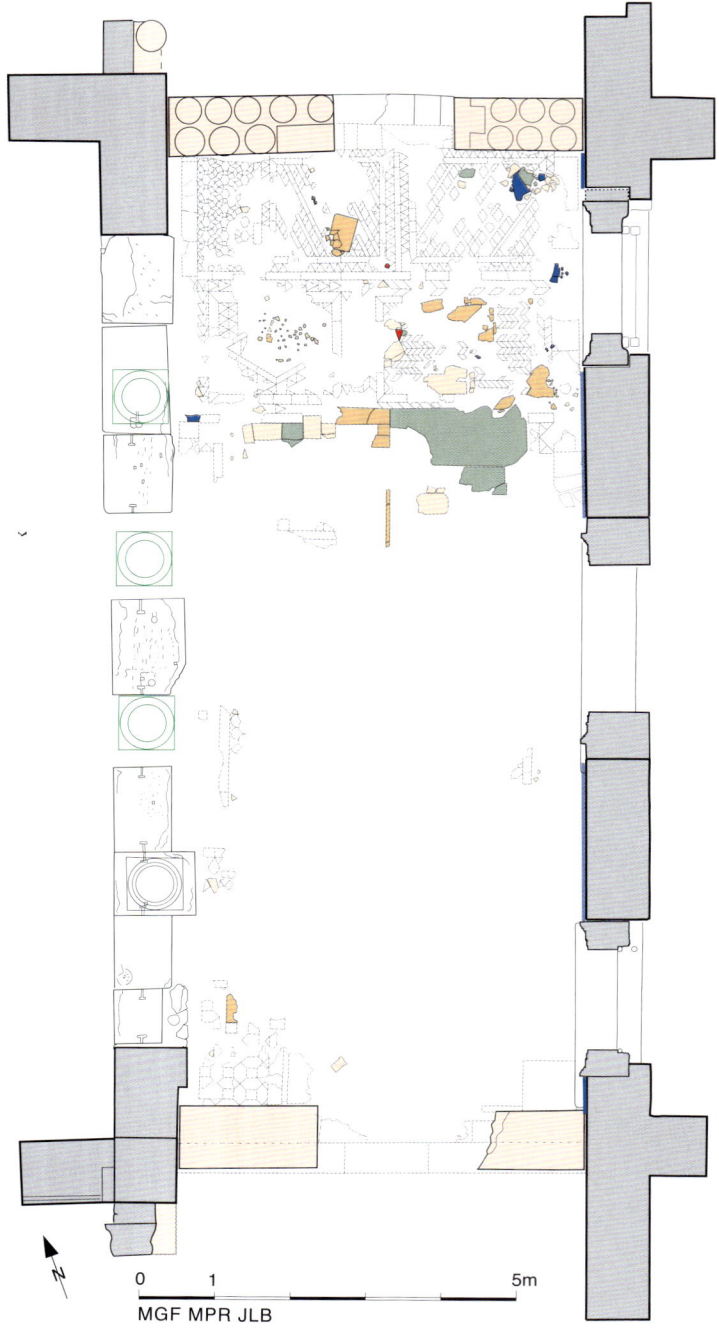

S door, skillfully filling a gap (ill.141). We also noted the restoration of a gap in the earlier part using two rectangular plaques of colored marbles (N conch; near the W wall) (ill. 142).

Commentary: the large plaques are mostly Proconnesian marble and are reused pieces probably coming from the original floor of the E conch, now hidden behind the *iconostasis*. Some large plaques are of white marble. Smaller plaques and small units of the *opus sectile* panels or bands are made of various reused marbles: we recognized white and Pentelic marble, a few greco scritto (Algeria) and Skyrian marbles, some cipollino pieces from Karystos, and nero scritto. Two plaques of middle size are made of breccia coralline (Bithynia), a colored marble that we also observed in one or two small pieces of the shield of triangles. We noticed in small units the use of dark blue or grey marble. A fragment of wall revetment with the rusty traces of its binding hook was reused in the medieval floor, as were a few fragments of marble with mouldings.

The main difference between these Middle Byzantine *opus sectile* floors and the pavements dating from the Early Byzantine period is the extremely reduced scale of the units in the later floors, even down to the size of splinters. These are not prefabricated pieces, carefully sawn to the exact shape. Rather, materials were extensively reused and the assembled pieces re-cut with a hammer to form squares and triangles, rather irregular (ill. 144). The triangles themselves were reworked into still smaller pieces to fill the leftover spaces with subdivided ornaments. Although the edges of pieces are not very even, this does not diminish the legibility of the overall design, whose structure remains clear. The chessboards and rows of poised squares alternate between single large pieces and other finely subdivided ones, creating the chief decorative effect of the pavement and giving it a varied appearance.

If the play of contrasting colors is less systematic than before, nevertheless the nuance of hues among the various materials is finely exploited.

Only marbles were used, and schist, limestone, terracotta or marlstone were abandoned as cheaper, less valuable materials, difficult to recut into very small pieces and not very durable. There is a rich assortment of stones, reflecting a preference for colored marbles in the recycling process. But we did not find precious classical marbles, such as rosso antico, porphyry (red and green), green breccia from Thessaly (verde antico), giallo antico (Chemtou), biggio antico, "flowering peach" from Iasos[5]. There were very few examples of

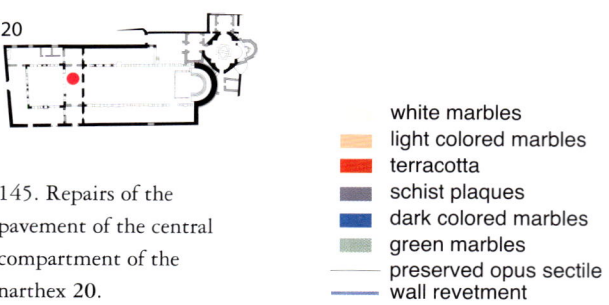

145. Repairs of the pavement of the central compartment of the narthex 20.

white marbles
light colored marbles
terracotta
schist plaques
dark colored marbles
green marbles
preserved opus sectile
wall revetment

---
5. In the contrary, in the Early Byzantine narthex, inv. **6**, these materials appear.

pavonazetto (or Skyrian) that were so appreciated in the Early Byzantine floors. Probably there no longer remained pieces of these materials at the moment when the Medieval Church was decorated.

The light grey mortar is very different from Early Byzantine mortar, appearing ashen and powdery and crumbling easily.

We also observed a great respect for the church's earlier pavements (which were restored and preserved), even to the extent of imitating their designs by using large plaques and panels separated by plain bands (ill. 140). The *opus sectile* floor from Early Byzantine times, preserved in the narthex and baptistery, probably influenced the repertory of the Middle Byzantine workshop at Xanthos. At the same time, the latter artists were well aware of new tendencies in making this kind of pavement, visible at Demre (Myra) and Amorium: patterns with large-scale interlacing, composed of bands of finely subdivided geometric ornament. Thus we may assume the existence of a local workshop influenced by contemporary fashions elsewhere.

Comparisons: this kind of medieval *opus sectile* floor[6] is composed of large interlaced centralized patterns, including large plain slabs of marble surrounded by geometric borders, and with the secondary spaces covered by geometric isotropic *opus sectile* patterns of very small scale. The diffusion of these pavements shows how they became very popular in all regions of the Byzantine world after the 9th c., especially the Near East, Asia Minor, Greece and the Balkans, but also in Italy and with less success, in Gaul or N Africa. The closest parallel, in style and distance is in St Nicholas of Demre (Myra, Feld 1975, pl III, figs. 1, 3-4; Demiriz 2002, pp. 26-30; Ötüken 2001, fig. 4; Ötüken 2002, fig. 1) with similar decorated bands made of interlocking squares and triangles surrounding plain marble plaques, and a similar shield of triangles. This pavement dates to the 11th c.[7].

We can cite some other pavements in Turkey, at nearby Amorium, Lower City Church (Lightfoot-Ivison 1995, figs. 1, 6; Lightfoot 2007, pp. 60, 85, 9th-10th c.). Also pavements in the area of Constantinople: the pavement of the Church on the Slopes of Yakacık in Istanbul (Demiriz 2002, pp. 73-83), Hebdomon, St. John Stoudios, Kalenderhane Camii, Pantocrator Monastery, area of Boukoleon Palace, and the well known examples of Iznik (*Nicaea*, St. Sophia) and Bursa. In Greece, the examples at Hosios Loukas, Mount Athos or Nea Moni on Chios. We found many examples in Sicilia (Church of the Martorana and Palatine Chapel at Palermo, Monreale), S Italy (Bari, Capua Cathedral - Speciale 2005, figs. 1-6 -, Reggio di Calabria, Montecassino), and a few cases in N Italy (S. Angelo in Formis, S. Vincenzo al Volturno, S Agata dei Goti, Salerno Cathedral).

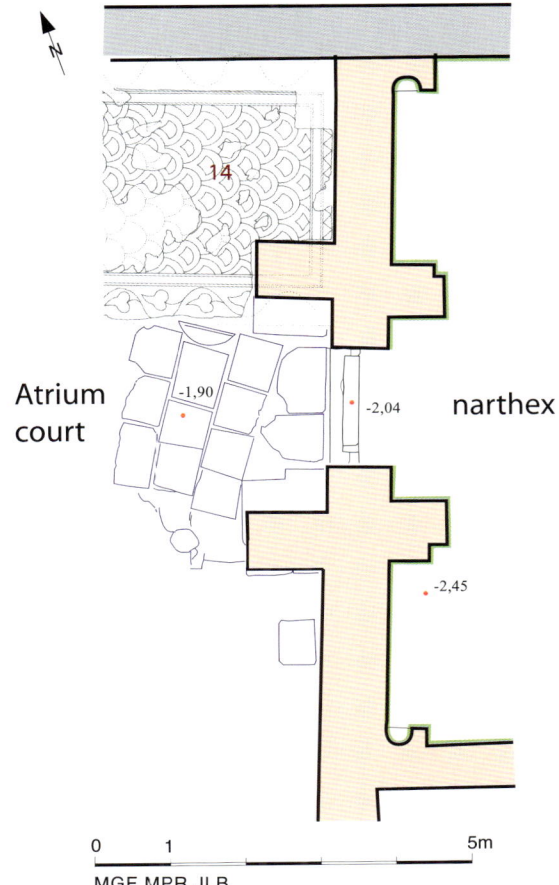

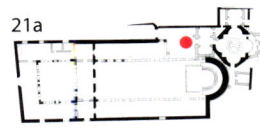

146. Pavement of rough stone slabs 21a (new narthex entry).

147. Pavement of rough stone slabs 21c.

---

6. In addition to the article already cited, Froidevaux-Raynaud 2005, see *infra* chapter "Synthesis".
7. See also Demiriz 1968 and Demiriz 2002.

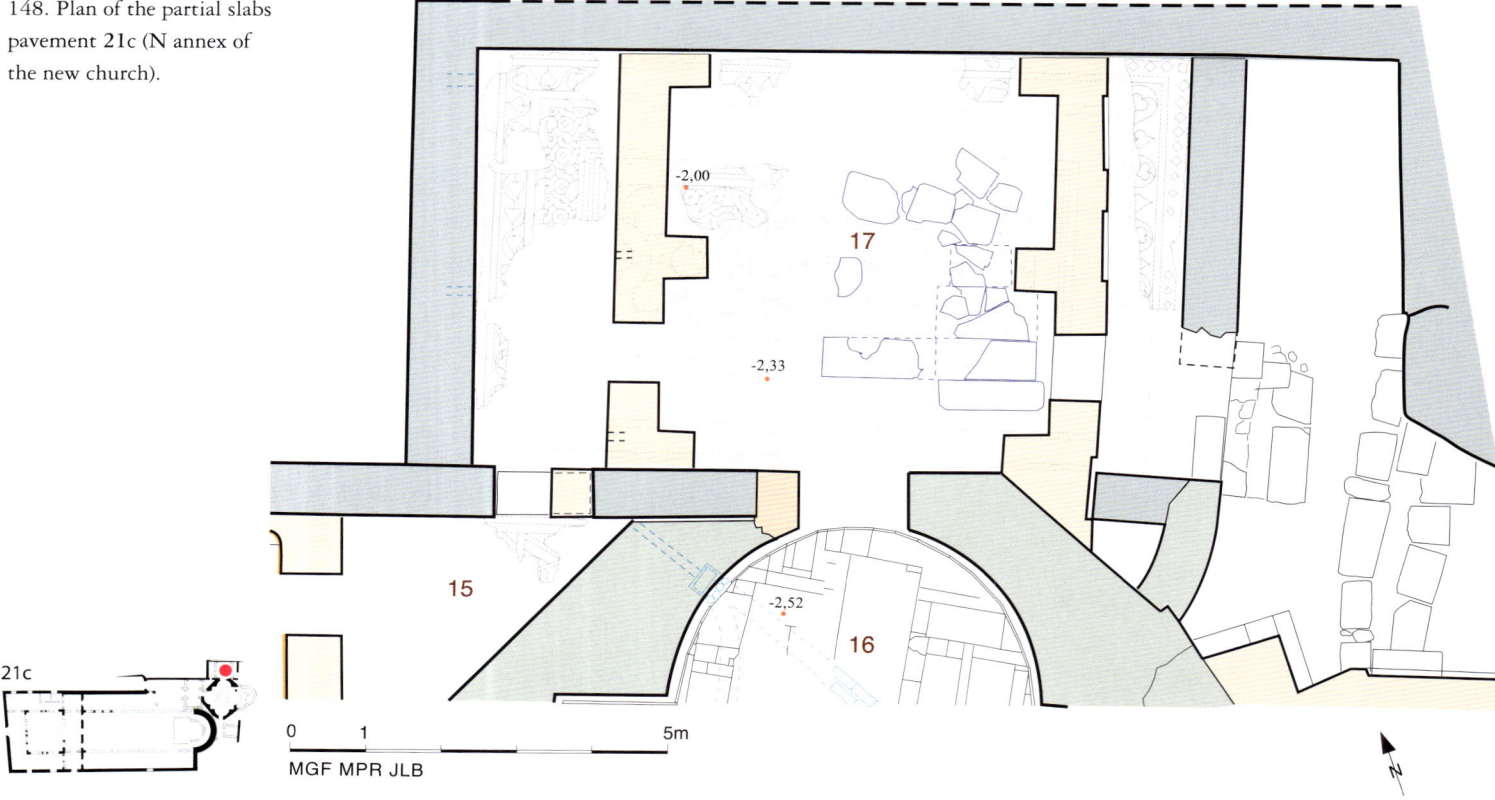

148. Plan of the partial slabs pavement 21c (N annex of the new church).

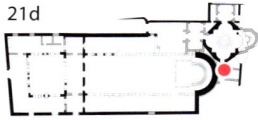

149. Pavement 21d of rough stone slabs and reused blocs (S annex of the new church).

Middle Byzantine Annexes

20. Restoration of the Ancient Narthex
Illustration 145.
During the Middle Byzantine period, the Early Byzantine *opus sectile* (inv. **6**) was partly destroyed, probably by the collapse of heavy architectural elements such as 2nd-story galleries, door jambs, lintels and beams. The Middle Byzantine workers, after clearing the overall space, roofing the best-preserved parts and building partition walls, chose to fill the gaps in the pavement with pieces of marble plaques (ill. 145), originally used as wall revetment (rather thin plaques) and here reemployed rather crudely; this made the room habitable. The restored patches do not follow the original design of the panels but simply seal the gaps. Nevertheless, the slabs were chosen carefully, with great attention given to colored marbles, in particular the very large green plaques (breccia from Thessaly) reused in panel 7. A few small, light-colored or green marble plaques were roughly aligned with the band separating panels 4 and 6; this repair work was done to prevent any further damage. It also underscores the taste for marble floors in general, demonstrated emphatically by the medieval pavement in the new church, considered the most luxurious pavement of all. This part of the building also probably received a new roof.

21. Pavements with plaques
Illustrations 146-149.
A few pavements made of stone plaques, more or less irregularly disposed and often surrounded by beaten-earth surfaces, complemented the remains from the earlier, damaged pavements in the medieval complex. They principally filled gaps rather than create elaborate pavements, and were often placed to be seen from the main rooms (in front of entrances). One finds some reused plaques before the entrance to the new narthex (**21**a), with the rest of the court's floor reusing the earlier mosaic (N part) or composed of beaten earth (S part) (ill. 146). A few plaques were also found

in the narthex itself during excavation, and were later removed (**21**b). Others occur in a small room arranged in the original N annex of the earlier baptistery (**21**c), in relation to carefully made new walls (ill. 147-148). This room is directly connected to the church through a door newly opened in the N conch. The last example (**21**d) is in the entrance to the original S annex of the baptistery, which also was subdivided by medieval walls. Plaques and walls were removed during excavation, and were found to be composed of many reused Early Byzantine fragments; it could be related to the late mediaeval occupation. A chancel post is visible in the excavation documents (ill. 149).

22. Leveling of the nave
Illustration 150.

It is an incomplete floor of small broken and reused materials (terracotta, marble and limestone), found during excavation and covering the nave mosaic in a few places (inv. **10**); elsewhere it covered the mortar of the earlier *opus sectile* pavement (ill. 150). This proves that, at the moment when this late pavement was laid, the mosaic was already partly destroyed. It follows the abandonment of the Early Byzantine church (after its roof collapsed), but we do not know if it originated in the later phase of the Early Byzantine period (contemporary with the cemetery's formation) or in the medieval reoccupation. A thin layer of lime mortar binds reused broken plaques of various shapes and sizes (ca. 2,5 cm thick). The result is haphazard and does not follow any design. The plaques are simply joined together (sometimes set on the edge) to form a flat surface, with no attempt at creating a decorative effect. We favor the notion of a medieval reworking of the area around the new mediaeval complex, together with removal of the rubble and fallen architectural features. The floor of the collapsed nave, flanking the access to the new church and no longer serving as a cemetery, was perhaps tamped down and covered with small gathered stones, all roughly leveled.

FINAL DESTRUCTION OF THE CHURCH

In the difficult period following the battle of Manzikert (1071), Turks from the interior occupied the region of Xanthos and pirates from the sea conducted frequent raids. The monks fled, closing the church's doors. Deserted, the site may have been inhabited from time to time by nomads, who dismantled the *templon* and reused its stones, aligning them in the N aisle and atrium. At the end of the 12th or later in the 13th c., a devastating fire destroyed the building and its annexes erected in the East Basilica, leaving a black layer of ashes and burned material everywhere.

OTTOMAN PERIOD

After a few centuries of subsequent abandonment, there occurred a few Ottoman settlements ca. 1 m above the previous level, as our excavations proved.

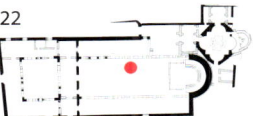

150. Leveling layer **22** (ancient nave).

III. A synthesis of the pavements

In this chapter I shall summarize the major characteristics of the basilica pavements, a study made possible by the number of floors preserved. After a brief review of other mosaics of the Byzantine period at Xanthos, I shall discuss the architectural setting of the various types of pavements, and suggest some conclusions regarding the *opus sectile* floors and the mosaics. For the mosaics, this includes the mosaic workshops and their style and influence, particular features of the basilica, the restoration program in progress, and some conclusions about iconography and chronology. Most of these points will be further developed in the forthcoming publication of the excavations in the East Basilica, prepared under the direction of Jean-Pierre Sodini.

OTHER PAVEMENTS IN THE CITY OF XANTHOS

Early Byzantine mosaics were recently discovered in the S portico of the city's main *decumanus*[1], linking the agora to the *dipylon* gate near the East Basilica (ill. 4). The N portico was probably also paved. The mosaics in the S portico consist of adjacent geometric carpets, employing simple repetitive patterns made of large tesserae. The type of décor and its treatment resemble what we observed in the church, particularly the N Atrium.

There were two other large churches, the church at the Top of the Hill[2] and the Triconch Church[3], but these have not yet been excavated.

The "civil basilica" recently discovered by J. des Courtils and L. Cavalier[4] presents an unusual figural panel within a geometric mosaic, and another pavement with a special type of inscription[5]. The geometric patterns closely resemble mosaics in the East Basilica (especially close to workshop A's production). The room situated to the N also contains contemporary mosaics[6].

The mosaics in the house on the Lycian Acropolis, to be studied in the next volume of Xanthos mosaics by A.-M. Manière-Lévêque, differ from the pavements of our church. The mosaic patterns and filler motifs are different as are all the materials used. However, the *opus sectile* floor of the apsidal *triclinium* contains panels with geometric patterns of small units, separated by schist bands, close to the baptistery floor and to parts of the nave floor of the East Basilica both of Early Byzantine date.

The mosaics in the Agora Church are very fragmentary and offer no direct parallels with the pavements in the East Basilica[7]. Nevertheless, the *opus sectile* floor of the sanctuary contains panels with geometric patterns composed of small-scale elements similar to the narthex pavement in the East Basilica, and the apse has a radial pattern of triangles like the pavement of the Byzantine Church in the Letoon[8].

Part of a mosaic carpet was recently discovered in the Agora, near the "pilier inscrit". On the basis of an excavation photograph[9], the style and the repertory seem so close to the mosaic of workshop B of the East Basilica (see particularly inv. **2**-8 and **4**) that we are tempted without further study to attribute the Agora mosaic to the same workshop.

ARCHITECTURAL SETTING OF THE VARIOUS TYPES OF PAVEMENTS IN THE EARLY BYZANTINE CHURCH

Regarding the location of the *opus sectile* pavements and the limestone and marble plaques[10], there appears a deliberate choice: they occupy systematically the most important areas of the ecclesiastical ensemble, such as the main axis of the church (atrium court, central compartment of the narthex, nave and sanctuary), and marble and schist plaques also compose the baptistery pavement. This choice reflects the special Early Byzantine taste for luxurious marble pavements. The mosaics were laid in areas of circulation (ill. 16, folding plans A and B), as a type of flooring of secondary importance.

OPUS SECTILE

Most of the kinds of pavements found in the area showing the influence of Constantinople also occur in the East Basilica at Xanthos[11].

---

1. Des Courtils-Laroche 2004, figs. 23-24.
2. This very large church is contemporary with ours. It has a plan very similar to the East Basilica, except for the extra galleries widening the building and confirming its use as a pilgrimage church, focused on a triconch chapel at its E end. Many similarities between the two churches suggest the work of a single architect (Canbilen-Lebouteiller-Sodini 1996).
3. This unexcavated church is situated near the East Basilica, on the other side of the *cardo* and a little further S.
4. Located south of the S portico lining the main *decumanus*.
5. Des Courtils-Laroche 2003, part. L. Cavalier, "L'agora supérieure", pp. 425-431, fig. 11: the N room of the civil basilica mosaic where is a verse from Homer...
6. Des Courtils-Laroche 2004, fig. 22.
7. The pavements of this church will also be included in the second volume of the Corpus of the mosaics of Xanthos (A.-M. Manière-Lévêque, Corpus Xanthos 2).
8. Metzger 1966.
9. Des Courtils *et alii* 2006, fig. 12.
10. See note 12, p. 105 (sanctuary).
11. Froidevaux-Raynaud 2005.

Early Byzantine pavements

- There is a good but fragmentary example of "*opus sectile* floor with panels made of small-scale units"[12] of the type found throughout Syria, Turkey, and Greece from the 5th c. onwards (ill. 59-62, central compartment of the narthex). The originality of the East Basilica pavement lies in its use of geometric borders. Even in similar pavements such as those found in the Byzantine Church of the Letoon and the sanctuary pavement of the Agora Church at Xanthos, which are contemporary, this feature is not present.

- The earlier nave pavement shows a combination of both "*opus sectile* floor with panels made of small-scale units" and large marble plaques separated by plain bands. This type of pavement is called a "mixed pavement" (ill. 92-93) ("un pavement mixte"[13] in French).

- The Early Byzantine baptistery pavement combines marble plaques with schist bands (ill. 124).

- The atrium court and the sanctuary are paved only with limestone and marble plaques (ill. 45).

Middle Byzantine *opus sectile* floor

The medieval fashion is well represented by the repair of the baptistery floor in order to install a new medieval church. It is a good example of this period's taste for large interlaced pavements (ill. 140, 151), made of bands with simple linear patterns of small-scale units surrounding large plaques, and panels containing a centralized pattern (shield of triangles, concentric patterns). This pavement shows that Lycian craftsmen remained in touch with contemporary artistic currents, as seen in the Church of St Nicholas at Demre (Myra), Lycia's provincial capital[14].

151. Medieval marble pavement, mixing large plaques and geometric borders.

Mosaic workshops in the Early Byzantine East Basilica

Various mosaic workshops (ill. 152-162) have been identified and are easily recognized in some places, but more difficult to distinguish in others, because of their mutual influence. These workshops are most easily differentiated in the first spaces to be paved, before there was any influence from the neighbor's style or repertory.

---

12. Type of *opus sectile* floor called "geometrico a piccoli elementi entro pannelli" in Guidobaldi-Guiglia Guidobaldi 1983, p. 319.
13. Donceel-Voûte 1988, p. 450.

14. Demiriz 1968 and Demiriz 2002, about Middle Byzantine pavements in Turkey.

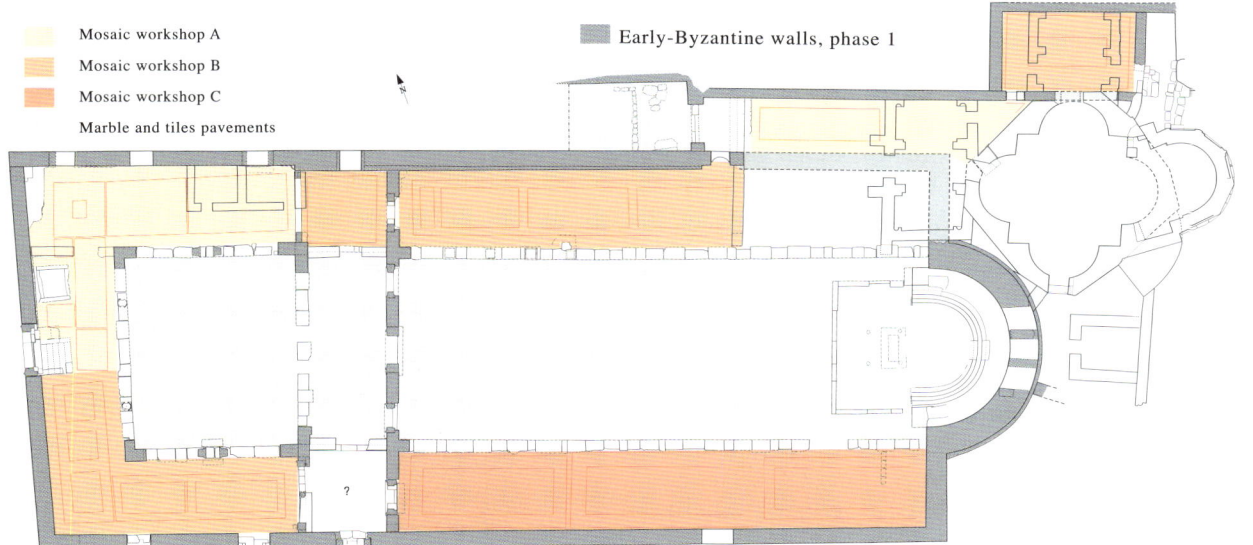

152. Plan of the first Early Byzantine phase mosaics: workshops A, B and C.

153. View of the N atrium, illustrating workshop A production (2007).

154. View of the S atrium, illustrating workshop B production (2007).

During the first Early Byzantine phase (ill. 152), three different workshops were working simultaneously. To workshop A we attribute the N atrium mosaics and perhaps also those in corridor **14**; to workshop B, easily distinguished in the S atrium, we add the N narthex mosaic, the entire pavements in the N aisle and those in the N baptistery annex. We attribute to workshop C the S aisle mosaic (first phase).

The reconstruction phase (ill. 158) of the Early Byzantine period (phase 2) is mainly represented by the activity of workshop D in the central nave and the S baptistery annex. We are tempted to join to this group the contemporary restoration of the S nave, whose style is less evident because it only intended to fill gaps by imitating earlier patterns that were partly destroyed.

A single carpet in the S narthex eludes this classification and can be attributed to an isolated workshop E, which may also have worked during the second phase.

1. Construction phase

The differences between workshop A and B are clearly visible in the atrium. Elsewhere it is more difficult to assign individual pavements unequivocally to one workshop or the other. The atrium appears to have received the first mosaic of the church[15].

Workshop A

Characteristics of the N part of the atrium:
These pavements mainly display simple, ordinary geometric patterns, and no borders frame individual fields. The patterns are linear without any original treatment of motifs. A few points help to give the workshop its identity and distinguish its designs.

- Unity of the ensemble

The carpets look simply juxtaposed since they are surrounded and separated by a white band, outlined on the wall side by a double black fillet. There is no decorated border (ill. 153) so prevalent in most Near Eastern mosaics (especially Syrian) and in other pavements of this church. The presence of decorated outer margins around this ensemble greatly unifies its appearance.

- Orthogonal organizing scheme

A strictly orthogonal scheme organizes the group of seven carpets on this L-shaped side of the atrium. There is a clear plan, overcoming the architectural intrusions (angle created by the W façade, presence of a few architectural features) (ill. 18, 153). These irregularities are discretely absorbed by the outer margins of the mosaics, whose dimensions vary.

- Illusionistic effects, depending on the use of polychromy, are a principal characteristic of this workshop, requiring ordinary patterns to be read in two different ways. An example is carpet **2-2**, ornamented with an ordinary scale pattern, transformed by the color scheme into a pattern of diagonal rows of scales (ill. 166).

- Most of the mosaics in the N atrium are drawn by white fillets, "negatively." This creates an airy design, sometimes making the pattern difficult to recognize. It is an original effect (ill. 24, 28, 29), since it is easier to draw a pattern in black and then fill in the motifs, the usual practice. This feature and the fact that the carpets are rarely framed in black, combined with the absence of borders and a limited range of motifs, give an impression of lightness and restraint to the entire ensemble.

---

15. The information in this chapter about workshops will be developed in the next archaeological publication of the East Basilica, under the direction of J.-P. Sodini. For a first study, see Raynaud 2008.

The mosaic of corridor **14** linking the church to the baptistery (ill. 121-122), below the N aisle, is very ordinary: the design consists of a very banal pattern of scales, done with very large *tesserae* (density about 25) and limited colors (black, red and white) that suggest perhaps an open-air area. The decoration of the outer margins recalls the scroll of *hederae* in the N atrium. The size of the *tesserae* has no comparison in the church and renders the attribution to a particular workshop merely hypothetical. The architectural features demonstrate that it belongs to the Early Byzantine period, and the overall impression is similar to the style of workshop A, but without any clear confirmation.

We found local comparisons in Gemiler Ada Church 1[16], namely, in the fruit tree and the pattern of oblong hexagons and squares treated as swastika meanders, which very closely resembles the N atrium mosaics at Xanthos. Another comparison was found at Patara[17], under the medieval church.

Workshop B

Characteristics of the S part of the atrium:
We initially notice the arrangement in two groups of panels (ill. 153) surrounded by dense, rich borders (ill. 18), whose importance is emphasized by their complex design on a white ground. They are sometimes richly colored. The fields have modest dimensions and display dense patterns of two types: interlaced designs with shaded bands (ill. 37-38, 156), or strictly repetitive designs of meanders and lozenges or squares (ill. 39, 42, 44). The ensemble of panels in the S half of the atrium is framed by a single external border surrounding the entire L-shaped space. Discrete and narrow outer margins link the ornamental mosaics to the walls.

- The repertory of patterns and borders features meanders, interlacing and centralized designs of intricate and complex type. In the S portico, geometric patterns display a linear effect, instead of exploiting color (ill. 43).

- Materials and colors are basic: black, white, red, pink, and blue, using *terracotta*, limestone, other local stones, and Proconnesian marble (ill. 40).

- Adaptation to the architecture: the arrangement of carpets follows the direction of the walls unlike the rigorous, orthogonal disposition visible in the N sector. Flexibility of pattern overcomes irregularities, as in the obtuse angle between the W and S porticoes. Special attention is given to carpet **2**-8, located to the immediate right of the entrance.

---

16. Ölüdeniz Area 1995, Asano 1998.
17. Woman Chapel, Işık 2000, p. 114, fig. 90.

155. Workshop B, N compartment of the narthex.

156. Workshop B, center of panel 2-8a (atrium); notice the very similar central motif.

- We also note this workshop's fine drafting skills, superb even in details. An example is the border of carpet **2**-9, where pairs of vertical spindles occur in the middle of the short sides (ill. 41), instead of the usual large horizontal spindles, thus shortening the border to fit the dimensions of the pavement. It is done in a natural way, unnoticeable at first. The way the architectural irregularities, creating the trapezoidal shape of certain carpets, are absorbed by the inner motifs of the pavements is very deft. This subtle adaptation is not visible *in situ*, but can be detected by the study of graphic layouts. One observes the remarkable overall conception of space.

The evolution of style is noticeable even within the S atrium, between carpet **2**-8 and carpet **2**-9. The latter shows an adaptation to a geometric style quite similar to the N atrium, with a distinct propensity

157. Workshop C, showing a predilection for fragmented lines; the black tesserae appear mostly in negative, made of a fragile material, different from the later neighboring panel 8-4, work of workshop D (top right).

for lines and fragmented motifs. In carpet 2-9, the design is created by a black double fillet.

The N narthex mosaic (ill. 155) presents close similarities to panels 2-8A (ill. 156) and 2-8B (S atrium), and is rich in interlaced motifs, with blue and red as the dominant colors. Some elements are different, such as the dark blue stone used instead of black to underline the motifs (ill. 47), the same stone occasionally used in the nave (workshop D). The pattern is traced in simple guilloche, a linear motif that does not appear in the atrium.

N aisle: we noticed many similarities with the work of the S atrium workshop, such as the choice of a small-module isotropic pattern (ill. 69, 73) (see atrium carpet 2-9), the same basic colors (see atrium carpet 2-8C and 2-9A and B), the taste for heavy borders (ill. 64), and a special propensity for interlaced pattern (see atrium carpet 2-8). In the N aisle, the grouping of carpets of the same size creates more unity (ill. 165). The characteristics noticed in the S atrium here seem better assimilated (more systematic), and we believe that it was finished after the atrium.

The N baptistery annex pavement is almost lost, but can be reconstructed. The organization within successive borders and the taste for interlaced motifs (ill. 128-129) are undoubtedly close to atrium carpet 2-8.

The floral filler motifs in the N narthex and the figural scene in the N aisle entrance have no parallels in the atrium; they show that this workshop excelled in making geometric patterns, but was less familiar with figural or floral motifs.

This workshop shows the greatest influence of the rainbow style. Locally, we can observe close parallels with Anemurium, especially in the church of the Holy Apostles there (module, organization, and repertory) [18].

Workshop C

Four main characteristics of this workshop can be observed in the first floor of the S aisle:

- Design traced negatively in white (ill. 83, 157) (double fillets), as we encountered in the N atrium (copying?); this is not common in mosaics, and it is one reason to insist on this point; here each carpet is surrounded by one or several borders.

- Linear network aspect of the patterns, often constituted by the blending of two patterns into a single one, giving rise to very fragmented motifs of small module. It concerns mainly panels 8-1 and 8-2 and their rare and complex patterns (of both border and field repertory), are barely legible and giving the impression of a tangle of lines (ill. 79, 81).

- Low importance given to colors, rare and light in hue, very different from workshop A, which takes more interest in colors than lines.

---
18. Campbell 1998, p. 23-26, fig. 102.

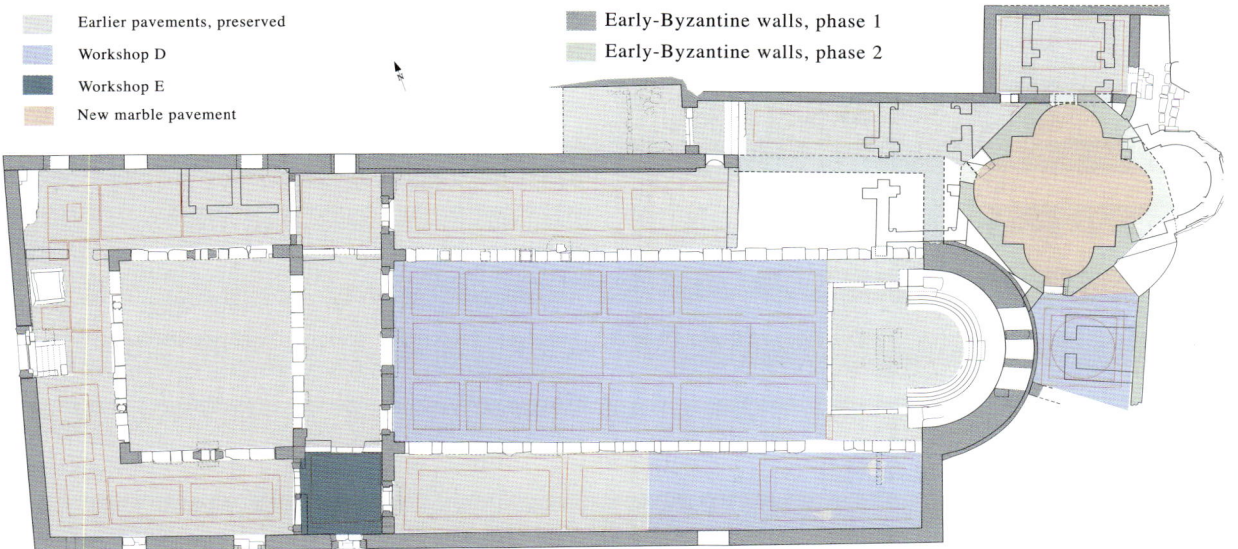

158. Plan of the second Early Byzantine phase mosaics: workshops D and E.

- Use of fragile marl for black tesserae (in reality, grey), which did not resist exposure to water, and today survives in "negative" form (ill. 157). Therefore, the mosaics are difficult to preserve, and the lack of the black tesserae causes instability.

Although the fragmentary and "linear" aspect of these mosaics could reflect some influences from workshop B (carpet Atrium 2-9), there is no overall unity of the space, since each carpet is treated independently of its neighbors, with an overall impression very different from the other workshop's production. In conclusion, the decorative aspect of these pavements is sophisticated but not pleasing.

The comparisons we found for these complex patterns come mainly from the Balkans, Greece and the islands (Thessalonica, Amphissa and Crete). For the rare border of carpet 8-2, we cite a parallel from Pisidian Antioch in Turkey.

2-Second phase: reconstruction after the earthquake

Workshop D

The large surface of the nave offers ample opportunity to observe the characteristics of this workshop: the overall pattern of this mosaic features a large grid (ill. 95) of square and rectangular panels. We note the taste for centralized patterns, small filler motifs, and colors. Observation of the support, directly borrowed from the earlier *opus sectile* floor, attests the urgency in making this pavement; it was nevertheless completed by a skilful and well trained workshop, well informed about the evolution of mosaic design, as the choice of repertory shows.

The varied repertory of isotropic and centralized patterns reflects its inventiveness: "cross of U's", wreaths of circles, stars of lozenges, and various modules of interlaced circles recall pavements of North Syria and Cilicia, both in their overall organization and in details. This taste follows the overall evolution of the repertory in the eastern Mediterranean world, at a time when simple isotropic patterns were replaced by grids of panels, with various filler motifs (ill. 159).

The S annex of the baptistery shows the same inspiration: the main border contains multiple rectangles, and the complex centralized wreath pattern of circles permits the insertion of small filler motifs such as small animals (ill. 163) and floral forms (ill. 160).

For chronological reasons, we are tempted to link this workshop with the restoration work done in the S aisle, after the earthquake that entirely destroyed the central nave, but only partly damaged the S aisle. The mosaicists here retained as much as they could of the damaged earlier carpets, sometimes creating a new décor, at other times imitating the previous work (ill. 87), but with no opportunity and no room to release their imagination and creativity. The clearer sign of this workshop in the nave — the choice of a new repertory — does not emerge in this sector of mosaics. The design, traced in white during the first phase, new becomes black in the repair (ill. 85): this is the main technical difference between the two phases of floors. We also observed that the design of the second phase is more convoluted and hesitant.

The nave mosaic recalls in a few details the mosaics found in Limyra. The overall arrangement in a grid of bands is representative of the 6th c.

159. a and b, filler motifs of the nave, typical of workshop D production.

160. S annex of the baptistery 18, floral filler motif characteristic of workshop D.

161. Detail of the support of S narthex; notice the division by lines of tile and brick sherds, and filling made of set-on-edge sherds and mortar.

fashion, here with large filler motifs attesting the survival of the rainbow style.

This new program of mosaics illustrates the way Early Byzantine mosaicists were able to improvise a new pavement with a single idea in mind: to limit the cost while maintaining a similar overall appearance[19].

Workshop E

One pavement is nonconformist: it is the floor in the S narthex compartment (inv. **5**), and it is very different from any other pavement of the church (ill. 49-58, 162). It reproduces the overall pattern of the N narthex, also present in the new nave ("U cross"), but this is the only similarity with these mosaics. The filler motifs, the colors and materials (many glass tesserae), the presence of a preparatory design, the density of tesserae, and even the way the support is carefully prepared contrast with all other mosaic activity in the East Basilica. It is the unique manner of workshop E.

The singular features of this precious pavement prevent our linking it clearly with the first or second phase, but a few elements allow us to date it to the second phase, after the earthquake.

- Use of glass tesserae could also imply the presence of mosaicists used to making wall mosaics. This material, unique in the church pavements because very fragile when walked upon, could suggest (as an hypothesis) attributing this pavement to the craftsmen who worked on the baptistery vault. The baptistery was definitely built right after the church, against its finished apse and thus could belong to the second phase after the earth tremor. But we must recall that the use of glass tesserae is frequent in pavement mosaics elsewhere, even if we do not find examples in the East Basilica at Xanthos.

- The support is totally different from traditional ones and two hypotheses are offered:

The use in the support of vertically laid fragments of tiles or bricks could be a response to the specific problem of frequent earthquakes; the resulting solution seems convenient for resisting seismic earth tremor, since it stays supple and durable (ill. 51-53, 161). It was perhaps as the result of a particularly difficult seismic experience that a sophisticated solution was found to address this recurring problem[20]. Another possible interpretation of this

---

19. Balty 1995, p. 51, « limiter les frais tout en sauvegardant les apparences », a precept that seems very relevant in most examples of Byzantine production.
20. Two similar examples of such a support have been observed in Albania, in very special conditions: the first one,

support is that this pavement was the product of a workshop not used to making pavement decoration, and not trained to create a traditional floor support, but rather wall or vault mosaics.

- Another factor, less evident, is the specific style of this mosaic and the way the pattern and the motifs are rendered here. As we observed before, it is likely that the overall pattern was copied from the symmetrical N compartment (ill. 164a), which did not suffer from the earthquake[21]. But if the overall organization is the same, the final result is very different. The "pictorial" way in which the motifs are represented, the constant use of illusionistic effects (for shadows and relief) and the striking realism of certain motifs (almost "trompe l'oeil") reflect the influence of painting, and especially recall ceiling or vault paintings. An obvious interest in relief effects and perspective, linked to the existence of a foreground and background (trees behind a fence), distinguishes this composition (ill. 57-58). In fact, it represents an exploded architectural view of a square room, with four lateral doors: surrounding the circle of the vault, the four lateral doors of the room radiate in a two-dimensional manner, with two of them opening onto an orchard (ill. 164c).

It is the realism of the rendering that permits this new interpretation of the pattern, and this was absolutely not the case in the N compartment of the narthex (ill. 155), where the linear rendering of the same pattern of a "U cross" restricts the composition to a geometric assemblage of motifs (there is no perspective and no depth). The third example of the same rare pattern in the church, very damaged, occurs in the central nave (carpet **10**-7B) (ill. 164b), but it is similar in its overall aspect to the latter – a geometric "circumcentric" pattern, more than an architectural projection. The interesting feature about this S compartment is its freedom and distance from the artistic model; it is a sign of an experience and a strong background in the representation of perspective and realism.

162. Workshop E, S narthex 5: the unusual taste for laurel garlands and acanthus scrolls can be noticed.

- This unusual use of illusionism is very surprising in the late antique pavement repertory, and it corresponds more to a new style in wall mosaics, as we observe in Ravenna or Thessalonica, to cite well-known examples of the same period.

- We noticed in this pavement the taste for floral motifs, less frequently used in Near Eastern regions than in western ones, including the laurel garland or acanthus wreath (ill. 162), which could reflect other influences than those seen in the rest of the church.

- The final observation is that the tesserae are more carefully cut and smaller than elsewhere in the church.

This room has the only pavement belonging to this workshop: is it because at that time it was the only pavement needing to be made as a replacement? Did its "sponsor" benefit from a wall workshop's presence on another job nearby (perhaps the baptistery vault), asking it to work here? Why was so much care taken at this particular location in the basilica? Some further excavations South of this space (staircases outside the church) may help provide an answer.

Repertory and influences

Most of border and field patterns are very common and ordinary, and in many cases, there is no reason for making comparisons of such grids, which would just consist of lenghty lists in order to be exhaustive. Such lists would not be instructive about dating or influences. However, in some cases the combination of patterns can be helpful for comparisons.

---

under the apse of basilica E of Byllis (excavated in 2006 under the direction of S. Muçaj and P. Chevalier, and studied by the author in May 2007), responded to a problem of stability linked to the steep slope of the hill: the declivity necessitated the building of a high foundation, and the choice of vertical sherds of terracotta correspond to a concern for solidity; we noticed here again the use of many glass tesserae. The second example occurs in the church of Vrina, near Butrint (Anglo-Albanian excavations directed by R. Hodges, in 2006), under the apse: this building lies in a flat and swampy plain and probably had to face problems linked to rising water. We thank A. Islami, restorer, who gave us this information concerning Vrina.

21. In this part of the slope there was no need for embankments, and the mosaic, well preserved, is laid almost directly on the rock.

What is usually called the "rainbow style"[22] is the most easily identifiable influence on the mosaics of the East Basilica. Most of its characteristics are reproduced here, with one feature preferred by one workshop and another by a neighboring atelier; it is remarkable that this style prevailed during both the first and the second phases, proof of its popularity. The characteristics of this rainbow style have been largely studied through mosaics of the Antioch region, Apamea, and all of N Syria. This new trend dominated mosaic art during the 4th and 5th c., all over the Mediterranean world, and very few centers of production escaped its influence. This style can be defined by the choice of geometric patterns (some often used before), and favoring the multiplication of compartments and allowing for the display of an infinite variety of geometric filler motifs. The treatment of these motifs exploits all possible gradations of color, using poised tesserae, iridescent chessboards, shaded bands, a profusion of interlaces and knots, and a taste for complex meanders. This fashion for rich geometric decoration is based on the play and sparkle of colors, with a taste for large interlaced patterns that become increasingly complicated (centralized designs)[23]. This style immediately spread abroad to Syria, Cyprus, the southern coast of Asia Minor, the Aegean islands and the whole of mainland Greece, as far North as Macedonia, Thrace, Dacia and Dalmatia. Its fullest expansion occurs in the first half of the 5th c., although this age-long tradition survived until the middle of the 6th c[24]. Its success soon extended beyond the stated region, to reach the mosaics of North Africa, Italy, and Spain and some southern parts of Gaul[25], where it, in principle, influenced the choice of small filler motifs.

It is noteworthy that the floors in the East Basilica of Xanthos, testifying to the presence of various workshops laboring during two phases of decoration, offer a good example of the variety of uses of the rainbow style.

"Workshop A" borrows the taste for "trompe l'oeil" effects, resulting in the distribution of colors in very simple patterns, although changing the original aspect of these patterns. Some shaded chessboard filler motifs directly demonstrate this influence.

"Workshop B" is probably the most affected by this style: centralized interlaced patterns, drawn by shaded bands; a taste for rich successive borders like meanders and strapworks, heavily surrounding the carpets, the use of filler motifs such as many kinds of knots, and motifs in a gradation of colors like chevrons and chessboards.

"Workshop D", which worked on the reconstruction of the Church's floors after an earthquake, had the opportunity to develop a large grid of bands on the great surface of the destroyed nave[26]. The resulting compartments are of good size, and their decoration is an alternation of centralized patterns (stars of lozenges, wreath of circles, starred octagons, U cross, concentric patterns, square of interlaced circles) and isotropic patterns, forming small-size compartments or constituted from interlaces, scales or peltae. Everywhere one sees the use of shaded bands, motifs in a gradation of colors, and knots of many sorts.

We also find in Xanthos a strong influence from mosaics of the Islands and Greece, especially in the overall design of pavements in the church: the decoration of each space or aisle is conceived as a whole. A common border unifies the succession of carpets and gives its homogeneity to the space. Symmetry plays an important role and equalizes the parts of the building, reflecting a taste for order and tranquility. This seems quite different from the Near Eastern habit of juxtaposing many carpets, varied in size and design, over all free spaces[27]. This discipline is clearly illustrated by Xanthos workshops A, B and D. The first phase is remarkable for its symmetrical organization of the overall decoration, as we observe in the reconstruction design of the aisles and probably the narthex[28].

---

22. Since the major publication of D. Levi about the Antioch mosaics, this term is in use in the study of mosaic. He defines this style as presenting "the dissolution of coloristic compactness, because of which we pass from the juxtaposition of solid spots of different colors, the succession of which is well discernible in the points of contact, to the expansion of the entire gamut of colors into parallel bands, with a predilection of zig-zag bands giving the impression of a quivering rainbow through the humidity of the air" (Levi 1947, p. 405ff).
23. The rainbow style was replaced in Syria around the middle of the 5th c. by a taste for figural scenes and animals shown on a neutral background or a *semis* of flowers.
24. Parallel to this rainbow style there developed a new trend characterized by the proliferation of animals and human figures as filler motifs. This is particularly noticeable in all regions of modern Greece and the Balkans in the 6th c., and also in the Near East, present day Jordan and Palestine.
25. The gradations of colors and other specific motifs of this style (silver-plate motif) appear in the mosaics of Aquitania, for example.

26. The grid of bands exists in all regions and periods, but it saw its most extensive use in the 6th c.; good illustrations of this trend occur in Illyria, Epirus and Macedonia. It favored the development of figural scenes, individualized in each compartment.
27. Among many examples, we can choose those of Hermione or Argos, in Epirus the sites of Nicopolis (Basilica A), Byllis (Churches A to E) or Saranda (*Onchesmos*, Church upon a synagogue), in Illyricum Caričin Grad, and in Macedonia, the churches of Stobi, Heraclea Lyncestis and Thessalonica, most of them from the 6th c.
28. Nicopolis (Basilica A) in Epirus is a good example of symmetry in the organization of the floor.

"Workshop C" (the S aisle in its first phase) displays geometric patterns, rare and complex, which favor lines over color. The comparisons for such designs are mainly found in Greece and the Islands with similar rendering. It is surely the workshop the most removed from Near Eastern influence.

The rare figural or symbolic motifs found in the basilica like the stags around a crater (workshop B) or the pomegranate tree (workshop A) are probably more commonly favored in the Balkans from the end of the 5th to 6th c.[29] than elsewhere, for example in the Near East (Syria, Jordan, or Palestine), where they mainly come into use later (end of the 6th and 7th c.).

The association of the different motifs or patterns encountered in the East Basilica shows a closer affinity to the Aegean repertory than to the Near Eastern one[30].

The last workshop, labeled "E", decorated the S compartment of the narthex. The fruit trees behind a garden fence, the acanthus clusters, and the laurel garlands all exhibit a western influence (North Africa, Spain or Gaul), a desire for realism, and the use of numerous glass tesserae recalling wall painting or vault mosaics.

The evolution of the repertory in the East Basilica is a good reflection of the overall evolution of Byzantine iconography through the 5th and 6th c. H. Maguire observed that "in the late 4th and 5th c., the dominant taste in ecclesiastical floor mosaics had been for geometric compositions, with relatively few living creatures. But by the 6th c. pavements were showing practically every type of animal, plant and fruit known to exist on earth…"[31]

This is illustrated in the Xanthos basilica by comparisons between the first-phase mosaics, almost exclusively geometric with only two symbolic scenes, and the second-phase ones, especially the pavement of the S annex. There one can observe the multiplication of pictorial and figural filler motifs, i.e., trees, birds and animals (ill. 159-160. The nave, probably executed by the same workshop, is too poorly preserved to reveal much of its content, but it demonstrates the same trend by the presence of craters, trees, and floral motifs. We can imagine that many other figures disappeared from the gaps of the fragmented floor.

163. S Annex of the baptistery. Motifs are mainly floral or animal.

This change closely reflects the evolution of theology and liturgy that we can perceive from texts, and it is common to all of the eastern Mediterranean, with differences in the results from one region to another.

The Lycian coast during late 5th to 6th centuries was a privileged place between Constantinople and the Near East and Egypt, and probably benefited, as did Cilicia, from this dual influence. The Xanthos mosaics seem a good example (melting pot) of these cultural exchanges between various regions.

A FEW RARE PATTERNS TO REMARK UPON

The "U cross" pattern has already been studied,[32] and it occurs three times in the church. These three mosaics derive from three clearly distinct workshops and were laid during both phases. This intricately interlaced pattern requires great skill. The earliest recorded examples outside Asia Minor are dated to the end of the 4th c. in Syria, and the latest ones originated in the first half of 6th c. in Greece. We have recorded 17 centralized patterns with this design, to which we add a new mosaic from Amisos (N Turkey)[33]. Overall, one finds 6 examples in Syria[34], 6 in Turkey[35], 2 in Greece[36], 1 in Bulgaria[37] and 3 in France[38]. We note a few

---

29. We can cite the pavements of Hermione, Akrini, and Longos in Greece, and of Edessa, Stobi and Heraclea Lyncestis in Macedonia.
30. For example the church of Argos, the « Hadrianic Library » (tetraconch) in Athens, or the mosaics found in Epidaurus (house and church) which show the choice of a closely related repertory.
31. Maguire 1987, p. 83.
32. See Raynaud 1996, pp. 69-102.
33. We only saw a photograph of the pavement in a short report : Akkaya 1997, fig. 3.
34. Apamea, Khirbet Muqa, Jerade, Murik, Qumhane, Dibs Faraj; Raynaud 1996, p. 69-82.
35. Misis (Mopsuestia), Sardis, Amisos, and the three examples inside the East Basilica of Xanthos (inv. **4**, **5** and **10**-7B).
36. Aigion and Delphi.
37. At Stara Zagora.
38. Two examples in Loupian (Narbonenses), and one in Séviac (Aquitania).

164. "U cross" paytern.
a: N narthex
b: nave panel
c: S narthex

variations of this pattern, based on the treatment of the angles of the design (*Décor* II, pls. 366-368). We also observed that the particular choice of filler motifs allows various readings of the pattern. With geometric and rainbow-style motifs, it is an ordinary decorative pattern (ill. 164b). With figural and floral motifs, it becomes a pretext for the multiplication of small compartments and can have a symbolic meaning (ill. 164a). With the representation of a garden behind a low fence in the U-shaped compartments, it suggests the flattened projection of a square room, opening through four arches onto an orchard (ill. 164c). This last reading occurs in the example from the S narthex at Xanthos: its originality, style and choice of motifs recall the repertory of mural paintings.

In the same vein is a carpet in the nave (panel **10**-7D) whose overall design is unknown (ill. 111) but it was obviously a complex and rare interlaced pattern[39].

The centralized pattern in the S baptistery annex seems unique (ill. 136), with a distant resemblance to a mosaic from Thessalonica, and some similarity to complicated interlaced patterns of the Near East (Jordan and Palestine).

The isotropic patterns of carpets **8**-1 and **8**-2 in the S aisle (first phase) and the border of carpet **8**-1 are quite original, especially in their linear, convoluted treatment (ill. 79, 81).

Particular choices of repertory: are they linked to the liturgy?

A few mosaic pavements in the basilica seem to reflect an artistic hierarchy through their location and the choice of iconography: they are treated more carefully and more richly than others. The most sophisticated and refined mosaics occur at what at first seem to be random locations. The first is the atrium carpet **2**-7 at the foot of the entrance stairs (ill. 18). The second area of interest is the panel in the center of atrium carpet **2**-3, located in NW corner of the atrium, at the intersection of two porticoes: it is one of the rare pictorial panels, showing a pomegranate tree. Both of these mosaics employ unusual materials, green and purple marbles, intended to attract attention. In addition, after the complex carpet with a "U cross"[40] in the N narthex, the entrance to the N aisle contains

---

39. It seems close to the centralized pattern next to the "U cross" in Amisos, Akkaya 1997, fig. 3.
40. This carpet was later imitated symmetrically in the S compartment, during the restoration phase.

another ambitious pictorial panel emphasizing the importance of that space and having symbolic meaning (ill. 165). It shows a crater representing the Fountain of Life flanked by stags and birds, meant to be seen from the door. It is badly damaged but perhaps contained the same rare materials as the previous atrium carpets. This entire arrangement may have indicated a special path of circulation, perhaps leading to the baptistery[41].

The last example of figural representation occurs in the S annex of the baptistery, where various animals, trees and birds occupy the small compartments of the composition. Their symbolical meaning is not obvious.

Polychrome effects

An original polychrome effect is observed in the atrium, particularly in what are thought to be the earliest mosaics of the church. It comes from the way common isotropic patterns use color to suggest a different reading. This is clearly evident in the N pat of the atrium (ill. 166), although the same feature occurs in a few isotropic patterns of the S atrium (**2**-8C, **2**-9A and **2**-9B), but in a lighter, less pronounced way. This tendency is absent elsewhere, even in mosaics attributed to the same workshops, as in the narthex and the N aisle. It is less noticeable in the later phase of the nave.

Mosaics-Technical features

We noticed a few technical characteristics that show the adaptability of the mosaics to disasters like earthquakes. We observed the unique support in the S compartment of the narthex, made of brick and tile sherds set on edge (ill. 51-53, 161). Various measures were taken to restore the church after the disaster, resulting from religious, economic and temporal constraints: in the nave the earlier mortar was reused to lay a new mosaic; in the S aisle, fragments of the partly destroyed mosaic were preserved by a simple filling-in of the gaps (ill. 77). These quickly reconstructed mosaics were rather fragile, due to the poor condition of their support.

We especially noted the choice of special colors and precious materials in some very significant places: rare marbles (purple or light green) were used in particularly refined mosaics (ill. 167), and an orange stone in the central part of the nave.

165. Overall view of the N aisle after restoration.

166. On this scales pattern, the unusual disposition of colors traces diagonal lines.

167. Light green and purple marbles (carpet 2-3).

---

41. This part concerning the link of the iconography with the liturgy will be developed in the publication of the East Basilica, in preparation under the direction of J.-P. Sodini.

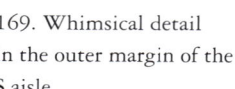

168. Restoration patch between carpet 8-1 and 8-2. The original design is not respected.

169. Whimsical detail in the outer margin of the S aisle.

170. Fragment of mosaic removed and reset with a large roll, in the nave (1988).

A few repairs, belonging to neither of the principal phases of mosaic construction, show that the repairs were made in the interval between those phases by non-professionals, who did not even try to imitate the pattern of the surrounding pavement. They consist of rough patches assuring the survival of the mosaics (ill. 168).

In two places, traces of preparatory drawings were discovered, respectively in the S aisle (carpet **8**-1, almost destroyed) and in the S compartment (**5**) of the narthex. The thin lines scored in the upper layer of the mortar are grid lines (ill. 53-54). The two pavements laid over these preparatory drawings had very complicated designs, whose completion was aided by the drawings.

The varied density of tesserae sometimes helped to determine which workshop executed a given mosaic. We provide a table of these in a supplementary chapter (Addenda).

An artist's whim?

A whimsical detail occurs in the outer margin of the S aisle, where a single flower (ill. 169) replaces the expected poised square (carpet **8**-2).

A second anomaly occurs in the common and sober design of carpet **7**-3 in the N aisle. The carpet begins on the W side with an ordinary pattern of scales, and without a formal transition (no line, band or border) it ends with a pattern of *peltae*. This would not be surprising if a boundary existed between the two parts, but here the design changes without real interruption: in fact the *peltae* are merely a different way of filling the scales (ill. 76). There is no other known example of this kind of transformation within a single pattern.

Recent restoration program

The French archaeological team in Xanthos decided to maintain the mosaics of the East Basilica *in situ*. They have been systematically reinforced during the excavations, and sometimes removed to change their support if necessary, but always put back in place. There has been consistent drainage of the pavements and experimentation with various types of protection for the floors, to prevent any walking on the surface and to preserve the mosaics from the elements and plant growth.

Three different teams worked in the church. The first French restorer, J.-M. Dupage of the Ateliers de Restauration de la Pierre et du Bois, came during the years 1986-1988. He removed a large fragment of the nave mosaic with a wooden roll (ill. 170), which permitted excavation below, the preparation of a new support, and a later resetting *in situ*. He also removed the mosaic in the S narthex compartment, which was very fragile (glass tesserae) and covered with lichen. In addition, he prepared a new support with efficient drainage and reset the mosaic in its original location, but he did not return to remove the canvas covering it.

Next, the team of P. Blanc and L. Krougly, Atelier de Conservation et de Restauration du Musée départemental Arles Antique, came on six different occasions between 1992 to 2001 and checked all of

171. Overall view of the atrium after restoration (2001).

the other mosaics in the church[42]. They filled and cleaned gaps (ill. 180-181), restored some sunken mosaics to their original level (ill. 172), removed fragments in order to replace the poorly preserved mortar (no longer waterproof), drained many areas (ill. 171), and halted plant growth. They also took special care to create temporary protection of the pavements, experimenting with various solutions before adopting the best technique under local conditions. It consisted of applying a thick layer of river sand on the mosaic (20 cm), and over that unwoven textile or plastic sheets covered by 20 cm of small pebbles[43]. The adhesive layer still covering the mosaic of the S compartment of the narthex was removed. They always tried to advise local residents about the maintenance of mosaics *in situ*, and to use local materials. In addition, they proposed returning from time to time to follow the evolution of the conservation and protection, but they have not had the opportunity to do so yet. The church was surrounded by a barbed wire fence to prevent tourists from entering it, but this type of protection is not very effective.

Since 2002, a Turkish team began to work on the mosaics of Xanthos under the direction of Ş. Yeşil Erdek. In 2007, they undertook an extensive

172. a and b: restoration of a sunken fragment, reset at correct level.

program of restoration dealing with the civil basilica, the S portico of the *decumanus*, the Baths of Leda and the protection of the residence on the Lycian Acropolis. This team also intended to begin restoring, once again, the atrium of the East Basilica, which had suffered from four or five years' constant exposure to the sun and

---

42. Concerning the restoration of mosaics *in situ*: Blanc-Krougly 1998, Blanc-Krougly 2003, Blanc 2003.
43. In 2007, ten years after this protection was put in place, the mosaics in N and S aisles were found intact. In the nave, a few bushes had grown in various places, and continue to be worrisome.

173. Narthex, central compartment 6, before and after restauration (2008).

rain[44] (ill. 153-154). They sought to cover all of the mosaics with sand and check their system of protection, in order to avoid further destruction. An annual inspection at the end of each tourist season is absolutely necessary to verify the condition of the pavements and assure their safety, while awaiting a more permanent solution. In 2008, Ş. Yeşil Erdek's team also worked on the narthex *opus sectile* which was in a very bad condition of preservation. Some wrong restorations (dating from the time of the excavation) were lifted and a unified mortar carried out, both to consolidate and to facilitate the reading of the N part of the pavement (ill. 173).

Various individuals have suggested a general program of restoration and presentation to the public, including putting roofs over certain areas and creating a path of circulation for tourists. In 1997, P. Blanc, L. Krougly and H. Canbilen (architect) proposed an overall project for restoration and presentation of the basilica floor[45]. Ş. Yeşil Erdek is now working with M. Türkeli (engineer) in a new project concerning the roofing of the western part of the basilica.

Chronology of the Building

We observed two main periods for the Early Byzantine pavements: a construction phase and a reconstruction one, both phases very close in time, and dated from the middle of the 5th to the second half of the 6th centuries[46], the presumed date of abandonment. The destruction that occurred between the two phases was due to a major earthquake,[47] frequent in these regions until today. The baptistery and its annexes, built on the east below the church, perhaps belong to this reconstruction phase.

This important campaign of rebuilding was carried out immediately, probably to re-establish in a very short time the worship in this important church: the nave pavement previously executed in *opus sectile* was entirely removed and replaced by a mosaic, a rare example of this kind. Usually it is an *opus sectile* floor which replaces a mosaic, being considered more valuable. In Xanthos, other factors influenced this choice, namely, the poor physical reaction of an *opus sectile* floor to an earthquake, linked with economic factors. A mosaic was much cheaper to produce, and the re-use here of the previous mortar attests to financial difficulties, as does the promptness of the work.

The urgency of the repairs to the church can also be seen in the S aisle mosaics, where more of the first pavement was preserved: here the gaps were filled by new mosaics, more or less following the original design. Here some parts of the earlier mosaic were deeply sunk and were

---

44. This pavement was the best preserved in the basilica, as can be seen in the photographs included in this corpus taken before damage occurred. It was carefully restored by P. Blanc and L. Krougly in 2001. It is a pity to see how quickly it has deteriorated, due to the uncovering for benefit of tourists and a lack of maintenance and yearly protection: it was in 2007 while the mosaics were at great risk of deterioration that Ş. Yeşil Erdek fortunately began its restoration.

45. Blanc-Krougly 1998.
46. This date is confirmed by the study of architecture, sculpture (capitals, chancel screens…) and ceramics, a study in course of publication.
47. Many earthquakes (Guidoboni 1994) occured in the eastern part of Mediterranean: in the surrounding region, one is recorded in 515-16 CE at Rhodes, in 518 at Sagalassos, in 529-530 at Myra, in 469 and 554 at Kos, in 560 at Arykanda and further East, at the end of 6th century at Anemurium, and in 515 and 526-528 at Antioch. The first half of the 6th c. was terribly destabilized by these repeated disasters. We are tempted to link the first disaster of Xanthos to the Rhodian one (515-516) and to place the second earthquake between 610 and 642 ; Foss 1996 II, p. 26; Duggan 2004, pp. 134-170.

covered by re-used, turned-over pieces of the destroyed mosaic (ill. 174), to re-establish the level of the new floor. It is possible that the earthquake happened before the end of the construction (phase 1), although we noticed that workshops changed between the two phases.

The church, after this reconstruction, was destroyed again in the second half of the 6th or beginning of the 7th c. by another tremendous earthquake: most of the roofs and orders of columns collapsed, and the site was abandoned as a place of worship. As the mass could no longer be celebrated any more in the Church, the sacred area near the ancient apse was used as an open-air cemetery from the middle of the 7th c.

The 11th c. witnessed the establishment of a new church inside the ruined walls, with a church installed in the preserved older baptistery and some partial reconstruction occurring in the W and N parts of the destroyed basilica. This period is interesting not only for its wall paintings representing standing saints and warriors (in the new narthex and the W annexes), but also for a fine *opus sectile* floor and an iconostasis erected in the church.

The church went out of use sometime between the end of the 11th and the first half of the 13th c., and after a period of sporadic reoccupation, a new disaster caused the total destruction of the complex, with much evidence of a major fire.

This last event marked the end of the church's use until the Ottoman period.

174. Collection of fragments reused in the second phase support, coming from the destroyed earlier mosaic: carpet 8-3 (a) and carpet 8-2 (b).

Conclusion

The decorative and technical quality of the mosaics in the East Basilica demonstrates the great experience of the various workshops that worked there at different periods, and showcases their high degree of skill. They probably had many opportunities to decorate other flourishing monuments of Xanthos in the Early Byzantine period, not only religious buildings but also secular structures. Houses of the late 5th and 6th c. are not numerous among the buildings excavated, but it is likely that mosaics also paved numerous dwellings of the aristocracy. Recent excavations clearly show how important the city was at this period, and we know that much remains to be discovered, such as the Episcopal complex located north of the East Basilica. These excavations and the study of an expanded number of mosaics of the same era could broaden our understanding of the workshops in Xanthos, and perhaps answer a question that is still outstanding: was Xanthos a center of mosaic production, as suggested both by the number of workshops laboring contemporaneously and their overall unity of style, despite their differences? Or were the workshops imported from abroad?

IV. Turkish abstract of the synthesis

MİMARLIK

KİLİSE ÖNCESİ YAPI

Kazılar sırasında, özellikle erken vaftizhanenin içine inşa edilen Orta Bizans kilisesinin narteksine yapılan derin sondajda daha erken dönemlere ait bir yapının izlerine rastlanmıştır[1]. Yamaçda halkın kullanımına açık oldugu tahmin edilen hamamsal mimarili anıtsal önemli bir yapıt görülmektedir. Orta Bizans Narteksinin altında bulunan bir mozaik fragmanının motif ve stilinin göstergeleri, zeminin büyük olasılıkla Roma yapıtına ait olduğunu göstermektedir. Ancak binaya ait hiçbir duvar ayakta kalmamıştır.

ERKEN BİZANS KOMPLEKSİ: DOĞU BAZİLİKASI

Doğu bazilikası yaklaşık 2400 metrekareyi kaplayan çok büyük bir yapıdır. *Cardo*'nun aşağısında bulunan merkez avluyla beraber üç portikli atrium ve narteksin bir bölümü olarak dördüncü portiğe sahiptir. Kilise 2/1/1 oranında bir orta nef ve iki yan nef, sunağa doğru U biçimli bölmeler ve *synthronon*'lu ve ortasında piskopos için bir cathedra olan bir apsisten oluşur.

Kuzey nefin ortasında bir kapı bulunur ve bu kapı kilisenin daha aşağıdaki bir düzeyde yandan çevreleyen ve apsisin kuzeydoğusunda ve iki metre altında *tetraconch* formundaki vaftizhaneye doğru yönlendiren bir koridora bağlıdır. Bu geniş kubbeli alan (100 metrekareden fazla) iki bölümlü çeşmeler içerir. Kuzey ve Güney ekleri bu yapının dinsel bütünlüğünü tamamlar ve kuzey ekindeki bir kapı güneydoğu yönündeki şehir kapısını bazilikaya bağlar. Olasılıkla merdiven içeren narteks'in yanındaki odalar henüz kazılmamasına rağmen sütunların, sütun kaideleri ve iki farklı ölçekteki sütun başlıklarının varlığı narteks ve neflerin üzerinde ikinci kat galerisinin olduğunu ispatlar. Heykel dekorasyon'larının çoğu (büyük oranda Marmara Adası mermerinden yapılan) istisnai olarak az sayıda yerel oval şekillendirilmiş yivli süsler ve devşirme malzemelerle beraber sütun başlıkları haricinde muhtemelen Marmara adasından veya İstanbul'dan ithal edilmiştir. Yapı bir bütün olarak genel form açısından ve birçok mimari detay bakımından İstanbul'daki St. John Stoudios Kilisesini anımsatır.

Önemli bir piskoposluk kompleksi muhtemelen başlıca kuzey tarafı olmak üzere kiliseyi çevreliyordu, ama bu yapıda henüz kazı yapılmamıştır.

Atrium

Atrium kireçtaşı levhalarla döşenmiş orta avluyu çevreleyen üç portiğe sahiptir. Kuzey, Batı ve Güney portiklerindeki mozaik döşemelerin kenardan kenara yerleştirilmiş geometrik halılar gibi sade bir şekilde düzenlendiği görülür. Keskin bir gözlemle iki ayrı atölyenin aktiviteleri ayırt edilebilir: bu farklılıklar genel olarak zeminlerin düzenlenmesi, bordür kullanılışı veya kullanılmaması ve basit desenlerle karmaşık desenlerin arasında yapılan seçimler, ayrıca malzemelerin seçimi, renkler ve mimari çevre hakkındadır.

İki homojen toplum etkisi görülmektedir:

Atrium'un kuzey yarısında kuzey portiğini ve batı portiğinin kuzey kısmının giriş merdiveninin ayağına kadar olan kısmını süsleyen yedi mozaik döşeme bulunur.

Bu sektördeki mozaikler env. 2-1'den 2-7'ye bir L oluşturur. Bitişik döşemeler birbirlerinden devam eden beyaz bir bantla ayrılır. Bu bant ayrıca dış kenarları da ayırır. Döşemeler arasında bordürler yoktur ve onların gruplanması batı portiğinin duvarı boyunca uzanan giriş merdivenlerini, bir temizlik havuzu veya *pediluve* ve bir künk etrafındaki duvar işçiliğini içeren çeşitli mimari özellikler tarafından belirlenir. Mozaiklerin döşenmesinden önce inşa edilen bu üç mimari özellik mozaik sanatçıları tarafından dikkate alınmak zorunda kalmıştır.

Atrium'un güney bölümü portik koridorlarını işgal edem mimari özelliklere sahip değildir, bu yüzden döşemelerin düzenlenmesi daha basittir. Mozaikler homojen bir topluluk biçiminde iki gurup panel halinde düzenlenmiştir: Batı portiğinde (köşeyi de içerir), üç panele ayrılmış uzunca bir yüzey vardır (env. 2-8 A'dan C'ye) ve güney portiğinde iki panelli bir grup (env. 2-9, A ve B) tarafından oluşturulan tek bir döşeme vardır. Her bir grubu kendi içerisinde de panellere ayıran geniş bordürleri vardır. İki uzun döşeme 8 ve 9 duvarlara paraleldir ve onlara dış bir kenar boşluğu ve devam eden mozaiklerin tümünü güney bölümünde geniş bir L içerisinde gruplayan ve kuzey atriumdan açıkça ayıran bir sarmaşık motifi tek bir dış bordürle bağlıdır.

Kuzeye doğru açılan üç kapı muhtemelen piskoposlara ait kompleksle ilişki içerisindedir; diğer ikisi güneye açılır ve portik stylobatının merkezinde merkezi bir avluya doğru üç açıklık daha vardır (env. 3) Bu üç kapının her birinin yanal bölümleri korkuluklarla düzenlenmiştir.

---

1. Jean-Pierre Sodini idaresinde hazırlanacak Doğu Bazilikası Kazı Çalışmalarının yayınlanması ile bu noktaların çoğu geliştirilecektir.

175. Kite view of the East Basilica/Doğu Bazilikası uçurtmadan görüntü (uçurtmadan çekilmiş genel fotoğraf).

Narteks

Narteks kilisenin güney ve kuzey duvarları arasındaki doğu portiğini bütünüyle kaplar (27 x 5.20 m.) üç bölümden oluşur, bölümler iki stylobat tarafından toprak seviyesinde açıkça ayrılmıştır: her biri narteksin bir köşesinde olan ve ortada hücreli kare şeklinde bölünmüş büyük bir dikdörtgen alanı çevrelemektedir. Alanın bu şekilde bölünmesinin oranlarıyla, atrium ve kilisenin oranları aynıdır. Bir ikinci kat galerisi bu doğu portiğini kaplar, bu yapı atriumun diğer portiklerinde varolmamaktadır.

Kuzey ve Güney bölümlerinin ikisi de Erken Bizans Dönemine tarihlenen mozaiklerle döşelidir (env. 4 ve 5). İkiz kompartımanlar dış alanlara açılan kapılarla bütün taraflardan açıktır, örneğin alanlar kiliseyi simetrik olarak sararlar ve muhtemelen ikinci kat galerilerine açılan merdivenler bulundururlar. Atrium'un portiklerinde, ilk giriş çok açıktı ve daha sonra yanal payandalar ve orta sütun tarafından desteklenen iki kemerle daraltıldı. Orta Bizans Döneminde, çoğu eşiklerle daraltıldı veya kısmi olarak örülen duvarlarla kapatıldı.

Ortadaki alanın genişliği, avlu ve orta nef'in genişliği eşittir. Batıda arşitrav ve ikinci kat galerisini destekleyen dört uzun sütun tarafından; stylobatın ortasında bir giriş ile çevrelenmiştir, bölmeler sütunlar arasındaki yanal alanları kapatmıştır. Doğuya doğru Likya arşitravlarıyla çevrelenerek büyük bir ihtişam etkisi veren yeniden kullanılmış olan üç kapı orta nefe açılır. Orta kapı özellikle geniştir (3.76 x 1.85 m.), oysa daha küçük yanal girişler yaklaşık iki metre uzunluğundadır. Narteksin ortasındaki döşeme yüzeyinin üçte biri korunmuş çok güzel bir *opus sectile* (env. 6) ihtiva eder. Bu döşeme kısmi olarak çoğunlukla kuzey tarafı olmakla birlikte, Orta Bizans yerleşiminde restore edilmiştir.

Kuzey Nef

Kilisenin kuzey nef'inin orijinal uzunluğunun yarısından biraz fazlası kadar bir bölümü Erken Bizans dönemindeki hali ile korunmuştur (env. 7-1'den 3'e kadar). Doğu bölümü, özellikle Orta Bizans döneminde orijinal vaftizhanenin üstüne inşa edilen yeni kilisenin önünde ek boşluklar açılmak istenmesi yüzünden tahrip edilmiş ve kazılmıştır. Erken dönem Bizans kilisesinin tabanının yaklaşık iki metre altında olan yeni kilisenin katına doğru açılan Kaba bir Orta Bizans merdiveni, yerdeki döşemenin 7-3'ünü keserek döşemenin altına inşa edilen yeni Bizans kilisesine bağlanmıştır. Muhtemelen başka bir döşeme 7-4 bir zamanlar nefin kaldırılan doğu kısmını süslüyordu. Aynı kapsamlı yenileme süresince, ilk Erken Bizans yapısına ait merdivenler ve vaftizhaneye giden koridor neredeyse tamamen tahrip edilmiştir. Ve nefin Kuzey duvarındaki kapı bir Orta Bizans dönemi nişiyle kapatılmıştır. Kuzey nefte yer alan diğer bir simetrik kapıda muhtemelen aynı dönemde kapatılmıştır.

Kuzey nefi, orta neften daha önce kullanılmış ve orta nef tarafında dikkatli bir şekilde, kuzey tarafında ise düzensiz bir biçimde dizilmiş bloklardan inşa edilmiş olan bir stylobat ile ayrılmıştır. Stylobatlar ikinci katta bir galeriyi destekleyen sütunları (veya sütunlar tarafından desteklenen altlığı) desteklemiştir, korkuluklar desteklerin arasındaki boşlukları kapatmıştır.

Önemli bir kubbe formlu havuz (sarnıç) kuzey nefin altında yer almaktadır. Mozaik ve stylobat, havuzu (sarnıcı) kısmı olarak kapattığından dolayı farz edebiliriz ki, havuz kiliseden önce inşa edilmiştir veya kilisenin kullanımı için yapılmıştır. Havuz (sarnıç)'un kaynağı muhtemelen Orta Bizans Döneminde, atriumun kuzeybatı köşesinden gelen ve havuzda biten künk tamir edildiği zaman yeniden inşa edilmiştir.

Daha önce belirtildiği gibi, Erken Bizans yapısının korunan kuzey tarafı her ne kadar kilisenin geriye kalan kısmı kısmen tahrip olmuşsa da Orta Bizans döneminde de kullanımda kalmıştır. Kuzey nefin korunan bölümünün üstüne Orta Bizans döneminde yeni bir çatı konmuştur. Modern kazılarda bu alanda yapının tamamen terk edilmesinden sonra dağılmış mimari öğeler (sütunlar, büyük bloklar) bulunmuştur ve bazı yerlerde bu öğeler büyük baş hayvanlar için kaba bir çit olarak yapıya direk olarak Erken Bizans zemininin üzerine adapte edilmiştir (Geçici Osmanlı Yerleşimi).

Güney nef

Kuzey nefte olduğu gibi, güney nef de orta neften, devşirme olarak kullanılmış blokların orta nefin iç köşesinde dizilmesiyle oluşan ve güney nef yönüne doğru düzensiz bir görünüm sergileyen stylobatla ayrılmıştır. Sadece bir yönde korunan alçak duvar, mozaiği nefin doğu kısmının bitiminden 2.80 m. önce kesmektedir. Bu duvar daha erken zeminlerden hemen sonra inşa edilmiş ve muhtemelen doğu ekini orta neften ayıran bir bölme olarak hizmet görmüştür (alçak korkuluk?). Geç bir banket ikinci bir safhada güney duvarının bir bölümüne karşı yerleştirilmiştir.

Kilisenin güney nefinin mozaikleri (env. 8-1'den 5'e) okunması ve yorumlanması, daha kötü korundukları için kuzey tarafındakilerden daha zordur. Dikkatli bir gözlemle motiflerin arasındaki devamsızlıklar görünebilir; birkaç örnekten biri olarak, bitişik parçalarda aynı motif farklı yollarla icra edilmiştir, bu da bize farklı 'ellerin' varlığını kanıtlamaktadır. Ayrıca bazı geç ve gelişigüzel antik onarımlar da gözlemlenebilmektedir.

Güney nefteki yakın dönem restorasyonları önemli birkaç keşife vesile olmuştur: bir hazırlık taslağının izleri ve mozaiğin iki temel safhası saptanmıştır, bu keşifler kilisenin arkeolojik tarihini açıklamaya yardımcı olmaktadır. Bu izler aynı zamanda bu alanda acele bir yeniden süsleme yapıldığını göstermektedir: döşemelerdeki boşluklar önceki dekoru taklit eden kaba bir tasarımla hızlıca onarılmıştır. Bu sektörde arkeologlar ve restoratörler arasındaki işbirliği onların yardımları ile mozaiklerin altında yapılan sondaj çalışmalarına izin vermektedir ve destekleme çalışmaları kendilerine önemli bilgiler sunmaktadır. Bu alandaki mozaiklerin gözlemi mimari kontekst ve heykel süslemeleri kolay yorumlanamadığı taktirde onların kronolojilerini daha iyi anlamamıza da yardım etmektedir.

Doğu kısmındaki 'açık alan' kazıları erken Bizans kilisesinin yıkımı ve bir tapım yeri olarak terk edilmesinden sonra oluşturulan mezarları bulmamıza olanak sağlamıştır. Mezarlardaki kalıntılar, bu mezarlığı 7. yüzyılın ikinci yarısına tarihlemektedir.

Bu yapının Erken Bizans dönemi için relatif kronolojisi, güney nefteki bu bölgedeki geniş kapsamlı çalışmalarına dayanmaktadır.

Orta Nef

Kilisenin orta nefi çok geniştir, girişten bitişik kutsal alana kadar 30.70 x 13.20 m. ölçülerindedir. Orjinal olarak devşirme sütunları ve neflerin üzerinde yer alan ikinci kat galerilerini destekleyen bir stylobat bu alanı iki nefe böler. Apsler, yüksek ve geniş pencereler ve üç geniş delikle aydınlatılmıştır. Orta kat kemerli bir kapıyla, merkez alana açılmıştır (kemer de chanceli taşımaktadır).

Orta nef kapatılmıştır ve sadece Erken Bizans dönemi sırasında tapım için kullanılmıştır, ama bu göreceli olarak kısa olan zamanda bile, zemin 5. ve 6. yüzyılın sonu arasında bir buçuk yüzyıl içinde döşenen iki çok farklı tipte döşemeye sahip idi. Yapının konstrüksiyonundan tarihlenen ilk döşeme, env. 9, *opus sectile*'nin elemanları ve taş plakaların karışımından oluşmaktaydı. Bu döşeme ani bir şekilde tahrip olmuştur ve bütün yıkılan ögelerin kaldırılmasından sonra daha erken zeminin

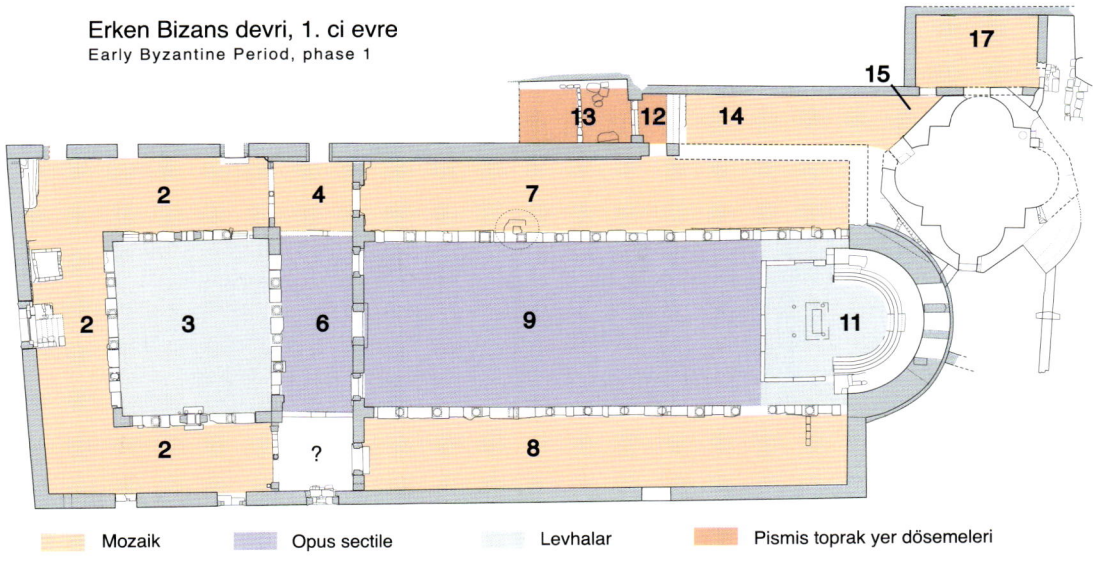

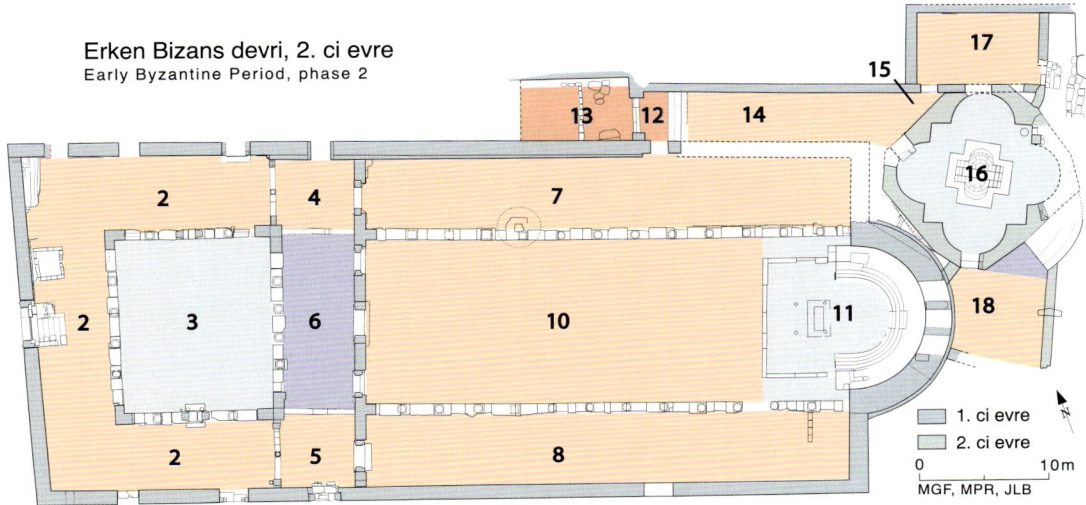

176. Plans of the two Early Byzantine phases of the floors/ Tabanların iki Erken Bizans evresine ait planları.

korunan desteğinin üzerine direk olarak konulan yeni bir mozaik döşeme ile yer değiştirmiştir (env. 10-1 to 13). Plakaların izleri mozaiğin boşlukları arasında görülebilmektedir ve bunlar kayıp *opus sectile*'lerin yeniden inşa edilmesini sağlar.

Yapının son terk edilişi muhtemelen 7. yüzyılın başında ani bir felaket sonucunda bazilikanın çatısının çökmesinden sonra gerçekleşmiştir. Eski kutsal alanın yanında olan bu kutsal yerin içine mezarlığın yapılışı, mezarlar kazılmasına bağlı olarak döşemelerin tahribine neden olmuştur. Mezarlarda 7. yüzyıl ortalarına tarihlendirilebilecek bazı kalıntılar bulunmuştur, bu mezarlardan birinin tarihi antropolojik çalışmalarla kanıtlanmıştır.

Orta nefteki hem birinci hem de ikinci döneme tarihlenen döşemeler iki stylobat arasındaki alanı Batı duvarından kutsal alandaki bölmeye kadar bütünüyle kaplar. Kutsal alan stylobatı *synthronon* ve apsisin önünde 9.00 x 5.40 metrelik dikdörtgen bir alanı kapsar. Kuzey ve Güney yönlerinden mermer plakalar döşenmiş dar koridorlarla çevrelenmiştir (env. 11), böylece yandaki antrelerden kutsal alana giriş sağlanmış ve bir eşikle orta neften ayrılmıştır. Kutsal alanın orta nefe bakan eksenel kapısı muhtemelen merkezi bir *ambo*'ya çıkmaktadır, bununla birlikte bu alandan hiçbir şey kalmamıştır: nefin doğu bölümünün tümü daha sonraki dönemlerde yapılan birçok mezarın inşası sebebiyle kötü bir şekilde *ambo* tabanından iz bırakmayacak şekilde tahrip olmuştur.

Vaftizhaneye giriş

Kilisenin kuzey nefinin kapısının kuzeyinde bir tür vestibulum (antre) yer almaktadır. Bu hem soldaki bir kapıya (Kuzey batı ekini meydana getirir) hem de üç basamak aşağıda yer alan sağdaki koridora girişi sağlar ve vaftizhaneye doğru açılır. Hem vestibulum hem de soldaki oda (env. 12 ve 13) pişmiş toprak kiremitlerle döşenmiştir. Kaba bir mozaik koridor zemini süslemiştir. (env. 14 ve 15).

Vaftizhane ve Ekler

Erken Bizans vaftizhanesi, kilise ve apsisin inşasının bitiminden hemen sonra kilisenin doğu ucunun altına inşa edilmiştir. Vaftizhane bir karenin içine yerleştirilmiş bir *tetraconch*[2]. Plana sahiptir, *tetraconch* karenin köşesindekilerden daha küçük gözükür. Vaftizhanenin dış şekli, hali hazırda olan kiliseye uyarlanması sonucunda bir takım düzensizliklerle beraber dengeli bir kare biçimindedir. Vaftiz kurnalarının üzerindeki tonoz mozaiklerle kaplanmıştır ve 13. yüzyılda Orta Bizans kompleksini tamamen harap eden aynı yangında tahrip olmuştur. Kemer mozaiği küçük parçalara bölünmüş bir biçimde zemini kaplayan yıkım tabakasının içinde bulunmuştur. Giriş kapısı çapraz bir biçimde batı *conch*'a açılır, ve kuzey koridoruna bir *tetraconch* ile bağlı (daha alçak bir seviyede) giriş koridoruna çıkar. Güney *conch*'un eksenindeki diğer bir kapı vaftizhanenin güney ekine açılır. Vaftizhanenin duvarları taş kaplama, mermer kaide ve pilasterlerle kaplı idi. İlk olarak, vaftizhaneye kuzey ekten herhangi bir geçiş yoktu, sadece koridor 15'e açılan bir alan vardı.

Vaftiz kurnaları: Kurnanın haç formlu bordürleri yeni Orta Bizans kilisesinin inşası sırasında bilinçli bir şekilde tahrip edilmiştir. İçi doldurulmuş ve yeni bir döşeme tarafından kapatılmış olan kurnalar iyi korunmuştur. Basamaklı formda iki yarım daire biçimli, her birinin sonunda üç basamak bulunan doğu-batı ekseninde dar bir koridorla ayrılan bir havuz şeklinde düzenlenmiştir. Bu koridor bitişik havuzların yanlarında bulunan dikey ince mermer paneller sayesinde sudan korunmuştur. Böylece dinsel tören esnasında havuz ağzına kadar doldurulduğunda bile rahip kuru kalabiliyordu. Merkezi koridorun her iki tarafında da dar beş basamaklı bir merdiven kurnaya doğu ve batı tarafından girişi ve diğer taraftan çıkışı sağlamaktaydı. İki yarım daire şeklinde havuz üç basamak vasıtasıyla yükselmektedir. Kurnalar çeşitli mermer tipleri ile düzenlenmiş zengin bir kaplamayla kaplanmıştır. Her bir havuzun dibi açık bir zemin üzerine kaba bir yeşil haçla süslenmiştir.

Zemin: Vaftizhanenin Erken Bizans döşemesi kurnaların kontürlerinin etrafında haç biçiminde düzenlenmiştir (env. 16). Bu kurnalar tam olarak *tetraconch*'un kuzey-güney ekseniyle dizilmemiş, vaftizhane girişine çapraz yerleştirilmesi için kuzey batı-güney doğu yönüne doğru sapmışlardır. Döşeme plakaları kurnaların köşelerine paralel ve dikey bir biçimde yerleştirilmiş ve merkezden köşelere doğru uzatılmıştır. Duvarların yanındaki rezidüel alanlar düzensiz formlu plakalarla doldurulmuştur.

Merkez kurnalar Orta Bizans döneminden bir döşeme tarafından tekrar kaplanmıştır. Bundan dolayı döşeme en iyi dış kenarlarda korunmuştur.

Kuzey ek: Geniş bir dikdörtgen oda (9.50 x 5.60 m. ölçülerinde) vaftizhaneyi kuzey tarafından çevreler ve Kilisenin Erken Bizans safhasındaki inşasıyla çağdaştır (mosaik 18) Ana ekseni doğu batı yönündedir; eke giriş güney duvarının batı ucundaki, bu bölümde keskin bir açı formu gösteren vaftizhanenin önündeki küçük vestibüle açılan bir kapı vasıtasıyla sağlanmaktaydı. Doğu duvarı dışa çıkışı sağlayan kaba ve dar bir kapı ile delinmiştir.

Güney ek: Bu alan kilise apsisinin hemen altında, direk olarak vaftizhaneye açılır bir şekilde yer alır (güney *conch*'taki güney kapısı). Zemini (env. 18) vaftizhaneyle aynı seviyededir. Bu odanın formu karmaşıktır, kilise apsisinin batı kıvrımı ile kuzeydeki vaftizhanenin küçük güney *conch*'u arasında sıkıştığından dolayı (poligonal dış duvarları), doğu sınırı bir açı oluşturur (muhtemelen yerin doğal eğimine bağlı olarak) güney sınır yamaca düştüğünden dolayı bulunamamıştır. Erken Bizans mozak ustaları bu alana geniş kare bir döşeme yapmaya karar vermişlerdir. Kuzeyde ve düzensiz batı tarafının geniş dış sınırında köşeleri ve çevreleyen bölümleri *opus sectile* ve mermer plakalarla doldurmuşlardır. Bu mozaiğin bir bölümü ortaçağ'da yeni yapılar inşa edildiği sırada bilinçli olarak tahrip edilmiştir.

ORTA BİZANS YAPISI

Muhtemelen 11. yüzyıl başlarında, Orijinal Doğu Bazilikasının göreceli olarak daha iyi korunmuş bölümlerinde bir yapı inşa edilmiştir ve daha eski zeminlerin çoğu bu dönemde tekrar kullanılmıştır. Kalıntıların genel bir temizliğinden sonra, yeni kurum eski atrium, narteks, kuzey nef ve vaftizhanenin yerini almıştır.

En önemli fiziksel değişiklikler kubbeli vaftizhanenin yeni bir kiliseye dönüşmesidir. Eski vaftiz kurnalarını çevreleyen bir *opus sectile* döşeme (env. 19) ve önceki Doğu *conch*unun yerini alan *synthronon*lu geniş bir Doğu apsisinden önce (farklı bir yönelimle), bir Deisis betimi ile süslenmiş bir templon inşa edilmiştir[3]. Ayrıca, kuzey *conch*undan kuzeydeki ek bölüme doğru bir kapı açılmıştır. Güney ve kuzey eklerinin her ikisi de duvarlarla daha küçük kısımlara bölünmüşlerdir (env. 21c, 21d).

Batıdaki girişin Yeni kilisedeki konumu, geçmişe nazaran önemli ölçüde değişmiştir. Yeni kilisede,

---

2. *Tetraconch*: dört conchdan oluşan yapı. *Conch*: üzeri yarım kubbeli yarım daire niş.

3. Sodini 1980.

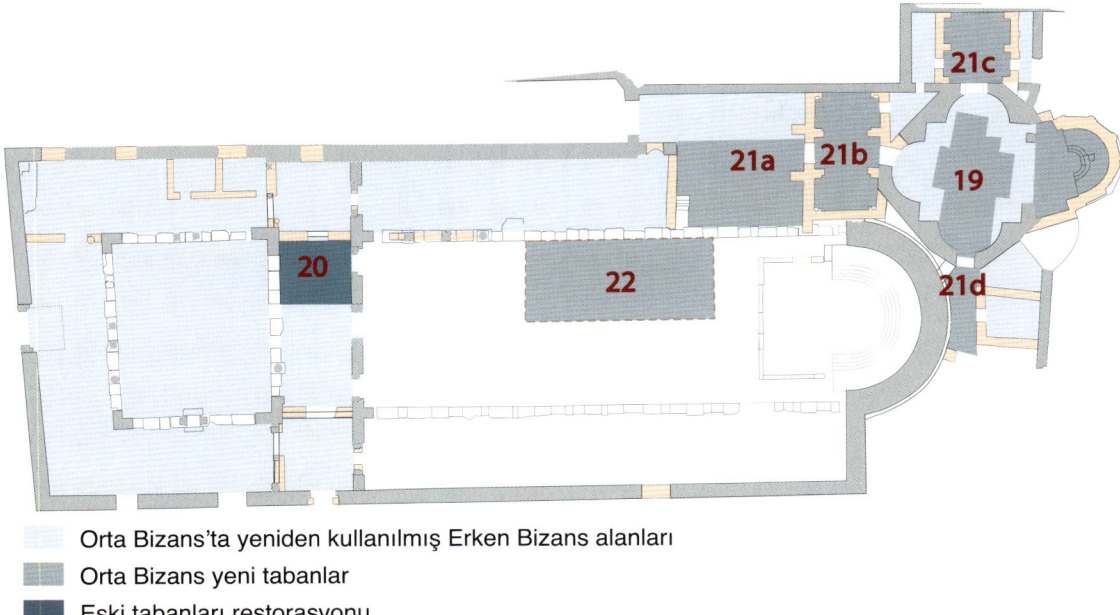

177. Plan of the Middle Byzantine complex with numbers of the floors/ Orta Bizans yapısı. Taban numaraları.

orijinal Erken Bizans yapısının altında 1.85 m. derinlikte kazılarak ortaya konan giriş batı yönü daha etkileyici kılmıştır (bu suretle kuzey nefin yarısı tahrip olmuştur) ve *tetraconch*un önünde 14.50 m. lik bir mesafe dönüştürülmüştür. Aynı zamanda, bitişik, daha erken döneme ait koridor güney yöne doğru uzanmış ve bu alanın tümü bir açık hava atriumu haline gelmiştir (ca. 10 x 11 m.), zeminin geri kalanı muhtemelen sıkıştırılmış toprak ve birkaç plakadan oluşmaktadır. Daha doğuda var olan tüm yapıların yerle bir edilmesinden sonra tamamen yeni bir narteks yaratılmıştır. Narteks üç paralel fıçı formlu kemer tarafından çevrelenen ve duvarları hiyerarşik olarak, piskoposlar, kutsal rahibeler ve şehitler figürlerinin bulunduğu duvar resimleriyle kaplı dikdörtgen bir odadır. Kaba kireçtaşı plakalardan bir döşeme narteksin batı eksenli kapısına kadar devam eder (env. 21a), fakat bu bölgedeki zemin (sıkıştırılmış toprak ve plakalar) kayıptır (env. 21b). Yeni kilisenin içine açılan doğu duvarındaki kapı yeniden yapılmış ve yapının ana eksenine çekilmiştir.

Erken Bizans kilisesinin atrium, narteks ve kuzey nefinin batı yarısı şimdi şehir *cardo*'su ve yeni kilise arasında bir dolaşım yolu olarak hizmet vermektedir. Çevresindeki alanlar ise küçük ek alanlar olarak bölümlendirilmiştir. En alt seviyede döşeli ve yapay bir teras üzerinde olmayan mozaiklerin iyi kondüsyonundan anlaşılabileceği gibi atrium muhtemelen iyi korunmuştur. Bu süre boyunca narteks ve kuzey nef muhtemelen ikinci kat galerilerini ve çatılarını kaybetmiştir, fakat orta Bizans döneminde yeniden kapatılmıştır.

Yeni alanları bölen duvarlar daha erken mozaiklerin üzerinde yer almaktadır. Bu duvarlar bazen sütunlardan kesilip alınan blokların yerleştirilmesiyle oluşan devşirme malzeme ile yapılmıştır. Ek olarak orijinal atriumun ve narteksin kuzey bölümündeki duvarlar çok ince Orta Bizans dönemi ayakta duran savaşçı azizleri tasvir eden fresklerle bezenmiştir.

İyi korunmuş durumda olan mozaikler herhangi bir restorasyon geçirmeden tekrar kullanılmıştır. Karşıt olarak, narteksin merkezi bölmesindeki *opus sectile* döşeme depremler ve kötü restorasyon sebebiyle büyük oranda hasar görmüştür (env. 20). Ayrıca orta ve güney nefin harap durumdaki durumu nedeni ile kullanılmadan kaldığı doğrudur ve gerçek şudur ki bu alan birkaç yüzyıl önce bir mezarlığa dönüştürülmüştür. Orta nefin yüzeyinin bölümleri kazılarda bulunan orta nefin mozaiği ortaya çıkarılan bazı bölümlerinde ve daha erken diğer *opus sectile* harcında (mortar) küçük kırık plakalardan oluşan kısmi bir zeminle (pişmiş toprak, mermer ve kireç taşı) düzeltilmiştir

KESİN YIKIM

Malazgirt savaşını (1071) takip eden zor dönemde, iç kısımlardaki Türkler bu Xanthos bölgesini ele geçirmişler ve denizden gelen korsanlar sık yağmalarda bulunmuşlardır. Keşişler kilisenin kapılarına kilit vurarak kaçmışlardır. Metruk bırakılan bu alan zaman zaman göçebeler tarafından yerleşim görmüştür ve göçebeler *templon*u söküp ve taşlarını kuzey nefi ve atriuma dizerek kullanmışlardır. 12. yüzyılın sonları veya 13. yüzyılın ilerleyen zamanlarında, büyük bir yangın Doğu bazilikasında kurulan yapıyı her yerde siyah bir kül tabakası ve yanmış materyaller bırakarak yok etmiştir.

Osmanlı Dönemi

Terk edişi takip eden birkaç yüzyıldan sonra, kazılarda birçok antik düzeyin yaklaşık bir metre üzerinde Osmanlıya ait yapılar keşfedilmiştir.

DÖŞEMELERİN BİREŞİMLİ İNCELEMELERİ

Xanthos Şehri İlave Döşemeleri

Son zamanlarda şehrin ana *decumanus*[4] güney portiğinde agorayı doğu bazilikası yakınlarındaki *dipylon* kapısına bağlayan Erken Bizans mozaikleri keşfedilmiştir. Kuzey portik de muhtemelen döşenmiştir. Güney portikteki mozaikler büyük boyutlu tesseralardan yapılmış basit, tekrar eden motiflerden meydana gelen bitişik geometrik döşemelerden oluşuyordu. Dekor tipi ve onun iyileştirilmesi Kilisede ve özellikle Kuzey atriumda gözlemlediklerimizi akla getirir.

İki kilise daha bulunmaktadır, bunlar tepenin üzerindeki kilise[5] ve *Triconch* kilisedir[6]. Fakat bunlar henüz kazılmamışlardır.

J. des Courtils ve L. Cavalier tarafından yeni keşfedilen "sivil bazilika" geometrik mozaiğin içinde alışılmadık bir figür paneli, ve özel yazı tipli diğer bir döşeme sunar[7]. Geometrik motifler açıkça doğu bazilika mozaiklerine benzemektedir. Ayrıca Kuzeyde yer alan oda çağdaş mozaikler içermektedir[8].

A.-M. Manière-Lévêque tarafından Xanthos mozaiklerinin sonraki cildinde çalışılmış olan Likya akropolisi evindeki mozaikler, bizim kilisemizdeki mozaiklerden farklılıklar gösterir. Mozaik desenleri ve doldurma motifleri kullanılan materyaller açısından farklıdır. Ancak, apsidal *tricliniu*mun *opus sectile*'si küçük birimler halindeki geometrik motiflere sahip olan paneller içermektedir. Bu paneller Erken Bizans dönemine tarihlenen doğu bazilikasının vaftizhane zemini ile benzer olarak şist bantlar tarafından ayrılmıştır.

Agora kilisesindeki mozaikler çok parçalıdır ve doğu bazilikasının mozaikleriyle direk paralellikler sunmaz. Bununla birlikte, sunak bölümü'nün *opus sectile*'si doğu bazilikadaki narteks döşemesindekine benzer küçük ölçekli öğelerle düzenlenmiş geometrik motifli paneller içerir ve apsis Letoon'daki Bizans kilisesinin döşemesi gibi ışınsal üçgen motifler içerir[9].

Yazılı sütun yanında yer alan Agoradaki mozaik döşemenin bir kısmı son zamanlarda keşfedilmiştir. Kazı fotoğraflarından birine dayanarak[10], stil ve repertuarın Doğu Bazilikasının atölye B'siyle benzerlikler gösterir (daha fazla bilgi için env. 2-8 ve 4).

Erken Bizans Kilisesinin Çeşitli Tipteki Döşemelerinin Mimari Düzenlemeleri

Opus sectile döşemelerinin ve kireçtaşı ve mermer plakalarının yerleri göz önüne alındığında, tartışmalı bir seçimin olduğu görülür: onlar sistematik olarak kilisenin genel ekseni (atrium'un avlusu, narteksin merkezi kompartımanı, orta nef ve kutsal alan) gibi dini topluluğun en önemli alanlarında yer almaktadırlar; mermer ve şist plakalar, vaftizhane döşemesini oluşturur. Bu seçim lüks mermer döşemelerde özel Erken Bizans zevkini yansıtır. Mozaikler ikinci derecede öneme sahip bir döşeme tipi olarak dolaşım alanlarına yerleştirilmiştir.

Opus Sectile

İstanbul'un etkisi altında bulunan döşemelerin çoğu Xanthos'taki doğu bazilikasında da bulunmaktadır[11].

---

4. Des Courtils-Laroche 2004, res. 23-24.
5. Bu büyük kilise bizimki ile çağdaştır. Doğu yönünde sonlanan Triconch şapel üzerine odaklanıldığında, hac kilisesi olarak kullanıldığını destekleyen ekstra geniş galerileri dışında yapının planı Doğu Kilisesine çok benzerdir. Bu iki kilise arasındaki birçok benzerlik tek bir mimari çalışmada yer almaktadır (Canbilen-Lebouteiller-Sodini 1996).
6. Bu kazı yapılmamış kilise Doğu Bazilikasının yakınında, *cardo*nun diğer tarafında ve güneyin biraz ilerisinde yer alır.
7. Des Courtils-Laroche 2003, L. Cavalier, "L'agora supérieure", s. 425-431, res. 11: Sivil Bazilikanın kuzey odasındaki mozaik Homer'in mısralarında yer alır...
8. Des Courtils-Laroche 2004, res. 22.

9. Metzger 1966.
10. Des Courtils et *alii* 2006, res. 12.
11. Froidevaux-Raynaud 2005.

Erken Bizans Döşemeleri

- Küçük ölçekli öğelerden oluşan panelli *"Opus Sectile"* Suriye, Türkiye ve Yunanistan boyunca 5. yüzyıldan itibaren görülen güzel ama parçalı bir örneği vardır[12]. Doğu bazilikasının döşemelerinin orjinalliği geometrik bordürlerin kullanımına dayanır. Bu döşemelerle çağdaş olan Letoon'daki Bizans kilisesinin ve Xanthos'taki agora kilisesinin sunak bölümü döşemeleri gibi benzer döşemelerde bile bu özellik yoktur.

- Daha erken nef döşemesi küçük ölçekli öğelerden oluşan panelli *opus sectile* ile düz bantlarla ayrılan büyük mermer plakaların kombinasyonunu gösterir. Bu tür döşeme 'karışık döşeme" olarak adlandırılır (fransızcada "un pavement mixte[13]" olarak adlandırılır).

- Erken Bizans vaftizhanesi döşemesi şist bantlı mermer plakalarla oluşturulmuştur.

- Atrium'un avlusu ve sunak bölümü sadece kireçtaşı ve mermer plakalarla döşenmiştir.

Ortaçağ *opus sectile*'si

Ortaçağ modası, yeni bir ortaçağ kilisesi inşa etmek için vaftizhane zemininin tamirinde güzel bir şekilde yansıtılmıştır. Büyük plakaları çevreleyen küçük ölçekli öğelerin basit çizgisel motifli bantlarından yapılmış geniş birleşik döşemeler ve merkezi bir motif içeren paneller bu dönemin döşeme zevkinin iyi bir örneğidir (üçgen biçimli kalkanlar, konsantrik motifler). Bu döşeme gösterir ki Likyalı zanaatkârlar Likya'nın eyalet başkenti olan Demre (Myra)'deki Aziz Nicholas kilisesinde görülebildiği gibi çağdaş sanatsal akımlarla ilişki içerisindedirler[14].

ERKEN BİZANS DOĞU BAZİLİKASININ MOZAİK ATÖLYELERİ

Çeşitli atölyeler tanımlanmış ve bazı yerlerde kolaylıkla tanınmıştır, fakat ortak etkileşimden dolayı bazılarını seçmek daha zordur. Bu atölyeler komşularının stili veya repertuarından olan etkilenmeler olmadan önce, ilk döşenen alanlarda en rahat biçimde birbirinden ayırt edilebilmektedir.

- İlk Erken Bizans dönemi boyunca, üç farklı atölye eş zamanlı olarak çalışıyordu. A atölyesine kuzey atrium mozaiklerini ve muhtemelen koridor 14'tekileri atfediyoruz; Güney atölyesinde kolaylıkla seçilebilen B atölyesine, kuzey narteks mozaiği, kuzey nef döşemelerinin tümü ve Vaftizhanenin kuzey ekinin döşemelerini ekliyoruz. C atölyesine Güney nef mozaiğini (ilk safhası) atfediyoruz.

- Erken Bizans dönemini (safha 2)'nin rekonstrüksyon safhası başlıca atölye D orta nef ve vaftizhanenin güney eki aktiviteleri tarafından temsil edilmektedir. Kısmen tahrip olmuş moziklerin erken motiflerin taklit edilmesi suretiyle onarılması yoluna gidilmesi sebebiyle stili daha az belirgin olan güney nefin modern restorasyonuna katılmak istedik.

Güney nartekseki tek bir döşeme bu sınıflandırmanın dışında kalır. Yalıtılmış olan ve ikinci safha boyunca çalışmış olması muhtemel atölye E ye atfedilebilir

1. Yapım aşaması

Atölye A ile B arasındaki farklılıklar atriumda rahatlıkla görülebilir. Başka yerlerde ayrı döşemelerin bir atölyeye ya da başka birine ait olduğunu net bir biçimde söylemek güçtür. Görünüşe göre atrium kilisenin ilk mozaiğinin yerleştirildiği yerdir[15].

Atölye A

Atriumun Kuzey tarafının Karakteristikleri:
Bu döşemeler genel olarak basit ve bayağı geometrik desenler teşhir eder, ve ayrı ayrı alanları çevreleyen bordürler yoktur. Motifler, üzerinde orijinal bir işçilik olmadan çizgisel bir şekilde ilerler. Birkaç nokta atölyenin kimliğinin oluşmasına ve kendi tasarımlarının ayırt edilmesine yardım eder.

Etki Birliği
Döşemeler duvarın yanında siyah bir çift kurdele ile çizgileri çizilmiş beyaz bir şerit tarafından ayrılıp çevrildiğinden dolayı basitçe birleştirilmiş gibi gözükür. Bu kilisenin diğer döşemelerinde ve çoğu Yakın Doğu (özellikle Suriye) mozaiklerinde olduğu gibi bordür yoktur. Bu etkinin etrafındaki süslenmiş dış kenarların varlığı görünüşünü büyük oranda benzerleştirir.

Ortogonal organizasyon şeması
Sıkı bir ortogonal şema, Atriumun L formlu kenarındaki 7 döşemenin oluşturduğu grubu düzenler. Burada mimari gereksizliklerin üstesinden gelen açık bir plan vardır (batı cephe tarafından yaratılan köşe, birkaç mimari özelliğin varlığı). Bu düzensizlikler, boyutları değişen mozaiklerin dış kenarları tarafından absorbe edilmiştir.

---

12. *Opus sectile* tipi Guidobaldi-Guiglia Guidobaldi 1983, s. 319 de "geometrico a piccoli elementi" olarak isimlendirilmiştir. Bkz. Froidevaux-Raynaud 2005.
13. Donceel-Voûte 1988, s. 450.
14. Demiriz 1968, Türkiye'de bulunan Orta Bizans Dönemi Döşemeleri hakkında. Demiriz 2002.

15. Atölyelerle ilgili bu kısım Doğu Bazilikası'nın J.-P. Sodini'nin yönetimi altındaki gelecek yayında geliştirilecektir. Raynaud 2008.

- Çok renk kullanımına bağlı olan göz yanıltıcı etkiler bu atölyenin başlıca özelliklerindendir ve sade motiflerin iki farklı şekilde okunmasını gerektirir. Döşeme 2-2 düzenli scale motifi ile süslenmiş, çapraz scale sıralarına renk şeması uygulanmasıyla dönüştürülmüş bir örnektir.

- Kuzey Atriumun içindeki çoğu mozaik beyaz kudelelerle 'negatif olarak' çizilmiştir. Bu saydam bir tasarım oluştursa da aynı zamanda desenin tanınmasını zorlaştırmıştır. Deseni alışılmış şekilde siyah ile çizip içini doldurmak daha kolay olduğundan bu orijinal bir etkidir. Bu özellik ve döşemelerin nadir olarak siyahla çevrelenmiş olması, bordürlerin yokluğu ve sınırlı sayıda motiflerin olması, hafiflik ve bütün etkinin kısıtlanması izlenimini verir.

Vaftizhaneyle kiliseyi bağlayan kuzey nefin altındaki koridor 14'ün mozaiği çok sıradandır: terazi motifi gayet büyük boyutlu tesseralarla (yoğunluğu yaklaşık 25'tir) ve sınırlı renklerle (siyah, kırmızı ve beyaz) muhtemelen bir açık alanı anımsatan bir şekilde yapılmış son derece sıkıcı bir motiftir. Dış kenarların dekorasyonu Kuzey atriumun hedera (orman sarmaşığı) taslağını hatırlatır. Tesseraların boyutu kilisedekilerle karşılaştırılamaz ve sadece hipotetik olarak belirli bir atölyeye atfedilmesi düşünülebilir. Mimari özellikler onun Erken Bizans dönemine ait olduğunu gösterir ve genel etki atölye A'nın stiliyle benzerdir fakat açık bir doğrulama yoktur.

Gemiler Ada Kilise 1'de yerel benzerlikler bulduk[16], şöyle ki, meyve ağacında ve gamalı haç kıvrımları şeklinde işlenen oblong (boyu eninden fazla) altıgenler ve kareler Xanthos'taki kuzey atrium mozaiklerine çok benzerlikler taşır. Başka bir benzer Patara'da, ortaçağ kilisesinin altında bulunmuştur[17].

Atölye B
Atrium'un güney kısmının özellikleri
İlk olarak panellerin iki grup halinde, koyu bir yüzey üzerindeki karmaşık tasarımının vurguladığı önemi ile, sık ve zengin bordürlerle çevrelenerek, düzenlendiğini fark ediyoruz. Onlar bazen zengin bir biçimde renklendirilmiştir. Alanlar iddasız ölçülere sahiptir ve iki tipte sık motifler gösterir: gölgeli bantlı halkalı tasarımlar veya sık bir biçimde tekrar eden meandır ve eşkenardörtgen motif tasarımları. Atriumun güney yarısındaki paneller topluluğu, L formlu bir alan oluşturup tek bir dış bordürle çerçevelenmiştir. Aralıklı ve dar dış kenarlar dekoratif mozaikleri duvarlarla birleştirir.

- Motiflerin repertuarı ve bordürler meanderler, birleşik ve merkezi karmaşık tipte tasarımlar

16. Ölüdeniz Area 1995, Asano 1998.
17. Işık 2000, p. 114, fig. 90.

gösterir. Güney portikte, geometrik motifler canlı renkler yerine çizgisel bir etki gösterir

- Materyaller ve renkler basittir: siyah, beyaz, kırmızı ve pembe, pişmiş toprak, kireç taşı, diğer yerel taşlar ve Prokonessos mermeri.

- Mimariye uyum: Döşemelerin düzenlenmesi kuzey sektöründe görülen sert ortagonal düzenden farklı olarak duvarların yönüne doğru devam eder. Desenin esnekliği güney ve kuzey portiklerin arasındaki geniş açıda olduğu gibi düzensizliklerin üstesinden gelir. Girişin hemen sağında yer alan döşeme 2-8'e özel ilgi gösterilmiştir.

- Ayrıca bu atölyenin taslak yapımındaki hüneri detaylarda bile muhteşem olması ile dikkatimizi çekmiştir. Genellikle kullanılan uzun yatay çubuklar yerine dikey çubuk çiftlerinin kısa köşelerin ortasında olduğu ve bu sayede bordürlerin döşemelerin boyutlarına uygun bir şekilde kısaltıldığı Döşeme 2-9'un bordürleri buna bir örnektir. Bu ilk bakışta görülemeyecek kadar doğal bir yolla yapılmıştır. Bazı döşemelerin yamuk şeklinde olmasına neden olan mimari düzensizlikler becerikli bir şekilde döşemenin iç motifleri tarafından gözden kaçırılmıştır. Bu zarif adaptasyon in situ haldeyken görülebilir değildir ama grafik yerleşiminin araştırılmasıyla, alanın olağanüstü bir şekilde kavranmasını sağlamıştır.

Stilin gelişimi güney atriumda döşeme 2-8 ve 2-9 arasında bile görülebilir. İkinci döşeme kuzey atriumdakine benzer bir şekilde geometrik stile adaptasyonunu çizgilere uzak bir eğilimle ve parçalanmış motiflerle gösterir. Döşeme 2-9'da tasarım siyah çift kurdele ile yapılmıştır.

Kuzey narteks mozaiği 2-8A ve 2-8B (güney atriumu)'daki panellere yakınlıklar gösterir ve halkalı motifler konusunda zengindir. Ayrıca baskın olarak mavi ve kırmızı renkler kullanılmıştır. Taslağı çizmek için kullanılan siyah taşlar yerine koyu mavi taşların kullanılması (aynı taşlar orta nefte de kullanılmıştır (Atölye D) gibi bazı öğeler değişiktir. Atriumda yer almayan bir motif olan bu desen basit birbirine geçmiş halatlar halinde çizilmiştir.

Kuzey nef: Güney atrium atölyesinin çalışmaları ile izotropik modülün küçük bir deseninin seçimi (bkz: atrium döşeme 2-9), benzer temel renkler (bkz: döşeme 2-8C ve 2-9A ve B), kuvvetli bordürlerin üslubu ve bitişik motiflere özel bir eğilim gösterilmesi gibi birçok benzerlikler görülür (bkz: atrium döşemesi 2-8). Kuzey nefte, aynı boyuttaki döşemelerin düzenlenmesi daha toplu bir görüntü yaratır. Atriumdaki mozaiklerin özelliklerinin daha iyi asimile (daha sistematik) oldukları fark edilmiştir ve düşüncemize göre bu mozaikler atriumdan sonra bitirilmiştir.

Kuzey ekteki döşeme hemen hemen kaybolmuştur ama tekrar kurgulanabilir. Birbirini izleyen

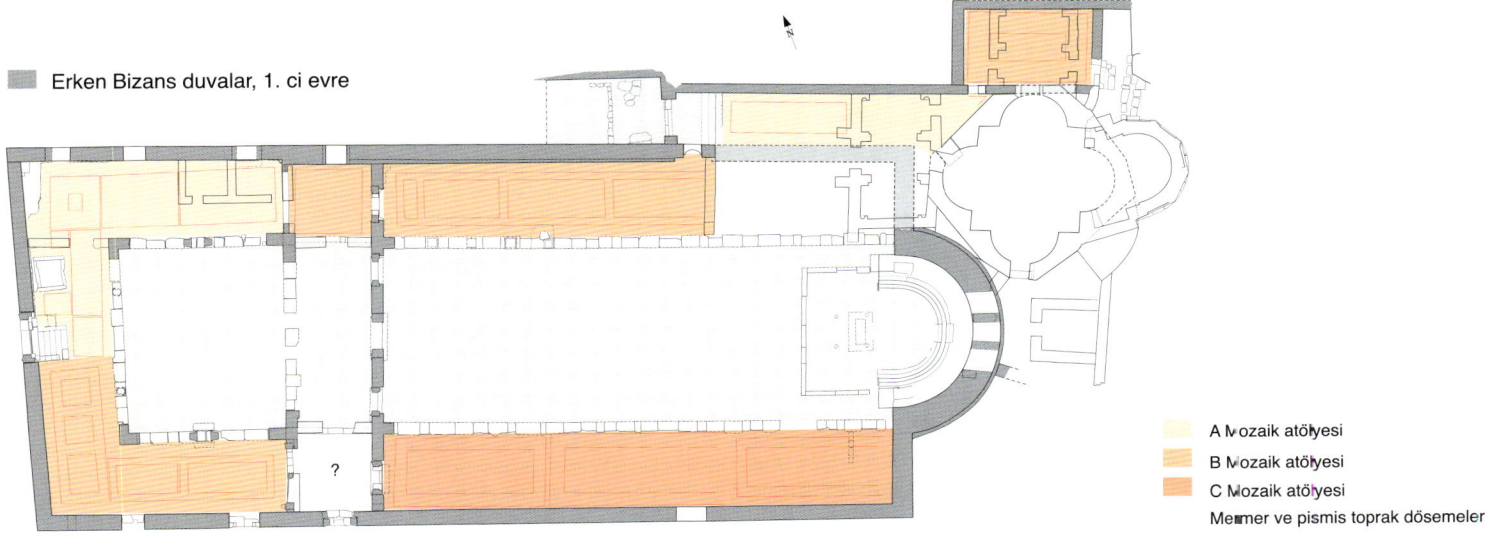

178. Plan of the first Early Byzantine phase mosaics: workshops A, B and C/ İlk Erken Bizans mozaikleri planı: A, B ve C atölyeleri.

bordürlerin düzenlenmesi ve bitişik motiflerin üslubu şüphesiz atrium döşeme 2-8'e yakındır.

Kuzey narteksteki bitkisel doldurma motifleri ve kuzey nefin girişindeki figürlü sahnenin atriumdakilerle bir paralelliği yoktur. Bunlar gösterir ki bu atölye geometrik motif yapımında ustalaşmış fakat figürlü ve bitkisel motiflere daha az aşinalardır. Bu atölye gökkuşağı sitilinin etkisini azami olarak gösterir. Yerel olarak, Anemurium ile olan yakın paralelliklerini özellikle oradaki Kutsal Havariler Kilisesinde (modül, organizasyon ve repertuar) gözlemleyebiliriz[18].

Atölye C

Güney nefin ilk zemininde bu atölyenin 4 ana özelliği görülebilir.

- Tasarım, kuzey atriumda rastladığımız gibi negatif olarak beyaz içerisine çizilmiştir (çift kurdele); bu mozaiklerde çok yaygın değildir ve bu nokta üzerinde ısrar edilmesinin bir sebebidir; burada her bir döşeme bir veya birkaç bordür tarafından çevrelenmiştir.

- Genellikle iki desenin kaynaştırılıp bir tane desene dönüştürülmesi ile oluşan motiflerin çizgisel ağ görünümü, küçük modülün çok parçalı motiflerini belirtir. Bu başlıca panel 8-1 ve 8-2 ve onların Güç bela görülebilen ve çigilerin karmaşıklık etkisini veren nadir ve karmaşık desenleri (bordürler ve alan repertuarının her ikisi) ile ilgilidir.

- Renklere verilen önemin azlığı, renk tonundaki açıklık ve nadirlik çizgilerden daha çok renklere önem veren atölye A'dan çok farklıdır.

- Suyun tahribatına karşı koyamayan kireçli toprak bazlı malzemelerin kullanımı, örneğin siyah tesseraların (gerçekte gri) yapımında kullanılan malzeme, dolayısıyla döşeme negatif halde günümüze ulaşmıştır. Bu yüzden, mozaiklerin korunması zordur ve siyah tesseraların eksikliği dengesizliğe yol açmıştır.

Eğer bu mozaiklerin parçaları ve çizgisel görünümü atölye B (atrium döşemesi 2-9)'nin bazı etkilerini yansıtabilseydi, alanın genel bir birleşimi yoktur, her döşeme komşularından bağımsız bir şekilde işlenmiştir, diğer atölyelerin üretiminden çok farklı bir görüntü sergiler. Sonuç olarak, bu döşemelerin dekoratif yönü karmaşık fakat göze hoş gelmez.

Bu karmaşık motiflerin benzerleri genel olarak Balkanlarda, Yunanistan ve adalarda (Selanik, Amphissa ve Girit) görülür. Döşeme 8-2'nin bordürü ile benzer olan bir örnek için Türkiye'deki Pisidia Antiocheia'sını zikredebiliriz.

2. İkinci Safha: Depremden sonra rekonstrüksyon

Atölye D

Orta Nef'in geniş yüzeyi (mozaik 10) bu atölyenin özelliklerini gözlemlemek için geniş olanaklar sunar: bu mozaiklerin genel motifleri geniş bir karenin ızgaralarını ve dikdörtgen panelleri gösterir. Merkezileştirilmiş motifler, küçük doldurma motifleri ve renklerin üslubu dikkatimizi çekmiştir. Burada desteklerin gözlenmesi, desteklerin direkt olarak erken *opus sectile*'den ödünç alındığını gösterir ve bu, döşemenin yapımındaki aciliyeti kanıtlamaktadır. Bununla beraber çok becerikli ve eğitimli olan ve repertuarın seçiminin bize gösterdiği gibi mozaik tasarımının gelişimi hakkında bilgisi olan bir atölye tarafından tamamlanmıştır.

---

18. Campbell 1998, s. 23-26, res. 102.

İzotropik ve merkezileştirilmiş motiflerin geniş repertuarı atölyenin yaratıcılığını yansıtır: "U'ların haçları", halkalardan çelenkler, eşkenar dörtgen yıldızları ve birleştirilmiş çemberlerin çeşitli modülleri, düzenlenme ve detaylarda Kuzey Suriye ve Kilikya döşemelerini hatırlatır. Basit isotropik motifler çeşitli doldurucu öğeler ile panel ızgaraları tarafından yeniden yerleştirildiği zaman, bu üslup Doğu Akdeniz dünyasının repertuarının genel gelişimini takip eder.

Vaftizhanenin güney eki aynı etkiyi gösterir: ana bordür çoklu dikdörtgenler ve çemberlerin küçük hayvanlar ve bitki formları gibi küçük doldurma motiflerinin eklenmesine müsaade ettiği karmaşık merkezileştirilmiş çelenk desenleri.

Kronolojik sebeplerden dolayı, bu atölyeyi kilisenin orta nefini tamamen yıkan ve kısmi olarak güney nefe zarar veren depremden sonra yapılan güney nefteki restorasyon işiyle bağdaştırmak isteriz. Mozaik sanatçıları burada ellerinden geldikleri kadar erken mozaikleri iyileştirmişler, bazen yeni bir dekor yaratarak, bazen eski dekoru taklit ederek ama hiçbir şekilde yaratıcılıklarını ve hayal güçlerini ortaya koyacak kadar alan veya fırsat bulamadan işlerini yapmışlardır. Bu atölyenin orta nefteki açık imzası (yeni repertuar seçimi) bu mozaik sektöründe ortaya çıkmaz. Tasarım, ilk safha boyunca beyaz ile çizilmiş, yenisi tamiratta siyahla yapılmıştır: Bu iki safha arasındaki ana teknik farklılıktır. Biz ayrıca ikinci safhanın tasarımının daha karmaşık ve daha kararsız bir şekilde yapıldığını gördük. Orta nef mozaiği Limyra'da bulanan mozaiği bazı detaylarda çağrıştırır. Izgara bantların genel düzenlenmesi 6. yüzyılın modasının temsilidir, burada büyük doldurucu motifler gökkuşağı stilini kanıtlar niteliktedir.

Mozaiklerin bu yeni programı Erken Bizans mozaik sanatçılarının aklında tek bir düşünce varken doğaçlama yoluyla yeni bir döşemeyi yaptığını gösterir: maliyet kısılmaya çalışırken genel görünüş korunmuştur[19].

Atölye E

Güney narteks bölümünün zemini komformist olmayan bir döşemedir (env. 5) ve bu döşeme kilisedeki diğer döşemelerden farklıdır. Kuzey narteksteki genel motifleri türetir ve ayrıca yeni orta nefte gözükür ("U cross"), ama diğer mozaiklerle arasındaki tek benzerlik budur. Doldurma motifleri, renkler ve materyaller (çok fazla cam tesseralar) hazırlayıcı bir dizaynın görüntüsü, tesseraların yoğunluğu ve doğu bazilikasındaki tüm mozaik aktivitelerine zıt bir şekilde dikkatli bir biçimde hazırlanmıştır. Bu atölye E'nin ünik tarzıdır.

Bu değerli döşemenin tekil özellikleri onu birinci veya ikinci safha ile bağdaştırmamıza engel olmaktadır, fakat birkaç element depremden sonraki ikinci safhaya tarihlememize izin verir.

Cam tesseraların kullanımı duvar mozaikleri yapmaya alışkın mozaik sanatçılarının varlığını ima ediyor olabilir. Bu materyal üzerinde yüründüğünde çok kırılgan olması sebebiyle kilise döşemelerinde üniktir. Bu döşemenin vaftizhane tonozunda çalışmış olan zanaatkârlara atfedilmesi (bir hipotez olarak) önerilebilir. Vaftizhane kesinlikle kiliseden hemen sonra, bitirilen apsisin karşısına inşa edilmiştir. Böylece depremden daha sonraki ikinci safhaya ait olması muhtemeldir. Ama biz anımsamalıyız ki döşemelerde cam tesseraların kullanılması Xanthos'un doğu bazilikasında bir örneğini göremesek bile başka yerlerde sıktır.

Destek geleneksel olanlardan tamamen ayrıdır ve iki hipotez sunulur:

- Dik olarak döşenmiş kiremit ve tuğla parçalarının destekte kullanılması sık depremlerin yarattığı problemlerin bir karşılığı olabilir; esnek ve dayanıklı göründüğünden; sonuç olarak bulunan çözümün sismik depremlere karşı uygun olduğu söylenebilir. Bu muhtemelen zor bir sismik deneyime karşı geliştirilen karmaşık bir çözüm olabilir[20].

- Diğer bir yorum ise, bu döşemenin döşeme süslemesi yapmaya alışkın olmayan ve geleneksel yer destekleri yaratmada duvar ve tonoz mozaikleri kadar ehil olmayan bir atölye tarafından yapıldığıdır. Birkaç sav bu hipotezi savunur: bunlardan biri döşemelerde fazla görülmemesine rağmen vaftizhanenin kemerinde gördüğümüz gibi kemerlerde sıklıkla kullanılan camın kullanımıdır.

Daha az belirgin olan başka bir faktör olarak, bu mozaiğin özgün stilini ve motif ve desenlerin işlenmesini söyleyebiliriz. Daha önce gözlemlediğimiz üzere genel olarak desenlerin depremden

---

19. Balty 1995, s. 51, « limiter les frais tout en sauvegardant les apparences », Bizans yapıtlarının pek çok örneğinde olduğu gibi, işlevsel bir kural.

20. Böyle bir desteğin iki benzer örneği de çok özel koşullarda Arnavutluk'ta gözlemlenmiştir: Birincisi Byllis (S. Muçaj ve P. Chevalier'in yönetimleri altında 2006'da kazıldı ve yazar tarafından Mayıs, 2007'de incelendi) Doğu bazilikasının altında, tepenin güçlü eğiminden kaynaklanan stabilite problemine karşılık olarak: Meyil yüksek bir kaide inşasını ve sağlamlık kaygısı sonucu toprak çanak çömleklerin dikey kırıklarının seçimini gerektirdi. Ve yine burada çok miktarda cam mozaiğin kullanımı dikkatimizi çekti. İkinci örnek Vrina'da ortaya çıktı, Butrint yakınında (2006'da R. Hodges başkanlığında İngiliz-Arnavut kazıları) yakınında, apsisin altında, düz ve bataklık bir alanda yatıyor ve muhtemelen suyun yükselmesinden kaynaklanan problemlerle yüzleşmek zorunda kalmış. Vrinia ile ilgili bu bilgiyi bize veren ve restorasyonu yapan A. Islami'ye teşekkür ederiz.

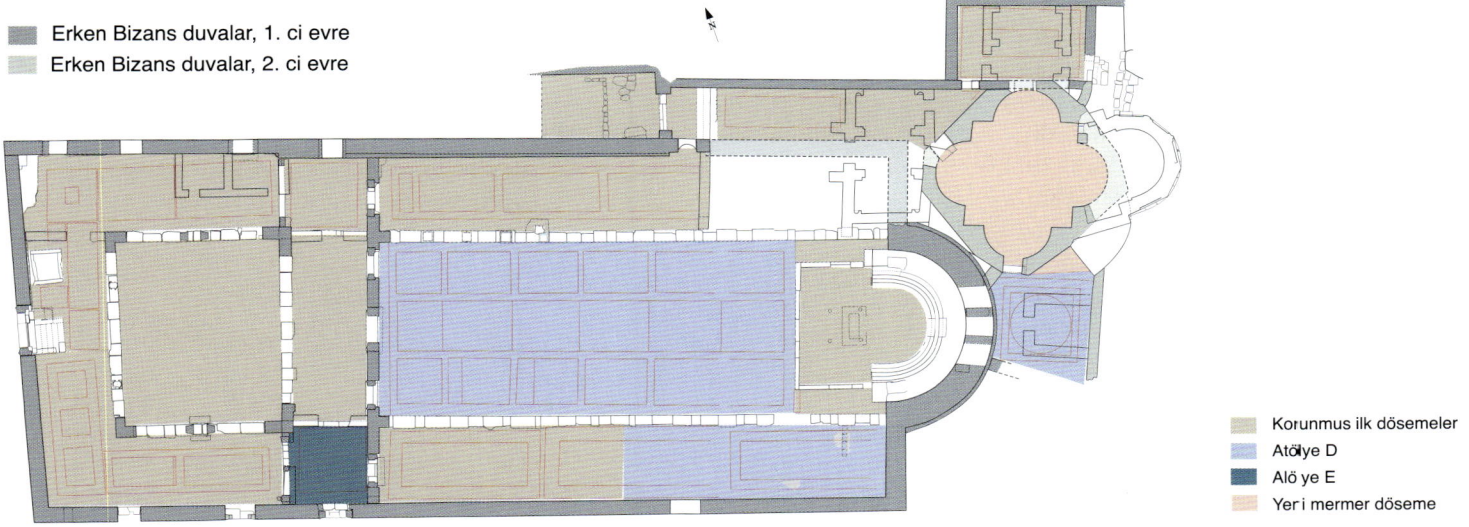

zarar görmemiş simetrik kuzey bölümünden kopya edildiği görülmektedir[21]. Fakat tasarım genel olarak aynı olmasına rağmen son sonucu farklıdır. Motiflerde tasvir edilen resimsel tarzda, göz yanıltıcı etkilerin sık kullanımı (gölgeler ve kabartmalar için) ve belirli motiflerdeki etkili gerçekçilik (hemen hemen 'trompe l'oeil') resmin etkisini yansıtır ve özellikle tavan ve tonoz resimlerini anımsatır. Kabartma etkileri ve perspektifteki açık bir ilgi ön plan ve arka planın varlığına bağlı olarak (bir çitin arkasındaki ağaçlar) bu kompozisyondan farklılaşır. Aslında 4 tane yanal kapısı olan kare bir odanın tahrip olmuş mimari görüntüsünü temsil eder. Tonozun çemberini çeviren bu dört yanal kapı iki boyutlu bir şekilde yayılır ve iki tanesi meyve bahçesine açılır. Bu desenin yeni yorumuna izin veren icranın gerçekliğidir ve bu durum asla "U cross" ya da U geçişli motiflerinin çizgisel icrası yüzünden kompozisyonun, motiflerin geometrik topluluğuyla sınırlandırıldığı narteksin kuzey bölümünde geçerli değildir (hiçbir perspektif ve derinlik yoktur). Kilisedeki bu nadir desenin üçüncü örneği ciddi tahrip olmuş bir şekilde orta nefte yer alır (döşeme 10-7B), ama genel görünüm itibariyle daha öncekilerle-bir geometrik 'circumcentric' desen bir mimari projeksyondan daha fazla benzerlik taşır. Bu güney bölümünün ilginç bir özelliği ise özgürlüğü ve sanatsal modelden uzaklığıdır; bu tecrübe ve perspektifin ve gerçekliğin sunumunda güçlü bir arka planın göstergesidir.

Bu ilizyonizm'in farklı kullanımı geç antik döşeme repertuarında çok şaşırtıcıdır ve daha çok Selanik veya Ravenna'da görülen yeni stil duvar mozaiklerine uyar.

Bu bitkisel motifler döşeme üslubu, Yakın doğu bölgelerinde daha az sıklıkta kullanılmıştır. İçerdiği defne çelengi veya akantus çelengi, kilisenin içinde gördüğümüz başka esinleri yansıtır.

Benim son gözlemim ise, tesseraların daha dikkatli bir şekilde kesildiğidir ve boyutlarının kilisenin herhangi bir yerinden daha küçük olmasıdır. Bu oda bu atölyeye ait olan sadece bir döşemeye sahiptir: acaba bu o zamanda döşeme ihtiyacı duyulan tek yer miydi? Acaba döşemeyi finanse eden kişi hemen yandaki başka bir iş için orda olan duvar atölyesinin varlığından (muhtemelen vaftizhane tonozu) mı yararlanmıştır? Niye özellikle bazilikadaki bu yere özel bir ilgi gösterilmiştir? Bu alanın güney bölümünde yapılacak kazılar buradaki sorulara cevap bulunmasını sağlayabilir.

Repertuar ve Etkiler

Bordür ve alan desenlerinin çoğu yaygın ve düzenlidir, pek çok örnekte ayrıntılı olması için uzun ve sıkıcı listelerden oluşabilen bu tür ızgaralar arasında karşılaştırma yapmak mantıklı değildir.

Bu tür listeler tarih koyma ve etkileri açısından aydınlatıcı olmayabilir. Ancak bazı durumlarda desenlerin kombinasyonu kıyaslamaya yardımcı olabilir.

Doğu bazilikası mozaiklerinde kolayca tanınabilen bir etkiye sahip olan mozaikler genellikle "rainbow style[22]" gökkuşağı stili olarak adlandırılır.

179. Plan of the second Early Byzantine phase mosaics: workshops D and E/ Ikinci Bizans evresi mozaikleri planı: D ve E atölyeleri.

---

21. Eğimin bu bölümünde bir bende ihtiyaç yoktu, tamamen kaya üzerine direkt döşenen mozaik iyi korunmuştur.

22. D. Levi'nin Antakya Mozaikleri hakkında yayınlamış olduğu ana kitaptan itibaren bu terim mozaik çalışmalarında kullanılmaktadır. O bu stili renk yoğunluğunun dağılımı olarak tanımlar. Farklı renklere sert noktaların birleşiminden geçtiğimizden dolayı bu bağlantı noktaları silsilesi iyi

Pek çok karakteristik özellik bir atölye veya başka bir yakın atölye tarafından tercih edilerek, bir özelliğiyle burada temsil edilmiştir ve bu üslubun birinci ve ikinci safhalar boyunca etkili olması popülerliğinin kanıtı olarak dikkate değerdir. Gökkuşağı stil üslubunun karakteristik özellikleri Antakya yöresi, Apamea ve bütün Kuzey Suriye mozaikleri üzerinde sık sık çalışılmıştır. Bu yeni akım tüm Akdeniz dünyasını 4. ve 5. yüzyıllar boyunca etkisi altına almış, çok az üretim merkezi bu etkinin dışında kalmıştır. Bu üslup, geometrik desenlerin tercihleri (genellikle önceden kullanılmış), doldurma motiflerinin sınırsız çeşitliliğe sahip olması ve bölümlerin çoğaltılabilmesi ile tanımlanabilir. Bu motiflerin uygulanışında elde hazır olan tesseralarla, renkleri değişen satranç tahtaları, gölgeli bantlar, sıkça görülen halkalama ve düğümler ve karmaşık kıvrımların uyumu kullanılarak, bütün olanaklı renk derecelendirmelerinden yararlanılır.

Bu zengin geometrik düzenleme modasının temelinde, artarak karmaşıklaşan iç içe geçmiş desenlerin (merkezileştirilmiş tasarımlar)[23] uyumu ile renklerin pırıltılı oyunları yatar.

Bu üslup, kuzey Makedonya, Trakya, Romanya ve Dalmaçya'ya kadar olan Suriye, Kıbrıs, Küçük Asya'nın güneyi, Ege denizi ve Yunanistan'ı kapsayan bölgenin tümüne doğrudan doğruya sıçramıştır.

Bu eski gelenek, 6.yy'ın ortalarına kadar yaşamış olmasına rağmen 5. yy'ın ilk yarısında en yoğun yayılımını gerçekleştirmiştir[24].

Başarısı belirli bölgelere kadar genişlemiş, kuzey Afrika, İtalya, İspanya'ya ve Galya'un[25] bazı güney bölümlerine ulaşmıştır, burada küçük doldurma motiflerin çeşitlerini etkilemiştir.

Xanthos doğu bazilikasının zemininde, süslemelerin iki safhası boyunca çeşitli atölyelerin varlıklarının vurgulanması yerine gökkuşağı stilinin çeşitli eğilimlerinin iyi örneklerini temsil edilmesi dikkate değerdir.

Atölye A, bu desenlerin orijinal halleri değiştirilse de, basit desenler içinde renklerin dağıtılmış, "trompe l'oeil" etkilerini ödünç almıştır. Gölgeli satranç tahtalarındaki bazı doldurma motifleri bu etkiyi doğrudan göstermektedir. Atölye B' nin, bu üsluptan son derece etkilendiği açıktır: gölgeli bantların kenarlarına çizilmiş, karmaşıklaşarak merkezileştirilmiş desenler; kıvrım ve şeritlerde olduğu gibi birbirini izleyen zengin bordürler, askerlerin rütbelerini gösteren kol işaretlerindeki ve satranç tahtalarındaki renk derecelendirmeleri içindeki motifler ve pek çok düğüm çeşidinde görülen doldurma motifler kullanılarak çevrelenmiş döşemeler.

Depremden sonra kilise zemininin rekonstrüksiyonunda çalışan "Atölye D", yıkılmış orta kısımdaki geniş dış yüzey üzerinde büyük bant ızgara gelişim imkânını bulmuştur[26].

Oluşan bölümlerin boyutları iyidir ve dekorasyonları, merkezileştirilmiş desenlerle biçimlenen (eşkenar dörtgen yıldızlar, halka çelenkleri, sekizgen yıldızlar, U haçlar, ortak merkezli desenler, karmaşık dairelerden oluşan kareler), küçük bölümlerden meydana gelen veya halkalanmalardan, terazi ya da *peltae*lerden oluşan izotropik desenlerin bir değişimidir.

Gölgeli bantların, renk derecelendirme içeren desenlerin ve çeşitli düğümlerin kullanıldığı herkes tarafından her yerde görülür.

Xanthos'ta, özellikle kilisenin genel döşemesinin tasarımında adalar ve Yunanistan'daki mozaiklerin güçlü etkisi görülebilir. Her boşluk veya nefin dekorasyonu bir bütün olarak düşünülür. Ortak bordürler, döşeme dizilerini birleştirir ve alana homojenlik katar. Simetri, çok önemli bir rol oynar ve binanın bölümlerini denkleştirerek sükûnet ve düzen hissi yaratır. Bu durum, çeşitli boy ve tasarımdaki döşemelerin bütün boş alanlarda yan yana bitiştirilmesi Yakın-Doğu alışkanlığından oldukça farklı görünmektedir[27]. Bu disiplin Xanthos atölyeleri A, B, ve D de açıkça gösterilmektedir ve bu ilk evre, neflerin ve belki de narteksin rekonstrüksyonundaki tasarıma baktığımızda, dekorasyonun genelindeki simetrik düzenleme açısından dikkate değerdir[28].

Atölye C'de, (ilk bölümündeki S nefi), renk üzerine çizgiler kullanılmış, seyrek ve karmaşık geometrik desenler göz önüne serilmektedir.

---

gözlemlenir, paralel bantlar içinde tüm renk serilerinin hava nemi arasından genişlemesi zig-zag bantlarla verilen titrek gökkuşağı etkisidir" (Levi 1947, s. 405 vd.)

23. Gökkuşağı stili 5. yüzyılın ortalarında Suriye'de tekrar yerleşmiş, figürlü ve hayvanlı sahneler için denenmiş nötr ya da yarı çiçekli arka planlarda gösterilmiş.

24. Bu gökkuşağı stiline paralel olarak, doldurucu motif olarak çoğaltılmış insan ve hayvan figürleri ile karakterize yeni bir akım gelişti. 6. yüzyılda Balkanlarda ve şimdiki Yunanistan'ın tüm bölgelerinde aynı zamanda Yakın Doğu, bugünkü Ürdün ve Filistin'de bu dikkate değerdir.

25. Örneğin, renklerin sıralanışı ve bu stile özgü diğer motifler (gümüş-kap motifleri) Aquitania mozaiklerinde görülür.

26. Bant ızgaraları tüm zamanlarda ve tüm bölgelerde var olmuştur, ancak en geniş kullanılışı 6. yüzyılda görmüştür; bu akımın en iyi örnekleri Illyria, Epirus ve Makedonya'da bulunur. Figürlü sahnelerin gelişimi tercih olundu, her kompartımanda kişilik kazandı.

27. Birçok örnek arasında, Hermione ya da Argos, Epirus Nicopolis mevkii (bazilika A), Byllis (A'dan E'ye kiliseler) ya da Saranda (Sinagog üzerinde kilise), Illyricum Caričin Grad ve Makedonya, Stobi Kiliseleri, Heraklea Lynkestis ve Selanik gösterilebilir, bu örneklerin çoğu 6. yüzyıldandır.

28. Epirus Nicopolis (bazilika A) zemin organizasyonunda simetriye iyi bir örnektir.

Söz konusu tasarımların temsilleri, çoğunlukla Yunanistan'da ve adalarda benzer yapılış şekillerine sahip olarak bulunmuştur. Atölyenin yakın doğu etkisinden en uzak atölye olduğu kesindir.

Bazilikanın içinde bulunan nadiren figürlü ya da sembolik motifler, bir kraterin etrafında geyikler (atölye B) ya da nar ağacı (atölye A) gibi, muhtemelen Balkanlarda bölgelerinde 5. yüzyılın sonu ve 6. yüzyılda yaygın olarak tercih olunmuşlardır[29]. Daha sonra Yakın-Doğu bölgelerinde (Suriye, Ürdün ve Filistin) 6. ve 7. yüzyılların sonunda kullanıma girmişlerdir. Farklı motifler veya desenler arasındaki ilişkiye, Ege repertuarından Yakın-Doğu'dakine doğru bir eğilim göstermekte olan doğu bazilikasında rastlanır[30].

Son E atölyesi narteksin güney bölümünü dekore etmiştir.

Bahçe çitinin arkasında kalan meyve ağaçlarının tümü - akasya salkımları ve defne çelenkleri- duvar resimlerini ve kemer mozaiklerini hatırlatan çok sayıda cam tesseranın kullanılması ve var olan gerçekçilik tutkusu açısından batı etkisini (kuzey Afrika, İspanya ya da Galya) yansıtır.

Doğu bazilikasındaki repertuarın gelişimi 5. ve 6. yüzyıllar, H. Maguire'a göre geç 4. ve 5. yüzyıllar boyunca genel Bizans ikonografisindeki evrimin iyi bir yansımasıdır. Dini zemin mozaiklerindeki baskın üslup, nispeten birkaç canlı varlık ile geometrik kompozisyonlar içermesiydi. Fakat 6. asırda, neredeyse her çeşit hayvan, bitki ve dünyada varlığı bilinen her türde meyve döşemeler üzerinde gösterilmekteydi[31].

Bu durum, Xanthos bazilikasında, neredeyse yalnızca iki sembolik sahneyle geometrik olan ilk bölüm mozaikleri ile özellikle döşemenin güney ekinde bulunan ikinci bölümdekiler karşılaştırılarak gösterilmektedir.

Ağaçlar, kuşlar ve hayvanlar gibi grafik biçimli ve çizgisel dolgu motiflerinin çoğalması gözlemlenebilir.

Aynı atölye tarafından tamamlanan kilisenin orta kısmı, içeriğinin açığa çıkarılmasında son derece yetersiz kalmıştır fakat kraterlerin, ağaçlar ve bitkisel motiflerin varlığı aynı akıma bağlı kalındığını göstermektedir. Pek çok başka figürün kırılan zeminin boşluklarında kaybolduğunu tahmin edebiliriz. Bu değişimler metinlerden anladığımız kadarıyla adım adım teolojinin ve toplu ayinlerin evrimlerine etki etmiştir ve bir bölgeden diğerine değişiklik gösteren tüm doğu Akdeniz için ortak bir durumdur.

Likya kıyı bölgesi, 5. yüzyıldan 6. yüzyıla kadar İstanbul, Yakın-Doğu ve Mısır arasında ayrıcalıklı bir bölgeydi ve Kilikya gibi bu iki taraflı etkiden istifade etmişti. Xanthos mozaikleri, çeşitli bölgeler arasındaki kültürel değişimlere iyi bir örnektir (erime potası).

ÜZERİNDE DURULMASI GEREKEN BİRKAÇ NADİR MOTİF

"U geçişli" motif daha önce araştırılmıştır[32] ve bu motif kilisenin içerisinde üç dönemde karşımıza çıkar. Bu üç mozaik açıkça üç farklı atölyeden türemiştir ve diğer safhalarda döşenmiştir. Bu karmaşık birleşik motif büyük beceri gerektirir. Küçük Asya'nın dışında kaydedilen en erken örnekler Suriye'de 4. yüzyıl sonuna tarihlenmektedir ve en geçlerinden biri Yunanistan'da 6. yüzyılın ilk yarısına aittir. Amisos'tan[33] bir mozaik ekleyerek bu tasarımla 17 tane merkezileştirilmiş motif kayıt ettik. Suriye'den 6 örnek[34], Türkiye'den 6 örnek[35], Yunanistan'dan 2 örnek,[36] Bulgaristan' dan 1 örnek[37] ve Fransa'dan 3 örnek bulunur[38]. Tasarımın köşelerinin iyileştirilmesinden (*Décor* II, lev. 366-368) uyarlanan motifin birkaç çeşidi dikkatimizi çekti. Ayrıca bizim gözlemlerimize göre doldurma motiflerinin özel seçimi motiflerin değişik algılanışına izin verir. Geometrik ve gökkuşağı stilli motifleri ile sıradan bir dekoratif motif halini alır. Figürlü ve bitkisel motifleri ile küçük bölümlerin çoğaltılmasına ve sembolik bir anlam kazanabilmesine vesile olur. U formlu bölümlerin içinde yer alan alçak bir çitin arkasındaki bir bahçenin gösterimi ile dört kemer vasıtasıyla bir bostana açılan kare bir odanın düzeltilmiş kesitini anımsatır. Bu son okuma Xanthos'un güney narteks örneğini hatırlatır: orjinalitesi, stili ve motif seçimi duvar resimlerinin repertuarını anımsatır.

Aynı düzlemde orta nefteki bir döşemedir (panel 10-7D). Bu döşemenin tasarımı bilinmemektedir

---

29. Hermione, Akrini ve Yunanistan'da Longos, Edessa, Stobi ve Makedonya'da Heraklea Lyncestis döşemelerinden bahsedebiliriz.
30. Örneğin Argos Kilisesi, Atina'da "Hadrianik Kütüphane" (*tetraconch*), Epidaurus'da bulunan mozaik (kilise ve ev) yakın ilişkili repertuar seçimlerini gösterir.
31. Maguire 1987, s. 83.
32. Bu patron çalışması Raynaud tarafından yapılmıştır, Raynaud 1996, s. 69-102.
33. Biz sadece bu taban döşemesinin fotoğrafını gördük: Akkaya 1997, res. 3.
34. Apamea, Khirbet Muqa, Jerade, Murik, Qumhane, Dibsi Faraj; Raynaud 1996, s. 69-82.
35. Misis (Mopsuestia), Sardis, Amisos ve Xanthos Doğu Bazilikası içinde üç örnek (env. 4, 5 ve 10-7B).
36. Aigion ve Delphi.
37. At Stara Zagora.
38. Loupian'da iki örnek ve Séviac'da bir örnek.

ama kesinlikle karmaşık ve nadir (seyrek) birleşik bir motiftir[39].

Vaftizhanenin güney ekindeki merkezileştirilmiş desen, Selanik'teki bir mozaiğe uzaktan benzerliği ve Yakın Doğu'nun (Ürdün ve Filistin) karmaşık birleşik motifleri ile olan benzerliği ile ünik görünmektedir.

Güney nefteki (ilk safha) 8-1 ve 8-2 deki döşemelerin izotropik desenleri ve 8-1'in döşemesinin bordürü özellikle çizgiler kıvrımlarıyla tamamen orjinaldir.

Belirli repertuar seçimleri: Onlar dini kitaba bağlı mıydı?

Bazilikadaki bazı mozaik döşemeler görünüşe göre yerleri ve ikonografi seçimi yoluyla sanatsal bir hiyerarşiyi yansıtırlar: bunlar diğerlerine göre daha dikkatli ve daha zengin bir biçimde işlenmişlerdir. En incelikli ve zarif mozaikler ilk bakışta tedadüfen dağılmış olarak gözükürler. Bu mozaiklerden ilki giriş merdivenlerinin tabanında bulunan 2-7 numaralı atrium döşemesidir. İlgili ikinci bölge 2-3 numaralı atrium döşemesinin merkezinde bulunan paneldir. Bu panel atriumun kuzeybatı köşesinde iki portiğin kesiştiği noktadadır: Bir nar ağacının gösterildiği bu panel nadir resimsel panellerden biridir. Her iki mozaikte de dikkat çekmek maksadıyla yeşil ve mor mermerler gibi alışılmadık malzemeler içerir. Ek olarak, kuzey narteksteki ''U geçişli[40]'' kompleks döşemeden sonra kuzey nefe giriş buranın önemini ve taşıdığı sembolik anlamı vurgulayan diğer bir iddialı resimsel panel içermektedir. Kapıdan görülmesi için yapılan hayat çeşmesini gösterir. Bu panel ağır bir şekilde tahrip olmuştur ama muhtemelen önceki atrium döşemeleriyle aynı nadir materyalleri içermektedir. Bütün düzenleme muhtemelen vaftizhaneye açılan özel bir dolaşım yoluna işaret ediyor olabilirdi. Figürsel sunumun son örneği kompozisyonun küçük bölümlerinde çeşitli hayvanlar, ağaçlar ve kuşların yer aldığı vaftizhanenin güney ekinde yer alır.

Çok renkli etkiler

Orijinal çok renkli bir etki özellikle kilisenin en erken mozaiklerinin olduğu düşünülen Atriumda gözlemlenir. Farklı bir algılama oluşturmak için yaygın izotropik motiflerde renk kullanması yoluyla

---

39. Amisos'daki merkez motif yakınındaki U geçişli tasarıma yakın görülmektedir, Akkaya 1997, res. 3.
40. Restorasyon safhasında bu döşeme S kompartımanı içinde daha sonra taklit edilmiştir.

olur. Bu güney atriumun birkaç izotropik deseninde ortaya çıksa da Kuzey atriumda açıkça görülür, fakat daha hafif ve az vurgulu bir şekilde yapılmıştır (2-8C, 2-9A ve 2-9B). Bu yönelim kuzey ve güney neflerde ve nartekste gibi aynı atölyeden olan mozaikler de dahil olmak üzere başka bir yerde yoktur. Bu, orta nefin daha geç safhalarında daha az dikkat çekicidir.

Mozaiğin Teknik Özellikleri

Mozaiğin depremler gibi doğal afetlere uyumunu gösteren bazı teknik özellikler dikkatimizi çekti. Narteksin güney bölümünde tuğla ve kiremit parçalarının köşe kısmına yerleştirilmesiyle oluşturulan ünik bir destek gözlemledik. Dinsel, ekonomik, geçici baskıların getirdiği felaketten sonra kiliseyi restore etmek için çeşitli önlemler alınmıştır: orta nefteki daha erken dönemdeki harç yeni bir mozaiğin döşenmesinde tekrar kullanılmıştır. Güney nefte, kısmi olarak tahrip edilen mozaiğin parçaları boşlukların doldurulması yoluyla basit bir biçimde korunmuştur. Bu hızlı bir biçimde yeniden inşa edilen mozaikler desteklerinin daha kötü durumda olmasına bağlı olarak daha kırılgandır.

Biz ayrıca bazı belirli yerlerde özel renk ve değerli materyallerin seçildiğini sezebiliyoruz: nadir mer-merler (mor ve açık yeşil) bazı zarif mozaiklerde kullanılmıştır.

Mozaik inşasının hiçbir ana safhasına ait olmayan birkaç tamirat gösteriyor ki, tamiratlar bu safhalar arasındaki zamanlarda çevredeki döşemelerin motiflerini taklit etmeyi bile denemeyen profesyonel olmayan kişilerce yapılmıştır. Mozaiğin günümüze ulaşmasını sağlayan kaba yamalardan oluşmaktadır.

İki alanda, her biri ayrı ayrı olarak, güney nefte (döşeme 8-1, neredeyse tamamen tahrip olmuş) narteksin güney bölümünde (env. 5) hazırlık çizimlerine ait izler keşfedilmiştir. Harcın üst katmanında çizilen ince çizgiler ızgara biçimindedirler. Çizimlerin tamamlanmasına yardım ettiği hazırlayıcı çizimlerin üzerinde olan bu iki döşeme oldukça karmaşık tasarımlara sahiptir.

Çeşitli yoğunluktaki tesseralar verilen bir mozaiğin hangi atölye tarafından yapıldığını belirlemesine yardımcı olur. Bunlardan bir tabloyu ek bir bölüm içerisinde sunuyoruz (Ek 3).

Bir sanatçının fantezisi (?)

Güney nefin dış kenarlarında dengeli bir kare olması beklenen yerde tek bir çiçeğin yer aldığı tuhaf bir etki görülmektedir (döşeme 8-2).

İkinci anormallik kuzey nefteki 7-3 döşemesinin alışılmış ve ölçülü tasarımında görülür. Döşeme batı yönünde sıradan bir pul motifi ile başlar ve geçişsiz bir şekilde *peltae* motifiyle son bulur. Bu iki parçanın arasında bir bordür var olsaydı bu durum şaşırtıcı olmazdı fakat buradaki tasarım bir kesintiye uğramaksızın değişmiştir: aslında *peltaeler* yalnızca ölçeklerin doldurulmasının farklı bir yoludur. Tek bir motifte bu tür bir değişimin başka bir örneği yoktur.

Güncel Restorasyon Programı

Xanthos'taki Fransız arkeoloji ekibi doğu bazilikasındaki mozaiklerin *in situ* halinde korunmasına karar vermiştir. Mozaikler kazılar süresince sistematik bir şekilde sağlamlaştırılmış ve bazen gerekli görülen yerlerde destekleri değiştirilmek amacıyla kaldırılmış fakat daima yerine geri konmuşlardır. Mozaiğin zemininin üzerinde yürünmesini önlemek ve mozaikleri çeşitli dış unsurlardan korumak için çeşitli koruma denemeleri yapılmış ve mozaiklerin ahenkli bir drenajı olmuştur.

Kilisede üç farklı ekip çalışmıştır. İlki, 1986-1988 yılları arasında çalışan, "Atelier de Restauration de la Pierre et du Bois" (Ahşap ve taş restorasyonu atölyeleri)'dan Fransız restoratör J.-M. Dupage'dı. Yuvarlak büyük bir ahşap parça ile orta nef mozaiğinin büyük bir kısmını kaldırdı. Bu sayede mozaiğin alt tabakalarında kazılar yapılabildi. Böylelikle yeni bir desteğin hazırlanması ve mozaiğin daha sonra in situ yerleştirilmesi mümkün oldu. O ayrıca güney narteks bölümündeki çok kırılgan olan ve üzeri likenlerle kaplı mozaikleri de kaldırmıştır. Ek olarak verimli bir drenaja sahip olan yeni bir destek hazırladı ve mozaiği in situ biçiminde bulunduğu yere koydu fakat mozaiği koruyan bezi kaldırmak için geri dönmedi.

Daha sonra P. Blanc ve L. Krougly'nin ekibi, "Atelier de Conservation et de Restauration du Musée d'Arles Antique" (Arles Antik müzesi Restorasyon ve Konzervasyon atölyesi) 1992-2001 yılları arasında altı defa bölgeye gelmişler ve kilisedeki diğer mozaiklerin tümünü kontrol etmişlerdir[41]. Onlar boşlukları temizlemişler ve doldurmuşlar bazı batık mozaikleri orijinal seviyelerine getirmişler, kötü bir şekilde korunan (su geçirmezliğini kaybeden) harcın değiştirilmesi için parçaları kaldırmışlar, bitkilerin yayılımını önlemek için birçok bölgeyi kurutmuşlardır. Mozaiklere geçici bir koruma yaratmak amacıyla özel bir ilgi göstermişlerdir, çeşitli çözümler bölge koşullarına uyum sağlayabilecek en iyi çözümü bulabilmek için çeşitli teknikler denemişlerdir. Bu teknikler, mozaiklerin üzerine kalın bir tabaka halinde nehir çakılları konulması ve üzerlerine dokunmamış tekstil veya 40 cm kumla kaplı plastik örtüler konulmuştur[42]. Mozaiklerin in situ hallerinde bakımları ve yerel materyallerin kullanımı konusunda bölge sakinlerini her zaman bilgilendirmeye çalışmışlardır. Ek olarak zaman zaman konservasyon'un gelişimini gözlemlemek için geri dönmeyi önermişler fakat bunu yapmaya fırsatları olmamıştır. Turistlerin kilise içine girmesini engellemek için, kilisenin çevresi dikenli telle çevrilmiş, fakat bu tür bir koruma çok etkili değildir.

Daha yakın zamanlarda, bir Ş. Yeşil Erdek yönetiminde Xanthos mozaiklerini çalışmak üzere bir Türk ekip bölgeye gelmiş. 2007'de sivil bazilika, decumanus'un güney portiği, leda hamamları ve Likya akropolisindeki yerleşimler ile ilgili geniş çaplı bir restorasyon programı uygulamışlardır. Ş. Yeşil Erdek ekibi 2008 senesinde narteksdeki *opus sectile* tabanında restorasyon çalışmaları sürdürmüştür.

Bu takım ayrıca 4 veya 5 yıldır güneş ve yağmurlardan dolayı zarar gören doğu bazilikasının atriumunda bir kez daha restorasyona başlamaya niyetlenmiştir[43]. S. Yeşil Erdek gelecek için döşemesi Doupage'ın restorasyonundan beri üzeri yapıştırıcı ve bezle kaplı güney narteksin durumunu araştırmayı planlamıştır-gelecek dönemde yapılacak kampanyada tamamlanmak üzere. O, daha fazla tahribi önlemek amacıyla mozaiklerin tümünü iyileştirmeyi ve korumalarını kontrol etmeyi düşünmüştür. Kalıcı bir çözüm getirilene kadar, her turist sezonunun sonunda yıllık bir tetkik yapılması mozaiklerin durumunu tasdik etmek ve güvenliklerinden emin olmak için kesinlikle gereklidir.

Çeşitli kişiler belirli alanlara çatıların yapılmasını ve turistler için yürüme yolu yapılmasını içeren genel bir restorasyon ve halka sunum programı yapılmasını önermişlerdir. 1997 senesinde P. Blanc, L. Krougly ve H. Cabilen (mimar) bazilika tabanına dair genel bir restorasyon ve sunum projesi önermişlerdir. Ş. Yeşil Erdek ve M. Türkeli (mühendis) halen bazilikanın batı bölümünün çatısına ilişkin bir projeyi sürdürmektedir.

---

41. Blanc-Krougly 1998, Blanc-Krougly 2003, Blanc 2003.

42. 2007'de, bu korumanın konulmasından on yıl sonra, Kuzey ve Güney sahanlar bozulmamış olarak bulundu. Nefte, çeşitli yerlerde bir kaç çalılık çıkmıştı ve bu endişe vermeye devam ediyordu.

43. Bu korpusta yer alan, tahribattan önce çekilmiş olan, fotoğraflarda görülebileceği üzere, bazilikada en iyi korunmuş olan taban döşemesi buydu. 2001 yılında P. Blanc ve L. Krougly tarafından dikkatlice restore edildi. Bakımsızlıktan ve yıllık koruması yapılmadığı için nasıl bu kadar çabuk kötüleştiğini görmek üzüntü verici ve şimdi büyük bir risk altında: 2007'de mozaikler bozulma tehlikesi altındaydı. Ş. Yeşil Erdek restorasyon çalışması başlatmıştır.

180. View of S atrium before restoration/ Güney atrium görüntüsü, restorasyon öncesi.

Yapının Kronolojisi

Erken Bizans döşemelerine ait iki ana dönem gözlemledik: bir yapım safhası ve tekrar yapım safhası. Bu iki safha birbirine yakındır ve tahmini terk ediliş tarihi olan 5. yüzyılın ortalarından 6. yüzyılın ortalarına tarihlenir[44]. İki safha arasında vuku bulmuş olan tahribat bugün de bu bölgede sıklıkla görüldüğü gibi büyük bir depreme bağlı olarak gelişmiştir[45]. Vaftizhane ve ekleri kilisenin doğusunun altına inşa edilmiştir ve belki de bu rekonstrüksyon safhasına aittir.

Bu önemli yeniden inşa etme seferberliği hızlı bir şekilde uygulanmış, bu kilise muhtemelen çok kısa bir süre içerisinde yeniden ibadete açılmıştır: daha önce *opus sectile* halinde konulmuş olan orta nef döşemesi tamamen kaldırılmış ve bu türde nadir bir örnek olarak bir mozaikle yer değiştirilmiştir. Genellikle daha değerli olarak görülen *opus sectile* döşemesi mozaiğin yerine gelir. Xanthos'ta, ekonomik faktörlere bağlı olarak, depreme karşı *opus sectile* döşemenin dayanıksızlığı gibi faktörler bu kararı etkilemiştir. Bir mozaiğin üretilmesi daha ucuzdur ve işi çabuklaştırmak adına ve finansal zorluklardan dolayı önceki harç burada yeniden kullanılmıştır.

Kilisenin tamiratlarının aceleye getirilmesi, döşemelerin daha iyi korunduğu güney nef mozaiklerinde de görülebilir: Burada boşluklar, az çok orijinal tasarımı takip eden yeni mozaiklerle doldurulmuştur. Burada da daha erken mozaiklerin bazı bölümleri oldukça derine batmış ve yeni döşeme seviyesi kurmak adına tahrip olmuş mozaikten alınan devşirme parçalarla kaplanmıştır. Burada inşa safhasının bitiminden önce bir deprem olması muhtemeldir (safha 1). Bununla birlikte iki safha arasındaki atölyelerin değiştiği gözlenmiştir.

Kilise, bu rekonstrüksyondan sonra tekrar 6. yüzyılın ikinci yarısı veya 7. yüzyılın başlarında vuku bulmuş başka bir büyük depremle tahrip olmuştur: çatının büyük bir bölümü ve sıra sütunlar çökmüş, bölge bir tapım merkezi olarak terk edilmiştir. Artık, kilisede kitleler halinde törenler yapılamadığından, eski apsis yakınındaki kutsal alan 7. yüzyılın ortalarından sonra mezarlık alanı olarak kullanılmıştır.

11. yüzyıl, harabe haldeki duvarlar içerisinde bir yapının kurulumuna tanıklık eder. Burada korunan eski vaftizhane ve tahrip olmuş bazilikanın

---

44. Söz konusu bu tarih mimari, heykeltıraşlık (başlıklar ve yüksek paravanlar) ve seramik çalışmaları ile yayın dizisi içindeki çalışmalarda doğrulanmıştır.
45. Akdeniz'in doğu bölümünde depremle ilgili birçok örnek biliyoruz: Rodos'ta İ.S 515-16 da, 518'de Sagalassos'da, 529-530 da Myra'da, 554 Kos'da, 560 Arykanda'da. 6. yüzyılın ilk yarısında tekrarlayan felaketler nedeniyle korkunç bir istikrarsızlık vardı. Foss 1996 II, p. 26; Duggan 2004, p. 134-170.

181. View of S atrium after restoration/ Güney atrium görüntüsü, restorasyon sonrası.

kısmi olarak yeniden oluşturulmuş batı ve kuzey bölümlerinde içinde bir kilise inşa edilmiştir. Bu kilise sadece ayakta duran aziz ve savaşçı betimlerini (yeni narteksin içinde ve bina topluluğunun girişinde) temsil eden duvar resimlerinden dolayı ilginç değil aynı zamanda güzel bir *opus sectile* zemin ve sunak bölümünde yapılmış *ikonostasi*sle sahneleri de ilgi çeker.

Yapı kompleksi 11. yüzyılın sonlarından 13. yüzyılın ilk yarısı arasında bir dönemde kullanılmamıştır ve aralıklı olarak bir yeniden iskân döneminden sonra büyük bir yangının izlerinin gösterdiği gibi yeni bir felaket, kompleksin tamamen tahrip olmasına sebep olmuştur.

Bu son olaydan sonra kilise Osmanlı dönemine kadar kullanım görmemiştir.

Sonuçlar

Doğu Bazilikasındaki mozaiklerin dekoratif ve teknik kalitesi, farklı dönemlerde burada çalışmış olan çeşitli atölyelerin yüksek tecrübe ve yeteneklerini sergilemektedir. Muhtemelen onlar, Erken Bizans döneminde, Xanthos'un sadece dini yapılarını değil, aynı zamanda dünyevi nitelik taşıyan gelişmekte olan diğer yapılarını da süsleme fırsatına sahipti. Geç 5. ve 6. yüzyıl evleri, kazı çalışması yapılmış evler arasında çoğunluğu teşkil etmemekle birlikte, aristokrat sınıfa ait çok sayıda konut da mozaiklerle döşenmişti. Son kazılar, şehrin bu dönemdeki önemini açıkça göstermektedir. Bunu da Doğu Bazilikanın kuzeyinde yer alan piskoposlara ait komplekste keşfedilen kanıtlardan anlıyoruz. Bu kazılar ve aynı dönem mozaiklerinin birçoğunun üzerine yapılan çalışmalar, Xanthos'taki atölyeler hakkındaki fikirlerimizi aydınlatabilirdi ve belki de halen yanıtlanmamış bir sorunun cevabını verebilirdi: Xanthos aynı dönemde çalışmış ve farklılıklarına rağmen genel bir üslup birliğine varmış birçok atölyeden oluşan bir mozaik üretim merkezi miydi? Yoksa atölyeler bölgeye dışarıdan mı getirilmişti?

Abbreviations

The abbreviations follow those used in the *Bulletin de l'Association internationale pour l'étude de la mosaïque antique*, vol. 1-20.

Institutions, revues…

AIEMA	Association internationale pour l'étude de la Mosaïque antique
AJA	American Journal of Archaeology
AnatoliaA	Anatolia Antiqua
AnTard	Antiquité tardive
AnzWien	Anzeiger, Österreichische Akademie der Wissenschaften, philosophisch, historische Klasse, Vienna.
ArchAnAth	Archaiologika Analecta Athènon
ArkST	Arkeometri Sonuçları Toplantısı
AS	Anatolian Studies
ASAA	Annuario della Scuola archeologica di Atene e delle missioni italiane in Oriente
AST	Araştırma Sonuçları Toplantısı
BAR	British Archaeological Report
BASOR	Bulletin of the American School of Oriental Research
BCH	Bulletin de Correspondance Hellénique
CIAC	Congresso internazionale di Archeologia Cristiana
CIEB	Congrès international d'études byzantines
CMGR	La Mosaïque gréco-romaine, Colloques internationaux de l'AIEMA
DOP	Dumbarton Oaks Papers
DossArch	Dossiers de l'Archéologie (les)
EFA	Ecole française d'Athènes
EHB	The Economic History of Byzantium from the Seventh through the Fifteenth Century
ENS	Ecole normale supérieure, Paris
ICCM	International commitee for the Conservation of Mosaics (conferences)
IFEA	Institut français d'Etudes anatoliennes, Istanbul
IM	Mitteilungen des Deutschen archäologischen Instituts, Istanbul
JbAC	Jahrbuch für Antike und Christentum
JÖByz	Jahrbuch des Österreichischen Byzantinistik
JRA	Journal of Roman Archaeology
KST	Kazı Sonuçları Toplantısı
MAMA	Monumenta Asiae Minoris Antiqua
MKKS	Müze Kurtarma Kazıları Semineri
MiChA	Mitteilungen zur christlichen Archäeologie
RA	Revue archéologique
RivAC	Rivista di Archeologia Cristiana
TAD	Türk Arkeoloji Dergisi
TM	Travaux et Mémoires

Authors of the plans and designs

JLB	Jean-Luc Biscop
MGF	Marie-Geneviève Froidevaux
MPR	Marie-Pat Raynaud
GB	Gérard Bernard

Other abbreviations

Rm.	room
Bas.	basilica
Ph.	Photograph

Bibliography and Abbreviations

Akıllı 1988
> AKILLI H., "Arykanda ve Perge Mozaiklerinin Bozulma Nedenleri ve Yerinde Koruma Sorunları," IV, *ArkST*, 1988, pp. 187-214.

Akkaya 1997
> AKKAYA M., "Amisos Antik Kenti Kurtarma Kazısı ve Mozaik Kaldırma Çalışmaları," VIII, *MKKS*, 1997, pp. 43-51.

Akyürek 2006
> AKYÜREK E., "The Bey Dağları in the Byzantine Period : Trebenna, Neapolis and their Territories," in Lycie antique 2006, I, pp. 1-18.

Andaloro 2005
> ANDALORO M., "Küçük Tavşan Adası: 2003 Report," *AST*, 23-2, 2005, pp. 41-53.

Antioch Mosaics 2000
> *Antioch Mosaics*, F. Cimok (ed.), Istanbul, 2000.

Armstrong 2006
> ARMSTRONG P., "Rural Settlement in Lycia in the Eight Century : New Evidence," in Lycie antique 2006, I, pp. 19-30.

Asano 1997
> ASANO K., "The Excavation of Church III on Gemiler Ada near Fethiye," *KST*, 18/2, 1997, pp. 449-470.

Asano 1998
> *Island of St Nicholas, Excavation of Gemiler Island on Mediterranean Coast of Turkey*, K. Asano (ed.), Karya, 1998.

Asano 2000
> ASANO K., "The Survey and Excavation Gemiler Adası Kaya Area near Fethiye (1999 season)," *AST*, 18/1, 2000, pp. 31-40.

Balty 1972
> BALTY J.-Ch., *Le groupe épiscopal d'Apamée, dit Cathédrale de l'Est. Premières recherches*, Bruxelles, 1972, pp. 187-208 (Fouilles d'Apamée de Syrie, 7).

Balty 1984
BALTY J., "Les mosaïques de Syrie au v{e} siècle et leur répertoire," *Byzantion*, LIV/2, 1984, pp. 437-467.

Balty 1989
BALTY J., "La mosaïque en Syrie," in *Colloque Archéologie et Histoire de la Syrie,* 1989, II, pp. 491-523.

Balty 1995
BALTY J., *Mosaïques antiques du Proche-Orient*, Besançon, 1995.

Barral I Altet 1985
BARRAL I ALTET X., *Les mosaïques de pavement médiévales de Venise, Murano, Torcello,* Paris, 1985.

Barrington 2000
Barrington Atlas of the Greek and Roman World, R.J.A. Talbert (ed.), Princeton-Oxford, 2000.

Bar Shay 1995
BAR SHAY A., "Un livre de modèles dans la mosaïque géométrique," in *CMGR* V, II, pp. 113-124.

Bayburtluoğlu 2004
BAYBURTLUOĞLU C., *Lycia*, Antalya, 2004.

Blanc 2003
BLANC P., "Découvertes de basiliques paléochrétiennes : expériences de conservation *in situ* des sols en mosaïques," in *Colloque Cathedral Workshops Project on Religious Arts and Crafts. "Mosaic Arts and Craftsmanship: their Value in Terms of Conservation and Promotion," Venice 1999,* Città del Vaticano/Conseil de l'Europe, 2003, pp. 50-54.

Blanc-Kroughly 1998
BLANC P., KROUGHLY L., "La conservation des pavements de la basilique épiscopale de Xanthos," *Xanthos, DossArch*, 239, déc. 1998, pp. 84-85.

Blanc-Krougly 2003
BLANC P., KROUGLY L., "La basilique épiscopale de Xanthos (Turquie). Problématique de conservation *in situ* et de coopération," in *ICCM* 6, pp. 31-39.

Borchardt 1977
BORCHARDT J. *et alii*, "Limyra: Bericht über die Abschlusskampagne 1974," *TAD*, XXIV-1, 1977, pp. 85-110.

Borchardt 1997
BORCHARDT J., "Bericht der Grabungskampagne in Limyra 1996," *KST*, 19/2, 1997, pp. 1-52.

Buchet-Manière Lévêque 2006
BUCHET L., MANIÈRE LÉVÊQUE A.-M., "La perception de phénomènes migratoires. La variation biologique intra-site: Xanthos (Turquie) à l'époque byzantine," in *La paléodémographie. Mémoire d'os, mémoire d'hommes, Actes des 8e journées anthropologiques de Valbonne, Juin 2003*, L. Buchet, C. Dauphin, I. Séguy (ed.),Valbonne, 2006, pp. 133-147.

Budde 1969
BUDDE L., *Antiken Mosaiken in Kilikien, I, Misis-Mopsuestia*, Recklinghausen, 1969.

Budde 1972
BUDDE L., *Antiken Mosaiken in Kilikien, II, Die Heidnischen Mosaiken*, Recklinghausen, 1972.

Campbell 1941
CAMPBELL W.A., *The Martyrion at Seleucia Pieria, The Excavation 1937-1939*, Princeton-Oxford-Den Hag, 1941 (Antioch-on-the-Orontes III).

Campbell 1988
CAMPBELL S., *The Mosaics of Antioch*, Toronto, 1988.

Campbell 1991
CAMPBELL S., *The Mosaics of Aphrodisias in Caria*, Toronto, 1991.

Campbell 1998
CAMPBELL S., *The Mosaics of Anemurium*, Toronto, 1998.

Canbilen-Lebouteiller-Sodini 1996
CANBILEN H., LEBOUTEILLER P., SODINI J.-P., "La basilique de l'Acropole haute de Xanthos," *AnatoliaA*, 4, 1996, pp. 201-229.

Céramiques Lycie 2007
Céramiques antiques en Lycie (VIIe s. a.C. – VIIe s. p.C.). Les produits et les marchés, Actes de la table-ronde de Poitiers (20-22 mars 2003), S. Lemaître (ed.), Bordeaux, 2007 (Ausonius Etudes 16).

Chypre du Nord 1995
Chypre du Nord, une mosaïque de culture, A Turism Yayınları & North Cyprus Museum Friends (ed.), Istanbul, 1995.

Crowfoot 1941
CROWFOOT J.W., *Early Churches in Palestine*, London, 1941.

Cvetković-Tomašević 2002
CVETKOVIĆ-TOMASEVIĆ G., *Corpus des mosaïques paléobyzantines de pavement*, I, Beograd, 2002.

Dauphin 2005
DAUPHIN C., "Ste Marie de la Probatique à Jérusalem (territoire français): Mosaïques de pavement, stratigraphie architecturale et histoire événementielle," in *CMGR* IX, 1, pp. 247-261.

Décor I
Le Décor géométrique de la Mosaïque romaine. I Répertoire graphique et descriptif des compositions linéaires et isotropes, Collectif (Balmelle C., Blanchard-Lemée M, Christophe J., Darmon J.-P., Guimier-Sorbets A.-M., Lavagne H., Prudhomme R., Stern H.), Dessins Prudhomme R., Paris, 1985.

Décor II
Le Décor géométrique de la Mosaïque romaine. II Répertoire graphique et descriptif des décors centrés, Collectif (Balmelle C., Blanchard-Lemée M., Darmon J.-P., Gozlan S., Raynaud M.-P.), Dessins Raynaud M.-P., Paris, 2002.

Dedeoğlu 1993
DEDEOĞLU H., "Lydia'da bir Kilise Kazısı," IV, *MKKS*, 1993, pp. 185-198.

Demiriz 1968
DEMIRIZ Y., "Demre'deki Aziz Nikolaos Kilisesi," *TAD*, XV-1, 1968, pp. 13-34.

Demiriz 2002
DEMIRIZ Y., *Örgülü Bizans Döşeme Mozaikleri / Interlaced Byzantine Mosaic Pavements*, Istanbul, 2002.

De Bernardi Ferrero 1995
DE BERNARDI FERRERO D.F., "Frigya Hierapolis'i 1993, Kazı ve Restorasyonu," *KST*, 16/2, 1995, pp. 345-360.

De Nuccio-Ungaro 2002
I marmi colorati della Roma Imperiale, Catalogo della Mostra, M. De Nuccio, L. Ungara (ed.), Veggiano (PD), 2002.

Del Bufalo 2004
DEL BUFALO D., *Marbres de couleur, pierres et architecture de l'antiquité au XVIIIe siècles*, Arles, 2004.

Des Courtils 2003
DES COURTILS J., *Guide de Xanthos et du Letôon*, Istanbul, 2003.

Des Courtils-Cavalier 2001
DES COURTILS J., CAVALIER L., "The City of Xanthos from Archaic to Byzantine Times," in *Urbanism in Western Asia Minor, New Studies on Aphrodisias, Ephesos, Hierapolis, Pergamon, Perge and Xanthos*, D. Parrish (ed.), Portsmouth, 2001, pp. 148-171 (*JRA, Supplementary Series* 45).

Des Courtils-Laroche 2003
DES COURTILS J., LAROCHE D., "Xanthos et Letoon: rapport sur la campagne 2002," *AnatoliaA*, 11, 2003, pp. 423-456.

Des Courtils-Laroche 2004
DES COURTILS J., LAROCHE D., "Xanthos et Letoon: rapport sur la campagne 2003," *AnatoliaA*, 12, 2004, pp. 309-340.

Des Courtils *et alii* 2006
DES COURTILS *et alii*, "La campagne 2005 à Xanthos," *AnatoliaA*, 14, 2006, pp. 275-291.

Di Matteis 2004
DI MATTEIS L.M., *Mosaici di Cos*, Athinai, 2004.

Donceel-Voûte 1988
DONCEEL-VOÛTE P., *Les pavements des églises byzantines de Syrie et du Liban. Décor, archéologie et liturgie*, Louvain-la-Neuve, 1988.

Duggan 2004
DUGGAN T.M.P., "A Short Account of Recorded Calamities (Earthquakes and Plagues) in Antalya Province and Adjacent", *Adalya*, VII, 2004, p. 123-170.

Dunbabin 1999
DUNBABIN K.M.D., *Mosaics of the Greek and Roman World*, Cambridge, 1999.

Equini Schneider 1997
EQUINI SCHNEIDER E., "Excavations and Research at Elaiussa Sebaste, 1995 First Campaign," *KST*, 18/2, 1997, pp. 367-381.

Equini Schneider 1998
EQUINI SCHNEIDER E., "1997 Excavations and Research at Elaiussa Sebaste, Turkey," *KST*, 20/2, 1999, pp. 385-402.

Equini Schneider 2008
EQUINI SCHNEIDER E., *Elaiussa Sebaste*, Istanbul, 2008.

Eyice 1963
EYICE S., "Two Mosaic Pavements from Bithynia," *DOP*, 17, 1963, pp. 373-383.

Fant 1988
Ancient Marble Quarrying and Trade, J.C. Fant (ed.), Oxford, 1988 (*BAR* International Series 453).

Farioli-Borboudakis 2005
FARIOLI CAMPANATI R., BORBOUDAKIS M., "La decorazione pavimentale e parietale della cattedrale di Gortina (Creta): nuovi elementi di datazione del pavimento musivo della navata," in *CMGR* IX, 1, pp. 165-171.

Feld 1975
FELD O., "Die Innenausstattung der Nilolaoskirche in Myra, der Opus sectile-Boden," in *Myra, eine lykische Metropole in antiker und byzantinischer Zeit*, J. Borchhardt (ed.), Berlin, 1975, p. 394-397 (Istanbuler Forschungen 30).

Foss 1996 II
FOSS C., "The Lycian Coast in the Byzantine Age," *DOP*, 48, 1994, pp. 1-52 (*Cities, Fortresses and Villages of Byzantine Asia Minor*, Variorum, Aldershot, 1996, Study II).

Foss 1996 III
FOSS C., "Cities and Villages of Lycia in the Life of St Nicholas of Holy Zion," *Greek Orthodox Theological Review*, 36, 1991, pp. 303-339 (*Cities, Fortresses and Villages of Byzantine Asia Minor*, Variorum, Aldershot, 1996, Study III).

Froidevaux-Raynaud 2005
FROIDEVAUX M.-G., RAYNAUD M.-P., "Les pavements en *opus sectile* de la cathédrale de Xanthos," in *Hommages J.-P. Sodini*, 2005, pp. 137-161 (*TM* 15).

Glass 1980
GLASS D.F., *Studies on Cosmatesque Pavements*, Oxford, 1980 (*BAR* International Series 82).

Gnoli 1971
GNOLI R., *Marmora Romana*, Roma, 1971 (reedition 1988).

Gough 1958
GOUGH M.R.E., "Report on Archaeological Work Carried out at Alahan in 1957," *TAD*, VIII-2, 1958, pp. 6-7, pls. I-IX.

Gough 1961
GOUGH, M.R.E., "Karlık and Dağ Pazarı, 1958," *TAD*, IX-2, 1961, pp. 5-6.

Grossman-Severin 2003
GROSSMAN P., SEVERIN H.G., *Fruhchristliche und byzantinische Bauten im südöstlichen Lykien. Ergebnisse zweier Surveys*, Tübingen, 2003.

Guidobaldi 1984
   GUIDOBALDI F., "Pavimenti in opus sectile di Corinto e Nikopolis, originalità e area di diffusione," in Xe CIAC (Thessalonique 1980), Città del Vaticano, 1984, pp. 167-182.

Guidobaldi-Guiglia Guidobaldi 1983
   GUIDOBALDI F., GUIGLIA-GUIDOBALDI A., *Pavimenti Marmorei di Roma dal IV al IX secolo,* Città del Vaticano, 1983.

Guidoboni 1994
   GUIDOBONI E., *Catalogue of Ancient Earthquakes in the Mediterranean Area up to the 10th Century*, Roma, 1994.

Guiglia-Guidobaldi 1984
   GUIGLIA-GUIDOBALDI A., "I pavimenti in opus sectile di Filippi, Tipologia i ascendenze," in Xe CIAC (Thessalonique 1980), Città del Vaticano, 1984, pp. 153-166.

Hadjichristophi 2005
   HADJICHRISTOPHI P., "La Basilique du Bord de mer à Kourion (Chypre)," in CMGR IX, 1, pp. 405-411.

Hanfmann 1973
   HANFMANN G.M.A., "Excavation and Restoration in Sardis," TAD, XX/1, 1973, pp. 100-101.

Hanfmann-Detweiler 1962
   HANFMANN G.M.A., DETWEILER A.H., "The Fourth Campaign at Sardis (1961)," TAD, XI/2, 1962, pp. 40-45.

Hanfmann-Detweiler 1968
   HANFMANN G.M.A., DETWEILER A.H., "Excavations at Sardis in 1966," TAD, XV/1, 1968, pp. 75-87.

Hawkins-Mundell-Mango 1973
   HAWKINS E., MUNDELL M., MANGO C., "The Mosaics of the Monastery of Mar Samuel, Mar Simeon and Mar Gabriel near Kartmin," DOP, 27, 1973, pp. 279-296.

Hellenkemper
   HELLENKEMPER H., "Early Church Architecture in Southern Asia Minor," in *Churches Built in Ancient Times-Recent Studies in Early Christian Archaeology*, K. Painter (ed.), London, without date, pp. 213-218.

Hellenkemper-Hild 2004
   HELLENKEMPER H., HILD F., *Lykien und Pamphylien, Tabula Imperii Byzantini* 8, Wien, 2004.

Herzfeld-Guyer 1930
   HERZFELD E., GUYER S., *Korykos und Meriamlik*, Manchester, 1930 (MAMA II).

Hill 1995
   HILL S., "The First Season of Rescue Excavation at Çiftlik (Sinop)," AS, 45, 1995, pp. 219-231.

Hörmann 1951
   HÖRMANN H., *Die Johanneskirche in Ephesos*, Wien, 1951 (Forschungen in Ephesos IV, 3).

Inan 1985
   INAN J., "Perge Kazısı 1984 Çalışmaları," KST, 7, 1985, pp. 397-420.

Işık 1999
   IŞIK F., "Patara 1997," KST, 20/2, 1999, pp. 159-171.

Işık 2000
   IŞIK F., *Patara*, Antalya, 2000.

Jacopi 1932-33
   JACOPI G., "Le basiliche paleocristiane di Arcassa (Scarpanto)," in *Clara Rhodos*, VI-VII, Rhodos, 1932-33, pp. 553-568, pls. LI, LII.

Jacopich 1925
   JACOPICH G., *Edifici bizantini di Scarpanto, mosaici e iscrizioni*, Rhodos, 1925.

Jobst 1977
   JOBST W., *Römische Mozaiken aus Ephesos I. Die Hanghäuser des Embolos*, Wien, 1977 (Forschungen in Ephesos VIII-2).

Jolivet 1981
   JOLIVET C., "Peintures byzantines inédites à Xanthos (Lycie)," in *XVI Internationaler Byzantinistenkongress*, II-5, JÖByz 32/5, 1981, pp. 73-84, pls. I et II.

Jolivet-Raynaud 2000
   JOLIVET-LEVY C., RAYNAUD M.-P., "Xanthos, mosaïques murales," AnatoliaA, 8, 2000, pp. 366-371.

Kadıoğlu 1997
   KADIOĞLU M., "Ankyra. Ulus Opus Sectileleri," TAD, XXXI, 1997, pp. 351-382.

Kier 1970
   KIER H., *Der mittelalterliche Schmuckfussboden unter besonderer Berücksichtung des Rheinlands*, Düsseldorf, 1970.

Kitzinger 1974
   KITZINGER E., "A Fourth Century Mosaic Floor in Pisidian Antioch," in *Mélanges Mansel (Mansel'e Armağan)*, I, Ankara, 1974, pp. 385-395.

Lassus 1938-1
   LASSUS J., "L'église cruciforme, Antioche-Kaoussié 12-F," Princeton, 1938 (Antioch-on-the-Orontes, II, The Excavations 1933-36).

Lassus 1938-2
   LASSUS J., "Une villa de plaisance à Yakto," Princeton, 1938 (Antioch-on-the-Orontes, II, The Excavations 1933-36).

Lazzarini 2004
   Pietre e Marmi Antichi: natura, caratterizzazione, origine, storia d'uso, diffusione, collezionismo, L. Lazzarini (ed.), Padova, 2004.

Lazzarini 2007
   LAZZARINI L., *Poikiloi Lithoi, Versiculores Maculae: I marmi colorati della Grecia antica,* Pisa-Roma, 2007.

Levi 1947
   LEVI D., *Antioch Mosaic Pavements*, Princeton, 1947.

Levi 1966
   LEVI D., "Le campagne 1962-1964 a Iasos," ASAA (bull 2) 44, 1966, pp. 413-414.

Lightfoot 2007
: Lightfoot C. and M., *Amorium, A Byzantine City in Anatolia*, Istanbul, 2007.

Lightfoot-Ivison 1995
: Lightfoot C.S., Ivison E.A. *et alii*, "Amorium Excavations 1994, the Seventh Preliminary Report," *AS*, 45, 1995, pp. 105-138.

Ling 1998
: Ling R., *Ancient Mosaics*, London, 1998.

Love 1972
: Love I.C., "Excavations at Knidos, 1972," *TAD*, XXI/2, 1974, pp. 85-129

Love 1973
: Love I.C., "Preliminary Report of the Excavations at Knidos, 1972," *AJA*, 77, 1973, pp. 413-424.

Lycie antique 2006
: *Actes du 3ᵉ colloque international sur la Lycie antique, Antalya, 7-10 Novembre 2005*, K. Dörtlük, B. Varkivanç, T. Kahya, J. des Courtils, M. Doğan Alparslan, R. Boyraz (ed.), Antalya, 2006.

Madrid 2001
: *Mosaico Romano del Mediterraneo*, Catalogue of the Exhibition, Madrid, 2001.

Maguire 1987
: Maguire H., *Earth and Ocean*, London, 1987.

Maiuri-Jacopich 1928
: Maiuri A., Jacopich G., "Rapporto generale sul servizio archeologico a Rodi e nelle isole dipendenti dall'nno 1912 all'anno 1927," in *Clara Rhodos*, I-1, Rhodos, 1928, pp. 98-104.

Mansel 1974
: Mansel A.M., "1972 Perge Kazısı Önraporu," *TAD*, XXI/1, 1974, pp. 109-113.

Megaw 1976
: Megaw A.H.S., "Interior Decoration in Early Christian Cyprus," in *XV* CIEB, Rapports et co-rapports*, Athinai, 1976, pp. 4-9.

Metzger 1966
: Metzger H., "Fouilles du Létoôn et de Xanthos (1962-65)," *RA*, 1, 1966, pp. 101-112.

Michaelides 1992
: Michaelides D., *Cypriot Mosaics*, Nicosia, 1992.

Michaelides 1993
: Michaelides D., "Opus sectile in Cyprus," in *The Sweet Land of Cyprus, Papers Given at the 25th Jubilee Spring Symposium of Byzantine Studies (Birmingham 1991)*, Nicosia, 1993, pp. 69-113.

Mikulćik 2003
: Mikulćik I., *Stobi, an Ancient City*, Skopje, 2003.

Miltner 1958
: Miltner F., "Bericht über die österreichischen Ausgrabungen in Ephesos im Jahre 1957," *TAD*, VIII, 1958, pp. 19-25.

Mitchell-Waelkens 1998
: Mitchell S., Waelkens M. *et alii*, *Pisidian Antioch, the Site and its Monuments*, London-Duckworth, 1998

Müller-Wiener 1977-78
: Müller-Wiener W., "Milet 1973-1975," *IM*, 27-28, 1977-78, pp. 93-125.

Nallbani-Raynaud
: Nallbani E., Raynaud M.-P., Foerster G., Lako K., Netzer E., "Une synagogue transformée en église," in *CMGR* X, (Conimbriga 2005), forthcoming.

Netzer-Weiss 1994
: Netzer E., Weiss Z., *Zippori*, Jerusalem, 1994.

Ovadiah 1987
: Ovadiah R. and A., *Mosaic Pavements in Israel*, Roma, 1987.

Ölüdeniz Area 1995
: *The Survey of Early Byzantine Sites in Ölüdeniz Area, (Lycia, Turkey)*, S. Tsuji (ed.), Osaka, 1995.

Ötüken 2001
: Ötüken S. Yildiz., Myra-Demre Nikolaos Kilisesi Opus Sectile yer Döşemesi ve Kazıda Ortaya Çıkan Opus Sectile Buluntular, in *Günışığında Anadolu, Cevdet Bayburtluoğlu İçin Yazılar / Anatolia in Daylight. Essays in Honour of Cevdet Bayburtluoğlu*, Istanbul, 2001, pp. 182-188, pls. 1-4.

Ötüken 2002
: Ötüken S. Yildiz., "2001 Yılı Demre-Myra Aziz Nikolaos Kilisesi Kazısı ve Duvar Resimlerini Belgeleme, Koruma-Onarım Çalışmaları," *KST*, 24/2, 2002, pp. 31-46.

Özet 2001
: Özet A., "Torba Manastırı Kazısı," in XII, *MKKS*, 2001, pp. 33-49.

Özgen 2000
: Özgen E., Helwing B., Engin A., "Oylum Höyük, 1998-1999," *KST*, 22-1, 2000, pp. 223-230.

Özyiğit 1999
: Özyiğit S., *Foça-Phocaea*, Izmir, 1999.

Pallas 1977
: Pallas D., *Les monuments paléochrétiens de Grèce découverts de 1959 à 1973*, Pontificio Istituto di Archeologia Cristiana, Vatican, 1977 (Coll. Sussidi allo studio delle antichità cristiane, 5).

Parrish 2001
: Parrish D., "An Early Byzantine Mosaic Workshop Based on Cos: Architectural Context and Pavement Design," *AnTard*, 9, 2001, pp. 331-349.

Pensabene 1998
: *Marmi Antichi II, Cave e technica di lavorazione, provenienza e distributione*, M. Pensabene. (ed.), Rome, 1998 (Studi Miscellanei 31).

Peschlow 1983
: Peschlow U., "Zum byzantinischen Opus Sectile-Boden," in *Festschrift für Kurt Bittel*, Mainz, 1983, pp. 435-447.

Petra Church 2001
: Fiema Z.T., Kanellopoulos C., Waliszewski T., Schieck R., *The Petra Church*, Amman, 2001.

Petrova 2007
   PETROVA E., *Stobi, Guide*, Skopje, 2007.

Piccirillo 1993
   PICCIRILLO M., *The Mosaics of Jordan*, Amman, 1993.

Pillinger 1996
   PILLINGER R., "Die christlichen Denkmäler von Ephesos," *MiChA* 2, 1996, pp. 39-70.

Pralong 1994
   PRALONG A., "La basilique de l'Acropole d'Amathonte (Chypre)," *RivAC*, LXX/1-2, 1994, pp. 412-455.

Prudhomme 1975
   PRUDHOMME R., "Recherches des principes de construction des mosaïques géométriques romaines," in *CMGR* II, pp. 339-347.

Ramage 1972
   RAMAGE A., "The Fourteenth Campain at Sardis (1971)," *BASOR*, 1972, pp. 9-39.

Raynaud 1996
   RAYNAUD M.-P., "La composition en croix de U dans la mosaïque de pavement," *RA*, 1996-1, pp. 69-102.

Raynaud 2008
   RAYNAUD M.-P., "Xanthos, East Basilica, Corpus of the Mosaics of Turkey, volume 1," in *Proceedings of IV. International Mosaic Corpus of Türkiye. The Mosaic Bridge from Past to Present, Gaziantep 6-10 June 2007*, M. Şahin (ed), Bursa, 2008, pp. 119-122.

Raynaud-Sodini 1998
   RAYNAUD M.-P., SODINI J.-P., "Basilique Est," *AnatoliaA*, 6, 1998, pp. 469-471.

Ristow 1998
   RISTOW S., *Frühchristliche Baptisterien*, Munster, 1998 (*JbAC* Ergänzungsband 27).

Roux 1998
   ROUX G., *La basilique de la Campanopetra*, Paris, 1998 (Salamine de Chypre, XV).

Russell 1988
   RUSSELL J., "Conservation and Excavation at Anemurium 1987," *KST*, 10-2, 1988, pp. 261-269.

Salona Christiana 1994
   Salona Christiana, arheološki Muzej, E. Marin (ed.), Split, 1994.

Sear 1977
   SEAR F.B., *Roman Wall and Vault Mosaics*, Heidelberg, 1977 (Mitteilungen des deutschen Archäologischen Instituts. Römische Abteilung, Ergänzungsheft 23).

Sevčenko 1984
   SEVČENKO I., SEVČENKO N.P., *The Life of St. Nicholas of Sion*, Brookline, 1984.

Sevim 1991
   SEVIM A., "Gümüşhane Ili, Kelkit Ilçesi, Yenice Köyü Kurtarma Kazısı," II, *MKKS*, 1991, pp. 373-376.

Slatter 1994
   SLATTER E., *Xanthus. Travels of Discovery in Turkey*, London, 1994.

Smith 1969
   SMITH L.C., "Excavation Report, Eski Anamur (Anemurium), 1968," *TAD*, XVII/2, 1969, pp. 177-184.

Sodini 1968
   SODINI J.-P., *Les pavements de mosaïque dans les basiliques de la Grèce continentale et du Péloponnèse*, Mémoire de l'EFA, 1968 (unpublished copy available in the Archaeology Library of the ENS, Paris).

Sodini 1970
   SODINI J.-P., "Mosaïques paléochrétiennes de Grèce," *BCH* 94, 1970, pp. 699-753.

Sodini 1980
   SODINI J.-P., "Une iconostase Byzantine à Xanthos," in *Actes du Colloque sur la Lycie antique*, Paris, 1980, pp. 119-148 (Bibl. IFEA, 27).

Sodini 1994
   SODINI J.-P., "Le goût du marbre à Byzance : sa signification pour les byzantins et les non-byzantins," in *Cahiers Balkaniques, Cahiers Pierre Belon, Actes du XVIIIe CIEB, (Moscou 1990)*, 1994, 1, pp. 177-201.

Sodini 2002
   SODINI J.-P., "Marble and Stoneworking in Byzantium, Seventh-Fifteenth Centuries," in *EHB* I, A. Laïou (ed.), Washington, 2002, pp. 129-146.

Sodini-Buchet 1996
   SODINI J.-P., BUCHET L., "Réoccupation et démographie médiévale d'édifices religieux paléochrétiens : les cas de Xanthos (Turquie) et Qal'at Sem'an (Syrie)," in *L'identité des populations archéologiques, XVIes rencontres Internationales d'Archéologie d'Antibes*, Sophia-Antipolis, 1996, pp. 367-388.

Speciale 2005
   SPECIALE L., "I sectilia della basilica Desideriana di S. Benedetto a Capua," in *CMGR* IX, 2, pp. 1179-1188.

Spiro 1978
   SPIRO M., *Critical Corpus of the Mosaic Pavements on the Greek Mainland, Fourth-Sixth Centuries, with Architectural Surveys*, New-York-London, 1978.

Stevens-Kalinowski-Vandeleest 2005
   STEVENS S.T., KALINOWSKI A.V., VANDELEEST H., *Bir Ftouha: a Pilgrimage Church Complex at Carthage*, Portsmouth, 2005.

Taşlıalan 1996
   TAŞLIALAN M., "Pisidia Antiocheiası 1995 Yılı Çalışmaları," VII, *MKKS*, 1996, pp. 221-252.

Tatlican 1996
   TATLICAN I., "Sinop, Çiftlik Köyü, Mozaik Kurtarma Kazısı," VII, *MKKS*, 1996, pp. 333-356.

Themelis 1977
   THEMELIS P., "Mosaics of Amphissa" (in Greek), *ArchAnAth*, 10, 1977, pp. 242-250.

Tok 2008
   TOK E., "Kuzey Lydia'da bir Kiliseye Ait Zemin Mozaikleri: Manisa Gördes Çağlayan Köyü Yakınındaki Kilise Kalıntısı," in *Proceedings of IV. International Mosaic Corpus of Türkiye. The Mosaic Bridge*

from Past to Present, Gaziantep 6-10 June 2007, M. Şahin (ed.), Bursa, 2008, pp. 155-159.

Tomaşević 1975
TOMAŞEVIĆ G.C., "Mosaiques paléochrétiennes récemment découvertes à Heraclea Lynkestis," in *CMGR* II, pp. 385-400.

Valeva 1995
VALEVA J., "Geometric Mosaics from Bulgaria," in *CMGR* V, pp. 251-264.

Vetters 1984
VETTERS H., "Vorläufiger Grabungsbericht 1983," *AnzWien*, 121, 1984, p. 215.

Vitti 2005
VITTI M., "Sectilia pavimenta di Salonicco," in *CMGR* IX, 2, pp. 695-711.

Vroom 2007
VROOM J., "Limyra in Lycia : Byzantine/Umayyad Pottery Finds from Excavations in the Eastern Part of the City," in Céramiques Lycie 2007, pp. 262-292.

Waelkens 2000
WAELKENS M., "The 1998-99 Excavation and Restoration Season at Sagalassos," *KST*, 22/2, 2000, pp. 159-180.

Waelkens 2003
WAELKENS M., "Report on the 2002 Excavation and Restoration Campaign at Sagalassos," *KST*, 25/1, 2003, pp. 215-227.

Waelkens 2005
WAELKENS M., "Report on the 2004 Excavation and Restoration Campaign at Sagalassos," *KST*, 27/2, 2005, pp. 271-286.

Ward Perkins-Goodchild 2003
WARD-PERKINS J.B., GOODCHILD R.G., *Christian Monuments of Cyrenaica*, J. Reynolds (ed.), London, 2003 (Society for Libyan Studies, Monograph 4).

Xanthos 1998
Xanthos, DossArch 239, dec. 1998.

Yıldız 1992
YILDIZ H., "Çömlekşaz Köyünde (Böceli) Bulunan Taban Mozayiginin Kurtarma Kazısı," II, *MKKS*, 1992, pp. 197-205.

Zeugma 2007
Belkis-Zeugma and its Mosaics, R. Ergeç (ed.), Istanbul, 2007.

Zikos 1989
ZIKOS N., *Amphipolis chrétienne et byzantine*, Athinai, 1989.

Zoroğlu 2003
ZOROĞLU K.L., ÇALIK-ROSS A., TEKOCAK M., EVRIN V., "Kelenderis 2002 Yılı Kazısı Raporu," *KST*, 25-2, 2003, pp. 451-466.

Corpus of mosaics: Algeria, Austria, Egypt, Gaul, Germany, Great Britain, Greece, Israel, Italy, Jordan, Macedonia, Portugal, Spain, Syria and Lebanon, Switzerland, Tunisia…

particularly:

Corpus Greece 1
PELEKANIDIS S. (coll. ATZAKA P.), *Syntagma tôn palaiochristianikôn psiphidôtôn dapedôn tis Hellados*, I, *Nisiôtiki Hellas,* Thessaloniki, 1974 (Byzantina Mnimeia 1, Kentron Byzantinôn Ereunôn).

Corpus Greece 2
ASIMAKOPOULOU-ATZAKA P., *Syntagma tôn palaiochristianikôn psiphidôtôn dapedôn tis Hellados*, II, *Peloponnisos - Sterea Hellada,* Thessaloniki, 1987 (Byzantina Mnimeia 7, Kentron Byzantinôn Ereunôn).

Corpus Greece 3
ASIMAKOPOULOU-ATZAKA P., *Syntagma tôn palaiochristianikôn psiphidôtôn dapedôn tis Hellados*, III, *Makedonia - Thraki,* 1, *Ta psiphidôta dapeda tis Thessalonikis,* Thessaloniki, 1998 (Byzantina Mnimeia 9, Kentron Byzantinôn Ereunôn).

Corpus Xanthos 2
MANIÈRE-LÉVÊQUE A.-M., *Corpus of the Mosaics of Turkey, I, Lycia, Xanthos,* vol. 2, forthcoming.

CMGR Proceedings

CMGR I
La Mosaïque gréco-romaine I, H. Stern, G.-Ch. Picard (ed.), Paris, 1965 (Actes du Ier colloque international pour l'étude de la mosaïque antique, Paris, 29 août-3 septembre 1963).

CMGR II
La Mosaïque gréco-romaine II, H. Stern, M. Le Glay (ed.), Paris, 1975 (Actes du IIe colloque international pour l'étude de la mosaïque antique, Vienne-Isère, 30 août-4 septembre 1971).

CMGR III
III Colloquio internazionale sul mosaico antico, R. Farioli Campanati (ed.), Ravenna, 1983 (Actes du IIIe colloque international pour l'étude de la mosaïque antique, Ravenna, 6-10 septembre 1980).

CMGR IV
La mosaïque gréco-romaine IV, J.-P. Darmon, A. Rebourg (ed.), Paris, 1994 (Actes du IVe colloque international pour l'étude de la mosaïque antique, Trèves/Trier 8-14 août 1984).

CMGR V
Fifth International Colloquium on Ancient Mosaics, 1 et 2, P. Johnson, R. Ling, D.J. Smith (ed.), Ann Arbor, MI, 1994 et 1995 (Actes du Ve colloque international pour l'étude de la mosaïque antique, Bath, 5-12 Septembre 1987) (*JRA*, suppl. 9).

CMGR VI
VI Colloquio internacional sobre mosaico antiguo, Palencia–Mérida, Octubre 1990, D. Fernández Galiano (ed.), Guadalajara, 1994 (Actes du VIe colloque international pour l'étude de la mosaïque antique, Palencia-Merida, octobre 1990).

CMGR VII
  La mosaïque gréco-romaine VII, M. Ennaïfer, A. Rebourg (ed.), Tunis, 1999 (Actes du VIIe colloque international pour l'étude de la mosaïque antique, Tunis, 3-7 octobre 1994).

CMGR VIII
  La mosaïque gréco-romaine VIII, D. Paunier, C. Schmidt (ed.), Lausanne, 2001 (Actes du VIIIe colloque international pour l'étude de la mosaïque antique et médiévale, Lausanne, 6-11 octobre 1997) (Cahiers d'Archéologie Romande, 85-86).

CMGR IX
  La mosaïque gréco-romaine IX, H. Morlier (ed.), Paris-Roma, 2005 (Actes du IXe colloque international pour l'étude de la mosaïque antique et médiévale, Rome, 5-10 novembre 2001) (CollEFR 351).

CMGR X
  La mosaïque gréco-romaine X (Actes du Xe colloque international pour l'étude de la mosaïque antique et médiévale, Conimbriga, 26 oct.-2 nov. 2005), forthcoming.

ICCM Proceedings (t. I to IX).

ICCM 1
  Détérioration et Conservation (Rome, Novembre 1977), Rome, 1978 (ICCROM, Mosaïques 1).

ICCM 2
  Sauvegarde (Carthage 1978, Périgueux 1980), Rome, 1981 (ICCROM, Mosaiques 2).

ICCM 3
  Conservation in situ, (Aquileia 1983), Rome, 1985 (ICCROM, Mosaics 3).

ICCM 4
  Conservación in situ (Soria 1986), Servicio de Investigaciones Arqueológicas, Diputación Provincial de Soria : Instituto de Conservación y Restauración de Bienes Culturales, Ministerio de Cultura, Soria, 1987 (Mosaicos 4).

ICCM 5
  Conservación in situ (Palencia, 1990), Excma, Diputación Provincial, Departamento de Cultura, Palencia, 1994 (Mosaicos 5).

ICCM 6
  Mosaics make a site. The Conservation in situ of Mosaics on Archaeological Sites, Proceedings of the VIth International Conference of the International Committee for the Conservation of Mosaics, (Nicosia, Cyprus, 1996), D. Michaelides (ed.), Rome, 2003.

ICCM 7
  Les mosaïques: Conserver pour présenter ? Mosaics: Conserve to Display ?, Actes de la VIIème conférence du Comité International pour la Conservation des Mosaïques, (Arles – Saint-Romain-en-Gal, 22-28 Novembre 1999), P. Blanc (ed.), Arles, 2004.

ICCM 8
  Wall and Floor mosaics: Conservation, Maintenance, Presentation, VIIIth Conference of the International Committee for the Conservation of Mosaics (Thessaloniki 29 October-3 November 2002). Proceedings. European Center of Byzantine and Post-Byzantine Monuments, Ephoreia of Byzantine Antiquities of Thessaloniki, Thessaloniki, 2005.

ICCM 9
  (Palerme, October 2008), forthcoming.

Bulletin de l'AIEMA, Paris, vol 1 to 20 (bibliographic bulletin about mosaic)

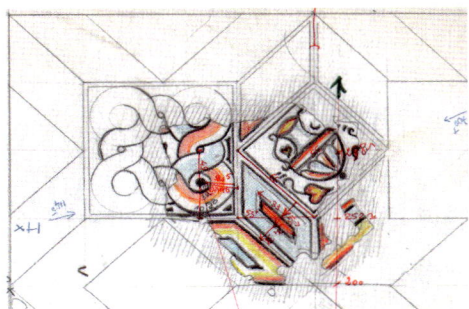

182. Draft plan of a mosaic of the nave.

Table of cube densities

Location	inv. n°	Density/dm²	Observations	Workshops
Roman mosaic	1	50		
N atrium	2-1	40		A
N atrium	2-2	43-48		A
N atrium	2-3	43	field	A
N atrium	2-3	52	pomegranate tree	A
N atrium	2-4	40-45		A
N atrium	2-5	40-46		A
N atrium	2-6	42		A
N atrium	2-7	45-48		A
S atrium	2-8	41	border	B
S atrium	2-8A	43-45	panel A	B
S atrium	2-8B	44-49	panel B	B
S atrium	2-8C	42	panel C	B
S atrium	2-9	43	border	B
S atrium	2-9A	42-45	panel A	B
S atrium	2-9B	39-43	panel B	B
N narthex	4	41-45		B
S narthex	5	51-57	glass tesserae smaller	E
N aisle	7	62	border	B
N aisle	7-1A	61-69	figural panel A	B
N aisle	7-1B	68	geometric panel B	B
N aisle	7-2	66		B
N aisle	7-3	56		B
S aisle	8-1	55	field	C
S aisle	8-2	53-55	border 1	C
S aisle	8-2	58	field	C
S aisle	8-3	45-47		C
S aisle	8-4	57-61		D
S aisle	8-5	56-57		D
nave	10	49-56	on average	D
nave	10-1	53-55		D
nave	10-2	56		D
nave	10-3	56		D
nave	10-4	53		D
nave	10-5	55		D
nave	10-7	49-88	on average	D
nave	10-7A	53	panel 7A	D
nave	10-7B	49	panel 7B	D
nave	10-7C	54	panel 7C	D
nave	10-7D	53	panel 7D	D
nave	10-7E	55	panel 7E	D
nave	10-11	56		D
N corridor	14	25-27		A?
N annex	17	54	field	B
S annex	18A	60		D

Individual Mosaic Entry or Fiche for Corpus of Turkish Mosaics

This format can be used for existing mosaics, and for those that are known but now lost:

When dealing with a building that has more than one mosaic, first describe the building overall (indicating its use or function) and provide architectural details, room by room, before documenting the mosaics decorating these spaces. There is needed a ground plan of the building, and individual rooms are to be numbered. Mosaic fiches should follow a logical path of circulation within the building.

Corpus No.: within a given site or area, mosaics should be numbered consecutively, with this numbering system continuing into additional volumes covering the same site.

Mosaic technique: pebbles, *opus tessellatum*, *opus sectile*, or other.

Title of mosaic (if one already exists, use it; if not, give the mosaic a generic title).

Provenance or name of archaeological site from which mosaic comes.

Present location of mosaic: *in situ*, in museum, in private or institutional collection, known only through archives and now lost.

Architectural context of mosaic: give location (i.e., room number) in building plan, and corpus number of mosaic decorating this room. Indicate room's function, if known. Describe shape of mosaic and its location within architectural space (for example, a square panel in center of a portico or in front of an apse) and relation of this space to adjacent rooms (threshold, part of dining area, etc.).

Dimensions of mosaic (in meters): present dimensions; if fragmentary, reconstructed dimensions.

Materials: - pebbles; - if tessellated, use of limestone, marble, terracotta, glass paste, etc.; - if *opus sectile*, types of marble or other stones used (having verified their identity); - type of foundations, if known.

Density (if tessellated): number of tesserae/dm^2 in various parts of field, in border, and in outer margin.

Colors of tesserae or pebbles (Munsell system probably will be adopted for this purpose):

Current state of preservation of mosaic: is mosaic complete, fragmentary, burned, etc.
1) Restoration of mosaic: restoration made in antiquity; modern restorations (describe what was done); if restoration is needed now, what type of treatment is recommended; indicate degree of urgency.
2) Present condition: *in situ*; protected by roof; removed from original setting and restored on new foundations; consolidated in other ways; covered by sand or reburied; or destroyed.
3) If in museum: museum inventory number; currently on display or not; stored in magazines; number of panels or fragments that exist.

Archival documentation of mosaic: this information must be detailed if mosaic is lost or partially destroyed. Location and type of archive (archaeological file; field notebook; watercolor drawing; ground plan, etc.), with author's name, title of source and artistic medium indicated.

Description of mosaic design and imagery:
1) Outer Margins
2) Border(s)
3) Field(s) or Carpet(s), with or without panels (if several panels, provide sketch numbering the panels)
4) Thresholds
5) Section added to mosaic carpet and adjusting it to room's dimensions (supplementary panel or *rallonge*). For geometric and floral designs, use descriptive terminology of *Le décor géométrique de la mosaïque romaine*, vols. 1-2, Paris, 1985, 2002.

Commentary: observations about mosaic's design, iconography, and style; comparisons should be made for all aspects of pavement.

Date: mention mosaic's archaeological context; stylistic criteria that help date the pavement; epigraphic or numismatic evidence.

Bibliography: a general bibliography can be given in the section of the text dealing with the building from which the mosaic(s) come. Subsequently, abbreviations can be used, with appropriate details added to each mosaic entry.
- Each mosaic requires its own bibliography with all published references to the pavement (an excavation report, articles in periodicals, books, other mosaic corpora mentioning this example, etc.), and the most important references should be printed in bold type.
- We recommend employing the usual abbreviations of AIEMA, found in the list attached to the *Bulletin de l'Association internationale pour l'étude de la mosaïque antique*, vol 1 to 20.
- Sample bibliographic form: J. Russell, "Mosaics of Anemurium," *AntK* 23, 1976, 242-256; D. Levi, *Antioch Mosaic Pavements*, Princeton, 1947, 23, pl. 56.

Illustrations:
1) plan of building from which mosaic comes (plans for all mosaic fiches should have a standardized size and type of labeling)
2) photograph giving overall view of pavement, in color if possible
3) few photographic details, if mosaic is of major importance and has a rich, complex design
4) if mosaic is fragmentary and evidence permits, make a reconstruction drawing of complete mosaic

Table of sites

Sites	ancient region	modern country	pages
Adana	Cilicia	Turkey	44, 95
Aigion	Peloponnese	Greece	139, 161
Aigosthena	Achaia (Attica)	Greece	103, 105
Akalissos (Asarcık)	Lycia	Turkey	18
Akrini	Macedonia	Greece	139, 161
Alacami (near Kadırlı)	Cilicia	Turkey	97
Alanya (Kalon Oros)	Pamphylia	Turkey	19
Amathous	Cyprus	Greece	66
Amisos	Pontus	Turkey	139-140, 161-162
Amorium	Phrygia	Turkey	125
Amphipolis	Macedonia	Greece	43, 71, 81
Amphissa	Achaia (Phocis)	Greece	81, 113, 135, 157
Andriake	Lycia	Turkey	17, 18
Anemurium (Anamur)	Isauria	Turkey	39, 41, 47, 71-72, 75, 81, 97-98, 101, 105, 114-115, 134, 144, 157
Ankyra-Ancyra (Ankara)	Phrygia	Turkey	65
Antikyra	Achaia	Greece	79
Antioch (Antakya)	Syria Prima	Turkey	44, 51, 79, 81, 96, 115, 138, 144, 159-160
Apamea	Syria Secunda	Syria	50, 66, 81, 95-96, 138-139, 160-161
Aphrodisias	Caria	Turkey	38, 41, 43, 47, 60, 72, 81, 98, 116
Apollonia	Lycia	Turkey	21
Arelate (Arles)	Narbonnensis	France	66, 142, 163
Argos	Achaia	Greece	44, 102, 138-139, 160-161
Arkaseia (Karpathos isl.)	Sporades	Greece	39, 79, 115
Arykanda	Lycia	Turkey	17-20, 38, 40, 43, 49, 73, 101, 144, 164
Astypalaia isl.	Cyclades	Greece	43-44
Athenae (Athens)	Achaia (Attica)	Greece	38, 44, 50, 73, 98, 105, 139, 161
Atrun	Cirenaica	Libya	66
Attaleia (Antalya)	Pamphylia	Turkey	21
Balboura	Lycia	Turkey	20
Barium (Bari)	Apulia	Italy	21, 125
Byblos	Phoenice	Lebanon	116
Byllis	Epirus Nova	Albania	57, 137-138, 158, 160
Caesarea Maritima	Palestine I (Samaria)	Israel	81
Çağlayanköy of Gördes	Lydia	Turkey	71
Capua	Campania	Italy	125
Caričin Grad	Illyricum	Serbia	138, 160
Carthage	Proconsularis	Tunisia	105
Chalchis	Achaia (Euboea)	Greece	44
Chios	Ionia	Greece	81, 125
Çiftlik (*Sinop*)	Hellenopontus	Turkey	103, 114-115
Cnidus, Knidos	Caria	Turkey	19, 43
Çomlekşaz (near Denizli)	Phrygia	Turkey	79
Constantinople (Istanbul)		Turkey	17-21, 35, 54, 65, 125, 130, 139, 148, 154, 161
Cyrene	Cirenaica	Libya	66
Dağpazarı (Koropissos)	Cilicia	Turkey	68, 71, 75, 115, 119
Daphnous	Achaia (Boeotia)	Greece	43, 52, 79

Sites	ancient region	modern country	pages
Deir el'Adas	Syria	Syria	116
Deir esh-Sharqi	Syria	Syria	96
Delphi	Achaia	Greece	51, 139, 161
Demetrias	Thessalia	Greece	81, 103
Dibsi Faraj	Syria Prima	Syria	139, 161
Echinos	Achaia	Greece	52
Edessa	Macedonia	Greece	66, 139, 161
Elaioussa Sebaste	Cilicia	Turkey	65
Elis	Achaia	Greece	79
Ephesus	Asia	Turkey	44, 48-50, 54, 65, 69, 79, 81, 90 105
Epidauros	Achaia	Greece	43, 97, 105, 139, 161
Gemiler Adası (*Levissos?*)	Lycia	Turkey	18, 20, 41, 47-49, 79, 105, 113-114, 116, 119, 133, 156
Gerasa	Arabia	Jordan	66
Gördes (*Platea Petra*)	Lydia	Turkey	49, 71
Gortyna	Creta	Greece	66, 98
Hama	Syria	Syria	51, 79
Heraclea Lyncestis, Heraklea Lynkestis	Macedonia	Macedonia	40, 44, 71 116, 119, 138-139, 160-161
Hermione	Achaia	Greece	38, 44, 71, 73, 98, 103, 138-139, 160-161
Hierapolis	Phrygia	Turkey	81
Hosios Loukas	Achaia	Greece	125
Iasos	Caria	Turkey	72, 98
Idyros	Lycia	Turkey	18
Isinda	Pamphylia	Turkey	21
Islamlar (near Elmalı)	Lycia	Turkey	20-21
Jerusalem	Palestine I	Israel	19, 66, 116
Jerade	Syria Prima	Syria	139, 161
Karabel	Lycia	Turkey	18
Karkabo (Asarlık)	Lycia	Turkey	18, 20
Karlık	Cilicia	Turkey	71
Karpasia	Cyprus	Turkey	65
Karpathos	Sporades	Greece	17, 39, 79, 115
Kartmin	Cilicia	Turkey	114
Kaunos (Caunus)	Lycia	Turkey	20
Kekova (Kaş)	Lycia	Turkey	17
Kelenderis	Cilicia	Tukey	65
Kelkit (near Erzincan)	Armenia	Turkey	43
Khirbet Muqa	Syria	Syria	93, 139, 161
Kislikçukuru (near Neapolis)	Lycia	Turkey	21
Klapsi	Thessalia	Greece	52, 119
Kos isl.	Sporades	Greece	43-44, 49, 72, 81, 98, 116, 119, 144, 164
Korydalla (Kumluca)	Lycia	Turkey	18
Korykos	Isauria	Turkey	65, 71
Küçük Tavşan Adası	Caria	Turkey	72
Kourion	Cyprus	Greece	97
Kyaneai	Lycia	Turkey	18
Laureotic Olympus	Achaia	Greece	40, 43, 51, 119

Sites	ancient region	modern country	pages
Letoon	Lycia	Turkey	18, 24, 65, 113, 130-131, 154-155
Limyra	Lycia	Turkey	17-18, 20, 49, 97, 135, 158
Longos	Macedonia	Greece	138, 161
Loupian	Narbonnensis	France	139, 161
Ma'ale Adomin	Palestine I	Israel	101, 116
Madaba	Arabia	Jordan	97, 116
Mastaura (near Dereağzi)	Lycia	Turkey	20
Mastichari (Kos isl.)	Sporades	Greece	72, 98, 119
Megalopolis	Achaia	Greece	51, 79
Meriamlik	Isauria	Turkey	52
Miletus	Caria	Turkey	72
Misis (Mopsuestia)	Cilicia	Turkey	51, 71, 115, 139, 161
Monreale	Sicilia	Italy	125
Montecassino	Campania	Italy	125
Mount Athos	Macedonia	Greece	125
Murik	Syria Prima	Syria	139, 161
Myra (Demre)	Lycia	Turkey	17, 19-21, 125, 131, 144, 155, 164
Mytilene	Lesbos isl.	Greece	66
Narli Kuyu	Cilicia	Turkey	95
Nea Anchialos (Thebes Phtiotides)	Thessalia	Greece	52, 97, 105
Nea Moni	Chios isl.	Greece	125
Neapolis	Lycia	Turkey	20-21
Nicaea (Iznik)	Bithynia	Turkey	18, 20, 125
Nicopolis	Epirus Vetus	Greece	38, 73, 98, 105, 116, 138, 160
Oenoanda	Lycia	Turkey	17
Olympos	Lycia	Turkey	17-18
Onchesmos (Saranda)	Epirus Vetus	Albania	72, 138
Oylum Höyük	Cilicia	Turkey	98
Palamutdüzü (near Doyran)	Lycia	Turkey	21
Paleopyrga (Argos)	Achaia	Greece	44, 102
Palermo	Sicilia	Italy	125
Patara	Lycia	Turkey	17-21, 38-39, 133, 156
Perge	Pamplylia	Turkey	17, 47, 97
Petra	Palestine I	Jordan	66
Phaselis	Lycia	Turkey	17
Philippi	Macedonia	Greece	43, 66, 79
Philippopolis (Plovdiv)	Thracia	Bulgaria	81
Phocaea (Yili Phokaia)	Asia	Turkey	81, 92
Phoinix (Fenike)	Lycia	Turkey	19
Pinara	Lycia	Turkey	18
Pisidian Antioch	Pisidia	Turkey	79, 93, 105, 135, 157
Prusa ad Olympum (Bursa)	Bithynia	Turkey	27, 125
Ptolemais	Cirenaica	Libya	66
Pydnai (*Cydnai*)	Lycia	Turkey	20
Qala'at Seman	Syria	Syria	66
Qumhane	Syria	Syria	48, 139, 161

Sites	ancient region	modern country	pages
Ravenna	Aemilia	Italy	114, 137, 159
Regium (Reggio di Calabria)	Calabria	Italy	125
Resafa	Syria	Syria	90
Rhodes	Rhodes isl.	Greece	17, 19, 43, 66, 79, 97, 144, 164
Rhodiapolis	Lycia	Turkey	17
Rihab	Arabia	Jordan	116
Rome	Latium	Italy	66, 114
S. Agata dei Goti (Rome)	Latium	Italy	125
S. Angelo in Formis	Campania	Italy	125
S. Vincenzo al Volturno	Samnium	Italy	125
Sagalassos	Pisidia	Turkey	65, 90, 144, 164
Salamis	Cyprus	Turkey	66, 90, 96
Salernum (Salerno)	Campania	Italy	125
Salona	Dalmatia	Croatia	72
Samos	Samos isl.	Greece	66
Sardis	Lydia	Turkey	32, 39, 65, 79, 139, 161
Seleukeia Pieria	Syria	Syria	66, 90
Sephoris	Palestine I	Israel	116
Séviac (near Montréal du Gers)	Aquitania	France	139, 161
Shavei Zion	Palestine I	Israel	79
Shunah al-Janubiyah (near Livias)	Arabia	Jordan	44
Sidyma	Lycia	Turkey	17, 20
Sipahi	Cyprus	Turkey	79
Sparta	Achaia	Greece	93
Stabia	Campania	Italy	58
Stara Zagora	Thracia	Bulgaria	139, 161
Stobi	Macedonia	Greece	66, 71, 116, 138-139, 160-161
Suhmata	Syria	Syria	115
Tarsus	Cilicia	Turkey	44
Tegea	Achaia	Greece	83
Telmessos (Fethiye)	Lycia	Turkey	17, 19-20, 23
Thessalonica-Thessaloniki	Macedonia	Greece	41, 44, 49, 52, 66, 81, 95, 114, 116, 119, 135, 137-138, 140, 157, 159
Thuburbo Majus	Proconsularis	Tunisia	66
Tlos	Lycia	Turkey	18
Torba Manastir-Bodrum (*Halicarnasse*)	Caria	Turkey	93
Tragalassos (Muskar)	Lycia	Turkey	18
Trebenna	Lycia	Turkey	20-21
Umm Qeis Gadara	Arabia	Jordan	66
Utica	Proconsularis	Tunisia	66
Veria	Macedonia	Greece	66
Vrina (near Butrint)	Epirus vetus	Albania	57, 137, 158
Yasilah	Arabia	Jordan	79
Zeugma	Osrhoëne	Turkey	44, 49, 102, 115

Photographic credits

Photographs and drawings are mainly by the author (MPR), except the following list:

Patrick Blanc: ill. 22, 56, 68b, 88, 157, 165, 171, 172, 180-181.
Bernard-Noël Chagny (aerial photograph): ill. 175.
Didier Dubois : ill. p. 185.
Şerigül Yeşil Erdek: ill. 62a, 173a-b.
Marie-Pat. Raynaud from Fabien Tessier, UMR7572: ill. 1.
Marie-Pat. Raynaud from the French team at Xanthos : ill. 4.
Marie-Pat. Raynaud, *Décor* II: ill. 136.
Engravings from Slatter 1994 (Drawings G. Scharf): ill. 2, 5, 7-10, 183.
Jean-Pierre Sodini : ill. 6, 11, 15, 50-53, 57-58, 93-94, 108, 120, 127, 139, 141, 143-144, 149-150 (150 photomontage MPR), 170, 162.

Plans have initials explained in the list of abbreviations, mainly prepared by M.-G. Froidevaux and the author. The plans published here are provisional as work is ongoing. The final versions will be contained in the overall publication of the Basilica currently being prepared under the direction of J.-P. Sodini; they might differ in some details.

List of illustration

1 Map of Turkey.
2 Plan of Xanthos by G. Scharf, 1843-44.
3 Map of Lycia.
4 Plan of the site of Xanthos.
5 Drawing of the Harpy Tomb and the "Sarcophagus on a Pillar" (by G. Scharf).
6 Overall view of the city from the top of the hill (1977).
7 View of the city of Xanthos in the time of Fellows' travels (by G. Scharf).
8 "G. Scharf sketching the Box Tomb" (by himself).
9 "Raffaelle casting the inscribed stele" (by G. Scharf).
10 Sketch of the archaeological house (by G. Scharf).
11 Overall photo of the East Basilica.
12 The East Basilica at twilight.
13 Draft plan of a mosaic of the nave.
14 Plan showing location of the Roman mosaic
15 Roman pavement.
16 Plans of the two Early Byzantine phases of the floors.
17 Scheme with the numbers of the Early Byzantine pavements.
18 Plan of the atrium (pavements 2 and 3) and the narthex (4 to 6).
19 Scheme of the atrium, with the numbers of the carpets and panels.
20 Outer margin with *hederae*.
21 Plan of carpet 2-1.
22 Ensemble view of carpet 2-1.
23 Plan of carpets 2-2 and 2-3.
24 Overall view of carpet 2-2.
25 Overall view of carpet 2-3.
26 Detail of carpet 2-3, pomegranate tree.
27 Plan of carpets 2-4 to 2-7.
28 Overall view of carpet 2-4 to 2-6.
29 Ensemble view of carpet 2-7, with the location of the main stairs on the left.
30 Detail with rainbow style filler motif.
31 Plan of carpet 2-8, with panels A, B and C.
32 Scheme of carpet 2-8, with numbers of the panels and compartments of the border.
33 Detail of the border, rectangle 2.
34 Detail of the border, rectangle 8.
35 Detail of the border, rectangle 10.
36 Detail of the border, rectangle 16.
37 Overall view of panel 2-8A.
38 Overall view of panel 2-8B.
39 Overall view of panel 2-8C.
40 Detail of panel 2-8C.
41 Plan of carpet 2-9, panels A and B.
42 Overall view of panel 2-9A.
43 Detail of panel 2-9B.
44 Overall view of panel 2-9B.
45 Plan of the atrium court, pavement 3.
46 Plan of the N compartment of narthex, pavement 4.
47 Overall view of the room.
48 Detail of an arch.
49 Plan of the S compartment of narthex, pavement 5.
50 Support on which the mosaic was laid.
51 Photo showing removal of the support.
52 Lines of tile and brick sherds shown after removal of the dividing bands.
53 Preparatory sketch on the mortar, below the mosaic: plan.
54 Preparatory sketch: détail.
55 Reconstruction of the design of the centralized pattern.
56 Overall view of the pavement.
57 Detail of the N arch, with a fruit tree behind a garden fence.
58 Detail of the S arch.
59 Plan of the central compartment of narthex, pavement 6.
60 Scheme with the numbers of the panels of pavement 6.
61 View of the first row of the *opus sectile* floor 6.
62 Detail of the *opus sectile* floor 6; a, panel 1; b, panel 4.
63 Plan of the N aisle, pavement 7, with the numbers of carpets and panels.
64 Outer margins, border and band between panels 7-1A and 7-1B.
65 Plan of carpet 7-1.
66 Ensemble view after restoration.
67 Panel 7-1A before restoration.
68 Details of the panel 7-1A, before (a) and after restoration (b).
69 View of carpet 7-1B, before removal of the fallen columns and the later structures built over the mosaics.

70	Detail of the carpet 7-1B.	116	Plan of carpets 10-10 to 10-12.
71	Detail of carpet 7-2.	117	Detail of the carpet 10-11
72	Plan of carpet 7-2.	118	Plan of the sanctuary and the apse (*synthronon* and altar socle). Pavement 11.
73	Overall view of carpet 7-2.		
74	Plan of carpet 7-3.	119	Plan of the access to the baptistery situated N of the N aisle: pavements 12-13.
75	Overall view of carpet 7-3 before restoration.		
76	Detail of carpet 7-3 after restoration, with a subtle change of pattern.	120	Pavement of tiles 13.
		121	Plan of the corridor leading to the baptistery, mosaic 14.
77	Plans of the S aisle, pavement 8, phase 1 (carpets 1 to 3); phase 2 (carpets 4 and 5).	122	View of the mosaic 14.
		123	Only preserved fragment of mosaic 15, in front of the door of the baptistery's N annex.
78	Plan of carpet 8-1.		
79	Overall view of carpet 8-1.	124	Plan of the Early Byzantine Baptistery, pavement 16.
80	Plan of carpet 8-2.		
81	Overall view of carpet 8-2.	125	Detail of the fonts.
82	Plan of carpet 8-3.	126	Overall view of the baptistery from the apse, showing pavement 16 at the periphery and Middle Byzantine *opus sectile* floor 19 in the center.
83	Deeply sunk fragment A of carpet 8-3, covered after an earthquake by the repairs 8-5.		
84	Detail of the different levels of the phases of the two floors.	127	Detail of the floor of the font showing a rough cross.
85	Overall view of carpet 8-3 and repair 8-5 (at left).	128	Plan of the N annex of the baptistery, pavement 17, and mosaic 15 at lower left.
86	Plan of carpet 8-4, phase 2.		
87	Photo of carpet 8-4.	129	Detail of the NW fragment of mosaic 17.
88	Carpet 8-4 during restoration: many fragments of the first phase mosaic (at right) were reused as foundation blocks for a second phase floor.	130	Plan of the S annex, pavement 18, mixing mosaic and *opus sectile* floor.
		131	Remains of pavement 18, view from the apse Medieval walls have destroyed part of the mosaic
89	Detail of an ancient part (from carpet 8-2), inexplicably preserved in the new carpet 8-4.	132	Detail of the dog.
		133	Detail of the stag.
90	Plan of repairs 8-5, bordering fragments of phase 1 (8-3).	134	Detail of the boar.
		135	Detail of trees.
91	Fragments of the two phases, the ancient parts (at right) are preserved inside the new pavement.	136	Reconstruction design of the centralized pattern.
		137	Plan of the Middle Byzantine complex with numbers of the floors.
92	Plan of the *opus sectile* pavement 9 (first phase of the nave).		
		138	Detail of a shield of triangles, from the Middle Byzantine *opus sectile* floor.
93	Detail of the upper mortar, showing the prints of the plaques.		
		139	The original fonts were entirely covered by the medieval floor, seen here partly preserved at the time of excavation; later these plaques were removed to study the fonts.
94	Support of the *opus sectile* floor, mainly composed of pebbles.		
95	Plan of the mosaic 10 (phase 2 of the nave).		
96	Scheme of the nave mosaic with the numbers of carpets, from 10-1 to 10-13.	140	Plan of the new church built within the old baptistery, pavement 19.
97	Detail of the band and the S outer margin.	141	Field detail.
98	Plan of carpets 10-1 and 10-2.	142	Panel with a circular medallion; notice a medieval restoration at top left, with two reused colored marble plaques.
99	Orthogonal view of carpet 10-1.		
100	Orthogonal view of carpet 10-2.		
101	Detail of carpet 10-2.	143	Example of field pattern.
102	Detail of a vase (carpet 10-2).	144	Detail showing the cutting technique of the marble units.
103	Plan of carpets 10-3 and 10-4.		
104	Orthogonal view of carpet 10-3.	145	Repairs of the pavement of the central compartment of the narthex, 20.
105	Detail of carpet 10-3a.		
106	Plan of the panel 10-5.	146	Pavement of rough stone slabs 21a (new narthex entry).
107	Plan of the W part of carpet 7: panels 10-7A and 10-7B.		
		147	Pavement of rough stone slabs 21c.
108	Panel 10-7A, before restoration.	148	Plan of the partial slabs pavement 21c (N annex of the new church).
109	Reconstruction of design of the panel 10-7Bb.		
110	Panel 10-7B, in great danger of disintegration.	149	Pavement of rough stone slabs and reused blocs 21d (S annex of the new church).
111	Plan of the central part of carpet 10-7: panels 10-7C and 10-7D.		
		150	Leveling layer 22 (ancient nave).
112	Overall view of the panel 10-7C.	151	Medieval marble pavement, mixing large plaques and geometric borders.
113	Deep depression between panels 10-7C and 10-7D, before the temporary removal, leveling and restoration.		
		152	Plan of the first Early Byzantine phase mosaics workshops A, B and C.
114	Plan of the panel 10-7E.		
115	Overall view of the fragment 10-7E, before temporary removal.		

153	View of the N atrium, illustrating workshop A production (2007).	171	Overall view of the atrium after restoration (2001).
154	View of the S atrium, illustrating workshop B production (2007).	172	a and b: restoration of a sunken fragment, reset at correct level.
155	Workshop B, N compartment of the narthex.	173	Narthex, central compartment 6, before (a) and after (b) restoration (2008).
156	Workshop B, center of panel 2-8a (atrium); notice the very similar central motif.	174	Collection of fragments reused in the second phase support, coming from the destroyed earlier mosaic: carpet 8-3 (a) and carpet 8-2 (b).
157	Workshop C, showing a predilection for fragmented lines; the black tesserae appear mostly in negative, made of a fragile material, different from the later neighboring panel 8-4, work of workshop D (top right).	175	Kite view of the East Basilica / Doğu Bazilikası uçurtmadan görüntü (uçurtmadan çekilmiş genel fotoğraf).
158	Plan of the second Early Byzantine phase mosaics: workshops D and E.	176	Plans of the two Early Byzantine phases of the floors / Tabanların iki Erken Bizans evresine ait planları.
159	a and b, filler motifs of the nave, typical of workshop D production.	177	Plan of the Middle Byzantine complex with numbers of the floors / Orta Bizans yapısı. Taban numaraları.
160	S annex of the baptistery 18, floral filler motif characteristic of workshop D.	178	Plan of the first Early Byzantine phase mosaics: workshops A, B and C / İlk Erken Bizans mozaikleri planı: A, B ve C atölyeleri.
161	Detail of the support of S narthex; notice the division by lines of tile and brick sherds, and fillings made of set-on-edge sherds and mortar.	179	Plan of the second Early Byzantine phase mosaics: workshops D and E / Ikinci Bizans evresi mozaikleri planı: D ve E atölyeleri.
162	Workshop E, S narthex 5: the unusual taste for laurel garlands and acanthus scrolls can be noticed.	180	View of S atrium before restoration / Güney atrium görüntüsü, restorasyon öncesi.
163	S Annex of the baptistery. Motifs are mainly floral or animal.	181	View of S atrium after restoration / Güney atrium görüntüsü, restorasyon sonrası.
164	"U cross" pattern; a: N Narthex, b: nave panel, c: S narthex.	182	Draft plan of a mosaic of the nave.
165	Overall view of the N aisle after restoration	183	Tomb of the lion (by G. Scharf).
166	On this scales pattern, the unusual disposition of colors traces diagonal lines.		
167	Light green and purple marbles (carpet 2-3).		
168	Restoration patch between carpet 8-1 and 8-2. The original design is not respected.		
169	Whimsical detail in the outer margin of the S aisle.		
170	Fragment of mosaic removed and reset with a large roll, in the nave (1988).		

Fold-out plan A : Early Byzantine East Basilica, Phase 1.
Fold-out plan B : Early Byzantine East Basilica, Phase 2.
Fold-out plan C : Medieval Complex.

183. Tomb of the lion (by G. Scharf).

La Tombe du Lion. A l'arrière-plan : le Pilier de l'acropole et le sarcophage de Payava.
(Dessin de G. Scharf, photo du British Museum.)

About the author

After completing her studies in art history and archaeology at the University of Paris-Sorbonne and the École du Louvre, Marie-Patricia Raynaud entered the Centre national de la Recherche scientifique (CNRS) in 1983, as a field engineer of the Henri Stern Center for the Study of Ancient Mosaics (UMR 8546 AOROC, located in the École normale supérieure, Paris). In 2006, she moved to the Center for Byzantine History and Civilization (UMR 8167 Orient et Méditerranée, College de France, Paris).

Ms. Raynaud has participated in numerous excavations at sites in France and abroad. Among the latter are Xanthos, the East Basilica (Turkey); Carthage, houses in the district of the Odeon, Jebel Oust, Haïdra and Acholla (all in Tunisia); Lixus (Morocco); Byllis and Saranda (Albania), and Caričin Grad (Serbia).

Ms. Raynaud has contributed to several mosaic publications, beginning with those produced by the Henri Stern Center as *Le Décor géométrique de la mosaïque romaine*, and she illustrated several volumes of the *Recueil général des mosaïques de la Gaule*. Currently, she is helping prepare the publication of excavations of the East Basilica at Xanthos under the direction of J.-P. Sodini, while also contributing to a second volume of the Corpus dealing with mosaics of Xanthos. She wrote the chapters on mosaics in publications of the excavation at Byllis (*Byllis* I is in press), a project led by S. Mucaj, J.-P. Sodini and P. Chevalier. Ms. Raynaud additionally is responsible for the study of mosaics from the synagogue-basilica at Saranda, in collaboration with an Albanian-Israeli team directed by E. Netzer, G. Foerster, E. Nallbani, K. Lako. She is planning several new research projects in the Middle East, focused primarily on Byzantine churches.